ALEXANDER PUSHKIN'S

Little Tragedies

PUBLICATIONS OF THE WISCONSIN CENTER FOR PUSHKIN STUDIES

David Bethea, Alexander Dolinin, Thomas Shaw
Series Editors

ALEXANDER PUSHKIN'S

Little Tragedies

The Poetics of Brevity

Edited by Svetlana Evdokimova

THE UNIVERSITY OF WISCONSIN PRESS

Funding for this book has been made possible by Brown University and the Wisconsin Center for Pushkin Studies at the University of Wisconsin–Madison.

The University of Wisconsin Press
1930 Monroe Street
Madison, Wisconsin 53711

www.wisc.edu/wisconsinpress/

3 Henrietta Street
London WC2E 8LU, England

5 4 3 2 1

Printed in the United States of America

Library of Congress Cataloging-in-Publication Data

Alexander Pushkin's Little tragedies : the poetics of brevity / edited by Svetlana Evdokimova.
p. cm. — (Publications of the Wisconsin Center for Pushkin Studies)
Includes bibliographical references and index.
ISBN 0-299-19024-2 (alk. paper)
1. Pushkin, Aleksandr Sergeevich, 1799–1837—Dramatic works.
I. Evdokimova, Svetlana. II. Series.
PG3357.A44 2004
891.72′3—dc21

2003007694

Contents

Acknowledgments

I would like to acknowledge my sincere gratitude to everyone who contributed to *Alexander Pushkin's* Little Tragedies*: The Poetics of Brevity.* Their contributions made my own work on this project both meaningful and pleasurable. I should also thank in particular a number of people who helped me to transform a mere phantom of a book into a tangible, three-dimensional reality. The idea of writing a book or editing a collection of essays on *The Little Tragedies* has been on my mind for nearly ten years, yet the gulf that separated the conception from realization began to narrow only when in 1998 Robert Louis Jackson, Vladimir Golstein, and I organized a Yale University conference on Pushkin's dramatic masterpieces. My foremost gratitude goes therefore to my two colleagues, who not only made this conference possible but also encouraged me to undertake the editing of the volume and provided me with invaluable advice at various stages of the manuscript preparation. I also owe a very special debt to Kerry Sabbag for her meticulous proofreading of the entire manuscript and her endless struggle with commas, periods, colons, parentheses, and various formal bibliographical requirements.

Earlier versions of parts 1 and 2 of Robert Jackson's essay appeared as "Beginnings: The Opening Lines of *Skupoi rytsar', Motsart i Salieri* and *Kamennyi gost',*" *Transactions of the Association of Russian-American Scholars in the U.S.A.* 30 (1999–2000): 85–96, and as "Moral-Philosophical Subtext in *Kamennyi gost',*" *Scando-Slavica* 35 (1989):

17–24. The author thanks the journals for their permission to use these materials. James E. Falen's translations of Pushkin's *Little Tragedies* were first published in the *Pushkin Journal* 2–3 (1994–95). They are reprinted here with the permission of the author, who owns the copyrights.

"Pushkin's *Stone Guest*" by Anna Akhmatova is translated by Janet Tucker and is reprinted from *Anna Akhmatova: My Half Century. Selected Prose*, edited by Ronald Meyer (Ann Arbor: Ardis, 1992) with the permission of the publisher. Excerpts from Marina Tsvetaeva's essay, "Art in the Light of Conscience" (in Angela Livingstone's translation), are reprinted here from *Eight Essays on Poetry by Marina Tsvetaeva* (Cambridge, Mass.: Harvard University Press, 1992), also with the permission of the publisher.

Finally, I would like to thank my home institution, Brown University, for kindly subsidizing a portion of this book's production costs. I would also like to express my gratitude for additional funding through the generous support of David Bethea and the University of Wisconsin's Slavic Department.

A Note to the Reader

Unless otherwise noted, all quotations from Pushkin's works are cited by volume and page number in his *Polnoe sobranie sochinenii*, 17 vols. (Moscow: Akademiia Nauk, 1937–58). When there are two subvolumes, the volume number is followed by a comma and the number indicating the subvolume, followed by a colon and the page number(s); for example, "Pushkin 9, 1: 37" refers to volume 9, subvolume 1, page 37. All translations of Pushkin's texts are mine unless otherwise specified. Whenever possible and unless otherwise specified, the contributors use James Falen's translations of Pushkin's *Little Tragedies*, which are included in this volume.

A modified Library of Congress system of transliterating Russian is used here, except for names whose Anglicized spelling is more familiar to readers, for example, Dostoevsky, Tolstoy, Meyerhold.

Ellipses within square brackets—[. . .]—indicate omissions of portions of authors' original texts; ellipses in the original appear without brackets. Except where noted, all italics are in the original.

ALEXANDER PUSHKIN'S

Little Tragedies

Introduction

"The Devil of a Difference"—Tragedies, Long or Short?

Svetlana Evdokimova

> I finally understood how to recite [*chitat'*] Shakespeare, but I do not know how to recite Pushkin.
>
> —Konstantin Stanislavsky

In the fall of 1830, trapped in his estate in Boldino by the cholera epidemic and, like Dante, finding himself at the crossroads of life, the thirty-one-year-old Pushkin experiences a surge of unprecedented creativity as he is forced to confront the timeless issues of sin, redemption, human happiness, love, death, poetic vocation, salvation, and faith with unparalleled scrutiny. Isolated from his friends and his fiancée, surrounded by the horror of death, and faced with a momentous life decision (his pending marriage to the first beauty of St. Petersburg), he composes a cycle of short stories, *The Tales of Belkin*, and the four compact plays that later became known as *The Little Tragedies*.[1] In these short stories and plays, Pushkin creates two alternative visions of human life that reflect his state of mind during his celebrated Boldino seclusion—his oscillation between a psychological *Paradiso* and *Inferno*: the happy endings of *The Tales of Belkin* and the tragic dilemmas and catastrophic climaxes of *The Little Tragedies.*

However, the two cycles share more than merely common themes and images; what also unites them is an exceptional brevity that bewildered many of Pushkin's readers. As a result of their unusual brevity, Pushkin's short stories were perceived as "somewhat bare" (Tolstoy's words), while his tragedies were deemed unfit for the stage. Consequently, neither of the cycles was fully appreciated and understood by Pushkin's contemporaries, generating a strange admixture of admiration, bewilderment, and frustration. A good example of how this bizarre perception of Pushkin's plays lingers even to the present day can be found in A. D. P. Briggs's introduction to the recent translations of *The Little Tragedies* published in *The Complete Works of Alexander Pushkin*:

> As may be seen from these brief summaries, the *Little Tragedies* stand on the brink of melodrama. Too much is squeezed into a small compass, so that events occur for which one needs to make allowances when arriving at an overall assessment. [...] The action of these playlets debars them from performance. It is hard to understand why they could have been so highly valued in comprehensive terms. Critics have waxed lyrical in their praise, using phrases like "a climax of perfection" and "admirable and perfect from whatever standpoint" to describe them; if you ask a well-read Russian, he or she is bound to place these pieces on a high pedestal. But this can only be because of their poetry. The poetry does indeed reach sublime heights of expressiveness. [...] They are pure gems of Russian speech, so beautiful and memorable that the learners forget how exaggerated and unconvincing is the action of the playlets in the midst of which they appear. Judgment is clouded, and we end up with great surges of enthusiasm for the goodness of language which sweeps away objective assessment. Thus the *Little Tragedies*, fine examples of poetic diction, are converted into unassailable masterpieces.[2]

Both a "well-read" Russian's unconditional praise and a British scholar's cavalier and condescending dismissal of the dramatic merits of the "playlets" are motivated, however, by the same lack of informed critical judgment. Indeed, few of Pushkin's works have stirred more controversy about their meaning and artistic merit than *The Little Tragedies*, which present numerous and diverse problems that plague literary and theater critics to this day. Among these critical difficulties, *The Little Tragedies'* genre, their unity, and their stageability are the least understood and therefore require elucidation. In what follows, I will discuss some of the reasons for *The Little Tragedies'* unsuccessful stage history and examine Pushkin's generic innovation as part of his romantic sensibility, focusing in particular on the plays' condensed form and Pushkin's treatment of character.

A Little Tragedy of *The Little Tragedies'* Reception and Stage History

The profound influence of *The Little Tragedies* on many Russian and Western writers could hardly be overestimated. Generations of Russian writers (Fyodor Dostoevsky, Anna Akhmatova, Marina Tsvetaeva, Osip Mandelshtam, and Andrei Bely) and Soviet and pre-Soviet Russian scholars (Dmitrii Darkii, Mikhail Gershenzon, Dmitrii Blagoi, Grigorii Gukovskii, Sergei Durylin, Boris Gorodetskii, Boris Tomashevskii, Stanislav Rassadin, Sergei Bondi, and Iurii Lotman), among many others, were engaged in the discussion of the plays' ideological and philosophical content.[3] During the last decades, especially since the mid-1970s, a number of valuable Russian and American essays have appeared dealing both with individual plays (Henry Kuchera, Robert Louis Jackson, Victor Terras, and Vladimir Golstein) and with the plays as a cycle (Barbara Heldt Monter, Richard Gregg, Vladimir Alexandrov, Valerii Tiupa, Nikolai Beliak, and Mariia Virolainen).[4] Yet, with all the critical attention that Pushkin has received in the past, especially in recent years, the four plays of the cycle—*The Covetous Knight, Mozart and Salieri, The Stone Guest,* and *A Feast in Time of Plague*—remain largely unknown to American students and scholars outside the field of Slavic studies.

Generally, the Western reader knows Pushkin's lyrics, narrative poems, and prose far better than his drama. While there is great familiarity on college campuses with recognized masterpieces such as *Eugene Onegin, The Bronze Horseman,* and *The Queen of Spades,* readily available in Penguin or Oxford World's Classics editions, Pushkin's theatrical works, including not only his *Little Tragedies* but even *Boris Godunov,* are rarely staged, read, and discussed. Pushkin's plays never became part of standard college curriculum. While the works of Turgenev, Dostoevsky, Tolstoy, and Chekhov are routinely taught here in the West even in non-Slavic literature, philosophy, and theater courses, Pushkin's literary heritage, with few exceptions, remains the domain of Slavists and connoisseurs. Even so, although a fairly extensive body of criticism deals with Pushkin's theater, English translations of his plays have been hard to find, and collections of essays or monographs on *The Little Tragedies* are simply nonexistent.[5] Moreover, although *The Little Tragedies* have attracted considerable attention from literary critics, there is an alarming dearth of scholarship by contemporary theater scholars on the history of the plays' productions or on the problem of the plays' stageability. Hence, despite their reputation as Pushkin's masterpieces among Russian readers and Slavists, these plays are virtually unknown to Western audiences, so much so that Peter Shaffer claims he composed his *Amadeus* without being aware that Pushkin's *Mozart and Salieri* had examined the same myth and dealt with similar issues almost a century and a half before.[6]

Why has Pushkin's theater been so unfortunate? Is it because Pushkin wrote "closet dramas" divorced from theatrical realities? Or perhaps because he created a new form of tragedy that was too far ahead of contemporary theatrical standards? Whatever the reason for Pushkin's failure to win the stage, the fact is that his plays are far more widely read than seen. For example, *Boris Godunov* was not staged for some forty-five years after it was written; *The Little Tragedies* in particular have never been sufficiently and successfully staged anywhere in the West or in Russia. Indeed, the history of their theatrical productions is scant at best. During Pushkin's lifetime *Mozart and Salieri* was staged only twice, while *The Covetous Knight* was only prepared for staging but then canceled in February 1837 due to the poet's unexpected and tragic death. With various degrees of success, attempts have been made to adopt *The Little Tragedies* for music, opera, and film, but theater productions have almost invariably failed to do justice to Pushkin's genius, and it became a commonplace to maintain that these "dramatic scenes" could not be considered theater works but instead were narrative genres only appropriate for recitation. Consequently, all too many stage productions were reduced to mere declamations.

This is not to say that *The Little Tragedies* were bypassed by Russia's most talented actors and directors. Among the actors of Pushkin's time, *The Little Tragedies* attracted V. A. Karatygin and M. S. Shchepkin. In the twentieth century, the Moscow Art Theater staged three of the plays—*Mozart and Salieri*, *The Stone Guest*, and *A Feast in Time of Plague*—within the so-called *Pushkinskii Spektakl'* (1915) designed by Alexander Benois, with Konstantin Stanislavsky playing the part of Salieri; and Vladimir Nemirovich-Danchenko produced a revised version of *A Feast in Time of Plague* and *The Stone Guest* in 1919. Despite these efforts, Stanislavsky viewed the Moscow Art Theater stage production as a failure and admitted that he could not resolve the problem of how to properly perform Salieri. Throughout the twentieth century, the best

Soviet actors such as N. Simonov, I. Smoktunovskii, S. Iurskii, and Iu. Liubimov played various parts in *The Little Tragedies*. Yet despite the individual actors' and directors' efforts to stage the plays, as late as 1995 critics were forced to admit that "there is a theater of Ostrovsky, there is a theater of Chekhov. But the theater of Pushkin still does not exist."[7] As one critic declares, Pushkin "resisted theater" and "generated neither a great theater tradition nor a stage history. [. . .] In a word, what makes a real drama, if not a tragedy, is precisely Pushkin's relations with theater."[8]

As the official Russian culture surrounded Pushkin with so much piety, Russian actors and stage directors never dared to question the suitability of Pushkin's plays for the stage; instead, for the most part they accepted responsibility for not being able to create a "theater of Pushkin." The difficulties presented by the staging of Pushkin's plays are obvious: they are too short; the monologues are too long (especially, for example, in *The Covetous Knight*, in which the Baron's monologues constitute one third of the entire text); the plotlines are undeveloped; and there is very little action, few theatrical effects, and a lot of silence. The troublesome formal aspects of these short dramas are topped with endings that are highly inconclusive and ambiguous. The plays seem to be too "literary," their language excessively aphoristic and evocative. It is hardly surprising, then, that one of the stage directors who attempted a production of *The Little Tragedies* in connection with Pushkin's jubilee in 1937, S. E. Radlov, complained that even Shakespeare "seems a simple and uncomplicated affair as compared to Pushkin."[9] Ultimately, though, Pushkin's drama is not the drama of silence or the theater of the absurd; he uses similar devices such as silence, economy, and undeveloped plotlines but produces very different effects.

Significantly, it is precisely the problem of staging Pushkin that fueled a polemic between Stanislavsky and Meyerhold about the goals of modern theater, a discussion of which provides an entryway into understanding the complexities of staging Pushkin. Both artists used Pushkin's observations about the nature of dramatic art as a point of departure for their own theories about dramatic acting: Stanislavsky defended the primacy of psychology and the "verisimilitude of emotions" (Pushkin's term) to support his Method and his naturalistic theater, while Meyerhold stressed the conventionality of theater (the very nature of which, according to Pushkin, "excludes verisimilitude") to advocate his "stylized theater." As a Russian critic, Oleg Feldman, points out, it is in Pushkin that Stanislavsky "found his formula of the main law of the psychological theater, a formula that, thanks to Stanislavsky, became so widely used."[10] In his essay "Rabota aktera nad soboi" (An actor prepares), Stanislavsky draws on Pushkin's often-quoted statement about the art of drama: "The truthfulness of passions, the verisimilitude of emotions in given circumstances—that is what our mind asks of a dramatist" (Pushkin 11: 178). He singles out Pushkin's notion of the "verisimilitude of emotions" as a key concept in his own approach to acting and concludes then that "that is exactly what we ask of an actor."[11] Ironically, Meyerhold relies on the same essay by Pushkin but focuses on a different passage: "Verisimilitude is still considered a chief condition of and the basis for dramatic art. What if they proved to us that the very essence of dramatic art excludes precisely this verisimilitude?" (Pushkin 11: 177).[12] Arguing against naturalism in theater, he refers to Pushkin's notion of "stylized improbability," which is more congenial to Meyerhold's own theatrical practices: "Pushkin, who drew particular attention 'to the ancients with their tragic masks and their dualistic portrayal of character,' who welcomed such 'stylized improbability,' is hardly likely to have expected real horses, previously schooled to fall injured and run wild, to be brought on to the stage."[13] Meyerhold lists Pushkin as the first one among those playwrights who created their works "not on the basis of the stage technique of their time but in anticipation of the inevitable transformation of this technique."[14] Neither Meyerhold nor Stanislavsky, however, confronted the main challenge that anyone who attempts to stage Pushkin has to confront, namely, the challenge of shortness.

There are two main approaches to the problem of the plays' extreme brevity. One way to resolve the problem of shortness is to stage *The Little Tragedies* as a tetralogy, as a cycle rather than as individual plays. The other is to stage individual plays but to focus not only on what they spell out but also on what they leave out. The first approach is more traditional and is grounded in a relatively extensive literary criticism, analyzing the plays in terms of their unity and identifying various links among the four "little" tragedies, including their recurrent themes, images, and leitmotifs.[15] This comparative approach, while not necessarily contradicting the interpretations of the plays as separate entities, is warranted not only by their thematic and formal unity but also by the fact that the four tragedies were written almost simultaneously (the four plays are dated 23 October, 26 October, 4 November, and 8 November 1830).[16]

The second approach has become increasingly subjective and appeals more to the twenty-first-century aesthetic sensibility with its postmodern fondness for marginality, ambiguity, open-endedness, and uncertainty and its distrust of final judgment and anything grand. Both approaches are fully legitimate, yet each also has certain limitations. By presenting the plays as a cycle, stage directors as well as literary critics run the danger of simplifying the plays by inevitably making generalizations in the search for a unifying idea, textual parallels, and links. On the other hand, the second approach risks being anachronistic, for by focusing excessively on what we imagine or wish Pushkin to say, we may completely lose sight of Pushkin's own concerns and artistic intents. More often than not in recent stage productions, the two approaches are combined, and the cycle of plays becomes fully subordinated to the director's artistic imagination (for example, the recent staging of *Mozart and Salieri. Don Juan. The Plague* by E. Niakroshius).[17] With the postmodernist "death of the author" and "death of the text," the stage director emerges as a new demiurge.

Whether Pushkin's plays are interpreted as "little tragedies" or as "one big tragedy," in most approaches to their staging the brevity of the plays is perceived more as an impediment than a strength. In contrast, I contend that it is precisely the shortness of the plays that is the focal element of Pushkin's theater of experimentation; that is, in order to do justice to *The Little Tragedies,* one has to fully appreciate Pushkin's generic innovation and to focus on the plays' shortness as the main shaping force of their genre and the key to their performative dimension.

Pushkin's Quest for a New Form

While the prevailing tendency in discussing genre peculiarities of *The Little Tragedies* is to focus on the relationship between the tragic and the comic and on the cyclical aspect of the plays, the generic aspect of their brevity has not been sufficiently addressed. Even if the cycle as a whole can be viewed as a "supergenre" or a "big epic form, similar in some respects to *The Divine Comedy,*" the genre of each individual play has to be addressed in its own terms.[18] Leaving aside for a while the argument about whether Pushkin's plays should be considered as tragedies, tragicomedies, or dramas, I will instead focus on the problem of their shortness.

In 1823, upon embarking on the composition of *Eugene Onegin,* Pushkin emphasized his generic experimentation in a letter to Viazemsky: "I am writing not a novel but a novel in verse—the devil of a difference. Something of the sort of *Don Juan*" (13: 73). To paraphrase Pushkin's own words, one could say that in 1830 Pushkin set out to write not tragedies but *short tragedies*—the devil of a difference. Just as *Eugene Onegin,* along with its Byronic and Sternian models, heralded the birth of a new lyrical-epic genre, the cycle of plays traditionally referred to as *The Little Tragedies* signifies the emergence of a new genre, one that I call a *short tragedy* in analogy to the short story. Pushkin frequently stressed the experimental nature of his "free novel," *Eugene Onegin.* It is precisely the writer's freedom to experiment outside of the genre system and to fuse various genres that characterizes the "motley stanzas" [sobran'e pestrykh glav] of *Eugene Onegin.* The same degree of experimentation applies to the "dramatic scenes" of *The Little Tragedies.* True to his concept of romanticism, Pushkin created a new form, a "free" tragedy that supercedes not only neoclassical tragedy but also Shakespearean tragedy; that is, it combines the elements of a tragedy, long narrative poem, lyrical poem, and tale.

In discussing the nature of romantic experimentation in general, Pushkin insisted that romanticism constitutes a body of formal characteristics rather than being merely a matter of content and that romantic poetry is first and foremost characterized by the emergence of new genres in opposition to the old classical literary genres. "What kind of poetry do we consider romantic?" Pushkin asks in his essay "O poezii klassicheskoi i romanticheskoi" (About classical and romantic poetry). And he answers: "The kind of poetry that did not exist among the ancients, as well as the kind of poetry in which the old forms have been changed or replaced with new ones" (Pushkin 11: 36). The romantics also sought to reconsider the classification of drama as part of their attempt to redefine genres. Pushkin was also profoundly interested in the transformation of Russian theater, and he believed that the creation of the new dramatic form corresponding to the Zeitgeist was the main task of the dramatist: "The spirit of the age requires crucial transformations on the dramatic stage" (11: 141). Pushkin's plays, therefore, cannot be viewed in isolation from contemporary romantic pursuits.

Thus, it is not surprising also that he shares not only the generic ambitions of his fellow romantic writers but also the common fate of romantic playwrights, even talented ones such as Shelley, Büchner, and Kleist: their plays were often dismissed as the works of lyric poets and deemed unfitted for the stage.

The romantics had a particular taste for the fragmentary, the inconclusive, and the ambiguous. Since modernity, according to them, represented an endlessly developing process, total perfection was deemed unattainable. The best form that could do justice to this sense of reality, therefore, had to be incomplete. Friedrich Schlegel's *Athenäum Fragments* and Novalis's *Aphorisms and Fragments* gave expression to this new sensibility and conveyed the authors' perceptions of reality as fragmentary and inconclusive. As Friedrich Schlegel put it in his Fragment #116: "Other types of literature are already complete and therefore can now be completely analyzed, but the Romantic type of literature is still becoming. Indeed, its unique essence is that it is always becoming and can never be completed.[. . .] It alone is infinite. It alone is free."[19] August Schlegel expressed a similar idea: "The classical is more simple, clear, and like nature in the self-existing perfection of separate works; the Romantic, in spite of the appearance of fragmentation, approaches the secret of the universe."[20] The conception of poetry as an endless becoming had crucial consequences for the romantics' sense of genres: genres were expected to be mixed and mingled; incompleteness was best represented by fragments and therefore, in many cases, shorter forms.

As disappointed as he was with the public's inability to appreciate his innovations in *Boris Godunov*, Pushkin was nevertheless convinced that his play could be performed. Although in *The Little Tragedies*, as opposed to *Boris Godunov*, Pushkin largely restored the classical unities, he further developed within them the Shakespearean structure as a simple sequence of scenes without divisions into acts, a strategy that he previously adopted for *Boris Godunov*. In fact, he pushed this device to the extreme in his Boldino cycle: the fragmentary nature of *Boris Godunov*, with its moves from one place to the next in a matter of minutes, becomes *The Little Tragedies*' dominant structural principle. It is clear that in 1830 he still sought to reform the stage and was fully aware of the experimental nature of his Boldino plays, to which his preliminary ideas for *The Little Tragedies*' titles testify: "Dramaticheskie stseny" (Dramatic scenes), "Dramaticheskie ocherki" (Dramatic sketches),

"Dramaticheskie izucheniia" (Dramatic investigations), or "Opyt dramaticheskikh izuchenii" (An experiment with dramatic investigations). Judging from the content of the plans that go back to 1826, Pushkin appears to have projected a cycle of at least ten plays: *The Miser, Romulus and Remus, Mozart and Salieri, Don Juan, Jesus, Beraldus of Savoy, Paul I, An Enamoured Devil, Dmitry and Marina,* and *Kurbsky.* The tentative subtitles of Pushkin's *Little Tragedies* point to the parameters of his reform of the genre of tragedy: the plays' scope (their shortness), their fragmentariness as an organizing principle of their composition (*stseny*), their experimental nature (*opyt, izucheniia*), and the hybridization of their form (a combination of drama and sketch—*dramaticheskie ocherki*). Although the hybridization of genres and the discovery of the artistic value of the fragment was part of the general romantic project, in Russia an intense generic awareness, which characterized the age of romanticism, extended even to most of modern Russian literature.[21] It is hardly surprising, then, that Pushkin delighted in this radical freedom from a codified hierarchical system of genres and explored the potentials of various dramatic and nondramatic forms.

Iurii Tynianov correctly intuited that Pushkin offers here "a new genre of classical tragedy, transformed in the style and scope of a technical fragment."[22] Most importantly, he linked the evolution of Pushkin's verse from extended descriptions to a more compact but voluminous discourse with a generic evolution. Similar to the way the word began carrying a variety of associations on the level of lexicon, a single scene or a fragment became representative of the whole drama: "In Pushkin's verse drama after *Boris Godunov,* the same thing happens as in epic: with a small number of verses, Pushkin produces a large verse form. In epic this is achieved in a moment of energetic shift from plane to plane; in verse tragedy this is achieved through the dramatic situation's ability to energetically color the speech."[23] A similar process, we may add, characterized Pushkin's evolving prose style. The semantic intensity and compactness of his verse found their counterpart in the extreme laconicism of *The Tales of Belkin,* with their economy of lexicon, syntax, and plot. Tynianov further argued that the condensed and pithy dialogue that distinguished Pushkin's drama did not evolve merely in separate lyric poems but instead emerged as a full-fledged drama as the dramatic elements were absorbed by the speech itself: "This application of dramatic accessories to speech turns the verse discourse of the dialogue into a verse gesture."[24]

Nonetheless, even though the fragment played a crucial role in the formation of the new genre of Pushkin's short tragedy, *The Little Tragedies* are not dramatic fragments. Rather, the generic peculiarities of the fragment are fully absorbed by and subordinated to the newly emerging form. Pushkin's *Little Tragedies* would combine several short forms in a new synthesis. It is not a coincidence that in addition to fragment Pushkin was also interested in the genre of anecdote and aphorism; he valued conciseness and economy in poetry as well as in prose and was acutely aware of the connection between length and modern sensibility. Speaking about the art of prose writing, Pushkin claimed, "Precision and brevity are the chief merits of prose" (11: 19). His fascination with brevity and simplicity was the result of his new aesthetics, which unfortunately was not immediately appreciated by his contemporaries. Indeed, the hybrid genre of *The Little Tragedies* has not been understood as intended neither by Pushkin's immediate contemporaries nor by his later audience.

The Impact of Shortness

What effects does Pushkin achieve by his plays' extreme brevity? The brevity both imposes certain limitations on format and subject and engenders new qualities and devices to the genre of tragedy. Pushkin's short tragedy—similar to a short story—has a limited number of characters, and its plot is collapsed into a single semantic knot. Pushkin almost completely dispenses with familiar comic or tragic types such as servants, buffoons, rogues, and villains (Leporello may be one exception), which in a longer play are used not only to create theatrical effects but also to reinforce the audience's sense of the particular patterns, themes, and images that may otherwise escape our attention. In a shorter play they are simply superfluous, because the audience's attention is not dispersed and the spectator easily remembers all the aspects of the play.

Its limited space also restricts a short tragedy's ability to present a portrait of an epoch. As interested as Pushkin may have been in historicity and in contemporary issues, he offers little information about the epochs that serve as background for the unfolding events. They could happen almost anytime, anywhere.[25] Indeed, although Pushkin preserves a degree of "local color" in his tragedies (for example, the

Mediterranean atmosphere of Spain in *The Stone Guest* and certain attributes of sixteenth-century Europe in *The Covetous Knight*), it would be naive to conclude that Pushkin's task in these plays is that of a historian who represents here a succession of the four historical periods (the Middle Ages, the Renaissance, the Enlightenment, and Romanticism) as suggested, for example, by Beliak and Virolainen.[26] Pushkin's settings are extremely scant and generalized. While references to helmets, tournaments, and knights make us think of the Middle Ages, there is little in the text of *The Covetous Knight*, for example, that would help us more precisely locate the events presented. While our understanding of the time period of *Mozart and Salieri* is facilitated by our historical knowledge of Mozart's life span, the play provides no information about the exact location of the events. References to place stress universality over historicity. Thus stage directions for scene 1, for example, merely state "A room," and scene 2 also opens with a rather general stage direction: "A private room at an inn; a fortepiano. Mozart and Salieri at a table." Apart from English names such as Jackson, Mary, and Jenny and Louise's comment about Mary's Scottish origin, there is practically nothing in *A Feast in Time of Plague* that would indicate that the action takes place in seventeenth-century London. Thus although Pushkin does not violate our sense of historicity by flagrant anachronisms, the historical aspect of the plays is toned down. The intentional temporal ambiguity of the final line of *The Covetous Knight*—"What dreadful times are these, what dreadful hearts!" [Uzhasnyi vek, uzhasnye serdtsa]—stresses the universal aspect of the play over the local color. Mikhail Alekseev was undoubtedly right when he insisted that behind Pushkin's images one should seek "not real historical personages but great generalizations, an outline of a vast philosophical plan."[27]

While reducing the cast and scope, the short tragedy increases the semantic polyvalence. Building on Tynianov's observation about the impact of the fragment on the evolution of genres in Pushkin's works, Iurii Chumakov concludes, "The profound thesis of Tynianov points to the ways in which Pushkin increases semantic intensity while reducing the length of the text. Generic transformations result in a peculiar collapse of genres, which is characteristic of both *Eugene Onegin* (novel) and *Mozart and Salieri* (drama). In both cases the plot is curtailed and condensed."[28]

Language is also treated differently. Since the reader and the audience are more likely than in the case of the longer tragedy to remember all the details of the short play, the vocabulary bears more than its normal significance, as the reader and the audience are more prone to assign symbolic value to individual images and to identify recurrent leitmotifs. As a result, Pushkin's short tragedies are close to lyrics. What makes them so close to lyrics is not, of course, their meter or poetic diction but the use of parallelism that confers on the text an expectation of the sequence. Recurrent images and words establish the rhythm of repetition and succession within both individual plays and the cycle as a whole, a formal peculiarity that provided an impetus for scholars' search for the unifying patterns.[29]

Similar to lyrics, Pushkin's short tragedies put an unusually heavy weight on their closing lines, which function as a *pointe* of sorts. In their aphoristic form, the final lines present a moral dilemma or a vision of truth. Such are Salieri's moral dilemma and his questioning of Mozart's maxim that genius and villainy are two things incompatible. Such is the Duke's indictment at the end of *The Covetous Knight*: "What dreadful times are these, what dreadful hearts!" Such are the intensely ambiguous endings of *The Stone Guest* and *A Feast in Time of Plague*, which leave the audience and the reader in a state of indecision about the protagonists' final gestures and motives. Are Don Juan's last words—"I perish.... All is done.... O Dona Anna!..."—an expression of his fear or his care and love for Dona Anna? Is his final exclamation an indication of his heroic and stoic defiance in the face of death and punishment or a sign of his belated regret and final moral transformation? What does the final exchange between Walsingham and the Priest signify? Whose truth prevails? Neither? Or both? At the end of *A Feast in Time of Plague*, Walsingham's silence speaks more than the characters' words. Similar to the celebrated silence at the end of *Boris Godunov*, *A Feast*'s final stage direction—"The Master of Revels stays, lost in thought"—is fraught with implication and explodes the sense of tragedy. With so much uncertainty in the plays' final lines, the sound and intonation with which they are pronounced profoundly affect the meanings of the plays.

The extreme compression of the form leads to intense ambiguity and polyvalence at the level of plot, ideas, images, and words that are also characteristic of Pushkin's lyrics and short stories. Every word, every move is carefully planned to bear the meaning. Every line is loaded with significance. It is not surprising then that in addition to common themes and motifs identified by critics, *The Little Tragedies* also share with the cycle of Pushkin's short stories, *The Tales of Belkin*, some generic similarities. The genre of the short story with which Pushkin experiments in his *Tales of Belkin* confers, as it were, some of its generic peculiarities on Pushkin's *Little Tragedies.* But his short stories in their own way were affected by a variety of genres, including anecdote, parable, and lyric poetry—the genres that, to use Mikhail Bakhtin's term, underwent "novelization" in nineteenth-century Russian fiction. As a result of this mixing of genres and Pushkin's generic evolution in general, *The Little Tragedies* become close to the short story, on the one hand, and to the lyric, on the other. While in his analysis of *The Tales of Belkin* Wolf Schmid lays the ground for a "poetic" reading of Pushkin's prose, one that focuses on various semantic potentials offered by each story, we could extend a similar approach to a "poetic" reading of *The Little Tragedies.*[30]

Finally, each of Pushkin's short tragedies is organized around a theme; it deals with single episodes and focuses on experiences that are extreme, not typical. Again in a way similar to the lyric, it puts emphasis on subjectivity and becomes more psychological and poetic. That is why the use of leitmotifs becomes one of the most essential aspects of *The Little Tragedies'* poetics. It is this evocative aspect of the plays' poetics that validates the critics' approach to the plays in terms of a cycle and their analysis of the plays' various leitmotifs and recurrent images, such as the feast, life, death, Eros, and happiness.[31] Thus, precisely because Pushkin's tragedies are short, they rely on implication, silence, elision, and stress—the qualities that we frequently associate with the genre of the short story or the lyrics.

Characterization and the Sense of Length

What are, then, the elements of characterization, plot, theme, and point of view that are characteristic of Pushkin's short tragedy? Or, to put it differently, what makes Pushkin's short tragedy short? If, as Bakhtin taught us, the initial concept always determines the shape of the narrative, we must assume that there is something in Pushkin's plays' subject matter and the manner in which it is presented that requires shortness. The brevity of Pushkin's plays, therefore, is not merely a matter of length. If we compare the tragedy of Salieri or the Baron to that of Macbeth or Hamlet, it will become clear why Shakespeare needs narrative space and time to convey the tragedy of his heroes and why Pushkin does not. Obviously, Pushkin's way of viewing reality in *The Little Tragedies* affects his choice of narrative structure and characterization and requires brevity of form.

Certainly, Pushkin's tragedies are not "little" in a sense of insignificance, but they are undoubtedly small in compass and scope. After all, the experiences of the Baron, Salieri, Don Juan, and Walsingham do not affect the fate of kingdoms; they are contained in the boundaries of the personal. While the traditional tragedy renders not only what a character feels but also how he acts (or does not act), what happens to him, and how he deviates from the norm (thereby requiring greater narrative space), there are no grandiose national or historical cataclysms, as in classical Greek tragedy and Shakespeare, in Pushkin's "little" plays. Similar to the dramatists who practiced monodrama, he is more interested in the complexity of human nature than in one person's actions or his deviations from the norm.

Scholars have observed that the form of *The Little Tragedies* owes some of its peculiarities to the *Dramatic Scenes* of Barry Cornwall but have failed to place them in the larger tradition of romantic drama.[32] The tentative titles of Pushkin's *Little Tragedies* demonstrate, however, their generic affinity with similar experimental pursuits by other European romantics, especially those who sought to explore the potential of the monodrama and to transform it into a new romantic tragedy such as Wordsworth and Byron, who created plays focusing on the extreme states of consciousness and owing much to monodrama for its potential to provide a close analysis of character. In this new psychological drama, the depiction of character takes precedence over action. Among the projects with the most revelatory experimental titles of this kind are Joanna Baillie's *Series of Plays: In Which It Is Attempted to Delineate the Stronger Passions of the Mind: Each Passion Being the Subject of a Tragedy and a Comedy*, Matthew Lewis's *The Captive, a Monodrama or Tragic-Scene*, and Frank Sayers's *Dramatic Sketches*. Discussing the significance of the genre of monodrama for romantic drama, Jeffrey Cox points out:

> The rise of the monodrama is clearly linked to broader changes in the critical definition of the drama: from drama as an imitation of an action to drama as a presentation of character. This transformation is perhaps

> most familiar in that movement within Shakespeare criticism—from Maurice Morgann's *Essay on the Dramatic Character of John Falstaff* (1777) to A. C. Bradley's *Shakespearean Tragedy* (1904)—which focuses upon Shakespeare's ability to create powerful individuals and to portray their inner lives; it is summed up in Browning's pronouncement in the preface to *Strafford* (1837) that drama should offer "Action in Character, rather than Character in Action."[33]

Like the romantics, Pushkin also dealt with "the stronger passions of the mind," and he made them the subjects of tragedies (*The Little Tragedies*) and comedies (*The Tales of Belkin*). In his *Little Tragedies*, Pushkin captured precisely "action in character," or a shift from the external event to the internal event, as he reduced the external events to a minimum and almost entirely focused on the hero's emotions. He completely destroyed what could be called the verisimilitude of length and development, as the characters are seen only in a few crucial moments. Instead, *The Little Tragedies* concentrate most on intense moments in the lives of the protagonists, not on what precedes the conflict and what follows afterward.

We may recall how this focus on human passions and the overall inward turn in the representation of character was typical of the European romantics' perception of the new drama. This inward turn was widely examined in many studies of romanticism, such as, for example, Erich Kahler's *Inward Turn of Narrative* and Alan Richardson's *Mental Theater: Poetic Drama and Consciousness in the Romantic Age.* Both European and Russian romantics never tired of stressing the primacy of emotions over action in their literary pursuits. Thus, commenting on German romanticism, Madame de Staël observes that introspection is a distinguishing feature of modern German theater and that Germans are more interested in that which the characters feel than in what happens to them. (See her extremely influential *On Germany* and *On Literature Considered in Its Relationship to Social Institutions.*)[34] A contemporary of Pushkin, a Russian poet and translator, Nikolai I. Gnedich, echoes this view by emphasizing the importance of emotions over events: "Why can't the emotions that characters experience be as interesting as the events that happen to them? When we derive interest uniquely from what occurs in the character's soul, then the slightest hint of stiltedness or any inappropriate word will strike us as a false sound."[35] It is for the considerations of the necessity to portray onstage the character's complexity that Vasilii Zhukovskii, for example, criticizes the classical French tragedy for not being suitable for acting: "In French tragedies it is impossible to be an actor. Everything consists in declamation of verses rather than in depicting whole characters with their nuances."[36] A typical view on the supremacy of human character and human passions in theater is expressed by Pavel Katenin: "The subject of art in general is man himself, and especially in the dramatic art, it is man in action. He who is able to depict the inner workings of these actions, customs, feelings, and passions with honesty, force, and fervor will earn the praise of experts, even if he costumes his characters according to local fashions. It is precisely by these merits that Sophocles, Shakespeare, and Racine earned their immortality."[37]

Pushkin's method, inspired as it was by the romantic "inward turn," was therefore inductive, from the particular and singular to the general. The particular is presented as a window to a larger philosophical problem, that of human nature. Tragedy emerges not as a result of the fall of great personages but as a result of a character's inner contradictions. Pushkin greatly admired Shakespeare's ability to create complex and contradictory characters and to depict individual psychology.[38] But although he claimed that Shakespearean characters served him as an inspiration for his own tragic heroes, the way Pushkin portrays his characters is fundamentally different from that of Shakespeare. Pushkin's tragic heroes do not need a long process of revelation in the manner of Lear, nor do they unfold gradually as do Macbeth and Othello. The sense of tragedy is conveyed not so much through tragic heroes or even tragic situations but through the perception of man's tragic predicament: the tragic disparity between man's aspirations and his limitations. The shorter form therefore results from character taking precedence over action. When we first encounter the protagonists of Pushkin's short tragedies, they already know what they are going to do: the Baron knows that he won't give money to his son, Salieri knows that he will poison Mozart, Don Juan knows that he will seduce Dona Anna, and Walsingham knows that he will stay with his blasphemous companions. We do not even view them pondering or deliberating upon a choice: Salieri does not hesitate over whether or not he should poison Mozart, Don Juan does not waver on seducing Dona Anna or on challenging the statue of the Commander, the Baron does not question his passion for accumulation, just as Walsingham does not seriously consider changing his ways. Throughout the plays, they undergo no dynamic change in their characters; they may experience intense identity crises in the end, but ultimately none of the characters grows to any greater awareness of life or gains any real insight into himself or the world around him. The characters' identity crises lead them to no revelation of truth, no final illumination or epiphany, but rather to an unresolved and probably insoluble existential uncertainty. Shakespeare's tragic heroes are different.

The disparity between Pushkin and Shakespeare exists in a change of consciousness that is experienced by many of Shakespeare's characters and not Pushkin's, a change that is not instantaneous and thus takes time and is explained by a variety of causes. In his short tragedy, Pushkin replaces the Shakespearean tragedy's gradual unfolding of character and extended analysis with synthesis. In other words, the short tragedy implies a special mode of understanding and confronting reality, one that is concentrated and thus revealed in a few emblematic moments. Pushkin concentrates almost entirely on the climax, which is why Durylin aptly observes that *The Little Tragedies* represent "the epilogues of great and complicated lives filled with tremendous struggle and rebellion of the human spirit." Rather than focusing on the process or development of conflict, they are merely "the resolutions of great tragedies that have been lived out before the raising of the curtain."[39] Pushkin dispenses here with the traditional arsenal of dramatic devices that are used to show the audience how a character gradually unfolds. An extraordinary tension and explosion of passions replace traditional movement and development.

This is apparently what Pushkin means by the "truthfulness of passions." Discussing the generic characteristics of tragedy, Pushkin claimed that tragedy as a genre is far from being based on verisimilitude as frequently believed; instead, it is the most conventional of all genres, because the spectator must forgo a sense of place, time, and language:

> I thought about tragedy in general; it is perhaps the least understood of all genres. Both the classicists and the romantics based its laws on verisimilitude, but that is precisely what the nature of a dramatic work excludes. Not to mention time, and so on, what kind of verisimilitude, for devil's sake, can there be in a hall divided into two halves, one of which is occupied by two thousand people who are supposed to be invisible to those onstage? [...] Tragedians of true genius never cared

> about verisimilitude. The verisimilitude of situations and the truthfulness of dialogues—that is the true law of tragedy. (13: 197)

Pushkin, therefore, was primarily interested in a "free and broad representation of characters"; he replaced traditional verisimilitude with psychological verisimilitude, the "truthfulness of passion," the "verisimilitude of emotions," and the "verisimilitude of characters and situations." He takes the characters of classical tragedy (such as the miser or the envious, as suggested by his draft titles *The Miser* and *Envy,* which evolved into *The Covetous Knight* and *Mozart and Salieri,* respectively) and "liberates" them into "free" types. Regardless of whether the reader, the audience, or the author justifies or condemns the protagonists of *The Little Tragedies,* it is impossible to ignore their charismatic nature, rooted in their complexity and in the heterogeneous nature of their personalities. As villainous, petty, vicious, promiscuous, or egotistical as the characters of *The Little Tragedies* may be, Pushkin also allows them to be attractive and even enticing. The "truthfulness of passions" is revealed in their multifacetedness, strength of character, and even dignity. As Alexander Turgenev testified to in his memoirs, Pushkin insisted on the complexity of evil, for vice has to be attractive in order to be tragic: "The key is what happens in our soul, in our conscience, and in the charm of evil. This charm would be incomprehensible were not evil endowed with a beautiful and pleasant appearance. I trust the Bible in all that concerns Satan. There is a great philosophical truth in the verses about the Fallen Spirit, who is both beautiful and perfidious."[40]

The tragedies of the characters of Don Juan and of Salieri would have required a longer narrative space if they were to account for character development. But the tragedies of "Don Juanism" or "Salierism" may dispense with a longer form in favor of a more compact genre. That is precisely what takes place in the universe of *The Little Tragedies.* Take, for example, *The Stone Guest.* In this play, Pushkin shows not so much a tragedy of Don Juan as the tragedy of "Don Juanism." The question of whether or not Don Juan changes is superfluous to the very essence of Pushkin's play, which focuses on the tragic nature of Don Juan's passion—his "Don Juanism"—and not on how his passion finds itself in conflict with other passions. The tragedy is in the contradictory nature of the passion itself. If the essence of "Don Juanism" consists in the odd combination of love and infidelity, then it is entirely irrelevant whether Pushkin's Don Juan is morally reborn or, on the contrary, if he lies to Dona Anna. Blagoi is certainly correct when he asserts that "if Pushkin's Don Juan indeed proved capable of loving one woman forever, he would ipso facto cease to be Don Juan."[41] Yet, in line with his notion of the "truthfulness of passions" and their charismatic nature, Pushkin shows how Don Juan's compulsive infidelity becomes ennobled as a high passion because he is not merely a seducer but instead a poet of seduction. Critics have commented on Pushkin's innovation in portraying Don Juan as a poet but have overlooked the connection between his poetic nature and his "Don Juanism." This connection is revealed, however, if we consider Pushkin's poem "The Poet" (1827). The poem describes how in the moment of poetic creation the poet transcends all others:

> But as soon as the divine word
> Touches the poet's sensitive hearing
> The poet's heart begins to throb
> As an awakened eagle.
>
> Но лишь божественный глагол
> До слуха чуткого коснется,
> Душа поэта встрепенется,
> Как пробудившийся орел.

The minute the inspiration deserts him, however, the poet could become the most insignificant of all human beings:

> As long as Apollo does not call the poet
> For a sacred sacrifice
> He is cowardly immersed
> In the concerns of the vain world
> His sacred lyre is silent
> His soul is consumed by a cold dream
> And of the world's worthless offspring
> He may be the most worthless of all.
>
> Пока не требует поэта
> К священной жертве Аполлон,
> В заботах суетного света
> Он малодушно погружён;

Молчит его святая лира;
Душа вкушает хладный сон,
И меж детей ничтожных мира,
Быть может, всех ничтожней он.

A similar metamorphosis occurs to the "poet of seduction," Pushkin's Don Juan. To paraphrase the poem, "As long as Eros does not call Don Juan for a sacred sacrifice," he is "worthless" (*nichtozhnyi*), but immediately after he experiences the touch of the divine Eros on his heart, he rises in stature and is ennobled by his love; as manipulative as he may be, he is also sincere. Is there then deceit in his love of Dona Anna? Yes and no. He is a skillful seducer, but in the process of his seducing he falls in love with the object of his seduction as Pygmalion falls in love with his own creation, Galatea. Yet his love can never endure the pressure of time. Thus Pushkin captures the tragic duality of Don Juan's personality: the fall from height is the same for the poet (or any artist) and for Don Juan; it is in their inability to sustain inspiration. This aspect of Don Juan's personality is best expressed through his female double, Laura, who is also an artist. Asked by Don Carlos if she is still in love with Don Juan, she replies: "This very moment? / Oh no . . . I never love two men at once; / Just now . . . it's you I love." This avowal does not prevent Laura from discarding Don Carlos and falling back in love with Don Juan exactly a minute later. Likewise, Don Juan may be indeed in love with Dona Anna as he claims he is, but the truth of his words has no permanency; it is good only for "this very minute." Don Juan's love then is presented as an equivalent of artistic inspiration: it is truthful but transient, intense but shifty, lofty but doomed. By portraying his Don Juan as a poet, Pushkin departs from the tradition precisely because he wants to show the tragic and artistic nature of "Don Juanism"—the tragedy of transiency. Significantly, Pushkin's Don Juan dies at the moment of his triumphant "Don Juanism," when he wins Dona Anna's heart after striping all of his masks—as a monk or as Don Diego. It is by affirming his identity as Don Juan (he stresses his identity by repeating three times that he is Don Juan: "I'm not Don Diego . . . I'm Don Juan"; "Don Juan am I"; "Don Juan am I, and I'm in love with you") that he precipitates his death. Don Juan is, and must be, destroyed by his "Don Juanism."

Likewise, the conflict in *The Covetous Knight* can be found in the clash between father and son or between two opposing impulses of human nature—avarice and wastefulness. But the essence of tragedy, as Pushkin stages it, is in the covetousness itself. The Baron attains the stature of a tragic hero because his very passion—his covetousness—emerges not only as a petty passion for accumulation but as a quest (as misguided as it may be) for a meaningful existence. He is a knight in the service of an ideal, although by serving his ideal he stops being a knight: "[O]r am I knight no more?" [Il' uzh ne rytsar' ia?] exclaims the Baron at the end of the play. This exclamation, marking the climax of the play and articulating that greed did not fully suppress his sense of honor, reveals the tragic nature of his passion best of all. The "poet of greed" falls from the height of his might only to realize that he may be a nonentity—not a knight ("ne rytsar'"). The oxymoronic tension between being a knight and a miser therefore destroys his sense of identity. The play ends with the Baron's unresolved uncertainty about his identity. Being a "covetous knight" proves to be an impossible task.

Similarly, in *Mozart and Salieri* another passion—"Salierism" (which should not be understood as mere envy)—destroys Salieri's sense of identity as a musician of genius. The play ends with a similar crisis of identity and an identity question: "Am I no genius?" [Il' ia ne genii?]. Although the critics frequently argue whether Pushkin's play as a whole supports or refutes Mozart's claim that genius and villainy are incompatible, this argument is irrelevant for our understanding of the sense of tragedy in the play.[42] The tragedy arises from Salieri's doubt and his existential uncertainty. No definitive answer is provided either to Salieri or to the audience. What disturbs Salieri's peace of mind is precisely the situation Pushkin describes in "The Poet." Salieri recognizes acutely that, in his creativity, Mozart rises above all—he is a genius. Yet "[a]s long as Apollo does not call [the poet] / For a sacred sacrifice," he may be "worthless"—or at least so he seems to Salieri. Salieri's conundrum exists in his simultaneous vision of Mozart as a genius and as a nonentity, a complexity and duality that cannot be maintained. Ironically, it is the manner in which he interprets or misinterprets Mozart—as a genius and as a nonentity—that suggests to Salieri the possible compatibility of villainy and genius and thereby confers on him a license to commit murder. Thus, the essence of "Salierism" is embedded in Salieri's concurrent, unconscious rebellion against and faith in the compatibility of villainy and genius. By murdering Mozart he wants to "monologize" him, to keep him alive only as a genius, yet he relies on this very notion, that is, the compatibility of villainy and genius, by committing villainy and believing himself a genius. Salieri's question "You think it so?" immediately after Mozart's philosophical maxim about the incompatibility of genius and villainy points to his complete confidence in the opposite, a confidence that is reaffirmed by his dropping poison into Mozart's glass. But what did he want to achieve by murdering Mozart? He wanted to reestablish the order of things when genius is *incompatible* with corruption, for the "immortal sacred gift" of genius, so he believes, should not be rewarded to a "foolish idler" and a "madman." Salieri's act of murder, therefore, negates his very goal and thus explodes his sense of identity.

Paradoxically, in their emphasis on the contradictory nature of human passions, *The Little Tragedies* are more akin to Bakhtin's view of Dostoevsky's novels than to typical plays that consist of four acts and unfold from exposition through complication to a definite and conclusive ending. The words that Bakhtin uses to describe Dostoevsky's major characters seem strangely relevant to a description of Pushkin's tragic heroes: "[A]s people of an idea, [they] are absolutely unselfish, insofar as the idea has really taken control of the deepest core of their personality. This unselfishness is neither a trait of their objectivized character nor an external definition of their acts—unselfishness expresses their real life in the realm of the idea (they 'don't need millions, they just need to get a thought straight'), idea-ness and unselfishness are, as it were, synonyms."[43] Indeed, if judged by these criteria, all four of the major protagonists of the four plays—the Baron, Salieri, Don Juan, and Walsingham—are unselfish in their "idea-ness" and embody the tragedy of an idea. Thus Salieri, for example, is closer in this sense to Raskolnikov than to his tragic predecessors, for he suffers because his theory—the compatibility of genius and villainy—may prove wrong.[44] Pushkin's technique of introducing very few main characters (in most plays only one or two) and presenting them as people of an idea or "passion," be it existential greed, envy, desire, or rebellion, does not lead him closer to realism, however, as some scholars have maintained. On the contrary, the elements of artifice and conventionality are further increased. That is precisely why it would be a mistake to blame the action of the plays for being "exaggerated and unconvincing" and approach them, as Briggs seems to do, with an expectation of a realistic drama. Instead, one should attend to the role of stylization in Pushkin's concept of drama and recognize that the smaller cast and the focus on "passions" lead Pushkin to a different genre or subgenre. Similar to

Dostoevsky, who, according to an apt observation of Viacheslav Ivanov, created "novels-tragedies," Pushkin created a hybrid genre, although on a smaller scale: that of "short stories–tragedies."

In his cycle of Boldino plays, Pushkin is interested in human nature as a philosophical issue. It is because Pushkin completely shifts the focus from the germination and development of passions to their contradictory nature that he needs a short form that excludes extended expositions. Indeed, as argued by theoreticians of the short story (the genre that, as I suggest, is in some respects analogous to the short tragedy), there is an obvious correlation between the nature of change and the length of the narrative. Short story scholars (Norman Friedman and Charles May, among others) point out that length also depends on how authors wish to treat their subjects. They conclude that the smaller the change, the shorter the narrative. A minor change requires less space because the author does not need to account for as many causes as in the case of a major change. Since Pushkin's tragedies do not focus on the characters' change or development, their narrative space could be easily collapsed into a few scenes. This is why Pushkin's short tragedies include very few scenes, and the crucial information about a protagonist's life is presented through very few episodes; much of his life is merely alluded to or altogether omitted. For example, Pushkin limits his Don Juan's seductions to only one amorous conquest, that of Dona Anna. All his other prey are either very briefly mentioned (Inéz, for example), or their seduction occurs before Don Juan first appears on stage (although he makes love to Laura, he does not conquer her but merely revisits her). There is almost nothing shown to us about Walsingham's life prior to his joining the reveling party on the streets of the plague-ridden city. Salieri's life is briefly summed up in his opening monologue. Likewise, the Baron's past is almost altogether concealed, and only vague allusions are made to his youth. Pushkin's concept of character therefore warrants a short form.

Staging Polyvalence

Since the short form of *The Little Tragedies* tends toward innuendo, silence, ellipsis, and understatement, it is oriented toward a more active reader or audience that would be able to fill out what is merely implied. Moreover, it requires a genius of an actor who would be able to deliver the plays' profound ambiguity or, to use Gogol's expression, the "abyss of space" [bezdna prostranstva]. Clearly, as a new genre Pushkin's *Little Tragedies* demanded new forms of dramatic acting. The problem with performing Pushkin's plays is ultimately the problem of the intense ambiguity of most of the plays' spoken utterances, which present great difficulties for delivery on stage. Since the complexity of character is presented by Pushkin not diachronically (as an evolution) but synchronically (as a simultaneous coexistence of various impulses within human nature), performance and enactment of the characters' complexity become a real ordeal for an actor. That is one reason why even such a talented actor as Stanislavsky claimed that it was harder for him to recite (*chitat'*) Pushkin than Shakespeare. Oral articulation and gesture, which constitute the essence of dramatic acting, tend to restrict the ambiguity characteristic of the written word, or, in Bakhtin's terms, they "monologize" discourse.[45] Pushkin himself was skeptical not only of the work being written for contemporary theater but of Russian theatrical life in general. He criticized conventions of performance that dominated the Russian stage in the 1820s and 1830s (lofty declamation, an emphasis on spectacle) and insisted on the necessity of developing a new technique of acting that would correspond to a new dramatic form: "But the actors, the actors!—Unrhymed five feet verses require a completely new type of declamation" (13: 45).

The unity of dramatic form and dramatic acting lies, therefore, at the core of Pushkin's dramatic experiment. But as Pushkin and his contemporary dramatists knew very well, the new forms of drama and acting also demanded a new type of audience. The new form of drama and the new type of acting, Pushkin maintained, emerged in response to the new demands of the audience: "The public shapes dramatic talents" (11: 9). Alexander Griboedov expressed a similar view: "In a wonderful poem, many things must be figured out; ideas and emotions that are not fully expressed affect the soul of the reader all the more so that in the very depths of his soul lurk those hidden strings that the author has barely touched, often with a mere hint. But he is understood; everything is distinct, clear, and powerful. For this the following is required: from one side, talent and art; from the other: receptiveness and attention."[46] Unfortunately, Pushkin's audience was not yet attuned to the new development of Pushkin's genius.

In his cycle of Boldino plays, Pushkin shows the ultimate that can be done with brevity. It is not my task here to make suggestions about the new ways in which Pushkin's plays could be performed. It is clear, however, that minimalist stage settings and overall minimalist productions would be most congenial to Pushkin's dramatic design. Since oral delivery and staging always somewhat limit semantic polyvalence of the written text, one way to sustain the text's ambiguity can be achieved by increasing the elements of conventionality and stylization that would allow for multiple points of view and by reducing excessively realistic details. Any new and successful staging of *The Little Tragedies* has to be sensitive to their generic peculiarities, their hidden semantic potentials, and their suggestive power. But to do so we have to create not only new stage productions and a new language for the stage but also a new audience, one that would be ready to engage in the plays' internal dialogues.

A Few Words about the Present Collection

Regardless of the plays' extreme prestige among Russian readers and specialists, comprehensive scholarship on Pushkin's "little" masterpieces represents a glaring lacuna in Western criticism. The present collection of essays began as a conversation among Robert Louis Jackson, Vladimir Golstein, and myself about the ways to remedy this situation. We realized that the best way to start would be to organize a conference that would create an occasion for various scholars to discuss the critical issues that a study of *The Little Tragedies* presents. A "little" conference on Pushkin's *Little Tragedies* held at Yale University for fourteen scholars in October 1998 was the first step in this direction. It set out to explore the principal ways of approaching Pushkin's plays in order to raise new problems, provide new readings, and address aspects of the plays seldom illuminated in previous scholarship. Most of the essays included in the present collection emerged from the papers delivered at this conference.

Most importantly, this minisymposium provided us with a focus and helped to identify the crucial gaps in *The Little Tragedies*' criticism. Thus, in addition to the questions of genre, the plays' unity, and their playability (issues I have discussed in some detail in this introduction), it became clear that the Western reader would benefit from a discussion of the plays' literary connections, their various cultural contexts, and the problems of their transposition to various media such as film and opera. The present collection of essays seeks to address all these issues. It opens with two classic essays by two remarkable Russian female poets of the twentieth century, Anna Akhmatova and Marina Tsvetaeva, essays that remain of great interest to the contemporary reader for the breadth of their insights into Pushkin's texts and for their influence on generations of Russian writers and scholars.

In the sections that follow, one set of essays—those of Vladimir Markovich, Sergei Davydov, and myself—investigates the problem of the plays' unity. Charting the main trends in Soviet and Russian approaches to *The Little Tragedies* and informing us of the major interpretations of the plays, Markovich's expert essay, "Scholarship in the Service and Disservice of *The Little Tragedies*," not only offers an excellent synthesis of previous scholarship and a glimpse into the dynamics of the critical and philosophical development of Russian intellectual thought during the second half of the twentieth century but also raises a number of larger theoretical questions. Through the prism of *The Little Tragedies*' criticism, he discusses the merit and limitations of various methodologies and literary theories that inform, implicitly or explicitly, the study of Pushkin's dramas. His account of the present state of *The Little Tragedies*' scholarship and his discussion of approaches that might be the most fruitful will be an invaluable source for anyone who would venture into further investigation of the plays.

Although Markovich suggests that the discussion of the unifying themes and motifs of *The Little Tragedies*, with its implicit attempt to posit their meaning as a "systemic, centralized, isomorphic unit," has been nearly exhausted by scholars, Davydov's essay, "'Strange and Savage Joy': The Erotic as a Unifying Element in *The Little Tragedies*," demonstrates that the fruitfulness of an approach is largely measured by the degree of the scholar's expertise. Analyzing the texts of the plays along the well-known axis of Pushkin criticism (Thanatos and Eros), Davydov finds many new details along the way. By pointing out that all four major protagonists of the plays are barren and fruitless, he suggests an intriguing connection between Eros and Thanatos. Curiously, in the universe of the plays, it is the woman's or, rather, Eros's "gift" that serves as the instrument or cause of death (Thanatos), be it the poison, the last gift of Salieri's Isora, or Dona Anna, who serves to precipitate Don Juan's downfall. To that one may add that the cause of the Baron's death, that is, his son, is also a "gift of love" left to the Baron by his wife. In the Baron's case, Eros indeed turns into Thanatos.

Instead of focusing on textual correspondences and cross-references between the plays, in "The Anatomy of the Modern Self in *The Little Tragedies*," I explore the ways in which the four plays overlap in terms of their treatment of the "passions" that shape modern selfhood. Placing Pushkin's interest in selfhood in the context of romanticism, I show how Pushkin transforms universal myths and types such as Cain, Don Juan, and the miser into a study of modern identity. The plays are held together, I suggest, by a polyphonic unity that puts into relief several dominant "passions" or "themes" that are refracted in all the plays of the cycle.

In tracing what unites the four plays it is easy, however, to lose sight of what makes them distinct. Thus a different approach, one that focuses on individual plays, complements the study of the plays as a cycle. In his analysis of *The Stone Guest*, Robert Louis Jackson concentrates on the text itself and unravels the "abyss of space" in just one "little" tragedy. Jackson concentrates on the issue of Don Juan's identity and thus the endless gallery of masks that Don Juan flaunts. While Pushkin follows the basic outline of the Don Juan story, his contribution lies precisely in raising the question of Don Juan's identity and depicting him as first and foremost a character who defies expectations. Do we know him? Does he know himself? Is not his shifty identity connected with his shifting values and priorities? By analyzing the way Pushkin makes his Don Juan systematically abuse freedom and avoid responsibility, even through seemingly innocent words or gestures, Jackson uncovers the larger moral and psychological dimensions of the play. If, in the well-known observation of Abram Lezhnev, Pushkin's prose is psychological without psychology, Jackson shows that Pushkin's dramas are also moral and psychological without morality and psychology.

Although Monika Greenleaf and Vladimir Golstein also focus primarily on individual plays, their methods of disclosing how the plays' meanings are generated differ from Jackson's in that they consider the various cultural contexts and literary subtexts that surrounded and shaped the texts in question. While I explore the cultural contexts that informed Pushkin's conception of modern selfhood in *The Little Tragedies* as a cycle, they deal with various aspects of modern sensibility as they are reflected in individual plays. Thus in her essay, "Feasting on Genius," Greenleaf investigates how Pushkin presents Mozart as "the unconscious victim of a peculiarly modern prosecution and ritual sacrifice." "Time or Money: The Paradoxes of Aging in *The Covetous Knight*" by Golstein deals with another "modern trait": man's failure to appreciate time and its calls and to respond to changing temporal circumstances. Both Greenleaf and Golstein, by unveiling particular cultural contexts and literary subtexts, greatly enrich our understanding of the individual plays and present them in a new light. By examining the cultural phenomena of the Mozart-Salieri rumor and the production of "national genius," Greenleaf's "Feasting on Genius" recontextualizes Pushkin's *Mozart and Salieri* and approaches the play within the context of the romantic christological view of the artist as a sacrificial victim of the crowd. According to Greenleaf, Pushkin is aware of what is involved in the construction of a romantic and national genius, both its glory and its danger, and he tries it on himself as he explores it in the character of Mozart. Salieri thus becomes an emblem of the public, ready to admire the genius but incapable of dealing with his purely human traits. The public as well as Salieri prefer their national geniuses dead so that they can comfortably analyze and compartmentalize their geniuses and their artistic input.

Golstein argues for the need to "recontextualize" *The Covetous Knight*, but to do so he draws not so much on an analysis of cultural phenomena (as Greenleaf does) as on literary subtexts and contexts. By placing *The Covetous Knight* in the larger context of European art and thought, ranging from Dante to Titian to Montaigne, Golstein seeks to disclose the larger philosophical and religious underpinnings that underlie Pushkin's notion of usury as it is embodied in the character of the Baron. When considered within the context of medieval and Renaissance thought, the Baron's tragic flaw—usury—emerges not only as a moral and economic breach, condemned as greed or exploitation, but also as a subversion of the divine order and violence against the callings of time and nature.

Whether or not the cycle of Pushkin's plays could be linked to Dante's *Divine Comedy* in terms of its treatment of human vices (greed, envy, lust, blasphemy), its free mixing of historical, mythical, literary, and purely imaginary personalities, and its hybrid genre, it is clear that each of the four plays is so rich and suggestive in its imagery, historical, literary, and cultural backgrounds, traveling motifs, and literary and historical allusions that it solicits, at least potentially, as much scholarly attention as Dante's particular cantos. Since the criticism of *The Little Tragedies* has not yet reached the level of Dante's voluminous scholarship, there is still room for the unraveling of the various literary and cultural subtexts, clues and leads with which Pushkin packed his short plays. One figure of colossal authority who was perennially on Pushkin's mind and against whom most romantic dramatists measured their achievements was, of course, Shakespeare. David Bethea revisits an old theme of Pushkin scholarship—Pushkin's Shakespearism—in a particularly fruitful way. In his "'A Higher Audacity': How to Read Pushkin's Dialogue with Shakespeare in *The Stone Guest*," Bethea approaches Pushkin's appropriation of Shakespeare in terms of his maturity and growth, his search for a new voice, and his liberation from the familiar restraints of French classicism. Exploring the way Pushkin rewrites in *The Stone Guest* the seduction of Anna by Gloucester in *Richard III* and paying particular attention to differences in Shakespeare's and Pushkin's renderings of the scene, Bethea reconstructs Pushkin's protagonists—Don Juan and Dona Anna—in all their human complexity. By rewriting the relatively simple case of power struggle that Gloucester and Anna embody in *Richard III*, Pushkin creates his own dramatic portraits of Dona Anna, Don Juan, and the statue of Dona Anna's husband that acquire a truly Shakespearean depth.

While Golstein and Bethea explore Pushkin's indebtedness to the preceding literary tradition, Susanne Fusso and Sofya Khagi delve into later literary texts that took Pushkin's *The Little Tragedies* as a point of departure. Even though Dostoevsky's indebtedness to Pushkin is well attested and analyzed in scholarship, Fusso's essay, "The Weight of Human Tears: *The Covetous Knight* and *A Raw Youth*" sheds new light both on Dostoevsky's design of his novel and on Pushkin's play as she invokes themes sketched out by Pushkin and then resurrected from oblivion by Dostoevsky. A similar goal is set in Khagi's essay, "Pleasures of the Plague: Pushkin and Camus," on *A Feast in Time of Plague* and its echoes in Camus's *The Plague.* She not only puts *A Feast in Time of Plague* on the map as an important subtext for Camus's novel but also reveals the existential underpinnings of Pushkin's play, which the modern age has found so congenial but which were not easily understood by Pushkin's contemporaries. Thus, both Fusso and Khagi offer examples of the two-way traffic between earlier and later texts: while the predecessors illuminate the texts to follow, the later texts help us read and better understand their antecedents.

An analysis of literary connections between the later texts and their antecedents also raises the larger problem of how the relationships not only between literary texts but between any "texts," whether they are the "texts" of music, opera, or film, could be considered mutually illuminating. Stephanie Sandler's and Caryl Emerson's essays articulate the ways transpositions in different media present possibilities for both the creation of new "texts" and a commentary on the old ones. The history of *The Little Tragedies*' transpositions to opera suggests a way of approaching the plays' alleged unplayability and reveals some important elements of the plays' poetics. By overviewing the history of composition and reception of the four chamber operas based on *The Little Tragedies* by four Russian composers (Alexander Dargomyzhsky, Nikolai Rimsky-Korsakov, César Cui, and Sergei Rachmaninoff), Emerson examines how these very different composers tried to solve the problem of fitting Pushkin's texts to music and his plays to the operatic stage. Their operatic works engendered a heated polemic as to whether a faithful reproduction of Pushkin's texts diminishes or enhances the value of his works. The conclusion that we can draw from Emerson's account of this polemic is paradoxical but not entirely unexpected: the most successful operatic adaptations of *The Little Tragedies* are those that are least faithful to its scripts. The relationship between a successful composer and Pushkin's original text is then similar to the strange friendship between Laura and her "faithful friend" and "fickle love," Don Juan. This relationship can only be sustained when freedom and even unfaithfulness are allowed. The example of Tchaikovsky's operas *Eugene Onegin* and *The Queen of Spades* is a case in point. Tchaikovsky, as Emerson notes, "sinned and achieved on a grand scale." To convey the spirit of Pushkin's plays frequently means to cocreate. The verbal compression of Pushkin's texts then both restricts and liberates.

In discussing Mikhail Shveitser's cinematic version of *The Little Tragedies* in her essay "*The Little Tragedies* on Film: Cinematic Realism and Embodied Inspiration," Sandler explores Shveitser's fascination with Pushkin's creativity, his rendering of the dynamic of the creative process, and the various aspects of his involvement in this process. As the audience observes artists creating in Shveitser's film, so do we, the audience of the film, observe Shveitser's creating through his film. As a result, Sandler suggests, we get a glimpse into a powerful creative impulse that is contained in Pushkin's plays. As Shveitser depicts the various artistic responses and creative acts that are generated by *The Little Tragedies*, we are made aware of their unlimited creative potential.

Pushkin's plays then seek to trigger coperformance, whether of the audience within the film or of the audience of the film. Sandler further argues that the creative impulse of Pushkin's works, which was captured by Shveitser, is part of Pushkin's own enterprise for his drama. Her essay therefore not only examines Shveitser's appropriation of Pushkin but also sheds light on Pushkin through Shveitser.

By considering various aspects of the poetics of Pushkin's *The Little Tragedies*—their verbal compactness, their cultural contexts and literary subtexts, the way they lend themselves to literary, operatic, and cinematic transpositions—the scholars of this collection demonstrate the tremendous artistic potential of Pushkin's "dramatic sketches" and their uncanny ability to infect. Pushkin engages in a dialogue with the past and future by simultaneously planting leads that connect him to the past tradition and throwing the ball into the hands of future poets, artists, actors, composers, stage directors, filmmakers, and scholars. Fraught with semantic potential and laden with allusions, echoes, cross-references, and ambiguities, Pushkin's cycle of short tragedies seeks to trigger a creative response from the reader and the audience. The ball is now in our hands.

Notes

1. The plays were united under the title of *The Little Tragedies* on the basis of Pushkin's brief reference to his short dramas as "several dramatic scenes or little tragedies" in a letter to P. A. Pletnev of 9 December 1830. *A Feast in Time of Plague* is different from the other three plays in that it represents a translation—with substantial modifications and additions—of a fragment from John Wilson's *The City of the Plague.*

2. Briggs, "Introduction," 25–26.

3. See Darkii, *Malen'kie tragedii Pushkina*; Gershenzon, *Mudrost' Pushkina*; Blagoi, *Sotsiologiia tvorchestva Pushkina*; Blagoi, *Tvorcheskii put' Pushkina* (1950); Blagoi, *Masterstvo Pushkina*; Gukovskii, *Pushkin i problemy realisticheskogo stilia*; Durylin, *Pushkin na stsene*; Gorodetskii, *Dramaturgiia Pushkina*; Tomashevskii, "'Malen'kie tragedii' Pushkina i Mol'er"; Rassadin, *Dramaturg Pushkin*; Bondi, "Dramaturgiia Pushkina"; and Lotman, "Iz razmyshlenii nad tvorcheskoi evoliutsiei Pushkina (1830 goda)"; among many others.

4. See Kuchera, "Pushkin and Don Juan"; Jackson, "Miltonic Imagery and Design"; Jackson, "Moral-Philosophical Subtext"; Victor Terras, "Pushkin's 'Feast during the Plague' and Its Original"; Golstein, "Pushkin's *Mozart and Salieri.*" For the plays as a cycle, see in particular Monter, "Love and Death"; Gregg, "The

Eudaemonic Theme"; Alexandrov, "Correlations"; Tiupa, "Novatorstvo avtorskogo soznaniia v tsikle Malen'kikh tragedii"; Beliak and Virolainen, "'Malen'kie tragedii' kak kul'turnyi epos novoevropeiskoi istorii."

5. Until 1999, when James Falen's translations of *The Little Tragedies* finally appeared in *The Complete Works of Alexander Pushkin*, translations of Pushkin's tetralogy were out of print or hard to find. Soon to follow Falen's translations were Nancy K. Anderson's translations of the plays. See Pushkin, *The Little Tragedies*, translated by Nancy K. Anderson.

6. Albert Camus's staging of Pushkin's *Stone Guest* with himself playing the role of Don Juan was clearly an exception motivated by the French writer's overall intense interest in Russian literature and the celebrations of the centennial of Pushkin's death in 1937. Note that in the 1930s several new stage productions of *The Little Tragedies* were planned in Russia and elsewhere in connection with the centennial of Pushkin's death. For a more detailed discussion of Camus's involvement with Pushkin, see Khagi in this volume.

7. Shakh-Azizova, "Pushkin kak teatral'naia problema," 226.

8. Ibid.

9. S. E. Radlov, "O stsenichnosti podlinnoi i mnimoi," *Rabochii i teatr* 2, no. 13 (1937). Cited in Feldman, *Sud'ba dramaturgii Pushkina*, 234.

10. Feldman, *Sud'ba dramaturgii Pushkina*, 8.

11. Stanislavskii, *Sobranie sochinenii v 8 tomakh*, 2: 61. All translations of Pushkin's texts are mine unless otherwise specified.

12. See Vsevolod Meyerhold's essay on Alexander Benois as a theater director in Meierkhold, *Stat'i, pis'ma, rechi, besedy*, 278.

13. Brown, trans. and ed., *Meyerhold on Theater*, 140.

14. Meierkhold, *Stat'i, pis'ma, rechi, besedy*, 2: 419–26.

15. See Gregg, "The Eudaemonic Theme"; Monter, "Love and Death"; Alexandrov, "Correlations"; Shapiro, "Journey to the Metonymic Pole"; Beliak and Virolainen, "'Malen'kie tragedii' kak kul'turnyi epos novoevropeiskoi istorii."

16. Analyzing *The Little Tragedies* in terms of symmetry and parallelism on the level of plot, structure, and images, a number of Russian scholars have suggested that the cycle could be viewed as one big tragedy. Moreover, the cycle could be interpreted as a new genre, or "supergenre." For a more detailed discussion of scholars' interpretations of the plays as a cycle, see Markovich in this volume.

17. See Shakh-Azizova's discussion of the series of innovative directors who have attempted to stage *The Little Tragedies* in recent years in "Pushkin kak teatral'naia problema," 231.

18. See Odinokov, *Khudozhestvenno-istoricheskii opyt v poetike russkikh pisatelei*, 138–45; Beliak and Virolainen, "'Malen'kie tragedii' kak kul'turnyi epos novoevropeiskoi istorii," 97; and a discussion of their ideas by Markovich in this volume.

19. Schlegel, "Athenäum Fragments #116, 139, 238," 12.

20. Schlegel, "From Lectures on Dramatic Art and Literature," 36.

21. We may recall Leo Tolstoy's frequently quoted pronouncement about Russian writers' defiance of generic norms: "From Gogol's *Dead Souls* to Dostoevsky's

Dead House, in the recent period of Russian literature there has not been a single artistic prose work, at all rising above mediocrity, that quite fits the form of a novel, a poem, or a story" (Tolstoi, "Neskol'ko slov po povodu knigi 'Voina i mir,'" in *Polnoe sobranie sochinenii*, 16: 7.

22. Tynianov, *Pushkin i ego sovremenniki*, 149.

23. Ibid., 148.

24. Ibid., 149.

25. See Tomashevskii, "'Malen'kie tragedii' Pushkina i Mol'er," 262–314. See also note 2 in my essay in this volume.

26. Beliak and Virolainen, "'Malen'kie tragedii' kak kul'turnyi epos novoevropeiskoi istorii," 77.

27. Alekseev, *Pushkin*, 285.

28. See Chumakov, "Dva fragmenta o siuzhetnoi polifonii *Motsarta i Sal'eri*," 37. See also Chumakov, *Stikhotvornaia poetika Pushkina*, 280. This potentially important observation leads Chumakov not to the examination of the plays' generic peculiarity but to the claim that *Mozart and Salieri* has two alternative fabulas. Chumakov does not sufficiently discuss Pushkin's generic innovation; instead, he uses this observation to suggest that "semantic intensity" in Pushkin is accompanied by "semantic uncertainty," a claim that validates his own reading of *Mozart and Salieri* in terms of semantic polyphony on the level of plot. One plot, he maintains, has several fabulas, at least two. Ultimately, *Mozart and Salieri* offers, according to Chumakov, a possibility not so much for various interpretations of the events but for various ways of telling the events.

29. Critics have commented extensively on rhyme patterns, repetitions, use of symmetry, and parallelism in *The Little Tragedies*. For an excellent account of this enterprise, see Markovich in this volume.

30. Wolf Schmid argues that Pushkin endows his *Belkin Tales* with some elements of poetic discourse by using three main devices: creations of the intratextual equivalencies and paradigms; activation of the intertextual equivalencies; and realization and unfolding of the phraseological expressions and semantic figures in order to transform them into larger plot units. See his *Puskins Prosa in poetischer Lektüre*, 49–50.

31. See Alexandrov, "Correlations"; Gregg, "The Eudaemonic Theme"; Monter, "Love and Death"; and Bethea and Davydov in this volume, among others.

32. Alekseev, *Pushkin*, 285.

33. Cox, *In the Shadow of Romance*, 44–45. In addition to monodrama, there were also experiments with old dramatic forms such as mysteries (see Byron's preface to his poem-play *Cain*).

34. Madame de Staël juxtaposes ancient Greek and Roman tragedies to modern drama by emphasizing the inward turn in the portrayal of modern characters:

> In epic poems and ancient Greek and Roman tragedies, there is a kind of simplicity coming from the way people then identified themselves with nature. [...] Reflecting very little, man would relate the action of his soul

> to the outside world. Consciousness itself was represented by external objects, and the torches of the Furies showered remorse on the heads of the guilty. In ancient times, the event was all-important; in modern times, character has become more important. The anxious reflection eating away at us like Prometheus's vulture would have looked insane among the clear, distinct relationships of the civil and social state in ancient times. (Folkenflik, ed. and trans., *An Extraordinary Woman*, 300)

35. Cited in Feldman, *Sud'ba dramaturgii Pushkina*, 71.

36. Zhukovskii, *Polnoe sobranie sochinenii v 3 tomakh*, 3: 584.

37. Pavel Katenin, in *Literaturnaia gazeta*, no. 71, 284.

38. In his drama, Pushkin was primarily interested in a "free and broad representation of characters" and "carefree and simple conceptions of plans"—the qualities that he associated with the dramatic art of Shakespeare. For the most part, his references to Shakespeare reflect the common trend in the romantics' theoretical discussions of using the English Bard as a vehicle against neoclassical conventions of unities and fixed types in dramaturgy. Shakespeare stood for freedom from rules and constraints and as a license to mix styles. "I imitated Shakespeare," Pushkin writes in 1830, "in his broad and free depiction of characters, in his carefree and simple compositions of types" (11: 140). Along with most other romantics, he opposed French neoclassicist norms in tragedy and shared the terms of the polemic about the new romantic tragedy with his early-nineteenth-century contemporaries, who formulated it—rather idiosyncratically—as an opposition between Racine and Shakespeare.

39. Durylin, *Pushkin na stsene*, 94.

40. Quoted in Darkii, *Malen'kie tragedii Pushkina*, 23.

41. See Blagoi, *Tvorcheskii put' Pushkina* (1967), 653.

42. The idea that genius and villainy are incompatible is, in fact, deeply rooted in romantic sensibility, with its notion of the poet as a prophet and its belief in the special vocation of the artist. Consider, for example, Shelley's famous lines from his *Defence of Poetry*: "A poet, as he is the author to others of the highest wisdom, pleasure, virtue and glory, so he ought personally to be the happiest, the best, the wisest, and the most illustrious of men" (Clark, ed., *Shelley's Prose*, 135).

43. Bakhtin, *Problems of Dostoevsky's Poetics*, 87.

44. Several Russian scholars approached *The Little Tragedies* through the prism of Bakhtin's ideas about polyphony and overall "novelization" of genres (Odinokov, Maimin, Tiupa). Thus Maimin, for example, discusses the polyphonic coexistence of various "truths" or "voices" in Pushkin's plays in his essay "Polifonicheskii roman Dostoevskogo i pushkinskaia traditsiia," 313–14. The critics' fruitful observations should be further developed to include the notion of internal dialogism that characterizes Pushkin's portrayals of his tragic characters. Interestingly, Caryl Emerson arrives at a similar conclusion in her discussion of *Boris Godunov*.

45. Bakhtin, *Problems of Dostoevsky's Poetics*, 198. It is no coincidence that in

her discussion of *Boris Godunov* Emerson arrives at an analogous conclusion about the difficulties that a successful stage production of *Boris Godunov* must face. Emerson explains these difficulties by the play's internal dialogism and supports her point with Bakhtin's observation about the language of novels, which, according to Bakhtin, resists oral delivery, "for loud and living intonation excessively monologizes discourse and cannot do justice to the other person's voice present in it" (*Boris Godunov*, 116–17).

46. Griboedov, *Sochineniia*, 527–28.

The Poets' Corner

Pushkin's *Stone Guest*

Anna Akhmatova
Translated by Janet Tucker

I

As is well known, Pushkin was revered by his contemporaries in the early period of his literary career (when *The Prisoner of the Caucasus, The Fountain of Bakhchisaray,* and the early lyrics came out); his literary career developed quickly and brilliantly. And then, sometime around 1830, the readers and critics forsook Pushkin. The reason for this lies first and foremost in Pushkin himself. He had changed. Instead of *The Prisoner of the Caucasus,* he was writing *The Little House in Kolomna,* instead of *The Fountain of Bakhchisaray—The Little Tragedies,* and later *The Golden Cockerel* and *The Bronze Horseman.* His contemporaries were perplexed; his enemies and those who envied him rejoiced. His friends kept mum. Pushkin himself writes in 1830:

> There are both almanacs and journals
> Where precepts are reprised to us,
> Where nowadays they abuse me so,
> And where I would encounter such madrigals
> About myself from time to time.

In precisely what way and how did Pushkin change?

In the preface proposed for the eighth and ninth chapters of *Eugene Onegin* (1830), Pushkin polemicizes with the critics: "The age may move forward," but "poetry stays in one and the same place. . . . Its means and ends are one and the same."

In that same year, however, in the drafts of an article about Baratynsky, Pushkin depicts the relationship between the poet and the reader in an entirely different way:

> The concepts and feelings of the eighteen-year-old poet are still near and dear to everyone; young readers understand him and are delighted to recognize their own feelings and thoughts, which are clearly expressed, alive, and harmonious in his works. But as the years go by and the youthful poet reaches manhood, his talent grows, his understanding becomes greater, his feelings change. His songs are no longer the same. But the readers are the same and have only become more coldhearted and indifferent toward the poetry of life. The poet grows apart from them and little by little withdraws entirely. He creates for himself, and if his works are still published from time to time, he encounters coldness or inattention, and he finds an echo of his sounds only in the hearts of a few admirers of poetry, who, like himself, are secluded and forgotten by the world.

It is odd that it has still not been noted anywhere that it was Baratynsky himself who suggested this idea to Pushkin in a letter in 1828, where he explains the failure of *Onegin* this way:

> I think that a poet in Russia can hope for great success only with his first immature experiments. All the young people, who find in him what are virtually their own feelings and thoughts, brilliantly expressed, are on his side. The poet develops, writes with greater deliberation and profundity, but the officers are bored by him, and the brigadiers do not accept him, because after all his poetry is not prose. Don't take these reflections as referring to yourself; they are general ones.[1]

Just how Pushkin developed Baratynsky's idea is evident from a comparison of these two citations.

Thus, it is not so much that poetry is static, as that the reader does not keep pace with the poet.

All of Pushkin's contemporaries enthusiastically recognized themselves in the hero of *The Prisoner of the Caucasus*, but who would agree to recognize himself in Eugene from *The Bronze Horseman*?

II

The *Little Tragedies* can be numbered among those of Pushkin's mature works that not only his contemporaries, but even the poet's friends did not know.[2] There is perhaps no single work of world poetry in which such formidable moral questions are presented so sharply and complexly as Pushkin's *Little Tragedies.* The complexity is so great at times that, when combined with the breathtaking conciseness, the sense is almost obscured, which invites various interpretations (for example, the denouement of *The Stone Guest*).

I believe that Pushkin himself provides an explanation for this in his note about Musset (October 24, 1830), where he commends the author of *Contes d'Espagne et d'Italie* for the absence of moralizing and in general advises against "tacking on a moral admonition to everything." This observation in part provides a key to understanding the supposedly humorous ending of *The Little House in Kolomna* (October 9, 1830):

> "Have you at least some moral admonition?"
> "No . . . well, perhaps . . . I'll think, with your permission . . .
> Here is a moral for you . . ."[3]

This is followed by a parody on a moral ending, clearly meant as a challenge: "Nothing more fine / Can be squeezed out of this plain tale of mine."

It is understandable that many of the standard ways of representing passions were closed to a poet who had thus posed the question about moralizing. Everything above is particularly relevant to *The Stone Guest,* which nevertheless represents an adaptation of the universal theme of retribution; and Pushkin's predecessors did not hesitate to moralize when dealing with this theme.

Pushkin takes a different path. He needs to convince the reader from the very first lines, and without resorting to explicit moralizing, that the hero must perish. The fact that *The Stone Guest* is a tragedy of retribution for Pushkin is proven by the very title he has chosen (*The Stone Guest,* not *Don Juan*). Therefore, all the dramatis personae—Laura, Leporello, Don Carlos, and Doña Anna—act only so as to prepare and hasten the death of Don Juan. The hero himself tirelessly pleads for the same:

> All's for the best. Unlucky enough to kill
> Don Carlos, taking refuge as a monk
> Within these cloisters . . .[4]

But Leporello says:

> That's the style.
> Now let's enjoy ourselves. Forget the dead.

Pushkin scholarship has shown us how Pushkin's Don Juan resembles his predecessors. And it makes sense for us to determine now in what way he is original.

It is characteristic of Pushkin that Don Juan's wealth is referred to only once, and in passing, whereas this is an essential theme for da Ponte and Molière. Pushkin's Juan is neither da Ponte's rich man, who wants "to revel in his money," nor Molière's doleful raisonneur, who deceives his creditors. Pushkin's Juan is a Spanish grandee whom the king would not fail to recognize if he encountered him on the street. Reading *The Stone Guest* attentively, we make an unexpected discovery: Don Juan is a poet. Laura sings his verses that have been set to music; and even Juan calls himself an "Improvisor of Love Songs."

This draws him nearer to the basic Pushkin hero. Charsky, repeating one of Pushkin's favorite thoughts, says in *The Egyptian Nights:* "Our poets do not enjoy the patronage of gentlemen, our poets are themselves gentlemen. . . ." As far as I know, no one else has thought to make his Don Juan a poet.

The situation at the tragedy's denouement is itself very close to Pushkin. In the 1820s Pushkin was tormented by the dream of a secret return from exile. That is precisely why Pushkin transferred the action from Seville (where it was set in the drafts—Seville is Don Juan's city of long standing) to Madrid: he needed the capital. Pushkin, through Don Juan, says of the king:

> Send me away again.
> I don't suppose I'll have my head chopped off.
> I'm not accused of crime against the State.

Read "political prisoner," on whom the death penalty is customarily imposed for an unauthorized return from exile. His friends said something of the sort to Pushkin himself when he wanted to return to Petersburg from Mikhailovskoye.[5] And apropos of this, Pushkin's Leporello, turning to his lord, exclaims: "Well, then, you should *have stayed in safety*."

Pushkin, it is true, does not put his Don Juan into the same ridiculous and shameful situation of every other Don Juan—no amorous Elvira pursues him and no jealous Mazetto intends to beat him; he doesn't even disguise himself as a servant to seduce the housemaid (as in Mozart's opera); he is a hero to the end, but this combination of cold cruelty and childish carelessness produces an incredible impression. Hence, Pushkin's Don Juan, despite his elegance and worldly manners, is far more terrifying than his predecessors.[6]

Both heroines note this, each in her own way: Doña Anna—"You are a real demon"; Laura—"Ruffian, fiend."

If Laura perhaps is simply scolding, then the word "demon" on the lips of Doña Anna produces just the impression that Don Juan must make, in accordance with the author's conception.

In contrast to other Don Juans, who treat all women absolutely the same way, Pushkin's Juan addresses each of the three very different women with different words.

The hero of *The Stone Guest* scolds his servant in the same way as both Mozart's and Molière's Don Juans, but the buffoonish scene in the opera's finale—the gluttony of servant and master—would, for example, be absolutely impossible in Pushkin's tragedy.

Pushkin originally wanted to emphasize the circumstances surrounding Juan's proposal to meet with the Commendador's widow near his statue, but then Leporello's indignant remark: "Atop a husband's grave . . . he is shameless; *it will turn out badly for him!*" seemed to smack too much of moralizing to Pushkin, and he left it to the reader to guess where the meetings take place.

In neither the final text nor in the drafts of *The Stone Guest* is there even a single word of explanation for the cause of the duel between Don Juan and the Commendador. This is odd. I dare say that the reason for this unexplained omission is as follows: in all the works preceding Pushkin's (save Molière's, where, in contrast to *The Stone Guest*, the Commendador is presented as an entirely abstract figure, not linked with the action in any way), the Commendador perishes defending the honor of his daughter, Doña Anna. Pushkin made Doña Anna the Commendador's wife, not his daughter, and he himself informs us that Juan has never seen her before. The former cause falls by the wayside, but Pushkin did not want to devise a new one that would distract the reader's attention from what was most important. He emphasizes only that the Commendador was killed in a duel

> When we two met behind the Escorial . . .[7]

and not in a scandalous nocturnal fight (in which even Doña Anna takes part), which would not have been in keeping with Juan's character.[8]

If the scene of Juan's declaration to Doña Anna can be traced to Shakespeare's *Richard III,* we must remember that Richard is a consummate villain and not a professional seducer; he is motivated by political considerations, not at all from amorous ones, as he explains to the onlookers then and there.

Pushkin thereby wished to say that thoughtlessness can lead his Juan to act like a villain, although he is only a society rake.

Second, to my mind a more significant link with Shakespeare that has gone unnoticed can be found in the closing scene of the tragedy *The Stone Guest:*

> Doña Anna
> How did you dare
> Come here? If someone recognized you—death.

In the draft:

> People could recognize you.

> Juliet
> How cam'st thou hither, tell me, and wherefore? . . .
> And the place death, considering who thou art,
> If any of my kinsmen find thee here . . .
> (*Romeo and Juliet,* Act II, scene 2)

Even the scene of inviting the statue, the only one that follows tradition, reveals the real abyss between Pushkin's Don Juan and his prototypes. Pushkin has transformed the inappropriate prank of the

Mozartian and Molièrian Don Juans, evoked and motivated by the fact that he read an insulting inscription on the monument, into demonic bravado.[9] Instead of the absurd and traditional invitation to dine offered to the statue, we see something unparalleled:

> My good Commendador, tomorrow evening
> Come to your widow's house—I shall be there—[10]
> And will you stand outside the door on guard?
> You'll come?

That is, Juan speaks to the statue as to a lucky rival.

Pushkin retained his hero's reputation as an atheist, a reputation proceeding from *l'Ateista fulminado* (the hero of a religious drama presented in churches and monasteries).

> Depraved and *godless* scoundrel named Don Juan (the monk)
> Your Don Juan is a *godless* scoundrel (Don Carlos)
> Don Juan is described to you as being without conscience, *without faith* (Don Juan himself)
> I have heard you are a *godless* libertine (Doña Anna)

Accusations of atheism were a usual refrain in the young Pushkin's life.

On the other hand, Pushkin completely banished from his tragedy another feature typical of Don Juans—the wanderings. It suffices to recall Mozart's *Don Giovanni* and Leporello's celebrated aria—the catalogue of conquests (641 in Italy, 231 in Germany, 100 in France, 91 in Turkey, and in Spain, a neat 1,003). Pushkin's grandee (his exile excepted, it goes without saying) leads a completely settled metropolitan way of life in Madrid, where every "tipsy fiddler or strolling gypsy-woman" would recognize him.[11]

III

Pushkin's Don Juan does not do or say anything that any contemporary of Pushkin's would not have done or said, aside from what is necessary to preserve the Spanish local color ("I'll take him out concealed beneath my cloak / And put him at a crossroads"). This is precisely how Daiti, the hero of Musset's *Portia,* deals with the corpse of his rival, which is found the next day "*le front sur le pavé*" ("face down on the road").

Laura's guests (obviously Madrid's golden youth—Don Juan's friends) are more like members of the Green Lamp, dining with some celebrity of that time, such as Kolosova, and discussing art, than like noble Spaniards of whatever era. But the author of *The Stone Guest* knows that this presents no danger for him. He is confident that his brief description of the night will create a brilliant and unforgettable impression that this is Spain, Madrid, the South:

> Come out upon the balcony. How clear
> The sky; the air is warm and still—the evening
> Wafts us the scent of lemon boughs and laurel;
> The moon shines bright upon the deep dark blue—

Juan sports with Laura like a Petersburg rake with an actress; he recalls Iñez, whom he has ruined, in a melancholy way; he praises the stern spirit of the Commendador, whom he has killed; and he seduces Doña Anna according to all the rules of "Adolphian" worldly strategy.[12] Then something mysterious happens that is not fully explicated. Don Juan's final exclamation, when there can be no question of pretense:

> I die—My end has come—O, Doña Anna!

convinces us that he has truly been reborn during his meeting with Doña Anna, and indeed the entire tragedy operates on the premise that at this moment he loved and was happy, but instead of salvation, from which he was but a step away, comes death. Let us note one more detail: "Leave her," says the statue. This means that Juan flings himself at Doña Anna; it means that he sees only her at this terrible moment.

Indeed, if Don Carlos had killed Don Juan, we would not have had a tragedy, but something on the order of *Les Marrons du feu,* which Pushkin so admired in 1830 for its absence of moralizing and where the Don Juanian hero ("*Mais c'est du don Juan*") perishes accidentally and senselessly. Pushkin's Don Juan perishes neither accidentally nor senselessly. The Commendador's statue is a symbol of retribution, but if it had carried Don Juan away while still in the cemetery, then we would have had not so much a tragedy as a theater of horrors or *l'Ateista fulminado* of medieval mystery plays. Juan is not afraid of death. We see that he is not in the least frightened of Don Carlos's sword and does not give even a second thought to the possibility of his own death. That is why Pushkin needed the duel with Don Carlos: to show Don Juan as he really is. At the finale of the tragedy we see him in a completely different way. And it is not at all a matter of whether the statue is an otherworldly phenomenon: the nod in the scene at the cemetery is also an otherworldly phenomenon, one to which Don Juan does not pay proper attention, however. Juan is not afraid of death or punishment after death, but of the loss of happiness. Hence his last words: "O Doña Anna!" And Pushkin places him in the only situation (according to Pushkin) in which death terrifies his hero. And we suddenly recognize something we know full well. Pushkin himself provides a motivated and comprehensive explanation for the tragedy's denouement. *The Stone Guest* is dated November 4, 1830, and in mid-October, Pushkin wrote "The Shot," the autobiographical character of which no one disputes. Silvio, the hero of "The Shot," says: "What use is there for me, thought I, to deprive him of life, when he in no way values it? A wicked thought came to mind (. . .) Let's see if he'll accept death as indifferently on the eve of his wedding as he once did when he was eating cherries!" We may conclude from this that Pushkin believed death to be terrible only if there was happiness. This is exactly how Juan responds to Doña Anna's question: "And have you loved me long?"

How long or lately
I cannot say. But *since that love began*
I've learned the price of every passing moment,
And what it means to speak of Happiness.

That is, he learned the price of every passing moment when he became happy. In both "The Shot" and *The Stone Guest,* the woman whom the hero loves is present at the moment of reckoning, contrary to the Don Juan tradition. In Mozart, for example, only the buffoonish Leporello is present, in Molière—Sganarel.

The problem of happiness troubled Pushkin greatly at this time (1830). "As far as happiness is concerned, I am an atheist; I don't believe in it," he wrote to P. A. Osipova the day after finishing *The Stone Guest* (the original is in French); "The devil himself tricked me into raving about happiness as if I had been created for it"—Pushkin's letter to Pletnyov; "Ah, what a cursed trick happiness is!"—to Vyazemsky (original in French). It would be simple to cite a whole series of such quotations, and one can even say, at the risk of seeming paradoxical, that Pushkin was as afraid of happiness as others are afraid of sorrow. And inasmuch as he was always expecting trouble of all sorts, he was uneasy in the face of happiness, that is to say, in the face of the loss of happiness.

IV

But that's not all. In addition to analogies with the autobiographical "The Shot," we should cite quotations from Pushkin's correspondence. The first is from a letter to his future mother-in-law, N. I. Goncharova (April 5, 1830): "I pictured in my mind the errors of my early youth; they were distressing enough just taken by themselves, but calumny has intensified them even more; unfortunately, the rumors about them have been widespread" (original in French). How close this is to Don Juan's confession:

> Maybe, report is not entirely false,
> Maybe, upon a tried and weary conscience
> There lies a weight of evil. Long was I
> A model pupil of debauchery . . .

And: "Poor thing! She is so young, so innocent, but he is such a frivolous, such an *immoral* man" (autobiographical fragment, May 13, 1830). Here "immoral," of course, is an extenuation of "debauched." And this is just what the voice of rumor communicates.

In that same year, Pushkin addresses the very same question in a poem that was not published during his lifetime, "At moments when your graceful form . . .":

> Too keenly mindful in your heart
> Of past betrayal's doleful mention . . .
> I curse the cunning machinations
> That were my sinful youth's delight . . .[13]

All of Doña Anna's rejoinders are implied in this verse. Pushkin, who had just gotten married, writes to Pletnyov: "I am . . . happy . . .

This state is so new for me that it seems I have been reborn"; compare with *The Stone Guest:* "My inmost being has changed." Juan says of the Commendador: "He . . . enjoys the bliss of *Heaven*!"; compare with Pushkin's letter to A. P. Kern: "How is it possible to be your husband? I cannot picture such a thing for myself, just as I cannot picture heaven" (original in French).

In *Eugene Onegin,* Pushkin promises that when he depicts declarations of love, he will recall:

> The language of impassioned pining
> Will I renew, and love's reply,
> The like of which in days gone by
> Came to me as I lay reclining
> At a dear beauty's feet . . .[14]

The similarity of these citations speaks not so much to the autobiographical quality of *The Stone Guest* as to the lyrical source of this tragedy.

V

If Pushkin did not publish *The Covetous Knight* for six years, afraid, as was then said, of "applications [to himself]," then we can assume the same of *The Stone Guest,* which he did not publish at all. (I shall note in passing that *The Feast at the Time of the Plague* was published in 1832, that is, almost immediately after it was written, and this is not because *The Feast* is a simple translation.) However that may be, *The Stone Guest* is the only one of *The Little Tragedies* not published in Pushkin's lifetime. It is easy to see that something that we can unearth now only with the very greatest difficulty was, in Pushkin's mind, floating right on the surface. He had invested too much of himself in *The Stone Guest* and treated it like several of his lyric poems, which remained in manuscript regardless of their quality. In his mature period, Pushkin was not at all inclined to expose "the wounds of his conscience" before the world (to which, to a certain extent, every lyric poet is condemned), and I dare say that *The Stone Guest* was not printed for the very same reason that Pushkin's contemporaries did not read until after his death the conclusion of "Remembrance," "No, no, those fierce delights I do not treasure," and "At moments when your graceful form," and not for the same reason that *The Bronze Horseman* remained in manuscript.[15]

Besides all the parallels I have cited, the lyrical source of *The Stone Guest* can be established by a connection with, on one hand, "The Shot" (the problem of happiness) and, on the other, with *The Water Sprite,* which is recounted in brief (as indeed befits a prehistory) in Juan's recollection of Iñez. Juan's rendezvous with Iñez takes place at the cemetery of the St. Anthony Monastery (as is clear from the draft):

> Wait: that is St. Anthony's Monastery—
> And the monastery cemetery . . .
> Oh, I remember everything. You used to come here . . .

Like the prince in *The Water Sprite,* Juan recognizes the place and recalls a woman he had ruined. In both works she is the daughter of a miller. And it is no accident that Juan says to his servant: "Just go to the village, you know, that one where the mill is." Later he calls the place the cursed *venta* (bazaar). The final wording of these lines partially erased this similarity, but now that the drafts have been studied, there is no doubt that Pushkin's tragedy begins with an obscured mention of the crime of a hero whom fate brings to the very same place where this crime was perpetrated and where he perpetrates a new crime. Everything has been predetermined by this, and the shade of poor Iñez plays a much greater role in *The Stone Guest* than has customarily been thought.

VI

The preceding remarks concern the Don Juan line of the tragedy, *The Stone Guest.* But this work obviously has another line as well—that of the Commendador. Pushkin breaks completely with tradition here as well. In Mozart, da Ponte's Don Juan does not want to be reminded of the Commendatore to such an extent that when Leporello asks permission to say something, his master answers: "All right, if you don't talk about the Commendatore."

But Pushkin's hero talks almost non-stop about the Commendador.

And what is even more important is the fact that, both in the legend and in all its literary adaptations, the statue makes an appearance in order to appeal to Juan's conscience, so that he will repent of his sins. This would not make sense in Pushkin's tragedy, because Juan confesses without being coerced:

> My inmost being has changed—in love with you
> I am in love with virtue, and at last
> On trembling knees I humbly bend before it.

The Commendador arrives at the moment of the "cold, peaceful kiss" to take his wife away from Juan. All other authors depict the Commendador as a decrepit old man and an insulted father. In Pushkin, he is a jealous husband ("And I heard that the deceased was a jealous man. He kept Doña Anna under lock and key"), and it does not follow from this that he is an old man. Juan says:

> Don't torment my
> Heart, Doña Anna, with the passionate mention
> Of your spouse—

to which Doña Anna protests: "How jealous you are."

We have every right to regard the Commendador as one of the characters in the tragedy, *The Stone Guest.* He has a biography, a personality and he takes part in the action. We even know what he looks like: "he was small, thin." He had married a beauty who did not love him and was able through his love to be worthy of her favor and gratitude. Not a word of this is from the Don Juan tradition. The thought about his jealousy enters Don Juan's head (in the draft when he does not yet even know Doña Anna) from the first moment; and it is then that Leporello says of his master: "Atop a husband's grave . . . he is shameless; it will turn out badly for him!"

And Pushkin's Commendador is more like the "incensed jealous man" of Pushkin's youthful poem "To a Young Widow," where a dead husband appears before a widow who is unfaithful to his memory (and where the deceased is also called a happy man, as in *The Stone Guest*), than like a phantom from beyond the grave who calls on the hero to renounce his impious life.

In the seventh chapter of *Eugene Onegin* Pushkin touches on the theme of jealousy from beyond the grave in connection with Lensky's grave and Olga's unfaithfulness:

Was the despondent bard perturbed
By the news of the betrayal?

At least, out of the grave
There did not rise on that sad day
His jealous shade,
And at the late hour dear to Hymen,
No traces of sepulchral visitations
Frightened the newlywed.[16]

It is as though Pushkin were disappointed (seeking a plot where an angered and jealous shade would appear). That is why he changes the plot of Don Juan and turns the Commendador into the husband, not the father of Doña Anna.

The moving widowed fiancée, Xenia Godunova, crying over the portrait of her dead betrothed whom she has never seen in life, says: "I will be faithful to the deceased."

Tatyana's celebrated rebuff:

But I was pledged another's wife,
And will be faithful all my life.[17]

is only a pale reflection of what Xenia Godunova and Doña Anna affirm ("a widow must be faithful to the grave").

But what is even more astonishing is the fact that, in the letter cited above to N. N. Goncharova's mother (April 5, 1830), Pushkin writes: "As God is my witness, I am ready to die for her; but to die and leave her a radiant widow, free to choose a new husband for herself the next day—this thought is hell for me." And still more striking: ". . . should she consent to give me her hand, I would see in this merely the proof of the serene indifference of her heart" (original in French).[18] Compare *The Stone Guest:*

No,
My mother gave my hand to Don Alvaro.

And further the entire situation is the same in the letter as in the tragedy.

Thus, in the tragedy *The Stone Guest,* Pushkin is chastising his young, carefree, and sinful self—and the theme of jealousy from beyond the grave (that is, the fear of it) resounds as loudly as the theme of retribution.

A careful analysis of *The Stone Guest,* therefore, leads us to the firm conviction that behind the external borrowings of names and situations, what we have in essence is not simply a new treatment of the universal Don Juan legend, but a deeply personal and original work by Pushkin, whose principal feature is determined not by the plot of the legend, but by Pushkin's own lyrical feelings, inseparably linked with his life experience.

We have before us the dramatic embodiment of Pushkin's inner personality, an aesthetic revelation of what tormented and captivated the poet. In contrast to Byron, who (in Pushkin's view) "cast a one-sided glance at the world and human nature, then turned away from them and became absorbed in himself," Pushkin, proceeding from personal experience, creates finished and objective characters: he does not shut himself away from the world, but goes out into the world.

That is why self-avowals are so inconspicuous in his works and can be identified only through painstaking analysis. Responding "to every sound," Pushkin absorbed the experience of his entire generation in himself. Pushkin's lyrical richness allowed him to avoid the error he had observed in the dramatic works of Byron, who dispensed "a single component of his personality to each protagonist" and who thus reduced his work "to several petty and insignificant characters."

Notes

[This essay is reprinted from Anna Akhmatova, *My Half Century*, 200–214. The majority of the notes belong to Akhmatova and are marked A.A. Commentary by Emma Gershtein from her edition of *O Pushkine* is marked E.G. The notes done by Ronald Meyer are marked Ed.]

Akhmatova's third Pushkin article, devoted to the little tragedy, *The Stone Guest,* is dated 1947. More than ten years had passed since the publication of her work on Pushkin and Benjamin Constant (1936). The essay, however, did not appear in print until 1958, though Akhmatova had read her new work to a number of the leading Pushkin scholars soon after its completion. Her analysis of *The Stone Guest* bears witness to her increasing interest in Pushkin's biography, to which she would turn in the 1950s. In the late 1950s Akhmatova returned to her essay on *The Stone Guest* and wrote a number of extended insertions. These interpolations were never fully integrated into the final text.

1. S. M. Bondi pointed this out in his study "Stat'i Pushkina o Baratynskom" (see his book: *Novye stranitsy Pushkina* [Moscow, 1931], pp. 123–24). [E.G.]

2. In his diary Vyazemsky coldly lists *The Little Tragedies* as new things Pushkin had brought from Boldino (P. A. Viazemskii, *Polnoe sobranie sochinenii*, St. Petersburg, 1884, vol. 9, p. 152), and Zhukovsky wrote to Pushkin in 1831: "There's no need for you to get angry at *The Plague:* it is scarcely better than *The Stone Guest.*" Belinsky's raptures date from 1841[:] "... Pushkin's greatest creation is his (play) *The Stone Guest*" (V. G. Belinskii, *Polnoe sobranie sochinenii*, Moscow, Publications of the Academy of Sciences of the Soviet Union, 1954, vol. 4, p. 424). [A.A.]

3. Alexander Pushkin, *Collected Narrative and Lyrical Poetry*, translated by Walter Arndt (Ann Arbor, 1984), p. 410. [Ed.]

4. Here and following the English translation of the final version of *The Stone Guest* is from *The Little Tragedies*, translated by Antony Wood (London: Angel Books, 1982), pp. 45–72. [Ed.]

5. "Sit still, write, write poetry" (P. A. Vyazemsky to Pushkin, May 10[,] 1826); "All in all, it would be more prudent for you to stay *quietly* in the country" (V. A. Zhukovsky to Pushkin, April 12, 1826). [A.A.]

6. If it is natural for all the discourse of Leporello and Laura to be based on popular speech, then the expressions of the Commendador's widow—"I'm dying of curiosity" and "No, I've never seen the likes of it"—are often explained by Pushkin's expressed conviction that popular speech is an absence of affectation and a sign of good breeding. Let us recall that in the sketch "Concerning All Sorts of Writing," Pushkin notes that in romantic tragedy the "blend of the comic and tragic sometimes necessitates expressions of popular speech for tension and refinement." [A.A.]

7. The Escorial is a royal palace, hardly a suitable location for a duel. Pushkin is probably alluding to the fact that the quarrel took place at the palace, thus emphasizing yet again Juan's closeness to the court. Does not Juan speak just as casually about the king: "The King still loved me when he banished me." [A.A.]

8. It seems to me that the much debated issue of whether Don Carlos was the Commendador's brother must be answered in the affirmative: it is difficult to imagine that Juan had two duels with two Spanish grandees and killed both, but for some reason he is afraid of only one family's vengeance and the King's anger about only one of these murders. Pushkin's laconicism again creates a certain reticence here. Moreover, any attempt to make this more concrete would have led to an additional confession by Don Juan in the concluding scene with Doña Anna, who at this time should be mourning the death of her brother-in-law. [A.A.]

9. See da Ponte: "Here I await vengeance against the godless one who killed me." Da Ponte's Don Juan (as well as Leporello) addresses the statue with the formal "you." Pushkin's Don Juan addresses the statue in the familiar form straightaway. This is not high style, but a remnant of their good relations in their lifetimes. It is the same with Carlos, too: Juan uses the familiar "you" straightaway. [A.A.]

In Pushkin's tragedy there is one more phrase that represents a literal translation of the libretto: "*L'ho voluto*"—"he wanted that himself." In da Ponte, Juan says this about the Commendatore whom he has murdered, but Pushkin's Juan—about the murdered Carlos.

10. It is even more terrible in the draft: "To your wife." [A.A.]

11. "Tipsy fiddler"—because the customers hired musicians to serenade and it was customary to treat the musicians to drink afterwards (see Le Sage's *Le Diable boiteux*). [A.A.]

12. See my article on *Adolphe.* Adolphe was the alter ego of Onegin and thus, to a certain extent, of Pushkin himself. [A.A.]

13. Alexander Pushkin, *Collected Narrative and Lyrical Poetry,* translated by Walter Arndt (Ann Arbor, 1984), p. 99. [Ed.]

14. Alexander Pushkin, *Eugene Onegin,* translated by Walter Arndt (New York, 1981), p. 67. [Ed.]

15. In spite of this, the theme of the wounded conscience appears in Pushkin's lyrics in the late 1820s: the mighty "Remembrance" (1828) and "A Georgian Song" ("Don't sing, my beauty, in my presence . . ."), which was written a few days later, where the "fatal" image of the "distant poor maid" resembles poor Iñez. [A.A.]

16. The variant lines from Pushkin are translated by Vladimir Nabokov in his monumental *Eugene Onegin,* translated from the Russian with commentary (New York, 1964), vol. 3, p. 80. [Ed.]

17. *Eugene Onegin,* translated by Walter Arndt, p. 220. [Ed.]

18. Let us recall that Pushkin wrote this letter right after he had received the consent of the bride's parents to his marriage to N. N. Goncharova, when these words sounded, to say the least, unexpected. Pushkin foretold his own fate with complete accuracy: he really did die because of Natalya Nikolayevna and left her a radiant young widow, free to choose a new husband. [A.A.]

Art in the Light of Conscience

Marina Tsvetaeva
Translated by Angela Livingstone

Excerpts

Poet and elements

Poetry is God in the holy dreams of the earth

There is an ecstasy in battle
and on the somber chasm's edge.

Ecstasy, that is to say, intoxication, is a feeling that is not good in itself, it is outside goodness, and anyway—intoxication with what?

Whatever threatens us with doom
hides in itself, for mortal hearts,
unspeakable pleasures . . .

Whenever you mention art's holiness call to mind this confession of Pushkin's.

—Yes, but further on it says . . .

—All right. Let's dwell on that line, then, the one trump card for goodness: ". . . guarantee / perhaps of immortality!"

What kind of immortality? In God? In such vicinity the very sound of the word is wild. A guarantee of the immortality of nature itself, of the elements themselves—and of us insofar as we are they, are it. A line, if not blasphemous, at least manifestly pagan.

And further on, in black and white:

> And so, all praise to thee, O Plague!
> We're not afraid of murky tombs,
> we're not confounded by your call!
> As one we lift our frothing cups
> and drink the rose maiden's breath
> although that breath be—breath of Plague!

Not Pushkin, the elements. Nowhere and never have the elements spoken out so strongly. Visitation of the elemental—upon whom, doesn't matter, this time upon Pushkin. It is written in tongues of flame, in ocean waves, in desert sands—in anything you like, only not in words.

And this capital letter for Plague: plague no longer as a blind elemental force, but as a goddess, the proper name and face of *evil.*

The most remarkable thing is that we all love these lines, none of us judges them. If one of us said this in real life or, better, did it (set fire to a house, for instance, blew up a bridge), we'd all come to and shout "Crime!" Yes, come to—from a spell, wake up—from a sleep, that dead sleep of conscience, with nature's powers, our own, awake within it, that sleep into which we were cast by these few measured lines.

Genius

Visitation of the elemental, upon whom? Doesn't matter. Today upon Pushkin. Pushkin, in the little song of the Wilson tragedy, is a genius primarily because it *came upon* him.

Genius: the highest degree of subjection to the visitation—one; control of the visitation—two. The highest degree of being mentally pulled to pieces, and the highest of being—collected. The highest of passivity, and the highest of activity.

To let oneself be annihilated right down to some last atom, from the survival (resistance) of which will grow—a world.

For in this, this, this atom of resistance (resistivity) is the whole of mankind's chance of genius. Without it there is no genius—there is the crushed man who (it's still the same man!) bursts the walls not only of the Bedlams and Charentons but of the most well-ordered households too.

There is no genius without will, but still more is there none, still less is there any, without the visitation. Will is that unit to the countless milliards of the elemental visitation thanks to which alone they *are* milliards (realize their milliardness) and without which they are noughts—bubbles above a drowning man. While will without the visitation is—in creativity—simply a post. Made of oak. Such a poet would do better to go for a soldier.

Pushkin and Walsingham

Walsingham was not the only one visited by the plague. To write his *Feast in Time of Plague* Pushkin had to *be* Walsingham—and cease to be him. Repentant? No.

To write the song of the *Feast,* Pushkin had to fight down in himself both Walsingham and the priest, and pass through into some third thing as through a door. Had he dissolved himself in the plague, he could not have written this song. Had he warded off the plague with signs of the Cross, he could not have written this song (the link would have snapped). From the plague (the element) Pushkin escaped, not into the feast (the plague's, that is, Walsingham's, triumphal feast over him) and not into prayer (the priest's), but into song.

Pushkin, like Goethe in *Werther,* escaped from the plague (Goethe from love) by giving his hero the death he himself longed to die. And by putting into his mouth a song that Walsingham could not have composed.

Had Walsingham been *capable* of that song, he would have been saved, if not for life everlasting, at least for life. But Walsingham, as we all know, is long since upon the black cart.

Walsingham is Pushkin with no way out into song.

Pushkin is Walsingham with the gift of song and the will to sing.

~

Why do I arbitrarily identify Pushkin with Walsingham and not with the priest, whose creator he also is?

This is why: in the *Feast* the priest doesn't sing. (—Priests never do sing.—Yes, they do: prayers.) Had Pushkin been the priest as much (as powerfully) as he was Walsingham, he could not have helped making him sing; he'd have put into his mouth a counter-hymn—a prayer to the plague—just as he put the delightful little song (of love) into the mouth of Mary, who is in the *Feast* (while Walsingham is what Pushkin *is*) what Pushkin loves.

The lyric poet betrays himself by song, and always will, for he cannot help making his favorite (his double) speak in his own, poet's, language. A song, in a dramatic work, is always love's give-away, an unwitting sign of preference. The author tires of speaking for others and gives himself away—in song.

What remains to us of the *Feast* (in our ears and souls)? Two songs. Mary's and Walsingham's. A love-song and a plague-song.

Pushkin's genius lies in his not giving a counterweight to Walsingham's "Hymn," an antidote to plague, a prayer. Had he done so, the work would have been stabilized, and we satisfied, from which no increase of good would have come; for by slaking our thirst for a counter-hymn Pushkin would have extinguished it. And so, with only the "Hymn to the Plague," God, the good and prayer remain—outside, as the place we not only aspire to but are thrown back to; the place to which the plague throws us back. The prayer Pushkin doesn't give is there, unavoidable. (The priest in the *Feast* speaks in the performance of his duty and we not only feel nothing, we don't even listen, knowing in advance what he will say.)

Pushkin could hardly have thought of all that. One can only plan a work backwards from the last step taken to the first, retracing with one's eyes open the path one had walked blindly. Think the work *through*.

A poet is the reverse of a chess-player. He not only doesn't see the pieces and the board, he doesn't see his own hand—which indeed may not be there.

~

In what lies the blasphemy of Walsingham's song? There is no reviling of God in it, only praise of the plague. Yet is there any blasphemy stronger than this song?

Blasphemy, not because from fear and despair we feast in a time of plague (thus children laugh from fear!), but because in the song—the apogee of the feast—we have lost our fear; because we turn punishment into a feast, turn punishment into a gift; because we dissolve not in the fear of God, but in the bliss of annihilation. If (as everyone believed, in those days, and we do too while reading Pushkin) the plague is God's will to punish and vanquish us; if it really is God's scourge.

We throw ourselves under the scourge, as foliage under sunbeams, as foliage under the rain. Not joy in the teaching, but joy in the beating. Pure joy in the blow as such.

Joy? More than that! Bliss, with no equal in all the world's poetry. Bliss of complete surrender to the elemental—be it Love, or Plague, or whatever else we may call it.

For after the "Hymn to the Plague" there was no longer any God. And having come in ("enter Priest"), what else is there for the priest to do, but to go out.

The priest went away to pray, Pushkin—to sing. Pushkin goes away after the priest, he goes away last, tearing himself with effort (as if by the roots) from his double, Walsingham; or rather, at this moment Pushkin divides: into himself as Walsingham and himself as poet, himself doomed and himself saved.

But Walsingham sits at the table eternally. But Walsingham rides on the black cart eternally. But Walsingham is dug in with a spade eternally.

For that song by which Pushkin was saved.

~

A terrible name—Walsingham. It's no wonder Pushkin named him only three times in the whole play (named as if invoking him and, like an invocation, thrice). The anonymous "President," which lends the work a sinister modern relevance, is still closer to us.

~

Walsinghams aren't needed by the elements. They defeat them in their stride. To conquer God in Walsingham is, alas, easier than to conquer song in Pushkin.

The plague, in *Feast in Time of Plague,* coveted not Walsingham but Pushkin.

And—*wonder of wonders!*—Walsingham, who is to the plague only an occasion for getting hold of Pushkin, Walsingham, who is for Pushkin only an occasion for his own elemental (his plaguey) self, that very Walsingham rescues Pushkin from the plague—into song, without which Pushkin cannot be his elemental self. By giving him the song and taking upon himself the end.

The last atom of resistance to the elemental, to the glory of the elemental, is what art is. Nature conquering herself to her own glory.

~

So long as you are a poet, you shall not perish in the elemental, for everything returns you to the element of elements: the word.

So long as you are a poet, you shall not perish in the elemental; for that is not to perish but to return to the lap of nature.

The poet perishes when he renounces the elemental. He might as well cut his wrists without ado.

~

The whole of Walsingham is an exteriorization (a carrying outside his limits) of the elemental Pushkin. You cannot live with a Walsingham inside you: either a crime or a poem. Even if Walsingham *existed,*— Pushkin would still have *created* him.

~

Thank the Lord the poet has the hero, the third person—*him*—as a way out. Otherwise, what a shameful (and uninterrupted) confession.

Thus, at least the appearance is saved.

~

The "Apollonian principle," the "golden mean": don't you see that this is nothing more than bits of Latin stuck in a schoolboy's head?

Pushkin, who created Walsingham, Pugachov, Mazeppa, Peter, who created them from inside himself, who didn't create them but disgorged them . . .

The Pushkin of the sea "of the free element."

—There was also another Pushkin.

—Yes, the Pushkin of *Walsingham's deep thought.*

(Exit Priest. The President remains, sunk in *deep thought.*)

~

November 1830. Boldino. A hundred and one years ago. A hundred and one years later.

Art's lessons

What does art teach? Goodness? No. Commonsense? No. It cannot teach even itself, for it is—given.

There is no thing which is not taught by art; there is no thing the reverse of that, which is not taught by art; and there is no thing which is the only thing taught by art.

All the lessons we derive from art, *we* put into it.

A series of answers to which there are no questions.

All art is the sole givenness of the answer.

Thus, in *Feast in Time of Plague,* it answered before I asked, plied me with answers.

All *our* art is in managing (in time) to put, to each answer before it evaporates, *our* question. This being outgalloped by answers is what inspiration is. And how often—a blank page.

~

One reads *Werther* and shoots himself, another reads *Werther* and, because Werther shoots himself, decides to live. One behaves like Werther, the other like Goethe. A lesson in self-extermination? A lesson in self-defense? Both. Goethe, by some law of the particular moment in his life, *needed* to shoot Werther; the suicidal demon of the generation needed to be incarnated precisely through Goethe's hand. A twice fateful necessity, and as such—without responsibility. And *very* fraught with consequences.

Is Goethe guilty of all the subsequent deaths?

He himself, in his profound and splendid old age, replied: no. Otherwise we wouldn't dare say a single word, for who can calculate the effect of any one word? (I'm putting it my own way, this is the substance of it.)

I too shall reply for Goethe: no.

He had no evil will, he had no will at all except the creative one. Writing his *Werther,* he not only forgot all others (that is, their possible troubles) but forgot himself too (his own trouble!).

All-forgetfulness, forgetfulness of everything which is not the work: the very basis of creation.

Would Goethe have written *Werther* a second time, after everything that had happened, if (improbably) he had again had just as urgent a need to? And would he then have been indictable? Would Goethe have written—knowingly?

He'd have written it a thousand times if he had needed to, just as he would not have written even the first line of the first one if the pressure had been the tiniest bit lighter. (Werther, like Walsingham, is a pressure from within.)

—And would he then have been indictable?

As a man, yes. As an artist, no.

Moreover, as an artist Goethe would have been both indictable and condemned if he had immolated Werther in himself with the aim of preserving human lives (fulfillment of the commandment: Thou shalt not kill). Here the law of art is exactly the reverse of the moral law. An artist is guilty in two cases only: in that refusal I have mentioned to create the work (for whoever's benefit), and in the creation of an inartistic work. Here his lesser responsibility ends, and his boundless responsibility as a human being begins.

Artistic creation is in some cases a sort of atrophy of conscience—more than that: a necessary atrophy of conscience, the moral flaw without which art cannot exist. In order to be good (not lead into temptation the little ones of this world), art would have to renounce a fair half of its whole self. The only way for art to be wittingly good is—not to be. It will end with the life of the planet. [. . .]

~

I don't want to be a springboard for others' ideas, a loudspeaker for other people's passions.

Other people's? But is anything "other" to a poet? In *The Covetous Knight* Pushkin made even miserliness his own, in *Salieri* even untalentedness. And it was not through being other, but precisely through being *related*, that Pugachov knocked at me. [. . .]

~

[. . .] In "Hymn to the Plague" there are two lines that are solely the author's—namely:

> And happy the one who finds and knows
> those pleasures mid this turbulence.

Pushkin was released by the demon for a second, and did not have enough patience. This and only this is what has happened when we discover in our own or other people's work a stop-gap line, that poetic "water" which is nothing other than the *shallows of inspiration.*

Take the whole passage:

> There is an ecstasy in battle
> and on the somber chasm's edge,
> and in the ragings of the ocean,
> the dreadful waves and thundering dark,
> and in the Arabian hurricane,

and in the breathing of the Plague.
Whatever threatens us with doom
hides in itself, for mortal hearts,
unspeakable pleasures—guarantee
perhaps of immortality!
And happy the one who finds and knows
those pleasures mid this turbulence.

Take it word by word: "and happy the one"—too small! small and limp after those absolutes of pleasure and ecstasy, an obvious repetition, a weakening, a lowering; "mid this turbulence"—what kind of? and again what a small word (and thing)! After all the hurricanes and abysses! An allegory of worldly turbulence after the authentic ocean waves. ". . . the one who finds and knows"—finds inexpressible delights—is this German? It's certainly not Pushkinian and not Russian. Next: "and knows" (a repetition, for if you've found, you already know). And how, in a situation like *that,* could one help finding them? A gallicism: "Heureux celui qui a pu les connaître," and altogether it's a piece *of* philosophizing, *preposterous* in such a whirlwind.

That is what happens when the hand overtakes the hearing.

The Little Tragedies as a Cycle

Scholarship in the Service and Disservice of *The Little Tragedies*

Vladimir Markovich
Translated by Kerry Sabbag

The large number of critical works on *The Little Tragedies* makes a comprehensive survey nearly impossible; therefore, predetermined specifications are necessary, and it seems to me that those suggested by this essay are the most natural and productive. First of all, let us limit ourselves to criticism written and published in Russia. The similarity of theoretical approaches and methodological skills of the majority of these authors makes these works more comparable and therefore more convenient for survey. The next restriction is that of chronology. It makes sense to consider works that appeared from the mid-1950s (when the so-called thaw began) through the present day. It may prove significant that the decade after the death of Stalin comprises a single historical epoch and a time of gradual disintegration of the Soviet social system, ideology, and culture; that is, a process of change began that has not yet reached its culmination. Focusing on the works of this time may lend the qualities of plot intrigue to a survey, thus providing an opportunity to observe a turning point that should have occurred in the understanding of *The Little Tragedies* and assess the reality and seriousness of this turning point. Finally, it is important to establish a fundamental thematic division and include in this study only those works that approach *The Little Tragedies* as a single entity, not focusing on the individual plays but on the structure, ideas, and functions comprising the dramatic cycle.[1] It is precisely this kind of approach that poses questions significant for the scholarly discussion and critical interpretation of *The Little Tragedies*.

In addition to the aforementioned stipulations, I would add the condition that the concrete works discussed be considered pieces of several general directions and patterns of study of the Boldino plays. Such an approach allows one to avoid the evaluation of individual merits or, conversely, errors of different authors; this essay will only focus on general trends of investigation and the patterns of their development. The result of such an approach must be a nearly colorless picture, really not a picture at all but a diagram or design. To the reader, this diagram may seem rather ascetic, but one hopes that it will be able to reveal the intrinsic logic of the processes that have sprung from and continue to develop in Russian Pushkin studies.

First of all, it is worth mentioning that during the period addressed in this survey, the notion of the connections between the various parts of the Boldino dramatic cycle became significantly more concrete. It had been noted occasionally that the four Boldino plays comprise a whole and complete unit (a tetralogy), but this idea remained only a vague declaration or was reduced to a consideration of the unity of the global problems addressed in *The Little Tragedies.* Sometimes these declarations were supported by visual comparisons based on parallels between the Boldino cycle and the symphonic form in music,[2] but, in general, they remained simple statements. Only in the late 1970s did researchers begin to describe how *The Little Tragedies* can be viewed as a single artistic unit and, at least partially, how the plays are linked compositionally.

At first, scholars were attracted to the motifs and themes (they rarely differentiated between these concepts) that link the different parts of the cycle. For example, it was noted that the motif of feast in the face of death is repeated in all the Boldino plays.[3] A similar observation by E. M. Taborisskaia suggested that "two themes—creation and death—permeate all four plays, with a variation of these themes in each."[4] Taborisskaia also revealed several other images that "migrate from one tragedy to another," for example, the "man in black," the messenger of death who is mentioned in *Mozart and Salieri* and then appears in the plot of *A Feast in Time of Plague.*[5] It is easy to see that fragmentary observations were already leading to the structuralist methodology of the determined search for constructive invariants. It was in the aforementioned work that Taborisskaia noted the pattern of the conflicts formed by the plot, conflicts that are implicit in the texts of *The Little Tragedies* and appear only when the plot is taken to a high abstract level.[6]

This abstract level of the text also revealed a compositional symmetry similar to a stanzaic formation. Taborisskaia found that the four titles of the Boldino plays combine contradictory concepts (e.g., *The Covetous Knight, The Stone Guest*) and that the first and last titles were accompanied by similar subtitles. Based on these observations, Taborisskaia concluded that Pushkin was creating his "tetralogy" similar to a quatrain with an enclosing rhyme (*abba*).[7]

Later, other rhymes or patterns in the plots were noted. In both *Mozart and Salieri* and *A Feast in Time of Plague*, on the eve of meeting with friends, the main characters "create works of art that turn out to be fundamental for them and powerful pronouncements in artistic form."[8] Certain word repetitions were identified for the first time, for example, the framing of Laura's and Mary's songs in *The Stone Guest* and *A Feast in Time of Plague*, respectively, by the same verbal design.[9] Perhaps most important was the description of the elusive symmetry inherent in the cycle itself (*arkhitektonika*). E. A. Vil'k noted the following symmetrical correlation: "If we arrange the plays in the order in which they were written, we find that the first two and last two plays each contain a total of five scenes."[10] It then became clear that each of the symmetrical pairs (*The Covetous Knight, Mozart and Salieri—The Stone Guest, A Feast in Time of Plague*) "constitutes an internal unity, and the corresponding scenes in the two pairs rhyme both in composition and theme."[11] Expanding the sphere of investigation resulted in a more radical conclusion regarding the compositional unity of the parts of the "tetralogy." Vil'k considered the possibility of interpreting Pushkin's cycle as, in the words of P. A. Katenin, "one big tragedy."[12] In other words, the concept of a "hypertext" had been introduced.

Scholars approached the study of the Boldino dramatic "hypertext" from different angles. As interest in the problem of the compositional unity of the works grew, scholars increasingly turned their attention to the question of the cycle's generic nature. The simplest solution to the question of genre was provided by the recognition of the generic homogeneity of all four plays. Not surprisingly, in the 1950s and 1960s this variant prevailed. At the time, nearly all conceptions of the genre of *The Little Tragedies* stemmed from the idea of the generically tragic nature of Pushkin's "dramatic experiences." This idea was not so much discussed as it was confirmed or rather illustrated by concrete observations or thoughts. One example of this phenomenon is found in the work of G. A. Gukovskii, who sought to demonstrate how in *The*

Covetous Knight the traditionally comedic theme of avarice unexpectedly turns tragic, both generically and otherwise.[13] Significantly, this reversal in theme was also noted by B. V. Tomashevskii, whose general perceptions of *The Little Tragedies* were usually contested by Gukovskii.[14]

Naturally, everyone recognized the unique construction of *The Little Tragedies* in terms of the tragic genre. As a group, scholars noted the structural features of *The Little Tragedies* that were considered "strange" within the context of tragedy (culmination not preceded by plot development, "open" endings, the lengths of the works, etc.).[15] However, any doubts about the purity of genre in *The Little Tragedies* that may have arisen due to the aforementioned aberrations were silenced by reference to V. G. Belinskii's famous formula: "In form and range *The Little Tragedies* are no more than dramatic sketches, but in content and development they comprise a tragedy in the full sense of the word."[16] Therefore, the idea of a uniquely formed tragedy was implied in the use of the words "scenes," "sketches," "essays," and "experiments" to describe Pushkin's cycle.

Already by the 1970s the situation had changed noticeably. G. P. Makogonenko brought to the forefront of scholarly discussion the question of the tragicomic treatment of characters and conflicts in the Boldino plays.[17] It was no longer a question of the transformation of the comic into the tragic but of the interaction and equality involved in the different types of pathos, that is, the equal presence of the fundamental characteristics of the comic and tragic genres. This idea was widespread, although Makogonenko considered all of the plays to be tragicomic, while other scholars only applied this label to some of them. The interaction of tragic and comedic elements began to be noted regularly first in *The Covetous Knight* and then in *The Stone Guest.*[18]

Now those who supported the idea of the tragic nature of all the Boldino plays were compelled to prove the legitimacy of this perspective. G. V. Moskvicheva resolved the question in a carefully formulated conception of the tragic nature of the "dramatic investigations" in that she saw the plays not as tragedies per se but instead as focused on the general tragic principle underlying them.[19] N. V. Beliak and M. N. Virolainen took a more straightforward position on this question in an article I shall address later. For now, suffice it to say that their thesis about the tragic nature of the Boldino plays was granted an extensive base and was accompanied by a significant stipulation. According to the authors, the four tragic plays, united in a cycle, found through their symbolic wholeness another generic quality: they became components of a "grand epic form" in some ways similar to *The Divine Comedy*.[20]

In later works, the concept of the generic homogeneity of *The Little Tragedies* survived only due to the quest for generic definitions that were as flexible as possible. For example, L. S. Mitina no longer characterized the Boldino plays as tragedies but did not yet see them as dramas. She suggested that the traditional signs of "pure" dramatic genres had lost their compulsory nature in the absence of the clear contours of a new genre.[21] The most important aspect of Mitina's essay is that she highlighted the precise moment of transition from one genre to another in the formation of the Boldino cycle.

This focus was even more pronounced in the works of scholars who had allowed for generic heterogeneity in the Boldino plays from the outset, for example, A. M. Garkavi and V. G. Odinokov. Garkavi believed that only *Mozart and Salieri* and *The Stone Guest* represented tragedies in the strict sense of the word; he (and many others at that time) found a combination of the comedic and the tragic in *The Covetous Knight* and *A Feast in Time of Plague*, which interweave elements of the tragedy and the poem.[22] Odinokov, trying to adhere more closely to Pushkin's subtitles, differentiated within the Boldino cycle tragedy and tragicomedy.[23] In general, the unique approach of these authors consists in how they pose the question of which factors determine the possibility for unity among such heterogeneous elements. One can easily imagine that the authors considered the most important of these factors to be the dynamic of the syntagmatic development of the cycle.

Garkavi and Odinokov believed that the order of the arrangement of the Boldino plays generated a dynamic succession endowed with a distinct teleological tendency. (The arrangement of the plays coincides with Pushkin's well-known plan and list of 1830, which in turn correspond to the date of completion of each play.) According to Garkavi, the aforementioned tendency is defined by thematic gradation: in the depiction of human passions and resulting pleasures one can see an ascent from passions and pleasures that are less valued to those that are more valued by the author. Garkavi noted another type of gradation in the rise of variations of a unified theme from one level of interpretation to a hierarchically higher level, for example, the ascent from a sociohistorical analysis of passions to a religious-philosophical interpretation. An implied "hypersujet" was discovered in the core of the structure of the tetralogy and was governed by the logic of the investigation ("dramatic investigations") of human passions.[24] The result was a real change in the understanding of the structural unity of the cycle.

Further development in this direction fell to Odinokov. He also noted a certain dynamic in the sequence of the four plays, one characterized by thematic gradation and a gradation of principles of depiction. It seemed natural that the tragicomedy of *The Covetous Knight* would act as a starting point because its tragic collision is "grounded" in society and social issues. The final point of the journey, *A Feast in Time of Plague,* moves toward a "universal character," and concrete characters "intermingle with the symbolic faces of fate."[25] However, the significance of Odinokov's analysis lies not only in his definitive position on the relationship between the beginning and the end of the dynamic series but, more importantly, in his ideas about the genre-forming nature of the transition from play to play.

Odinokov focused on the idea that the construction of the cycle marks the origin of a new generic form. The cycle forms a "supergenre" in relation to its parts. Odinokov saw this supergenre as a "dynamic state," simultaneously existing as a "transitional phase" and a "new generic modification."[26] Although the meaning of the supergenre was not sufficiently defined by Odinokov, much was explained by his accompanying reminder about the general "novelization" of genres in the nineteenth century. Mention of the novelization of literature made it clear that a special dramaturgical form had been born in Boldino, one that was in process and not completely formed but in its own way whole. In this case, the influence of Bakhtin on Pushkin studies is clear.

The question of the unity of content and function in the Boldino cycle was even more enthusiastically discussed than the aforementioned ideas; however, the concepts of content and function were understood differently throughout the period surveyed here. They had already become a presence in the 1950s and 1960s. Two clear but contrasting conceptions emerged from the many vague and eclectic interpretations, and each, to some degree, found support in preceding traditions.[27] One approach is embodied by the works of B. V. Tomashevskii,[28] whose conception of the unity of content and function was to some extent similar to that of I. M. Nusinov.[29] Tomashevskii viewed the Boldino dramaturgical cycle as an experiment intended to pave the way for analysis of the spiritual life of man and, first and foremost, for the analysis of human passions and the battle of subconscious motives.

In comparison to Pushkin's earlier work, *Boris Godunov*, Tomashevskii perceived the Boldino tetralogy as the author's departure from social issues into the sphere of pure psychology. The idea that this departure represented a rejection of the ideological goal of art was purposely not emphasized but nonetheless was felt strongly by the reader. No less important to the aforementioned concept of content and function was the high level of abstraction in the Boldino plays. Tomashevskii believed that in *The Little Tragedies* Pushkin explored general human passions, those that exist eternally and universally, regardless of concrete historical circumstances. According to Tomashevskii, the focus on universal concepts in the Boldino plays explains the use of "eternal" images and plots.

This conception of *The Little Tragedies* stood in stark contrast to that of G. A. Gukovskii, whose position consisted of two fundamental theses.[30] First, he insisted that, for Pushkin, the passions depicted in *The Little Tragedies* were not common to all mankind. Second, the content of *The Little Tragedies* was not so much an analysis of the passions it depicted as an objective explanation of said passions. According to Gukovskii, the explanation consisted of Pushkin's revelation of the concrete condition of passions considered to be universal and eternal. Instead, the nature of these passions depended on historical circumstances and objective reality as combined in different eras. In other words, the passions portrayed by Pushkin "were created by the environment."[31]

Gukovskii suggested that in the majority of the Boldino plays this environment is revealed to be a fixed cultural system. It is a cultural complex that shapes the psyche of Don Juan, Salieri, Mozart, and, of course, Walsingham. Environment is understood as "the problem of the social definition of man" only in *The Covetous Knight.*[32] Gukovskii was convinced that Pushkin's ideological evaluation of what was portrayed in *The Little Tragedies* was connected to history. Pushkin had not abandoned ideological evaluation; rather, in the Boldino plays he utilized a new approach. Pushkin does not judge his characters but explains their psyche and behavior in terms of historical circumstances, thereby sitting in judgment of the historical structure that shaped them. Gukovskii proclaimed such an approach to characterization to be a prerequisite for the subsequent revolution in Russian literature.

This direction in the interpretation of *The Little Tragedies* found its most extreme expression in the work of Makogonenko, who agreed with Gukovskii's basic theses but saw some inconsistencies in the latter's analysis, which he sought to correct.[33] Makogonenko was convinced that the sociohistorical interpretation of man in *The Little Tragedies* was in no way connected with the aspect of tragedy, the existence of which in the Boldino plays was unquestionable to Gukovskii. Makogonenko insisted that for Pushkin the realist the two most important generic characteristics of tragedy would have been unacceptable. These features were the canonization of the exceptional and fatalistic catastrophism, which Makogonenko defined as the existence of irreconcilable contradictions and problems in the life of man. According to Makogonenko, the generic laws of tragedy produce two unavoidable results: an apologia for individualism, since surely it is individualism that cultivates exceptionality, and the author's position, which rejects a judgment of reality based on the idea that if the problems and contradictions in life are irresolvable, then how can one judge reality? In characterizing the special nature of the Boldino plays, which he believed to be generically homogeneous, the scholar proposed three complementary definitions. The term *dramatic scenes* characterizes the compositional organization of the texts; *tragicomedy* is the principle of idea formation, which does not allow for ideas about the unresolvability of the contradictions depicted in the text; and *drama* characterizes the function of the plays, which were intended to serve as a means for the analytic study of reality. Makogonenko believed that it was the final definition that was meant to be the basis for the exploration of the characters' psychology and for the judgment of their formations by historical systems. Here the socialization and ideologization of the unified meaning of "dramatic investigations" unquestionably achieved fulfillment. Makogonenko saw the sole meaning of Pushkin's plays as the judgment of the "bourgeois ideal of man" and the discovery of the nonbourgeois, nonindividualistic path to spiritual development.[34]

Among Pushkin studies of the 1970s, Makogonenko's work already stood out as an exception. It was a relic of an earlier stage in Russian literary studies, that is, a relic of a time during which scholarly attention was focused on how sociohistorical phenomena and processes in literary works could be explained and appraised. The line between epochs in Russian literary studies was drawn in the 1960s, when a new goal was proposed: the discovery of Pushkin the philosopher (although it should be noted that on the basis of the tradition of the late nineteenth and early twentieth centuries this approach was already quite old).[35] A real change in course followed, but it developed over time. In the majority of works devoted to *The Little Tragedies* during the 1970s, sociological and ideological aspects had already faded to some degree.[36] For example, it was mentioned that "Pushkin was not trying to evaluate the passions and ideas of his characters so much as he wanted to depict them artistically."[37] In other instances the topic of discussion was the re-creation of a concrete cultural-historical atmosphere in which the characters of *The Little Tragedies* functioned as a manifestation of the romantic interest in the exotic nature of other worlds and distant epochs.[38] However, all these changes were only "baby steps" that did not truly affect the essence of the scholarly approach to *The Little Tragedies.* Noticeable changes took place only during the late 1980s and early 1990s, as demonstrated by two late works of Iu. M. Lotman.[39]

Lotman tested one of Gukovskii's main theses—the idea that in *The Little Tragedies* passions and characters were "created by the environment." He argued that in the Boldino plays a dependence on the external environment represented only the lowest level of interrelation between man and the world: "The destiny of a lofty personality is the refusal to take the inhumanity of a 'century' for the norm" and "the battle with the environment for spiritual freedom."[40] Lotman himself considered his objections to be only a clarification of Gukovskii's ideas, but his correction undermined one of the fundamental sociological interpretations of *The Little Tragedies.* A more extensive review of the tradition started by Gukovskii was unavoidable. Such a review, without a direct polemic with Gukovskii, can be found in the aforementioned work of Beliak and Virolainen.

Beliak and Virolainen strayed even farther from the idea that *The Little Tragedies* demonstrate the influence of the environment on the plays' characters. They believed that the Boldino plays revealed the opposite phenomenon—an unprecedented independence of the characters from the surrounding world and its objective laws. Pushkin's tragic hero "creates his own personal cosmos in which he emerges as the epicenter, a cosmos that stands in contrast to the rest of the world."[41] At its very essence this thesis contradicts not only Gukovskii but also Lotman. According to Lotman, the hero maintains his humanity in the face of the triumphant inhumanity all around him, thereby rejecting one norm out of loyalty to another. Beliak and Virolainen suggested that Pushkin's tragic heroes deny the existing system of distinguishing the reference points of values and, accordingly, the distinguishing criteria of humanity and inhumanity. One cannot even address the concept of a norm in such a situation. Lotman also wrote that Pushkin's tragic hero battles with the surrounding world for spiritual freedom. Beliak and Virolainen believed that the heroes of *The Little Tragedies* already demonstrated independence and sovereignty to such a degree as to signify complete autonomy "to the point of dropping out of the world."[42]

Beliak and Virolainen, like Gukovskii, perceived the Boldino dramaturgical cycle as a representation of journeys through cultural systems. However, if to Gukovskii each such system arose from an objective force that formed and defined the hero from without, Beliak and Virolainen believed that it was a "cultural cosmos" or new world created by the sufferings and actions of the hero himself through his relationships with men and God. As a result, the hero exists in a world that springs from his own existence.

Equally radical is the reconsideration of Gukovskii's proposed transfer of guilt onto the historical system in Pushkin's plays. Beliak and Virolainen insisted that this transfer of guilt from the individual to the surrounding world is realized not by the author but by the hero, from whom the author distances himself in each play. They believed that Pushkin shows the falsehood and depravity of transferring the guilt of the individual onto the world while suggesting the individual's willingness to take responsibility for the evil in the world as the saving grace of that world. Pushkin's highest truth was "the truth of genuine culture, which emerges as the only guaranteed solution to the tragic conflict."[43]

The conception of Pushkin's worldview as reflected in *The Little Tragedies* was also radically altered. Gukovskii identified two elements, the individual and social history, while Beliak and Virolainen uncovered other dimensions to Pushkin's vision of the world. They posited that each hero of *The Little Tragedies* in creating his "individual cosmos" brought about "a distortion and substitution of a sacred idea."[44] For example, the Baron turns ascetic restraint into a means of achieving control over the world. Don Juan distorts the idea of the Middle Age cults of the Lady (*dama*) and Madonna in order to force the path to heavenly love to serve earthly goals. Salieri blasphemously links the pagan conception of priesthood with the Christian idea of redemptive sacrifice. Walsingham turns the idea of immortality into a source of blasphemous ecstasy through death. Beliak and Virolainen suggested that the aforesaid does not simply represent an event occurring in the sphere of consciousness or worldly deeds. They were convinced that Pushkin was demonstrating the use of magical means for the regulation of existence. However, as these means were not used for their intended purpose, they produced not construction but destruction. In each instance, these magical means functioned in a completely realistic and quite frightening way, and, therefore, their effects could lead to a total and irreversible destruction of life. This was the eschatological warning that Beliak and Virolainen found in the plays of the Boldino cycle. If in Gukovskii's analysis the author of *The Little Tragedies* appeared to be an underdeveloped Marxist or at least a capable student of several precursors of the Marxist understanding of history (Guizot, Thierry, Mignet), then in Beliak and Virolainen's work he assumed the features of a fully developed mystic.

This revolution coincided with the general cultural process taking place in Soviet society at the juncture of the 1980s and 1990s. A significant segment of the Russian intelligentsia, parting with the stereotypical Marxist view of the world, was turning to the world of religious thought and in its own way returning to the traditions of the Russian religious-philosophical Renaissance. In 1990, one year before the introduction of Beliak and Virolainen's work, the anthology *Pushkin v russkoi filosofskoi kritike: Konets XIX–pervaia nolovina XXvv* (Pushkin in Russian philosophical criticism: The end of the nineteenth century to the first half of the twentieth century), edited by R. A. Gal'tseva, was published in Moscow and included essays by V. S. Soloviev, V. V. Rozanov, P. B. Struve, S. N. Bulgakov, G. P. Fedotov, S. L. Frank, and I. A. Il'in. Naturally, the appearance of this book can be seen in the interpretation of texts replete with spiritual problems. Religious-philosophical language plays only a minimal role in Beliak and Virolainen's work, but in the later essays of V. S. Nepomniashchii and several likeminded critics connected with the journal *Moskovskii pushkinist* (Moscow Pushkinist) (e.g., M. Novikova and sometimes M. Kostalevskaia), religious-philosophical discourse is viewed as the only acceptable approach to *The Little Tragedies.*[45]

Now the Boldino dramatic cycle was interpreted as an artistic theodicy imbued with an indestructible surety in the harmonious nature of Creation. The question of the providential meaning of the dramatic action in the Boldino plays was posed. Two categories were introduced into the analysis of dramatic conflicts: "law" and "grace." Psychological interpretation of the plots of *The Little Tragedies* was now considered not only inadequate but even so convoluted as to lead one away from the truth. "Self-sufficiency of the intellect," the recognized university-academic scholarly approach to literature, clashed with religious intuition as the surest path to understanding the Boldino plays.[46]

In short, much has changed over the last fifty years. However, it is important not to lose sight of what has remained constant at the heart of all the changes. Careful investigation of the coexisting and intermingling variants reveals a certain invariant. Despite the conceptual differences between the works of Beliak and Virolainen and Gukovskii and Makogonenko, there are certain shared features; for example, there are some aspects of their analyses in which the language and meaning of their descriptions coincide. After all, Beliak and Virolainen's work reveals that all distortions of the magical mechanisms for regulating existence, a phenomenon discovered by Pushkin, are, in the authors' view, manifestations of "extreme individualism."[47] In essence, this represents a judgment of individualism or of the "bourgeois ideal of man." The same pattern can be seen in the search for paths leading to changes in individualism and in the return of ancestral unity to the history of humanity, a unity that was torn apart by the individualistic conscience. (Makogonenko linked this idea with the search for the nonbourgeois path of development.) Both cases address this dangerous crisis, the search for its roots, and the possibility of reversing it. Only Gukovskii and Makogonenko considered this phenomenon on the sociohistorical level, while Beliak and Virolainen looked at it from an ontological perspective. Naturally, in each case the proposed point of view was ascribed to Pushkin himself.

In the end, almost all the works mentioned here (Gukovskii, Makogonenko, Lotman, Beliak and Virolainen, Nepomniashchii, etc.) can be viewed as concrete variants of the realization of the same understanding of the meaning of *The Little Tragedies*. The meaning of the four Boldino plays, both as a whole and individually, was perceived by all the aforementioned scholars as a systemic, centralized, isomorphic unit. In the final analysis, one finds that all the Boldino plays are written about the same topics and make the same assertions. They all create a single picture of the state of the world as sickly and abnormal. The plays diagnose the illness plaguing the world and simultaneously restore an understanding of the authentic norm of human existence and show people the path to salvation. The nature of this understanding varies with the changing epochs and the concrete positions of the individual scholars, but fundamentally it remains stable. Clearly, it reflects the primary trajectory in the study of *The Little Tragedies* in Russian literary studies in the second half of the twentieth century. A similar trend is observed in the aforementioned opinions on the composition and genre of the Boldino cycle. Of course, the dominant role of this direction in literary studies is not accidental. It primarily corresponds to the well-known traditions of Russian culture and is characterized by the conception in Russian literary studies of nature, the purpose of art, and so on. Therefore, it is all the more interesting that this scholarly approach was never the only one; other, perhaps less noticeable approaches developed and existed along with the dominant one.

Earlier in the essay, I mentioned that in the 1950s and 1960s Gukovskii's conception of *The Little Tragedies* resisted another approach, that of Tomashevskii. This refers to Pushkin's transition to purely psychological themes and to the search for the paths (just the paths!) of their analysis—in other words, to a search with an unforeseeable result. Such an understanding of the artistic goal of the author of *The Little Tragedies* could not coexist with the idea of diagnosis and judgment, the establishment of norms of human existence, and so on. It is not difficult to see how Tomashevskii's line of investigation might veer in another direction.

If Tomashevskii's idea about Pushkin's departure from societal problems and social or ideological evaluation was more implied than formulated, then in 1969 E. A. Maimin expressed this same idea directly and definitively. (Maimin connected Pushkin's transition to the universal and eternal to a general shift in the orientation of the Russian cultural consciousness after the defeat of the Decembrists.)[48] However, the transition to universal-philosophical problems was not the only issue; the new approach to these problems emerges as no less significant. According to Maimin, the "dramatic investigations" undertaken by Pushkin at Boldino practically excluded simple solutions and evaluations as well as the opportunity to judge anything. Therefore, Maimin posited that Pushkin's plays did not and could not contain any completed ideological concept. Maimin took his idea a step farther in a 1976 work in which he posed the question of the resonance in the Boldino plays of different but equal voices.[49] These voices were not subordinate to the author's position but completely independent of it. Their synchronic sound does not create a single picture of the world but instead the impression of several different truths. Maimin did not deny the obvious influence of Bakhtin, directly stating that *The Little Tragedies* were closer to the polyphonic novels of Dostoevsky than any dramatic construction.

Maimin introduced the thesis of the polyphonic meaning of *The Little Tragedies* briefly and tentatively, but a concretization and detailed reworking of the thesis followed. V. I. Tiupa uncovered, as a kind of invariant of the Boldino cycle, the dialogical relationships of two types of consciousness: "solitary," negating any possible moral establishments and bans and including egocentric and demonic characteristics, and "role playing," which centers around the universally recognized norms and forms of authority such as patriarchy and stereotypes.[50] According to Tiupa, both forms of consciousness receive equal treatment in the Boldino plays in that each is equally acceptable and unacceptable to the author. One is valued for its moral purity and the other for its individual character, but both are deficient because they are incomplete. However, Tiupa suggested that the coexistence of the different truths was secondary in importance to the dialogical nature of their interaction. Along with situations in which these two truths collided silently, Tiupa discovered other cases in which different truths answer each other and even are illuminated through mutual understanding. The result is not their merging but rather another effect. The author's consciousness, and sometimes even that of the characters, opens itself to the two truths and becomes a forum for their never-ending dialogue.

Another aspect of this same idea was revealed in the works of Iu. N. Chumakov at the end of the 1970s and beginning of the 1980s.[51] While supporting Maimin's idea of the polyphony of meaning in the Boldino plays, Chumakov proposed the use of this approach in the search not only for different voices of different characters but also for the interpretation of the same plot situations. This suggestion was based on the idea that plot situations might simultaneously inspire several different meanings in the mind of the reader. Take, for example, the poisoning of Mozart. Chumakov posited that, "along with the traditional version of the plot, according to which Salieri secretly poisons his unsuspecting friend, another perfectly correct version exists, in which Salieri throws the poison into the glass before Mozart's eyes."[52] Chumakov sees this gesture as a bold challenge with unclear results. He tries to show that this new version significantly expands the meaning of the play and is in keeping with Pushkin's position. This interpretation differed from that of Maimin (the concept of voices was not discussed) and also, to some degree, from Tiupa's point of view. While the dialogical relationships of the truths were important to Tiupa, Chumakov focused on the variety of plot and on the many semantic levels, realized without conflict or discussion, as a coexistence of autonomous meanings.

Even in the case of such a tolerant or open variant (or perhaps because of its tolerance), the idea of the polyphony of *The Little Tragedies* elicited a sharp rebuff from the current promoter of the centralized and isomorphic unity of their meaning, namely, Nepomniashchii, who categorically rejected Chumakov's idea.[53] Interestingly, Nepomniashchii found grounds for a polemic with the discussions of Beliak and Virolainen, whose position was closer to his own than that of Chumakov. In Nepomniashchii's criticism of Beliak and Virolainen, he fulfilled approximately the same function as had Makogonenko regarding Gukovskii's ideas. A war against inconsistency had begun. Nepomniashchii found inconsistencies in a 1995 article by Beliak and Virolainen about *Mozart and Salieri* that differed from its predecessors in that it contained the idea of tragic double meaning as one of the fundamental principles of the formation of meaning in Pushkin's plays.[54] The authors suggested that in the development of the plot in *Mozart and Salieri* it was possible to see how Mozart himself, through his words, actions, and even his music, provoked and pushed Salieri to commit the crime. In other words, genius gives rise to villainy. Since such an understanding of the plot seems possible, the concept of the incompatibility of genius and evil acquires a shade of doubt. "Music and death, creation and destruction [. . .] are captured here in a moment of tragic unity."[55] According to Nepomniashchii, the idea of tragic double meaning questions Pushkin's entire "artistic theodicy," and in a play "everything becomes an unsteady quagmire."[56] The critic's reaction was particularly harsh. Nepomniashchii viewed the tendencies leading to the conception of *The Little Tragedies* as having many meanings as "the expansion of postmodernism into the realm of Pushkin studies." He categorized postmodernism as eschatological perception, noting that "postmodernism is an illness of the human soul on a worldwide scale" and "positivism in the process of decay."[57] "Having begun with an attempt to create an orderly, nonreligious picture of the world and suffered a fatal defeat, it [positivism (V.M.)] behaves like a Gogolian sorcerer dreaming, while dying, of destroying the whole world."

Nepomniashchii clarified his position by adding that as an outgrowth of positivism, postmodernism "has a sanction, from a world viewpoint, to further destroy the universe."[58]

However, Nepomniashchii did not attach serious meaning to still another direction in the analysis of *The Little Tragedies*, a direction that posed no less danger to the idea of the single, centered meaning of each of the Boldino plays and the cycle as a whole. This dangerous potential went unnoticed because it remained just that, potential. It took the form of criticism that concentrated on the poetic form of the Boldino plays. Most often, this approach dealt with well-known and obvious structural features of poetic dramaturgy such as the dominant role of the monologue, the reduction of the plot, the singularity of the characters' language, and so on.[59] However, one author who took this approach uncovered a structural feature that led to a new understanding of the formation of meaning in the Boldino plays. In a 1974 article, V. Solov'ev posited that the principle of fragmentariness appears throughout *The Little Tragedies* not only at the level of individual plays or the cycle as a whole but within each scene composing individual plays.[60] For example, within the parameters of a scene, a character's monologues sometimes seem like completed and independent poems. Such monologues are not only independent in relation to each other but also act independently within the scenes. Such fragments can be understood as lyric utterances, the closest approximations of the author's intentions. The conclusions that logically follow Solov'ev's ideas are, first, that the fragmentariness of the speech "part" of a character might result in a lack of coordination between the meanings of his individual monologues or even a rejoinder to them; second, that these contradictory meanings might be perceived by the reader as autonomous (and, therefore, not requiring agreement), and their combination can be read as unstructured and illogical. In short, the "figurative characteristic" of the character might lose its centering unity, thereby failing to assume an internal dialogic. The same effect could be felt by the meaning of the play as a whole, because a lack of coordination between the monologues signifies the similar state of the author's intentions, or by the meaning of the cycle as a whole, which becomes chaotic. In essence, these conclusions are similar to the aims characteristic of the practice of text reconstruction, one more variant of the "destruction of the universe," according to Nepomniashchii.

However, Solov'ev did not reach these conclusions, and, therefore, his particular approach to the interpretation of *The Little Tragedies* went unnoticed and received no further development.

It is only possible to discuss the degree of productivity of each of the aforementioned directions in interpretation of *The Little Tragedies* briefly and hypothetically. The prevalence of the approach, as represented by a survey of the works of Gukovskii, Makogonenko, Lotman, Beliak and Virolainen, and Nepomniashchii and his followers, brings one closer to a sense that this approach has been exhausted to a greater degree than the other potential directions. In my opinion, further development in this direction is possible only in the form of variation or clarification of already established concepts (it is only possible for the invariant on which the concepts are based to veer into the sphere of some other methodology).

The consideration of the question of the polyphony and the dialogical nature of *The Little Tragedies* is, in reality, still only in the early stages. There have been only a few attempts in this direction. In front of us lies a wide-open space, open to a systematic study of the dialogic relationship in the Boldino plays; for example, the dialogues of different truths, as expressed by the voices of the characters, might correspond to the dialogues of different meanings found in the same plot situations and also to the dialogues of the encompassing meanings in the individual plays.

The least elaborated upon approach promises the most surprises. Deconstructionism is an approach that reveals the unregulated mutual relationship of autonomous fragmentary meanings and frees Pushkin's texts from "the yoke of (structural) unity" (in the famous words of Roland Barthes).

Still another perfectly reasonable question arises. Are the quests for synthesis of all the different approaches productive? We still lack a convincing answer to this question. In general, is it possible to combine in "ecumenical harmony" (E. D. Hirsch) the structural study of a work (and to some degree that includes the structure of meaning) with the attempt to decentralize the text? It is only clear that such a combination would mean the relativization of mutually exclusive methods and their transformation into compatible working methods. On what foundation could such a transformation be based? I will relegate this question to the as yet unknown future.

Notes

1. The reader will notice several exceptions to this rule in the essay. Exceptions were made for works in which the author combined an analysis of one of the Boldino plays with several generalizations characterizing general attributes of *The Little Tragedies.*

2. See, for example, Nepomniashchii, "Simfoniia zhizni."

3. Ustiuzhanin, *Malen'kie tragedii A. S. Pushkina,* 49.

4. Taborisskaia, "*Malen'kie tragedii* Pushkina kak tsikl," 140.

5. Ibid., 143.

6. Ibid., 139.

7. Ibid., 140.

8. Beliak and Virolainen, "'Malen'kie tragedii' kak kul'turnyi epos," 75.

9. Ibid.

10. Vil'k, "Malen'kie tragedii—odna bol'shaia tragediia?" 245.

11. Ibid.

12. Ibid., 244.

13. Gukovskii, *Pushkin i problemy realisticheskogo stilia,* 311.

14. Tomashevskii, "'Malen'kie tragedii' Pushkina i Mol'er," 275–76. This essay was first published in 1936.

15. I. M. Nusinov, for example, saw in the Boldino plays a special form of tragedy ("authorial") and insisted on the similarity of this form to the prosaic novella ("Tragediia skuposti," 438).

16. Belinskii, *Polnoe sobranie sochinenii,* 5: 59.

17. Makogonenko, *Tvorchestvo Pushkina,* 162–63, 216–18.

18. See, for example, Ustiuzhanin, *Malen'kie tragedii A. S. Pushkina,* 46; Fomichev, "Dramaturgiia Pushkina," 281–83; Stepanov, "*Skupoi rytsar'* A. S. Pushkina," 32–34.

19. See Moskvicheva, "Problema zhanra *Malen'kikh tragedii* A. S. Pushkina"; Moskvicheva, "Osobennosti konflikta v tragedii Pushkina *Motsart i Sal'eri*"; Moskvicheva, "Tragicheskaia kolliziia v *Kammenom goste* A. S. Pushkina."

20. Beliak and Virolainen, "'Malen'kie tragedii' kak kul'turnyi epos," 97.

21. See Mitina, "Tragedii Pushkina," 14. Several other works follow the same principles. For example, N. I. Ishchuk-Fadeeva connected the generic conception of the Boldino plays with the idea that they embodied "a very particular genre, anticipating the principle of montage" ("*Stseny* kak osobyi dramaticheskii zhanr," 84–97). L. A. Kazakova considers the Boldino plays to be "lyric dramas," that is, homogeneous texts according to a new definition, on the basis of the internal synthesis of literary genres ("*Malen'kie tragedii* A. S. Pushkina kak khudozhestvennaia tselostnost'," 14). The strongest expression of this tendency can be found in the opinions of O. G. Lazaresku, who believes that it is practically impossible to give generic definition to each of the Boldino plays and to the cycle as a whole (*Boldinskie dramy A. S. Pushkina,* 21).

22. Garkavi, "*Malen'kie tragedii* Pushkina kak dramaturgicheskii tsikl," 68–69.
23. Odinokov, *Khudozhestvenno-istoricheskii opyt*, 138–45.
24. Garkavi, "*Malen'kie tragedii* Pushkina kak dramaturgicheskii tsikl," 64–65.
25. Odinokov, *Khudozhestvenno-istoricheskii opyt*, 140–45.
26. Ibid., 138.
27. See, for example, Gorodetskii, *Dramaturgiia Pushkina*, 267–310; Iof'ev, "Profili iskusstva," 246–76; Blagoi, *Tvorcheskii put' Pushkina* (1967), 579–672.
28. Tomashevskii, "'Malen'kie tragedii' Pushkina i Mol'er"; Tomashevskii, "Pushkin," 43–44.
29. Nusinov, "Tragediia skuposti," 438–40.
30. Gukovskii, *Pushkin i problemy realisticheskogo stilia*, 298–325.
31. Ibid., 300.
32. Ibid., 309.
33. Makogonenko, *Tvorchestvo Pushkina*, 153–240.
34. Ibid., 199, 230–34.
35. Nepomniashchii, "Simfoniia zhizni," 113.
36. See, for example, Ustiuzhanin, *Malen'kie tragedii A. S. Pushkina*, 46; Feldman, *Sud'ba dramaturgii Pushkina*, 154–64; Fridman, *Romantizm*, 146–76; Fomichev, "Dramaturgiia Pushkina," 279–90.
37. See Fridman, *Romantizm*, 163.
38. Ibid., 166.
39. Lotman, "Pushkin: Etapy tvorchestva," 22–24; Lotman, "Tipologicheskaia kharakteristika realizma pozdnego Pushkina," 131–46.
40. Lotman, "Pushkin: Etapy tvorchestva," 23.
41. Beliak and Virolainen, "'Malen'kie tragedii' kak kul'turnyi epos," 86.
42. Ibid.
43. Ibid., 94.
44. Ibid., 87.
45. See, for example, Nepomniashchii, "Iz zametok sostavitelia," 843–912; Novikova, *Pushkinskii kosmos*, 163–254; Kostalevskaia, "Duet—diada—duel'," 55.
46. See Nepomniashchii, "Iz zametok sostavitelia," 877.
47. Beliak and Virolainen, "'Malen'kie tragedii' kak kul'turnyi epos," 86.
48. Maimin, "Filosofskaia poeziia Pushkina i liubomudrov."
49. Maimin, "Polifonicheskii roman Dostoevskogo i pushkinskaia traditsiia," 313–14.
50. Tiupa, "Novatorstvo avtorskogo soznaniia v tsikle *Malen'kikh tragedii*."
51. Chumakov, "Remarka i siuzhet"; Chumakov, "Dva fragmenta o siuzhetnoi polifonii *Motsarta i Sal'eri*."
52. Chumakov, "Remarka i siuzhet," 69.
53. Nepomniashchii, "Iz zametok sostavitelia," 877–79.
54. Beliak and Virolainen, "*Motsart i Sal'eri*."
55. Ibid., 118.
56. Nepomniashchii, "Iz zametok sostavitelia," 896.

57. Ibid.

58. Ibid.

59. See, for example, Shervinskii, *Ritm i smysl*, 219–21; Rassadin, *Dramaturg Pushkin*, 178–89; Kazakova, "*Malen'kie tragedii* A. S. Pushkina," 15–16.

60. Solov'ev, "Opyt dramaticheskikh izuchenii."

"Strange and Savage Joy"

The Erotic as a Unifying Element in *The Little Tragedies*

Sergei Davydov

Je suis l'Athée du bonheur.

—Pushkin's letter from Boldino, 1830

The famous autumn of 1830, which Pushkin spent at his ancestral estate in Boldino, was the most inspired and fruitful season of Pushkin's life; had he written nothing else but what he wrote during that season, he would still be Russia's greatest poet. In Boldino, Pushkin found himself at a crossroads. The thirty-one-year-old poet was about to end his bachelor life by marrying an eighteen-year-old paragon of beauty, Natalie, who probably did not love him. In his Boldino elegies Pushkin bade farewell to his bachelor past, to women, living or dead, whom he once loved—his "Don Juan list" consisted of thirty-four names at this point. The impecunious bridegroom came to Boldino in order to take possession of two villages, which he received before the wedding from his "miserly father," and, by mortgaging two hundred "souls," to collect a dowry for his bride, for such was the condition of his future mother-in-law. In addition, severe epidemics of cholera morbus broke out that fall, casting an ominous shadow over the blithe prospect of marriage. Thus, financial worries, courtship of a young beauty, parting with his promiscuous past, an unprecedented eruption of creativity, and ever-present death reverberate throughout the Boldino writings with a strong biographical note. The "mystery of happiness and grave" [tainy schast'ia i groba] can be seen as the leitmotiv of the Boldino season, which opened with this eerie question: "Are they burying a house-goblin? Marrying off a witch?" [Domovogo li khoroniat, / Ved'mu l' zamuzh vydaiut?] from the poem "Besy" (The demons).

Separated from his fiancée by seven quarantines, the poet pondered in life and art the unpredictability and limits of happiness in the face of a destructive force. A brief sampling of his letters shows how this quest monopolized Pushkin's mind: "Ha la maudite chose que le bonheur!"; "The devil pushed me to hallucinate about happiness, as if I was meant for it"; "Baratynskii says that only fools are blissful as bridegrooms"; "Notre mariage semble toujours fuir devant moi, et cette peste avec ses quarantaines n'est-elle pas la plus mauvaise plaisanterie que le sort ait pu imaginer"; "Mais le bonheur... c'est un grand *peut-être,* comme le disait Rabelais du paradis ou de l'éternité. Je suis l'Athée du bonheur."[1]

Doubting the possibility of happiness in real life, Pushkin tests such a prospect on paper in prose and verse. The Boldino season opens with the upbeat cycle of *The Tales of Belkin,* Pushkin's debut in prose, and concludes with the verse cycle of *The Little Tragedies.* In four out of the five *Tales* ("The Shot," "The Blizzard," "The Stationmaster," and "The Lady Peasant") an ominous force threatens the happiness of the "true hearts," but in the epic space of the *Tales* all situations fraught with doom are happily resolved. In "The Shot," "The Blizzard," and "The Stationmaster," Pushkin unites the true hearts (the Count with the Countess, Maria with Burmin, and Dunia with Minsky) literally over the grave of the adversary who threatened their happiness (Silvio, Vladimir, and Vyrin, respectively). In "The Lady Peasant," the happy epilogue to the *Tales,* Pushkin marries Vladimir and Liza offstage over the "grave," as it were, of the ancient family feud, thus dodging the Romeo and Juliet scenario.[2] In Anna Akhmatova's words, these "toy denouements" were a "bizarre conjury of destiny" [svoeobraznoe zaklinanie sud'by] through which Pushkin "prompted fate how to save him, showing it that there are no hopeless situations and that happiness, in spite of all odds, is attainable."[3]

Having finished *The Tales of Belkin* by 20 October, Pushkin writes in one breath the four *Little Tragedies* from 23 October to 6 November; they conclude the Boldino season. In these experimental verse dramas Pushkin continues to explore in a new generic key the same theme of happiness, sometimes referred to as the "eudaemonic theme."[4] However, in the tragic space of these "dramatic experiments," as Pushkin called his *Little Tragedies,* the poet comes to diametrically opposed results. In each play the heroes doggedly pursue happiness, but when they are on the very brink of attaining the object of their desire, a fatal calamity invariably strikes. Mozart's musical idea captures the crux of this situation:

> Now picture . . . let me see? . . .
> Well . . . *me,* let's say—a somewhat younger version,
> In love—not overmuch, but lightly so;
> I'm with a lady . . . or a friend . . . say, *you;*
> I'm cheerful . . . then . . . some vision from the grave . . . [viden'e grobovoe]
> A darkness comes . . . or something of the kind.[5]

In each of the four tragedies Pushkin stages this conflict as a contest between Eros and Thanatos.[6] I will use these two terms as a convenient shorthand for the complex forces involved in each conflict.

The main protagonists of *The Little Tragedies* pursue happiness through the gratification of some Eros-inspired desire. In each case, the essence of their passion is dualistic: "The heroes give themselves to the chaotic and orgiastic force of passion and simultaneously suffer as they try to absolve themselves from it. Thus the tragic hero becomes both a criminal and an expiatory victim."[7] The four objects of their passion form a well-marked crescendo in the four dramas: gold, music, love, and life. Each becomes an idol, is worshiped in a quasi-religious, shamanistic manner, and acquires highly erotic attributes.

The old Baron in *The Covetous Knight* now ranks gold above love, yet we know that there was a time when the knight cherished his lady's love. Unfortunately, the gift of her heart, their profligate son, Albert, only poisons his father's late years by threatening to squander his inheritance once his father dies. The Baron's love was displaced by a craving for gold, into which the widower invests what remains of his flaccid libido. The Baron awaits his rendezvous with his treasures "[t]he way a youthful rake awaits a tryst / With some licentious harlot." The Baron's "trusty chests" [vernye sunduki] are his underground harem: each time he is about to unlock a chest, he "fall[s] into a fever and [. . .] shudder[s]" [vpadaiu v zhar i trepet], an ardor worthy of Don Juan (or of Fedor Karamazov). However, the Baron's "lust for wealth,"[8] underscored by Pushkin's sexual pun, takes a sudden morbid turn:

> Physicians claim that there are certain men
> Who find a pleasure in the act of murder.

> When I *insert* my key inside the lock,
> I feel what murderers themselves must feel
> As they plunge dagger into flesh: excitement . . .
> And horror all at once.[9]

In his cellar the Baron tests the compatibility of pleasure and crime, the two things that, like "villainy and genius," should not go together in the moral universe of *The Little Tragedies.* Like a high priest performing sorcery, the Baron lights candles before each coffinlike trunk and conducts a Black Mass. His underground requiem includes a Litany and an Eternal Memory in commemoration of the victims from whom the various gold pieces were extracted. At the same time, the Baron keeps his own son on the verge of poverty, driving him into dealings with money lenders and into contemplation of patricide. The father's lust for gold has an emasculating effect on the son; the young knight, admired for his prowess at the tournaments by both rivals and ladies, shies away from other courtly merriments because of his lack of seemly attire. By denying his son his inheritance, the father foils, in a proto-Karamazovian manner, the son's romantic prospects with the lady of his heart, Clotilda.

The Baron's castrating touch also affects the object of his own passion. By burying the gold in his cellar, the miser has withdrawn it not only from his wastrel heir but also from its natural economic circulation.

> Go home—you've roamed the world quite long enough
> In service to the needs and lusts of men.
> Sleep well in here—the sleep of peace and power,
> The sleep the gods in deepest Heaven sleep. . . .

The Baron's Eros breeds death. Arrested in its procreative flow, the gold has become emasculated, sterile, and barren; Thanatos has won over Eros.

Salieri, in the next "little tragedy," too once loved a woman, but instead of an offspring, Isora has bequeathed to him a ringful of poison. For eighteen years Salieri carries with him Isora's "prophetic gift [of love]" [zavetnyi dar liubvi], waiting for a worthy occasion on which to employ it. By now music has displaced love in Salieri's life, but his ardor is once again unrequited.

O Heaven! Where is justice to be found?!
When genius, that immortal sacred gift,
Is granted not to love and self-denial,
To labor and to striving and to prayer—
But casts its light upon a madman's head,
A foolish idler's brow?... O Mozart, Mozart!

A similar pathology that once defiled Salieri's love now afflicts his passion for music, an infatuation with a dash of necrophilia: "[Killing] potent sounds, / I disassembled music like a corpse" [Zvuki umertviv, / Muzyku ia raz"ial, kak trup]. The autopsy of his beloved object climaxes in an actual murder, the thrill of which the Baron had only dreamed about. The melomaniac kills his beloved musician and something else:

I feel both pain and joy,
As if I'd just fulfilled some heavy debt,
As if a healing knife had just cut off
An aching limb!

The word *chlen* (limb or penis) that Pushkin uses here suggests that Salieri has performed a metaphoric castration.[10] The progression from autopsy to murder to self-mutilation allows for the conjecture that Salieri might have contemplated both murder and suicide. His words to Mozart—"No, wait! / You've drunk it down!... and could not wait for me?" [Postoi, / Postoi, postoi!.. Ty vypil!.. bez menia?]—suggest that Mozart, having drunk the poisoned wine alone, preempted Salieri's doubly morbid scheme.[11] Salieri's Eros, misplaced and disfigured by pathology (necrophilia, masochism, homicide, self-castration, suicide), breeds death.

Both the Baron and Salieri are proud and lonely misers, willing to endure privations in order to attain their goals. However, if the Baron has buried his treasure too deep in his underground vault, Salieri has placed his too high on a pedestal. Salieri considers it a sacrilege when a street fiddler plays one of Mozart's tunes: "I cannot laugh—when some benighted hack / Besmirches Raphael and his Madonna" or "[w]ith parody dishonors Alighieri." Salieri would like to withdraw music (just like the Baron would withdraw the gold) from the public domain. Mozart, on the other hand, is wasteful and promiscuous, sharing his gift and wine with the initiated and the commoner alike. Just as Albert sends his last bottle of wine to the sick blacksmith, Mozart gives the blind musician money for a drink. However, in his reluctance to part with his Requiem, commissioned by the "visitor in black," Mozart unexpectedly shares with the Baron and Salieri a touch of miserliness.[12]

Salieri is the true incarnation of Thanatos. His condemnation of Mozart—"And no successor will he leave behind. / What profit then his life?"—lays bare his own creative and procreative impotence as a childless composer of stillborn music. By contrast, Mozart, the true incarnation of Eros, "is not a slave of music [. . .] but its lover, unfettered by his own attachment to it."[13] He is also happily married and has sired a son with whom he plays and romps. Although death ultimately triumphs, the offspring of Mozart's biological and creative Eros live on, and his music resounds throughout the theaters and taverns of Salzburg and crosses the borders to Spain—the next "little tragedy" opens with an epigraph from Mozart's *Don Giovanni.*[14]

In *The Stone Guest* both gold and music make way for a higher value: "Of all the happy pleasures life supplies, / To love alone does music yield in sweetness." Bacchantes and pious women, wives and widows, husbands and bachelors, the ascetic friar, and even the marble tomb slab—each has been allotted its own share of Eros. Nevertheless, all is not well under the passionate Castilian sun. The Commander is dead, his lovesick widow pines away, while the paragon of Eros idles in exile in frigid France. Dona Anna was given in marriage to the rich Commander: "The lucky man!" grumbles the covetous Don Juan.

> He brought but worthless wealth
> To lay before an angel—and for this
> He tasted all the joys of paradise!

However, as we are led to believe, Dona Anna has found true love in marriage, and her passion eventually extends beyond the grave:

> How happy he, I think, whose frigid grave
> Is warmed by such an angel's airy sighs
> And watered by her sweet and loving tears.

The Commander, who "tasted all the joys of paradise" in Dona Anna's arms, knew how to cherish it. He was as miserly with his treasure as the Baron and Salieri were with gold and music, cloistering Dona Anna within the walls of his home, guarding her chastity, and barring access to others. In this one-woman "harem," the couple produced no offspring, implying perhaps impotence, barrenness, or both. When Dona Anna becomes a widow, the dead Commander confines her within the cemetery walls, and when even this "chastity belt" loosens its grip, his stone ghost rises from the dead—awesome and castrating—and claims his own.

Don Juan, the happy-go-lucky bachelor, may have been denied love beyond the grave, but he enjoyed a lion's share of earthly love. If the Baron's and Salieri's libidos were misplaced, Don Juan has dispersed his among too many targets. He "collects women the way the Baron collects gold."[15] Incapable of leaving the objects of his desire unserenaded and unmated, he keeps his seraglio happy. In his northern exile among Gallic "waxen dolls," he pines away for his Iberian sweethearts, remembering every fleeting shade of their charms, from the "lowest peasant girl in Andalusia" to the beautiful Inéz. To his darlings, Don Juan is always an uninvited, though welcome, guest. In contrast to the Commander, he is generous and supremely lacking in jealous feelings, sharing his sweethearts with other men. He is as generous with his love as Albert would be with gold or as Mozart is with music. A true master in verbalizing Eros, Don Juan is an inspired improviser of love songs, which Laura performs with such artistry. He falls in love very much to the tune of Mozart: "not overmuch, but lightly so" [ne slishkom, a slegka]. Laura, the high priestess of love and song, prefers him to all other men. Even the coy widow, whose husband and brother-in-law he has killed, gladly receives him, heedless of the ruin he has brought many a fine lady.

One question, however, remains. Shall we believe that this "devoted slave of lust" [pokornyi uchenik razvrata], as he calls himself, is capable of stepping out of his time-honored role to discover true love for the first time?

> But ever since the day I saw your face
> I've been reborn, returned once more to life.
> In loving you, I've learned to love true goodness,
> And now for once I bend my trembling knees
> And kneel in awe before almighty virtue.

Should we believe him if in the same breath he forswears all his former attachments: "But not a one till now / Have I in truth adored"? Dmitrii Blagoi and Friedeberg Seeley do not, and Barbara Monter declares Don Juan's theatrical gestures "a travesty of the romantic concept of redemption through love."[16] However, accepted wisdom has it that Don Juan, "far from being an unreconstructed lecher, is [...] in the process of falling sincerely, even virtuously, in love." Without this, the argument goes, there would be no tragedy.[17]

Regardless of Don Juan's ardor, his Eros, like that of his predecessors, is contaminated by pathology. His serial penetration of women has its morbid counterpart in his intercourse with men; Don Juan stabs the Commander in a duel and pierces his rival in love, Don Carlos, just when the latter is on the verge of possessing Laura—Don Juan will be paid back in kind. The description of the duel and of Don Carlos's wound are rife with sexual innuendoes: "Get up, my dear; it's finished now" [Vstavai, Laura. Koncheno]—*konchit'* (to finish) also means to climax. These words are followed by Laura's impish comment about Don Carlos's naked torso: "You didn't miss . . . you pierced him through the heart. / There's not a drop of blood [from this three-cornered wound]." The presence of the cadaver in Laura's bedchamber has an aphrodisiac effect on Don Juan: "(He kisses her.) Laura: 'My sweet! . . . / Oh, stop . . . before the dead!'" [Postoi!.. pri mertvom!]. The corpse ends up being a witness to their tryst and will be disposed of "before the break of day."

Consistent with Don Juan's morbid erotic slant, it should come as no surprise that his romance with the late Inéz (murdered by her jealous husband) took place at a cemetery. Recalling Inéz's charms, Don Juan invokes her pale, lifeless, nymphlike allure in terms that border on necrophilia:

> I always found
> A strange attraction in her mournful eyes
> And pallid [dying] lips. How strange it is, how strange.
> You never thought her beautiful, I know,
> And yes, it's true—she wasn't what you'd call
> A dazzling beauty. But those eyes of hers,
> Those eyes . . . her searching look. I've never known
> So beautiful a gaze. And then her voice—
> As soft and weak as some poor invalid's . . .

The proximity of death seems to be a catalyst for Don Juan's Eros.[18] He courts Dona Anna at the very cemetery where he used to meet with Inéz and experiences an erotic thrill as he observes the widow prostrate herself and "drape with raven locks the pallid stone" of her husband's sepulcher. Inviting the dead husband to attend the seduction of his widow—to his postmortem cuckolding—heightens this "strange and savage joy" [neiz"iasnimoe naslazhdenie] to a new degree. Apparently, Don Juan would like to relive the thrill of lovemaking in the presence of a dead man. Small wonder that the climax of his courtship with Dona Anna—their first frigid kiss ("kholodnyi, mirnyi potselui")—is interrupted by the entrance of the stone ghost with its castrating handshake: "How cold and hard his mighty fist of stone! / Away from me.... Let go.... Let go my hand ..." [O, tiazhelo / Pozhat'e kamennoi ego desnitsy! / Ostav' menia, pusti, pusti mne ruku...].

The Old Church Slavonic word *desnitsa* (right hand) has the connotation of God's righteous hand, and Vladimir Golstein is right on the mark when he writes: "The cemetery rendezvous, the Commander as a guard for [Don Juan's] lovemaking, or the corpse of Don Carlos as a silent witness of it—these are not exotic paraphernalia used to spice up a sexual act but consistent attempts to debase the mystery of death, to mock its power, to dismiss its inevitability. By mocking death Don Juan strives to overcome it, to ignore the power of time over his life, to conquer his way to heaven."[19]

Don Juan dies with Dona Anna's name on his lips, but in the moral universe of *The Little Tragedies* the fornicator and atheist, who mocks both love and death and debases their mystery, is not admitted into the paradise of true love, the realm where Eros is able to transcend the grave and attain immortality. Because Don Juan has squandered his gift of love in transient, nonprocreative, and morbid pursuits, Eros again loses to Thanatos. Don Juan's music, his love songs, may live on, but their creator perishes. The vagabond lover and his paramours remain childless and will pass their barrenness, along with their Eros-inspired art, to the revelers of the last "little tragedy."

Pushkin ends *The Stone Guest* just when the widow's vow of fidelity is on the verge of being broken. In the last tragedy, *A Feast in Time of Plague*, the widower Walsingham and the orphaned revelers have already broken all their vows. Seated around the banquet table on the town street are the English clones of Inéz, Laura, Dona Anna, and Don Juan, but the object of desire has been raised a notch higher. Facing death point-blank, the revelers crave the ultimate substance: life—or what's left of it. The feast among the corpses releases in the revelers an unprecedented eruption of creative Eros. The singers, dancers, poets, and lovers perform, under the baton of the Master of Revels, a highly artistic rite. Walsingham is himself a newborn poet, his "hymn to plagues" being his first poetic attempt. In their celebration at the edge of the grave of song, dance, poetry, wine, love, and life, the revelers abandon all time-honored pieties and cross over into that uncanny realm beyond good and evil, where "strange and savage joy" [neiz"iasnimy naslazhden'ia] can be had. It seems that no guest—invited or uninvited, made of flesh or stone—can stop the Dionysian feast, the revelers' last bastion against the onslaught of Thanatos.

As their ranks grow thinner, the revelers pretend that death does not exist, proposing a "ringing toast" to the empty chair of the jolly Jackson, "as if he lived." Walsingham rebukes their hackneyed trick—one does not clink when honoring the dead—and proposes a more devious scheme by which to tame fear and fool death: not by mocking it, like Don Juan, but by actually embracing it. In his "hymn to plagues" the Master of Revels bids his moribund congregation to taste the savage delight and merge with the elemental forces of destruction:

> There's bliss in battle and there's bliss
> on the dark edge of an abyss
> and in the fury of the main
> amid foam-crested death;
> in the Arabian hurricane
> and in the Plague's light breath.
>
> All, all such mortal dangers fill
> a mortal's heart with a *deep thrill*
> *of wordless rapture* that bespeaks
> maybe, *immortal life,*
> —and happy is the man who seeks
> and tastes them in his strife.
> (Vladimir Nabokov's translation; emphasis mine)[20]
>
> There's rapture on the battleground,
> And where the black abyss is found,

And on the raging ocean main,
Amid the stormy waves of death,
And in the desert hurricane,
And in the Plague's pernicious breath.

For all that threatens to destroy
Conceals *a strange and savage joy*—
Perhaps for mortal man a glow
That promises *eternal life.*
And happy he who comes to know
This rapture found in storm and strife.
(J. Falen's translation; emphasis mine)

Есть упоение в бою,
И бездны мрачной на краю,
И в разъяренном океане,
Средь грозных волн и бурной тьмы,
И в аравийском урагане,
И в дуновении Чумы.

Все, все, что гибелью грозит,
Для сердца смертного таит
Неизъяснимы наслажденья—
Бессмертья, может быть, залог!
И счастлив тот, кто средь волненья
Их обретать и ведать мог.
(Pushkin 7: 180–81, stanzas 4, 5; emphasis mine)

Like Mozart's Requiem, Walsingham's hymn reveals an uncanny fascination with death, but Mozart's creation is a Christian Mass, whereas Walsingham's hymn is a thoroughly pagan conjury. Moreover, its logic is pure sophistry: if in the realm of the living Death alone is immortal, then by embracing Death and blending with her primal forces we too shall render ourselves immortal. But Death won't be fooled by this ingenious "metaphysical camouflage," and Walsingham is doomed to repeat Don Juan's fatal blunder of inviting Death to his feast. Walsingham outdoes Don Juan in his audacity: the latter was a mere serial seducer of women and killer of men; Walsingham, the self-anointed high priest, is a mass seducer of an entire death-bound congregation. He ignores the entreaty of the Anglican priest to stop the revelry and to save their souls for the sake of eternal life, and he curses all who would follow the priest, knowing full well, perhaps (just as the Grand Inquisitor once knew), that "beyond the grave they will find nothing but death" [za grobom obretut lish' smert'].[21]

For the time being, Eros has the upper hand, and the feast goes on. The revelers are all inspired poets and life-artists striving to prolong their earthly joy. But their carousing among the corpses seems to have contaminated their Eros and impaired its ability to transcend death. From the Scottish ballad about some bygone plague that the harlot Mary sings, we learn that their ancestors once possessed this ability. Jenny, the heroine of the ballad, entreats her beloved not to come near her or to kiss her lips if she dies. She begs him to leave the village and, once the plague is gone, to visit her grave. For her part, Jenny pledges to remain true to her sweetheart even in Heaven. ("A Edmonda ne pokinet Dzhenni dazhe v nebesakh!") For the revelers such a paradise has been lost; the ancestral wisdom of the ballad, just like the priest's appeal, falls on deaf ears.

Defiant, devil-may-care brinkmanship has replaced the chastity of the ancients and their reverence before death. Unperturbed by the contagion, the revelers embrace their dead ("Can that be you, good Walsingham? / Who on your knees but three weeks since / Embraced your mother's corpse and sobbed?") and engage in licentious acts in front of their deceased. Walsingham explains to the priest:

I cannot leave
To take your path. What holds me here
Is foul despair and memories dread,
Awareness of my lawless ways,
The horror of the deathly hush
That now prevails within my house—
And yes, these fresh and frenzied revels,
The blesséd poison of this cup,
And kisses sweet (forgive me, Lord)
From this depraved but lovely wretch....
My mother's shade will call me back
No more.... Too late ... I hear your plea
And know you struggle for my soul....

Too late.... Depart, old man, in peace;
But cursed be all who follow thee.

Admittedly, Walsingham retains a measure of conscience even in his sacrilege. Unlike Don Juan, who wanted to seduce Dona Anna in front of her dead husband, Walsingham would like to "[c]onceal this scene" from the "deathless eyes" of his dead wife, Mathilda. But in his hymn Walsingham outdoes even Don Juan in metaphysical audacity. In the final and erotically most animated lines of the hymn, the plague becomes a maiden brimming with desire:

And so, Dark Queen, we praise thy reign!
Thou callest us, but we remain
unruffled by the chill of death,
clinking our cups, carefree,
drinking a rose-lipped maiden's breath
full of the Plague, maybe!
(Vladimir Nabokov's translation)

So hail to you, repellent Pest!
You strike no fear within our breast;
We are not crushed by your design.
So fill the foaming glasses high,
We'll sip the rosy maiden [literally, And we drink the breath of the Rose Maiden] wine
And kiss the lips where plague may lie!
(J. Falen's translation)

И так—хвала тебе, Чума!
Нам не страшна могилы тьма,
Нас не смутит твое призванье!
Бокалы пеним дружно мы,
И Девы-Розы пьем дыханье—
Быть может—полное Чумы!
(Pushkin 7: 181, stanza 6)

Paradoxically, in the contest of Eros and Thanatos in *The Little Tragedies* a beloved woman becomes a direct or indirect accomplice of death. Mozart was poisoned by Isora's gift of love, Dona Anna's frigid kiss triggers the entrance of the stone Commander, and in *A Feast in Time of Plague* the fornication with the miasmic Rose Maiden portends death. Although the revelers are still alive, dancing and ringing "around a rosie," their circle narrows, and the moment when the next "falls down" is just around the corner. Be that as it may, the revelers are already barren, childless, and their society all but extinct.

A Feast in Time of Plague was Pushkin's final and most daring experiment with happiness in the face of death. The protagonists of *The Little Tragedies* sought to gratify some *Eros-inspired desire.* The objects of their desire followed a *crescendo* (gold, art, love, and life), and all acquired highly *erotic attributes.* The protagonists *worshiped their idols* with shamanic abandon and aspired to attain *earthly paradise and immortality.* In each "little tragedy" *Eros temporarily triumphed,* and the idol-worshipers celebrated with a *feast.* But because their passion was defiled by *pathology* (misplaced libido, sterility, barrenness, morbid sexuality, masochism, castration, suicide, murder, necrophilia), the victory of Eros was short-lived and the ability to transcend death lost. The triumph of Thanatos is not complete, though; the fate of the four major *survivors* remains open at the fall of the curtain. The poetic justice will be meted out to Albert, Salieri, Dona Anna, and Walsingham offstage in the unwritten elliptical hypothetical "fifth act" that constitutes the true tragic space of each of Pushkin's experimental "little tragedies."

Death has robbed the Baron of his gold, but in the implied fifth act Albert's complicity in the death of his father might despoil his joy over his guilt-ridden inheritance. Until his doomsday will Salieri agonize over Mozart's last words about the incompatibility of villainy and genius. Don Juan's punishment is death and damnation, but the final destination of Dona Anna remains moot. Pushkin may have chivalrously spared his Anna the destiny prescribed by the classical scenario; his stage remark, "(They sink into the ground)" [(Provalivaiutsia)], may refer just to Don Juan and the Commander. If this is the case, then, after the curtain falls, Dona Anna has to face the same anguish and agony as the rest of the survivors of *The Little Tragedies.* Physical death is the most likely outcome for the revelers, who possibly also forfeited their chance for Christian afterlife. Their prospect for an alternative immortality through the pursuit of strange and savage pleasure remains iffy, to say the least. Their revelry continues, but their master has already distanced himself. As the curtain falls, we find him "lost in [deep] thought" [pogruzhennii v glubokuiu zadumchivost'], pondering, perhaps, his "grand peut-être," as Rabelais used to call paradise or eternity. The content of Walsingham's silent reverie constitutes fifth act of this last "little tragedy."

Walsingham's vision of his late wife, Mathilda, which triggered his reverie and sent a metaphysical shudder through his bones, offers an arcane glimpse into the contents of this rumination:

> Where am I now? *My blesséd light!*
> I see you . . . but my sinful soul
> Can reach you there no more. . . . (emphasis mine)

Mathilda, who tasted the earthly paradise in Walsingham's embrace ("znala rai v ob"iatiakh moikh"), is now in Heaven, where Walsingham's arms no longer reach. Walsingham calls her the "blesséd [child of] light" [sviatoe chado sveta], while her real name casts an additional glimmer on Walsingham's reverie. Dante used the name Matilda in *The Divine Comedy.* It belonged to the "radiant lady" who at the end of *Purgatory* guided the Poet to the river Lethe, which erased the memories of his evil deeds, and to the river Eunoë, which revived the memory of his virtues. The Poet is now "pure and prone to ascend to the stars" to Paradiso, to Beatrice (Dante, *Purgatory,* canto 33).

Thus the "fifth act" of Pushkin's gloomiest "little tragedy" is not without a ray of hope. Mathilda, privy to both earthly and heavenly paradise, could be signaling to *her* poet—"The Hymn to the Plague" is Walsingham's first poetic creation—that he too is not beyond salvation.

Surrounded by cholera morbus and cherishing hopes of marrying the beautiful eighteen-year-old Natalie, Pushkin tested in Boldino the challenge of happiness in the face of doom. The autumn opened with a prose cycle, *The Tales of Belkin,* of which "The Coffinmaker" was written first (8 September), and concluded with a cycle of verse tragedies, of which *A Feast in Time of Plague* was written last (6 November). These two liminal texts, straddling the Boldino season, emblematically echo its dominant theme—the contest of Eros and Thanatos. The plump Cupid with an inverted torch, painted on the sign over the coffinmaker's shop in "The Coffinmaker," can be seen as the emblem uniting the remaining four *Tales of Belkin,* in which love of the true hearts each time defeated death. As an analogous emblem of unity for *The Little Tragedies,* in which Thanatos invariably triumphs over Eros,

I propose, from *A Feast in Time of Plague,* the "somber cart" laden with corpses, which,

> as you well know,
> Has right to travel where it will,
> And let it pass we must.

As if to mark the significance of these two texts within their respective cycles, the poet left his cryptic signature on both of them. In the *Tales* Alexander Pushkin endowed his coffinmaker, Adrian Prokhorov, with his own initials (in the drafts even the first letters of their patronymics matched: Simeonovich and Sergeevich). Pushkin also lent to Adrian his own erstwhile profession—all members of the infamous Arzamas society were undertakers.[22] In addition, the poet has his coffinmaker begin his profession in 1799, that is, the year Pushkin was born. Adrian's counterpart in *A Feast in Time of Plague* is the undertaker pulling the somber cart. This black man shares with Pushkin an additional biographical detail: both are of African origin. In the English original (John Wilson's *The City of the Plague,* 1816), the undertaker is a Negro because he comes from the colonies, whereas in the Russian context this detail, I believe, begs for an autobiographical interpretation. Thus in both key texts of the two experimental Boldino cycles, the poet himself merrily plays at being the undertaker, and in tragedies, even "little" ones, the last laugh belongs to those who remove the corpses.

Notes

1. From letters 518, 519, 523, 525, 535 (Pushkin 14: 110, 113, 114, 123; see also Pushkin, The Letters, 309, 310, 314, 315, 323).
2. For the unity of the Tales, see Bethea and Davydov, "Pushkin's Saturnine Cupid."
3. Akhmatova, "*Kamennyi gost'* Pushkina," 166–68.
4. See Gregg, "The Eudaemonic Theme." The centrality of the concept of pleasure and happiness in *The Little Tragedies* was discussed by Blagoi, *Sotsiologiia tvorchestva Pushkina,* 219–23; Akhmatova, "*Kamennyi gost'* Pushkina," 89–109; and Beliak and Virolainen, "'Malen'kie tragedii' kak kul'turnyi epos," 73–96.
5. All translations are by James E. Falen. I have occasionally inserted in square brackets a literal translation of Pushkin's words.

6. For the "love and death" theme, see Blagoi, *Sotsiologiia tvorchestva Pushkina,* 206–18; Terras, "Introduction," 5–12, 105–10, 12; and Monter, "Love and Death."

7. Beliak and Virolainen, "'Malen'kie tragedii' kak kul'turnyi epos," 86.

8. Vladimir Alexandrov's expression in his "Correlations in Pushkin's *Malen'kie tragedii,*" 183.

9. Emphasis mine. The pun involves the verb *vlagat'* (to insert) and *vlagalishche* (vagina).

10. See Smirnov, *Psikhodiakhronologika,* 30.

11. Suggested by Aikhenval'd, *Pushkin* (1908), 86, and Vatsuro, "Introduction," 50.

12. Noticed by Ermakov, *Etiudy po psikhologii tvorchestva A. S. Pushkina,* 174.

13. Aikhenval'd, *Pushkin* (1908), 82.

14. Libretto by Lorenzo Da Ponte, 1787.

15. Alexandrov, "Correlations in Pushkin's *Malen'kie tragedii,*" 183.

16. Blagoi, *Sotsiologiia tvorchestva Pushkina,* 213; Seeley, "The Problem of *Kamennyi Gost'*"; Monter, "Love and Death," 210.

17. Gregg, "The Eudaemonic Theme," 189; Kotliarevskii, "Kamennyi gost'"; Bem, "Boldinskaia osen'"; Akhmatova, "*Kamennyi gost'* Pushkina," 100, 163.

18. Blagoi, *Sotsiologiia tvorchestva Pushkina,* 212–13, 215; Siniavskii, *Progulki s Pushkinym,* 70; Lotman, "Tipologicheskaia kharakteristika realizma pozdnego Pushkina," 140.

19. Golstein, "Pushkin's *Mozart and Salieri,*" 170.

20. Nabokov, *Three Russian Poets,* 15–16.

21. Dostoevsky, *The Brothers Karamazov,* 240.

22. For the concept of the poet as an undertaker, see my "The Merry Coffinmaker."

The Anatomy of the Modern Self in *The Little Tragedies*

Svetlana Evdokimova

Pushkin referred to his four dramas—*The Covetous Knight, Mozart and Salieri, The Stone Guest,* and *A Feast in Time of Plague*—as "studies." Although it is traditionally understood that by designating his plays as studies Pushkin implied the experimental nature of their form, it is equally important to consider that which Pushkin "studied" in them pertaining to subject matter. In this essay I will try to demonstrate that, although many of the themes and issues central to *The Little Tragedies*—such as the themes of love and death, personal happiness, and the problem of financial difficulties—may have been inspired by Pushkin's personal experiences, the four plays represent studies of "passions" that Pushkin viewed as constituents of the modern self.[1]

In discussing *The Little Tragedies* as a cycle, a number of critics have claimed that in the characters of the Baron, Salieri, Don Juan, and Walsingham Pushkin offered an analysis of universal human passions independent of specific historical circumstances that may have shaped the protagonists of the plays.[2] Others, on the contrary, insisted that Pushkin depicted passions in their historical manifestations as they are grounded in and motivated by concrete historical epochs.[3] In my approach I will try to navigate between the Scylla and Charybdis of the purely psychological and purely sociological interpretations and avoid both the perspective that characters are radically free from their environments as well as vulgar Marxist attempts to fully explain character by milieu. Instead, I will consider the role of romantic ethos in

Pushkin's representation of his protagonists; whether or not Pushkin presents his characters as being shaped by their environments, he nonetheless remains himself a legitimate member of his milieu and age and, as such, expresses many of the concerns that animated his fellow romantic writers. Profoundly interested in modernizing Russian theater, Pushkin believed that drama had to respond to the spirit of the age and had to be connected to the social and cultural conditions of its day. In other words, I suggest that *The Little Tragedies* are not antihistorical; instead, their historicism is not that of a historical play but of the sort we find, for example, in Goethe's *Faust.* Although the setting of *Faust* is explicitly medieval, the title character reflects the mentality that Goethe identifies with his own times. That is why I take the concluding line of *The Covetous Knight*—"What dreadful times are these, what dreadful hearts!"—as emblematic of *The Little Tragedies*' temporal ambiguity, which may be applicable to the modern age.[4]

Thus I submit that *The Little Tragedies* engage the tragedy inherent in the nature of modern life, understood broadly as a post-Renaissance phenomenon, one that coincided for Pushkin with the perceived collapse of traditional order, characteristic of the end of eighteenth-century and the beginning of nineteenth-century Europe and that was central to romanticism as a whole. Scholars seem to agree that the modern self as we recognize it now owes a great deal to romanticism. As Charles Taylor notes in his *Sources of the Self: The Making of the Modern Identity,* "These two big and many-sided cultural transformations, the Enlightenment and Romanticism with its accompanying expressive conception of man, have made us what we are."[5] Significantly, among the four plots Pushkin explores in his plays, two deal specifically with myths central to the age of romanticism: *Mozart and Salieri* draws on the myth of Cain, celebrated by Byron's *Cain,* which inspired generations of followers, and *The Stone Guest* delves into a myth that fascinated many romantics, from Byron and E. T. A. Hoffmann to Alfred de Musset and José Zorrilla—the legend of Don Juan.[6] It is also worthwhile to note that Pushkin was profoundly interested in the figure of Faust and wrote *A Scene from Faust,* which is close thematically and generically to the cycle of *The Little Tragedies,* although it was composed earlier, in 1825. Identifying the four most important myths of "modern individualism" as Faust, Don Quixote, Don Juan, and Robinson Crusoe, Ian Watt claims that these four myths "derive from the transition from the social and intellectual system of the Middle Ages to the system dominated by modern individualistic thought, and this transition has itself been marked by the remarkable development from their original Renaissance meanings to their present Romantic meanings."[7] As the romantics began to evaluate the concept of the modern self, a significant change in the general perception of these myths occurred. By turning to universal passions and myths, Pushkin presents them not as relics of a past age but as the basis for shaping our modern identity.

In what follows, after discussing the cultural and historical context that informed Pushkin's conception of modern selfhood, I focus on several major facets of the tragic identity of Pushkin's protagonists. As I have suggested in the introduction, *The Little Tragedies* are not dramas of events but rather tragedies of ideas or particular aspects of human nature. Each of the four plays puts forth a dominant passion, such as covetousness (*The Covetous Knight*), "Salierism" (*Mozart and Salieri*), "Don Juanism" (*The Stone Guest*), or religious apostasy (*A Feast in Time of Plague*), that cannot be reduced to mere greed, envy, lust, or blasphemy. Dominant in one play, each passion may also be reflected in other plays of the cycle. By being developed and acquiring additional meanings in one or more of the four plays, each of these representative passions creates a sense of an almost polyphonic unity holding the cycle together. Thus, for example, apart from being the dominant passion of *The Covetous Knight,* the "theme" of covetousness is also reflected in *Mozart and Salieri* and, with a curious twist, in *The Stone Guest.* The passion of "Don Juanism," whose key component is sensuality, finds its most powerful embodiment in *The Stone Guest,* but this passion also has links with religious apostasy, "Salierism," and covetousness. While a form of religious apostasy is present in all four plays, it becomes a dominant theme in *A Feast in Time of Plague.* By overlapping his treatment of individual passions, Pushkin achieves a more complex and dialectical representation of the "myths" that constitute the modern self.[8]

The Sources of the Modern Self: In the Shadow of Napoleon's "Somber Brow"

Clearly, the formations of a modern identity and a new type of mentality were themes that preoccupied European romantics no less than they did Pushkin. Many European romantics exhibited a near obsession with the problem of the identity of the nineteenth-century man. In addition to Byron, Pushkin credits several other European writers, or "two or three novels," as he puts it in *Eugene Onegin*, for accurately representing the modern man. Commenting on Onegin's appreciation of Byron's unique ability to capture the most typical features of the century and of the contemporary man, the narrator of *Eugene Onegin* articulates the romantic concern with the representation of the spirit of the age:

> Don Juan's and Giaour's creator,
> two or three novels where our later
> epoch's portrayed, survived the ban,
> works where contemporary man
> is represented rather truly,
> that soul without a moral tie,
> all egotistical and dry,
> to dreaming given up unduly,
> and that embittered mind which boils
> in empty deeds and futile toils.[9]
>
> Он из опалы исключил:
> Певца Гяура и Жуана
> Да с ним еще два-три романа,
> В которых отразился век
> И современный человек
> Изображен довольно верно
> С его безнравственной душой,
> Себялюбивой и сухой,
> Мечтанью преданной безмерно,
> С его озлобленным умом,
> Кипящим в действии пустом.
> (Pushkin 6: 148)

The "two or three novels" that Pushkin mentions in this stanza are traditionally interpreted as referring to *Melmoth the Wanderer* (1820) by Charles Robert Maturin, *René* (1802) by François René de Chateaubriand, and *Adolphe* (1815) by Benjamin Constant de Rebecque, but the list, of course, could go on. The titles or subtitles of many writers of the romantic period speak for themselves: *The Red and the Black: A Chronicle of the Nineteenth Century* (1830) by Stendhal, *The Confession of a Child of the Century* (1836) by Alfred de Musset, and *La Comédie humaine* (1841) by Honoré de Balzac.

Throughout his literary career and especially in his later works, Pushkin also grappled with modern identity and selfhood. As early as 1820–21, when writing his *Prisoner of the Caucasus*, Pushkin was, as he later acknowledged, motivated by a desire to depict the distinctive traits of the younger generation of the nineteenth century. ("Ia v nem khotel izobrazit' eto ravnodushie k zhizni i k ee naslazhdeniiam, etu prezhdevremennuiu starost' dushi, kotorye sdelalis' otlichitel'nymi chertami molodezhi 19-go veka.")[10] In 1833, in *The Queen of Spades*, an already mature Pushkin dealt again with a typical representative of the nineteenth century, whom he characterizes as "Homme sans moeurs et sans religion!" (See an epigraph for chapter 4, which starts with a symbolic date, "7 Mai 18**.") In most cases, the nineteenth century received little praise from the poet who referred to it as the "pernicious century" [gnusnyi vek] ("K Viazemskomu," 1826), the "cruel century" [zhestokii vek] ("Ia pamiatnik sebe vozdvig nerukotvornyi . . . ," 1836), "our merchant-century" [nash vek-torgash], or the "century of iron" [vek zheleznyi] ("Razgovor knigoprodavtsa s poetom," 1824).

Having lived during a time characterized by momentous transformations of culture and society, Pushkin sought to comprehend the impact of such crucial events of European history as the French Revolution and the rise of Napoleon. For Pushkin, the emergence of the contemporary man was first and foremost connected with a crisis of traditional aristocratic values ushered in by these events. Pushkin contemplated the receding values of the past centuries and often specifically the century of Catherine the Great with great anxiety and concern. This concern is probably best exemplified in his poem "K vel'mozhe" (To a noble, 1830) written in the same year as *The Little Tragedies*. The poem eulogizes some of the past centuries' aristocratic values: enlightened hedonism, with its light and playful attitude toward life, its balance and poise, as well as the appreciation of all kinds of beauty. By contrast, the nineteenth century's new generation is criticized for its failure to respond to a good joke, poetry, or love, for its calculation and thriftiness:

For see: around thee now
All things are new, the past doth ever distant grow,
And having witnessed yesterday's annihilation
The time is scarce recalled by this new generation.
In gathering late harvest from those cruel days,
They judge the good and bad to see which greater weighs.
They have no time to jest, to dine at Fortune's table,
Or talk of verse. E'en Byron's lyre is hardly able
To please and entertain them with its wondrous note.[11]

Смотри: вокруг тебя
Все новое кипит, былое истребя.
Свидетелями быв вчерашнего паденья,
Едва опомнились младые поколенья.
Жестоких опытов сбирая поздний плод,
Они торопятся с расходом свесть приход.
Им некогда шутить, обедать у Темиры
Иль спорить о стихах. Звук новой, чудной лиры,
Звук лиры Байрона развлечь едва их мог.
(Pushkin 3, 1: 219)

The implied watershed that separates the old and the new man is, of course, the French Revolution and the Napoleonic Wars. Thus, in the second chapter of *Eugene Onegin,* Pushkin outlines the impact of Napoleon on the consciousness of the modern man in the following way:

For we've outgrown
old prejudice; all men are zeros,
the units are ourselves alone.
Napoleon's our sole inspiration;
the millions of two-legged creation
for us are instruments and tools;
feeling is quaint, and fit for fools.[12]

Все предрассудки истребя,
Мы почитаем всех нулями,
А единицами—себя.

Мы все глядим в Наполеоны—
Двуногих тварей миллионы
Для нас орудие одно,
Нам чувство дико и смешно.
(Pushkin 6: 37)

While it is a commonplace of literary criticism that the emergence of the Byronic hero was directly connected with historical and social developments of Europe at the end of the eighteenth to the beginning of the nineteenth century, one must also acknowledge that the same historical circumstances were also responsible for the rise of the middle class, or the "class of industry and skill," a phrase coined by Ralph Waldo Emerson in his famous essay "Napoleon, or the Man of the World." The type of hero that best represented this class was an achiever—an ambitious, serious, calculative, and rational individual—like Napoleon, who Emerson maintained was the "incarnate Democrat."[13] Thus, both the type of the demonic rebel (such as Byron's Cain or Corsair) and the type of the achiever (such as Stendhal's Julien Sorel) develop from the same source: the myth of Napoleon. It is no coincidence then that in Onegin's library Byron and Napoleon merge in the image of the fashionable cult figure:

Lord Byron's portrait on the wall,
the iron figure on the table,
the hat, the scowling brow, the chest
where folded arms are tightly pressed.[14]

И лорда Байрона портрет,
И столбик с куклою чугунной
Под шляпой, с пасмурным челом,
С руками, сжатыми крестом.
(Pushkin 6: 147)

The "somber brow" (*pasmurnoe chelo*) of Napoleon is symbolic of the type of man who emerges as the result of European revolutionary upheavals.[15] Disregard for tradition, self-centeredness, immoralism, egoism, the subordination of means to ends, emotional coldness, and utilitarian rationalism are among the features that characterize him; his mind is "rebellious" (*miatezhnyi*) and "gloomy" (*sumrachnyi*), one that spreads the "cold poison all around" [khladnyi iad krugom] (drafts of stanza 22, chapter 7); he is always taciturn and preoccupied with economy. Pushkin clearly identifies the source of this mentality with the French Revolution and Napoleonic Wars. In other words, he links the appearance of the nineteenth-century man with precisely those historical circumstances that were responsible for the rise of the middle class, on the one hand, and the emergence of the Byronic hero, on the other. Whereas Pushkin discusses the shaping force of these events for Russian and European social and political institutions in some of his essays, the impact of these events on human nature could be best studied in drama, with its focus on character, and in the novel, with its focus on character development. It is for this reason that Pushkin treats the problem of the modern self with particular intensity in *Eugene Onegin* and *The Little Tragedies.*

Along with many other romantic dramatists, Pushkin sought tragedy in a close analysis of character. What defines the protagonists of Pushkin's plays is their romantic ethos, revealed first and foremost in their rebellious nature and in the inward turn of their personalities. The four plays engage the key themes of romanticism, that is, selfhood and revolt. As Jeffrey N. Cox points out in his *In the Shadow of Romance,* "Romantic art was, after all, born in an age of revolutionary individualism, an age that experienced the isolation brought on by the disappearance and even the 'death' of the divine, that felt the old ties of mutual family and community obligations threatened by the greedy atomism of the capitalist marketplace, that saw nature in retreat before technology and industry."[16] The four main characters of *The Little Tragedies*—the Baron, Salieri, Don Juan, and Walsingham—are proud individuals who, by breaking with family ties and "community obligations," try to bend the world to their will. They emerge as heroes not because of their superior achievements or position in society but because they are able to free themselves from the limits that define and restrict other men. They rise to the status of tragic heroes because they transgress against the limits of their own selves.

From God to Mammon, from Art to Crime

What makes the Baron, the miserly protagonist of *The Covetous Knight,* different from his literary predecessors is the ideological aspect of his passion. The tragedy of the Baron results from his obsession with gold, but his avarice is a passion that is much more complex than mere greed or striving for accumulation. Were his covetousness no more than financial thriftiness, the Baron would have remained a comic type, one that has been portrayed in countless versions of the Western comedy. But despite some comic elements, the play hardly ends on a comic note. The Baron is stricken dead, and the audience is left with the Duke's final indictment: "He's dead. O God in Heaven! / What dreadful times are these, what dreadful hearts!" The Baron's miserliness grows into a trait that has tragic repercussions beyond his personal fate. It grows into a tragedy of an "age" ("times") or century (*vek*) and a tragedy of this century's selves, or hearts (*serdtsa*).

In his *Defence of Poetry*, Percy Bysshe Shelley makes an observation that puts the Baron's passion for acquisition in the context of the romantic concept of selfhood: "Poetry, and the principle of Self, of which money is the visible incarnation, are the God and Mammon of the world."[17] Whatever the Baron's final goal, it is clear that his misguided worship of gold results in a number of reversals: he strives for absolute power and freedom (or independence) but turns out to be a slave (as Albert explains to his father, money serves not as a servant but as a master; "he himself serves it" [Pushkin 7: 106]); there is something religious in his service to his ideal, but his religious zeal becomes a form of blasphemy; his intense eroticism is displaced from coveting a human body or a Beautiful Lady to coveting chests filled with gold [bleshchushchie grudy]. While the Baron is endowed with a poetic nature, as the expressive power of his speech indicates, the "principle of Self" destroys the poet in him and makes him turn from God to Mammon.

As scholars have frequently observed, the Baron is not merely a miser but also a knight, and his passion for accumulation is almost mystical and selfless; it becomes a form of philosophical quest.[18] By interpreting the Baron's obsession with gold from the point of view of occult philosophies of medieval Europe, Marina Kostalevsky sees the Baron's tragedy as his attempt to achieve the absolute through his intimate association with gold, which represents the ultimate goal of alchemical transformations. This convincing reading connects the events of the play to medieval Europe, but it does not fully account for Pushkin's conception of covetousness in its modern manifestation. What makes the Baron's miserliness so unique is the way his greed is contaminated by other passions, asceticism and eroticism in particular. The Baron's wealth is the result of self-discipline and his ascetic life of privation:

> But oh, what human woes, what bitter tears,
> Deceptions, orisons, and imprecations
> This heavy-weighted gold is token of!
> [. . . . . .]
> No! Suffer first! and earn the wealth you crave.
>
> Кто знает, сколько горьких воздержаний,
> Обузданных страстей, тяжелых дум,
> Дневных забот, ночей бессонных мне
> Все это стоило?
> [. . . . . . .]
> Нет, выстрадай сперва себе богатство.
> (Pushkin 7: 113)

By grounding his wealth in his ascetic lifestyle, the Baron implicitly presents his covetousness as a form of "bourgeois" virtue. That is why neither financial nor sexual waste is tolerated. There is no need to discuss in detail the connection between the Baron's accumulation of gold and his sexual abstinence. That the Baron eroticizes gold and experiences some form of sexual gratification when he opens his drawers has frequently been observed by scholars. The Baron almost consciously casts himself in the role of the lover in relation to his treasures, as he envisions a "tryst" with his gold-filled chests similar to "[t]he way a youthful rake awaits a tryst / With some licentious harlot." Moreover, as he pictures his encounter with these chests, sexual innuendoes become prominent—the opening of the chests is perceived as penetration, in anticipation of which the Baron is burning with desire and quivers: "Each time I come to open up a chest, / I fall into a fever and I shudder" [Ia kazhdyi raz, kogda khochu sunduk / Moi otperet', vpadaiu v zhar i trepet] (Pushkin 7: 111). The bliss from opening the chest is generated by an "inexplicable feeling" that grips his heart ("no serdtse mne tesnit kakoe-to nevedomoe chuvstvo...") and that is both pleasant and dreadful ("priiatno i stráshno vmeste"). The act is completed by pouring gold into the chest. The erotic allusion between pouring in the gold and ejaculation is reinforced by stage directions that synchronize the Baron's verbal avowal of his extreme delight with an act of opening and pouring gold coins into the chest:

> (He opens the chest.)
> My ecstasy!
> (He slowly pours in his coins.)

What needs to be further stressed is that eroticization of power and money as a symbol of power is a phenomenon that Pushkin specifically associated with the age of industry and skill. The eroticization of power was, in fact, a well-known trait of Napoleon, who allegedly articulated his erotic attitude toward power in the most vivid terms: "I have only one passion, one mistress, and that is France. I go to bed with her."[19] Pushkin's greatest insight into the psychology of the modern self lies precisely in his demonstrating how miserliness grows from merely a vice into a complex passion under the impact of asceticism, on the one hand, and the eroticization of power and money, on the other. The eroticization of money and asceticism are intricately connected, for the eroticization of money occurs as a result of displaced and suppressed sexuality, that is, sexual asceticism. The suppression of sexuality in its turn is frequently explained by social historians as a form of bourgeois conservation of energy. Thus in his *History of Sexuality*, Michel Foucault, for example, argues that beginning with the seventeenth century the repression of sexuality became an integral part of the bourgeois order: "If sex is so rigorously repressed, this is because it is incompatible with a general and intensive work imperative. At a time when labor capacity was being exploited, how could this capacity be allowed to dissipate itself in pleasurable pursuits, except in those—reduced to a minimum—that enabled it to reproduce itself?"[20] In his imperative to accumulate, the Baron does not allow himself even the slightest of "pleasurable pursuits" and resents most of all any form of dissipation. Thus the dread of spending and wasting lies at the center of the Baron's reluctance to pass on his wealth to his son:

> I rule the world! . . . But who, when I have gone,
> Will reign in this domain? My wretched heir!
> A raving madman and a spendthrift youth,
> The comrade of licentious debauchees!
> Before I'm cold, he'll come! He'll hurry down,

With all his crew of greedy sycophants,
To enter these serene and silent vaults.
He'll rob my corpse and, when he has the keys,
He'll cackle as he opens all the chests.
And all my treasured gold will quickly flow
To pockets satin lined and full of holes.
He'll desecrate and smash these hallowed vessels,
He'll feed the regal balm to dirt and dust—
He'll squander all! . . . And by what proper right?!

Я царствую—но кто во след за мной
Приимет власть над нею? Мой наследник!
Безумец, расточитель молодой,
Развратников разгульных собеседник!
Едва умру, он, он! сойдет сюда
Под эти мирные, немые своды
С толпой ласкателей, придворных жадных.
Украв ключи у трупа моего,
Он сундуки со смехом отопрет.
И потекут сокровища мои
В атласные, диравые карманы.
Он разобьет священные сосуды,
Он грязь елеем царским напоит—
Он расточит... А по какому праву?
(Pushkin 7: 112–13)

The Baron's fear of wastefulness is closely linked with his fear of being sexually disempowered or castrated by his son: "He'll rob my corpse and, when he has the keys [. . .]" [ukrav kliuchi u trupa moego]. If, as Sergei Davydov aptly observes, his chests are his "underground harem," then it becomes clear why the Baron feels the need to hide and protect this "harem" from the immodest gazes of strangers: "If only I could hide this sacred vault / From worthless eyes!" [O, esli b mog ot vzorov nedostoinykh / Ia skryt' podval!] (Pushkin 7: 113).[21] He is afraid of the intruders—his son, specifically—who could offend the "serene and silent vaults" and open, that is, assault, his chests.

With a curious twist, the Baron's jealousy concerning his treasures and his desire to guard and protect his wealth even from beyond the grave ("If only from the grave / I might return and, like a watchful shade, / Secure my chests and from all living souls / Protect my treasured gold as I do now! . . .") is also echoed in *The Stone Guest*—a play that focuses predominantly on erotic passion. The Baron pictures himself as the dead husband of a beautiful widow (his treasure), that is, as a kind of "stone guest" or Commander who, being always possessive and jealous, visits his wife from the grave to protect her chastity and to punish the intruder.[22] While most critics interpret *The Stone Guest* as a play solely dedicated to Don Juan, it may be worthwhile to conceive of it in broader terms as a play about sexual passion in general. If one takes the title of the play seriously and considers the importance of the Commander or "the stone guest" as a character, one could say that this tragedy establishes two different attitudes toward sexuality: wastefulness and conservation, represented by Don Juan and the Commander, respectively.[23] Just as in *The Covetous Knight* the Duke indicts both Albert and the Baron, in *The Stone Guest* neither Don Juan nor the Commander is victorious, as both are doomed to the underworld. Curiously, however, the Baron's passion of covetousness is developed in *The Stone Guest* not only in the character of the Commander but also in the character of Don Juan himself. Like the Baron, for whom wealth matters only as a potential, providing no interest in its practical use ("I stand above all longings and all cares; / I know my might, and in this knowledge find / Enough reward . . ." [Ia vyshe vsekh zhelanii; ia spokoen; / Ia znaiu moshch' moiu: s menia dovol'no / Sego soznan'ia]) (Pushkin 7: 111), Don Juan, a knight of love, also values the potential and the process more than the actual realization of his erotic capacity. What Don Juan covets most of all is an infinite confirmation of his ability to seduce, that is, the sensation of his potential power rather than the practical result of the conquest itself. Don Juan is just as able to experience an imaginary gratification as the Baron. As Leporello observes, Don Juan does not even need to see the woman of his choice; it is "enough" for him to get a glimpse of her "narrow heel" to complete the picture. Similarly, a consciousness of one's potential as a supreme form of power is precisely what satisfies Silvio, a character drawn from contemporary life and depicted by Pushkin in *The Tales of Belkin*, also written during the Boldino autumn. When Silvio has a chance to finally get even with his rival, he withdraws from action and prefers to contemplate his imaginary might; he conceives of his power as an unrealized potential: "I am perfectly satisfied: I've seen your confusion and fright [. . .] that is quite enough for me" [ia dovolen:

ia videl tvoe smiatenie, tvoiu robost' [...] s menia dovol'no] (Pushkin 8, 1: 74).[24]

Asceticism as an extreme form of economy and the eroticization of money and power are phenomena that Pushkin associates with the age of industry or the "century of iron." Both of these features he explores in detail in his portrayal of the typical representative of the nineteenth century, Hermann from *The Queen of Spades*, whose mentality Pushkin links explicitly with Napoleon: "This Hermann [...] is a truly romantic character: he has the profile of Napoleon and the soul of Mephistopheles."[25] Similar to Lord Wellington, who admitted that "Napoleon was not a personality, but a principle," in his portrayal of Hermann Pushkin was interested in that which constitutes the "Napoleonic principle." He gives expression to this principle by formulating Hermann's motto as follows: "Calculation, moderation, and industry; these are my three reliable cards. They will treble my capital, increase it sevenfold, and bring me ease and independence!"[26] Hermann's ascetic attitude toward life (his "moderation" [*umerennost'*]), like the Baron's, is reflected not only in his parsimony but in his attitude toward sex: "Hermann did not touch even the interest earned by these funds; he lived on his salary alone, denying himself even the slightest extravagance. [...] He had strong passions and a fiery imagination, but his resoluteness saved him from the usual lapses of youth."[27] Again, like the Baron, Hermann conserves all his resources: he does not spend money, does not gamble, and is careful not to waste his sexual energy. The Baron's fear of wasting is also echoed in Hermann's opposition between his own ideal of economy and the aristocrats' wastefulness. While trying to convince the Countess to share with him her secret, Hermann reasons that her relatives do not need the secret of the three winning cards because they are already wealthy and do not value money: "They don't even know the value of money. A Spendthrift will not benefit by your three cards."[28] Thus, what is peculiar to the Baron's covetousness and Hermann's modern mentality, typical of the nineteenth century, is that their miserliness becomes a life principle, one that is perceived by the miser himself as an ethical and proper way of life.

The passion of covetousness, which is dominant in *The Covetous Knight* and which also features in *The Stone Guest*, is further developed in *Mozart and Salieri* in a different key. Its ominous meaning fully emerges only when we consider how it is refracted in the character of

Salieri. Salieri's identity is shaped by conservation of energy, suppression of sexuality, and utilitarian asceticism. Similarly to the Baron, Salieri leads an ascetic life, "[n]ot having slept or fed for days on end" [pozabyv son i pishchu]. Salieri's room is a monk's cell (*kel'ia*). He acquires great skills in music through labor, privations, and self-discipline, that is, by the same means that the Baron accumulates wealth:

> I early turned away from idle pleasures;
> All studies far from music I despised;
> And, scorning them with chill and stubborn pride,
> In music I invested all my hopes.
> First steps to any goal are always hard,
> And arduous and long the path ahead.
> But all my early trials I o'ercame,
> And craft I made the basis of my art.
> [. . . . . .]
> Through constancy of deep intense endeavor,
> In time I proved successful and attained
> The limitless and lofty realms of art.
>
> Отверг я рано праздные забавы;
> От них отрекся я и предался
> Одной музыке. Труден первый шаг
> И скучен первый путь. Преодолел
> Я ранние невзгоды. Ремесло
> Поставил я подножием искусству;
> [. . . . . .]
> Я наконец в искусстве безграничном
> Достигнул степени высокой.
> (Pushkin 7: 123–24)

He even decides to poison Mozart on grounds very similar to the Baron's desire to disinherit his son. Although he admits that he envies Mozart, envy is something Salieri is able to control. (He did not envy Gluck, who may be as talented as Mozart.) A more deep-seated and powerful cause of Salieri's crime is that he perceives Mozart as a "spendthrift" of sorts who is unable to accumulate and conserve the results of his labor:

O Heaven! Where is justice to be found?!
When genius, that immortal sacred gift,
Is granted not to love and self-denial,
To labor and to striving and to prayer—
But casts its light upon a madman's head,
A foolish idler's brow?...

О небо!
Где ж правота, когда священный дар,
Когда бессмертный гений—не в награду
Любви горящей, самоотверженья,
Трудов, усердия, молений послан—
А озаряет голову безумца,
Гуляки праздного?..
(Pushkin 7: 124–25)

In his eyes, Mozart is a "fool" (*bezumets*) and an "idle reveler" who wastes his talent. Compare this with Albert, who threatens to waste the Baron's gold ("bezumets, rastochitel' molodoi, on rastochit"). Mozart, by contrast, exemplifies a nonutilitarian approach to art and is, therefore, a "spendthrift" in the eyes of Salieri. Significantly, Salieri envisions art in terms of accumulation, as a linear progression or a cumulative growth:

What good if Mozart live? Or if indeed
He soar to such a height as none before?
Will he, by this, exalt the realm of art?
Not so! For fall it must when he departs,
And no successor will he leave behind.
What profit then his life?

Что пользы, если Моцарт будет жив
И новой высоты еще достигнет?
Подымет ли он тем искусство? Нет;
Оно падет опять, как он исчезнет:
Наследника нам не оставит он.
(Pushkin 7: 128)

The existence of Mozart disrupts Salieri's whole worldview. In a curious twist, both the Baron and Salieri think not only about themselves but also about posterity, that is, their "heirs" or "successors." A true heir, they feel, should continue to accumulate and in this way validate their efforts. Albert and Mozart, on the other hand, represent a threat to the stability and security of the achiever. In the character of Salieri, then, Pushkin shows a more refined form of miserliness—an artistic covetousness. Moreover, the connection between this passion and his crime becomes even more explicit. Salieri's artistic miserliness and his lack of generosity direct him to poison his friend and destroy his sense of self as an artist of genius:

> Who would say that proud Salieri
> Was ever a contemptible envier.
> [. . .] No one! But now—I say it myself—I am now
> An envier.
>
> [Кто скажет, чтоб Сальери гордый был
> Когда-нибудь завистником презренным.
> [. . .] Никто! . . А ныне—сам скажу—я ныне
> Завистник.]
> (Pushkin 7: 124)[29]

An observation that Pushkin wrote in his notebook—"An envier who was capable of booing *Don Giovanni* was also capable of poisoning its creator" [Zavistnik, kotoryi mog osvistat' "Don-Zhuana," mog otravit' ego tvortsa]—further confirms the connection that Pushkin establishes between the lack of artistic generosity and crime (9: 218). In *Mozart and Salieri*, miserliness is transformed into a poisonous envy. To use Shelley's expression once again, the "principle of Self" destroyed the poet (or the musician) in Salieri by turning him into a murderer.[30]

"Salierism," or the Tragedy of Being Earnest

The passion of "Salierism," however, is not limited to envy or "artistic covetousness," just as the passion of covetousness is not limited to greed. What makes Salieri not merely feel envy but act upon it? What is the nature of "Salierism"?

Of the four plays of the cycle, only *Mozart and Salieri* opens with a soliloquy. In fact, common theatrical practice avoids openings with long and important monologues because the audience requires time to fully concentrate on what is happening onstage, while latecomers may even completely miss the important lines. A frequent theatergoer, Pushkin would not have risked wasting some of the most powerful lines of the play if he did not hope to gain something in return. Indeed, by beginning his play with Salieri's lengthy soliloquy, Pushkin immediately draws our attention to the protagonist's dominant trait—his inward personality, his introspection, and his self-analysis. Salieri at once emerges as a character completely absorbed by his self: he tells us the story of his achievements, admits that he is overwhelmed with envy, and rebels against God's injustice that rewards with "an immortal genius" an idle reveler, Mozart, rather than a craftsman and a hard worker, Salieri. Since the play centers upon the conflict between Salieri and Mozart, it is significant that the ways in which they are presented are drastically different from the start. Salieri's most powerful moments onstage are expressed through his soliloquies; even when he talks to Mozart, his conversation could hardly be called a dialogue, for he is entirely focused on himself.

By contrast, Mozart is fully open to his interlocutor; his readiness to initiate dialogue and to maintain a relationship with Salieri is manifested eloquently in his desire to share his experiences with his friend and to literally *relate* them to him. As Mozart first appears onstage he declares that he brought "a treat" for his friend: "Aha! You've seen me then! And here I'd hoped / To treat you to an unexpected jest" [a mne khotelos' tebia nezhdannoi shutkoi ugostit'] (Pushkin 7: 125). Mozart visits Salieri precisely in order to show him some of his work and solicit his opinion about it: "And I'd come / To ask for your opinion" [Khotelos' tvoe mne slyshat' mnen'e] (Pushkin 7: 126). That Mozart's imagination is explicitly dialogical and oriented toward the other is further confirmed during the final scene of the play by Mozart's description of his musical fragment:

Now picture . . . let me see? . . .
Well, . . . *me*, let's say—a somewhat younger version,
In love—not overmuch, but lightly so;
I'm with a lady . . . or a friend . . . say, *you*.

> [Представь себе . . . кого бы?
> Ну, хоть меня—немного помоложе;
> Влюбленного—не слишком, а слегка—
> С красоткой, или с другом—хоть с тобой.]
> (Pushkin 7: 126–27)

The fact that Mozart never engages in a soliloquy demonstrates his resistance to Salieri's obsessive analysis and self-centeredness. Mozart reveals himself creatively and constructively, through music, while Salieri reveals himself deconstructively, through self-anatomy and the autopsy of music: "I disassembled [literally, "dissected"] music like a corpse" [muzyku ia raz"ial, kak trup] (Pushkin 7: 123).

To be sure, in the first scene, after Salieri disapproves of his "joke," Mozart correctly observes that Salieri is too absorbed with himself to be able to appreciate his music: "You're out of sorts today" (literally, "you are not in the mood for me" [tebe ne do menia]). Thus what the first scene reveals about Salieri is that, apart from envying his friend, he is entirely preoccupied with himself and is thereby unable to appreciate a good joke. Moreover, what the audience may miss from the opening monologue in terms of its content is compensated by what we learn dramatically and theatrically: we see Salieri immersed in self-analysis and resistant to humor and irony. Indeed, what makes the passion of "Salierism" distinct from mere envy and also representative of the modern self is that under the impact of seriousness and self-centeredness a simple vice (envy) grows into an ontological rebellion and results in murder.

Salieri's seriousness stems from his inability to accept his limitations. While awareness of one's weaknesses or inadequacies often takes the form of irony and playfulness, the refusal to admit uncertainty in respect to one's own possibilities or the world at large leads to a consciousness that leaves no room for jokes. Although all the protagonists of *The Little Tragedies*, with the exception of Mozart, exhibit a strange seriousness in respect to themselves and their endeavors, this feature is revealed best of all in the character of Salieri. Salieri's deadly seriousness and inability to laugh are contrasted with Mozart's playful nature and his joyful attitude toward life. Pushkin emphasizes the earthly aspect of Mozart: he is a husband and a father, he likes the simple pleasures of life such as food, wine, and good jokes. But he is also aware of the complexity of life and its contrasts:

I'm cheerful . . . then . . . some vision from the grave . . .
A darkness comes . . . or something of the kind . . .
Now listen. . . .

Я весел... Вдруг: виденье гробовое,
Незапный мрак иль что-нибудь такое. . .
Ну, слушай же...
(Pushkin 7: 127)

By contrast, Salieri methodically excludes from his life those elements that detract from his narrow aims: "I early turned away from idle pleasures" [Otverg ia rano prazdnye zabavy]. He dismisses merriment on the same grounds as he dismisses the "idle reveler," Mozart: entertainment is "idle," it has no purpose, it merely wastes the energy that should be fully subordinated to the achievement of one's goal.

Indeed, Salieri completely lacks a sense of irony or humor. As opposed to Mozart, who delights in jokes about himself and his art, Salieri dreads caricatures and parodies:

Oh no!
I cannot laugh—when some benighted hack
Besmirches Raphael and his Madonna;
I cannot laugh—when some repellent clown
With parody dishonors Alighieri.
Begone, old man.

Нет,
Мне не смешно, когда маляр негодный
Мне пачкает Мадонну Рафаэля,
Мне не смешно, когда фигляр презренный
Пародией бесчестит Алигьери.
Пошел, старик.
(Pushkin 7: 126)

By contrast, even though Mozart knows the worth of his talent and it is clear that the creative process for him is not an effortless enterprise, he still is able to refer to his piece of music rather nonchalantly as a "trifle":

Indeed, it's nothing much [literally, "just a trifle"]. For some nights past,
As sleeplessness tormented me again,
A phrase or two kept running through my mind.
I wrote them down [literally, "jotted them down"] this morning.

Нет—так; безделицу. Намедни ночью
Бессоница меня томила,
И в голову пришли мне две, три мысли.
Сегодня я их набросал.
(Pushkin 7: 126)

Salieri would have never called his work a "trifle" (*bezdelitsa*), for the very term *bezdelitsa* means, literally, "without work" or "without effort" (*bez dela*) and contradicts, therefore, his whole worldview. Mozart's *intentional insouciance* and his love of understatement contrast sharply with Salieri's self-righteous seriousness and pompous pathos:

You were bringing *this* to me!
And yet could loiter at a wretched inn
To hear some blind old fiddler play! O God!
O Mozart, you're unworthy of yourself.
[. . . . . .]
What richness and what depth!
What boldness of design and grace of form!

Ты с этим шел ко мне
И мог остановиться у трактира
И слушать скрыпача слепого!—Боже!
Ты, Моцарт, недостоин сам себя
[. . . . . .]
Какая глубина!
Какая смелость и какая стройность!
(Pushkin 7: 127)

Salieri claims that he understands Mozart, but, in fact, he understands (or so he believes) only his "depth" (*glubina*) while refusing to see the other side of Mozart's genius: his playfulness, irony, humor, and lightness. Consequently, Salieri insists that it is unlikely that Beaumarchais would have poisoned someone: "I doubt it's true—he seemed too droll a man / For such a crafty deed" [Ne dumaiu: on slishkom byl smeshon / Dlia remesla takogo] (Pushkin 7: 132). (Incidentally, Salieri calls himself a craftsman [*remeslennik*] in his opening soliloquy.) Salieri senses intuitively that it is precisely his seriousness and his inability to laugh that make him, Salieri, capable of murder.

Salieri's consciousness forms the center of the play, and Pushkin presents it not only as a tragedy of a musician, obsessed with envy, but also as a tragedy of modernity. In fact, it is an intense preoccupation with one's purpose and an inability to joke that lead not only Salieri but also other rebellious protagonists of *The Little Tragedies* as well as many other "gloomy" and "somber" characters of Pushkin's texts to crime and doom. The "somber brow" of Napoleon, which Pushkin alludes to in *Eugene Onegin*, prefigures Salieri, the "severe soul" (*surovaia dusha*) of Hermann, and Silvio from "The Shot." Pushkin unequivocally links their inability to appreciate jokes and frivolous playfulness with their crimes. Thus, it is no coincidence that in his short story "The Shot," written in Boldino along with *The Little Tragedies*, Pushkin depicts the conflict between the Count (who has both the title and wealth of aristocracy) and Silvio (whose social status is very uncertain) as a clash between a lighthearted playfulness and gaiety and extreme seriousness and gloominess.[31] As Silvio himself admits, "He was joking, while I seethed" [On shutil, a ia zlobstvoval] (Pushkin 8, 1: 69).[32] The duel itself is a duel of consciousnesses: of the Count's nonchalant attitude toward life and of Silvio's extreme seriousness and determination. Silvio takes very seriously that which the Count is turning into a farce and also reveals a very pragmatic and business-like approach to dueling: "'What's the use of depriving him of his life, thought I, if he himself doesn't cherish it?'"[33] Silvio's utilitarian approach to killing his offender contradicts the very premise that stands behind the aristocratic institution of dueling, that is, the defense of honor but not the pursuit of "use" (*pol'za*). That the whole conflict between Silvio and the Count is grounded in Silvio's inability to joke and his resentment of playfulness becomes clear in the scene of their last confrontation. Once again, the Count pretends that they are joking: "'Dear heart,' I said to her, 'can't you see we're just joking [*shutim*]?'" Silvio's reply reveals the true reason of his revenge: "'He's always joking [*shutit*], Countess,' Silvio answered her. 'He once jokingly [*shutia*] slapped me on the face, he jokingly [*shutia*] sent his bullet through this cap of mine, and a minute ago his shot jokingly [*shutia*] just missed me. Now I feel like cracking a joke [*poshutit'*].'"[34] Thus Silvio's failure to joke translates into his readiness to kill.

We see a very similar dynamic in Hermann's ominous threat to the old Countess as he forces her to reveal her secret: "'That was a joke [*shutka*],' she said at last. 'I swear to you it was only a joke [*shutka*]!' 'It is no joking matter [*etim nechego shutit'*],' rejoined Hermann angrily."[35] Hermann's Napoleonic gravity kills the frivolous old Countess.

In a more subdued form, excessive seriousness also characterizes other protagonists of *The Little Tragedies.* Significantly, when the Baron contrasts his own ascetic and economical way of amassing his wealth with other forms of enrichment such as gambling or inheriting, he specifically resents acquisition that does not involve labor and that happens "as a joke":

> Have I, indeed, attained all this by naught [*shutia*]?
> Or through a game, as if I were a gambler
> Who rattles dice and rakes the booty in?
>
> [Мне разве даром это все досталось,
> Или шутя, как игроку, который
> Гремит костьми да груды загребает?]
> (Pushkin 7: 113)

As lighthearted as Don Juan may seem, he too is unable to understand jokes. Significantly, when Leporello, who is trying to preserve the incognito of his master, playfully suggests that Don Juan, along with other rakes, should be thrown into the sea, Juan does not recognize Leporello's humor and protests: "What drivel's this?" [Chto, chto ty vresh'?] (Pushkin 7: 141). Moreover, it is precisely Juan's persistent violation of the laws of literary tropes ("proud tomb" [gordyi grob]; "marble spouse" [mramornyi suprug]) and his inability to differentiate between literal and figurative meanings, between the signifier and the signified, between the object of the representation and the representation that leads Don Juan to his "bad joke" in the monastery. It is no coincidence that Leporello, who is a master of ironical and humorous discourse, does not approve of his master's ill-conceived "prank": "Be careful, sir, / With whom you jest!" [Okhota vam shutit', i s kem!] (Pushkin 7: 160). Juan, however, does not joke. Similar to Hermann, who with his deadly seriousness implores the Countess to reveal the secret of the three winning cards to him, Juan dispatches Leporello to bid the statue of the Commander to come to Dona Anna's and stand at the door. Juan refuses to sustain the ambiguity of the metonymy and, as a result, treats the Commander's statue not as a marble image of the real man but as a marble man ("mramornyi suprug"), as living stone. Thus, what activates the Commander is not only an offense of the dead but Juan's own linguistic blunder, his persistent realization of the metonymy. (I use this term by analogy with the "realization of the metaphor.")

Similar to Hermann, who refuses to view the anecdote about the three cards merely as a joke, Juan fails to distinguish between art and reality. The realization of the metonymy turns out to be a deadly joke; literalness punishes Juan with a vengeance. His expressed wish to be buried "over there—by the door—next to the threshold" [tam—u dverei—u samogo poroga] turns out to be a self-fulfilling prophecy: Juan meets his "stone guest" on the threshold of Dona Anna's room. Don Juan's propensity to obliterate the line separating figurative and literal meaning ultimately results in his refusal to accept the line separating the dead from the living. The way he persistently treats his dead rival as alive provides a curious twist to the motif of envy and "Salierism." Don Juan takes his dead rival very seriously; he refers to him as if he were alive, and his seriousness ultimately animates the commander: "Without her, to be sure, / The good Commander here seems rather bored" [Bez nee— / Ia dumaiu—skuchaet komandor]; "the man was always sane, / And surely since he died, he must have cooled" [on chelovek razumnyi / I, verno, prismirel s tekh por, kak umer] (Pushkin 7: 159). Moreover, he repeatedly confesses that he envies Dona Anna's late spouse: "How happy he, I think, whose frigid grave / Is warmed by such an angel's airy sighs / And watered by her sweet and loving tears" [I dumaiu—schastliv, chei khladnyi mramor / Sogret ee dykhaniem nebesnym]; "Happy man! [...] He tasted heavenly bliss!" [Schastlivets! (...) Vkusil on raiskoe blazhenstvo!] (Pushkin 7: 164). To Dona Anna's amazement, he is so jealous that with deadpan seriousness he calls her husband that "lucky dead man" [mertvyi schastlivets]. Thus, the motif of envy, which is dominant in *Mozart and Salieri*, acquires in *The Stone Guest* new overtones: it becomes both morbid and absurd.

How do we explain Pushkin's incessant interest in a type who is always serious and gloomy and who, as a result, ends up committing some form of crime? Aleko from *The Gypsies* kills Zemfira and her lover, Onegin (who is, incidentally, also characterized as gloomy ["Kak Child-Harold, ugriumyi, tomnyi"]) kills his friend in a duel, Silvio commits terribly inconsiderate actions, Salieri poisons his friend, and Hermann indirectly kills the old Countess. As rational as these characters may seem or even profess to be, their behavior often verges on absurdity—Hermann, after all, ends up in the madhouse. Pushkin's interest in this trait is too pervasive to be simply accidental.[36] Clearly, Pushkin identifies seriousness with a mentality triggered by the crisis of aristocratic values. It is for this reason that in *The Queen of Spades* he explicitly juxtaposes the frivolous eighteenth century (represented by the old Countess) with the nineteenth century's gravity (Hermann). A good explanation for the importance of the opposition between frivolous and serious attitudes toward life is provided by Alexis de Tocqueville, whom Pushkin read and admired and who presents this opposition in terms congenial to Pushkin—as a clash between aristocratic and bourgeois values. Among the various aspects of American democracy that Tocqueville discusses in his book *Democracy in America*, he dwells in particular on two interconnected trends in democratic societies: seriousness and obsession with the acquisition of a private fortune. I quote from two chapters entitled "Why the Americans Are So Restless in the Midst of Their Prosperity" and "On the Gravity of the Americans, and Why It Does Not Prevent Them from Often Doing Inconsiderate Things":

> In aristocratic communities the people readily give themselves up to bursts of tumultuous and boisterous gaiety, which shake off at once the recollection of their privations. The inhabitants of democracies are not fond of being thus violently broken in upon, and they never lose sight of themselves without regret. Instead of these frivolous delights they prefer those more serious and salient amusements which are like business and which do not drive business wholly out of their minds. [...] [T]o preserve their dignity, they think it necessary to retain their gravity. [...] [A]ll free nations are serious because their minds are habitually absorbed by the contemplation of some dangerous or difficult purpose [...] and those whose thoughts are not engaged in the matters of the commonwealth are wholly engrossed by the acquisition of private

> fortunes. Among such a people a serious demeanor ceases to be peculiar to certain men and becomes a habit of the nation. [. . .]
>
> I am next led to inquire how it is that these same democratic nations which are so serious sometimes act in so inconsiderate a manner. The Americans, who almost always preserve a staid demeanor and a frigid air, nevertheless frequently allow themselves to be borne away, far beyond the bounds of reason, by a sudden passion or a hasty opinion and sometimes gravely commit strange absurdities.[37]

Pushkin shared Tocqueville's aristocratic antibourgeois sensibility. In one of his letters, Pushkin expresses his concern about the "overflow of a democracy worse than that of America" and adds: "[H]ave you read Tocqueville? I am still all hot and frightened from his book" (16: 260–61).[38] In *The Little Tragedies,* gravity and seriousness appear as indispensable constituents of the modern self.

From "Don Juanism" to Religious Apostasy and Rebellion

I have traced so far how Pushkin portrays simple vices such as greed or envy as "passions" of "covetousness" and "Salierism" that are not just timeless but representative of the modern age and modern self. As different as Don Juan may seem from the Baron or Salieri, there are threads that tie these characters together. Although Don Juan, who indulges compulsively in all pleasurable pursuits, seems to contradict the Baron's and Salieri's ascetic thriftiness and fear of spending and wasting, some of their traits—such as envy and jealousy, a strange seriousness, and a lust for power—are curiously refracted in his personality. Moreover, what makes Pushkin's Don Juan and his "Don Juanism" representative of the romantic ethos is what he shares with three other protagonists of the cycle—his inability to accept his limitations and the ensuing rebellion. Pushkin's Don Juan is neither comic (as in much of the previous tradition) nor melodramatic (as in much of the romantic tradition). Having himself indulged in Don Juanesque pursuits, even composing his own Don Juan's list, Pushkin takes Don Juan's passion seriously and makes his protagonist worthy of tragedy, even if just a "little" one.

Just as Pushkin was trying to establish a connection between the passion for acquisition, "Salierism," and the modern self, so he also sought to reevaluate the meaning of "Don Juanism" and its two most important components—insatiable sensuality and religious apostasy—as it may be representative of modern identity. Most important, Pushkin shows that the phenomenon of "Don Juanism" is not purely a male principle, as it had been portrayed in the previous tradition. It is for this reason that in *The Stone Guest* "Don Juanism" transcends the boundaries of gender, for Pushkin creates Don Juan's female counterpart in the character of Laura—a completely new personage that is absent from the Don Juan legend. Functioning as Don Juan's female double, the character of Laura puts in relief the universal aspect of the myth as it applies to the modern self. Laura chooses her lovers as freely and as unscrupulously as does Don Juan. Like him, she is both sincere and fickle and embodies the main tension of "Don Juanism": love and infidelity. Like Juan, she is entirely focused on the present and scorns death and mortality: "Why think about such things? What talk is this?" (Pushkin 7: 148).

But Pushkin's Don Juan is not merely an erotic adventurer or an irreverent monster offending the dead. What characterizes Don Juan's "passion" in *The Stone Guest* is not simple lust or a disregard for moral, social, and religious laws but his extreme independence and a strong assertion of selfhood that is affirmed against all limits. In discussing Maturin's *Bertram* in his *Biographia Literaria*, Coleridge makes a number of important observations about Maturin's romantic portrayal of Don Juan, observations that also are relevant to Pushkin's play. Bertram, according to Coleridge, demands to be loved for his own self: "Love me, and not my qualities, may be a vicious and an insane wish, but it is not a wish wholly without a meaning."[39] Likewise, Pushkin's Don Juan is not content with conquering Dona Anna without fully disclosing his self. As opposed to Tirso de Molina's *burlador*, all of whose sexual encounters are presented in *El Burlador de Sevilla* under false pretenses, Pushkin's Don Juan, even though he willingly chooses deception as a safe strategy of seduction, needs to be recognized and loved as Don Juan, not as a hermit or Don Diego. Moreover, by revealing his real name, he also discloses his identity as a murderer and a rake: "I killed your husband—and regret it not; / I feel no true repentance in my soul" [Ia ubil / Supruga tvoego; i ne zhaleiu / O tom—i net raskaian'ia vo mne] (Pushkin 7: 167). That he shows no remorse at having murdered the Commander is perhaps the most shocking aspect of the play. This is a recognizably romantic individualistic stance. Significantly, while treating the myth of Don Juan as one of the myths representing modernity, Ian Watt demonstrates that this myth reflected its period's "new emphasis on the social and political primacy of the individual."[40] Indeed, Don Juan is author of his own fate; he creates his life. He exalts his selfhood through a stubborn adherence to self, even if it is marred by crime and vice. Showing no repentance at the end of the play, he proudly confronts the statue of the Commander: "I invited you and I am glad to see you." As the Commander requests his hand, he does not shiver: "Here it is . . ." (Pushkin 7: 171).

Although in presenting Don Juan's fearlessness and lack of repentance Pushkin follows Tirso, Molière, and Mozart and Da Ponte's script (cf. "Dammi la mano in pegno! Eccola"), there is no happy ending and reconciliation in Pushkin's play of the sort we find in Tirso and Mozart. By ending his play abruptly when Don Juan and the Commander descend into the underworld, Pushkin calls our attention to Don Juan's defiant nature. Were Pushkin's goal merely poetic justice punishing the unredeemed villain, he would impose on the audience a feeling of comfort and satisfaction with God's punishment. But the ending is disturbing as it not only allows Don Juan to rise to the occasion by demonstrating his knightly valor and strength of character but also leaves too many uncertainties and ambiguities unresolved. Does Juan truly love Dona Anna? Is he about to reform?[41] Since Dona Anna seems to be in love with Don Juan regardless of all his crimes, whom does his death really benefit? In Tirso's *El Burlador*, Don Juan's death is presented somewhat comically as he pleads pathetically to the statue, first by arguing that he did not actually harm his daughter and then by asking for a priest to absolve him. More importantly, an entire scene follows, depicting those who have been wronged to be finally revenged and able to happily marry. While Molière's version dispenses with happy marriage scenes and, therefore, puts more emphasis on Don Juan's revolt, its power is somewhat undermined by a comic and reconciliatory final remark by Sganarelle, who specifically calls for the audience's satisfaction with Don Juan's punishment:

> Oh! my wages! my wages! Everyone gets satisfaction from his death: Heaven he offended, the laws he violated, the girls he seduced, the families he dishonored, the parents he outraged, the wives he harmed, the

husbands he drove to despair. Everyone is satisfied except unlucky me, who after all my years of service, have no other reward than seeing before my eyes the wickedness of my master punished in the most terrible way. My wages, my wages,—oh! my wages![42]

Similarly, Mozart and Da Ponte's *Don Giovanni* ends with the sense of relief the characters experience after all have been avenged. Even though Pushkin preserves the punitive element in his version of the myth, he leaves no characters onstage that would delight in this retribution.

What distinguishes Pushkin's version of the Don Juan myth is that Don Juan's contempt for conventional mores, which underscores his indifference to the divine order, is presented not as an aberration—not as a deviation from the norm, which could be comfortably corrected in the interests of society—but as part and parcel of the world we live in and of the very instability of the divine order. Even though the romantics did not officially proclaim yet that God was dead, the providential order began to erode, and the sense of the loss of the divine became one of the central themes of romantic art. Pushkin tackles a similar set of issues that animated European romantic experiments in the tragic mode: the tragedy of man in a world bereft of traditional order and isolated from the divine. This sense of uncertainty, which was connected with the collapse of unifying values, directly affected Pushkin's sense of the tragic.[43]

It is when the religious order crumbles that the individual and self fill the vacuum. "Don Juanism" becomes a tragedy of modernity when insatiable erotic desire—a counterpart to Faust's insatiable intellectual aspirations—becomes a form of man's attempt to triumph over death and providential order. Don Juan's necrophilic tastes, which Pushkin so thoroughly emphasizes in his play, and his disrespect for the dead could be seen then as an ultimate desire to assert himself and to challenge mortality through his sexual omnipotence. Significantly, as opposed to the legend in which the Commander—the metaphor of death—appears as Dona Anna's father, Pushkin makes the Commander Dona Anna's husband and therefore Don Juan's rival. The motif of rivalry with the "lucky dead man," whom he invites not for a supper or a feast as in the legend but to stand guard at his wife's door, emphasizes Don Juan's ultimate aspiration to assert sexual dominance over death itself.

As in the case with other "passions," the dominant "passion" of *The*

Stone Guest, that is, "Don Juanism," understood as self-assertion through sexual omnipotence and challenge of death, is also refracted in other plays of the cycle. It is in the fourth play, *A Feast in Time of Plague,* however, that it receives its ultimate form of metaphysical rebellion. Curiously, the motif of death's or the dead man's invitation to a feast, which is replaced by Pushkin in *The Stone Guest* with an invitation to stand at the door, reappears in *A Feast in Time of Plague* in Walsingham's Dionysian dithyramb to the Queen of Death, the Plague. By showing contempt for the "darkness of the grave" and defiantly ignoring the call of death ("You strike no fear within our breast; / We are not crushed by your design" [Nam ne strashna mogily t'ma, / Nas ne smutit tvoe prizvan'e!]), Walsingham proudly challenges the underworld "commander," the Plague. In fact, he conjures it up to his feast as he proposes to "drink" a breath of a beautiful maiden "[a]nd kiss the lips where plague may lie!"

Similar to all the protagonists of *The Little Tragedies,* Walsingham seeks to triumph over the limits set by nature and religion; his is the ultimate theological revolt, that is, a rebellion against the evil of death. To be sure, Walsingham is not an atheist; he seems to acknowledge the existence of heaven as he refers to the "immortal eyes" of his beloved Mathilda and appeals to the spirit of his late wife: "My blesséd light! / I see you . . . but my sinful soul / Can reach you there no more. . . ." His metaphysical rebellion is revealed precisely when, being aware as he is of the existence of heaven and hell, he consciously chooses—like Byron's Cain—to break all divine and human laws to remain among the "godless madmen" and their "godless feast." Walsingham engages in the ultimate rebellion, for he denies traditional Christian immortality by replacing it with the immortality understood only as the pleasure of gambling with death. The proximity of death, so he proclaims, gives man a heightened awareness of life and, therefore, affords him intense pleasure:

For all that threatens to destroy
Conceals a strange and savage joy—
Perhaps for mortal man a glow
That promises eternal life.

Всё, всё, что гибелью грозит,
Для сердца смертного таит

> Неизъяснимы наслажденья—
> Бессмертья, может быть, залог!
> (Pushkin 7: 180)

Anticipating Nietzsche's praise of war and strife over peace and tranquility and "living dangerously" over an ascetic fear of life, Pushkin's Walsingham delights in freely submitting to death in order to reaffirm life. In fact, Nietzsche's notion of the Dionysian man helps us to understand the degree of Walsingham's religious apostasy.

A detailed discussion of Nietzsche's concept of Dionysus is clearly beyond the scope of this essay; I will mention only several notions that are central to Nietzsche's concept of Dionysian man and that also inform Pushkin's *Feast in Time of Plague*: death and eternity; the connection between destruction and the height of existence; the opposition between the weak and the strong and between Christianity and paganism; the motif of eternal recurrence (the seasons); and finally, the importance of the poetic form that Pushkin and Nietzsche chose for their heroes. Nietzsche considered the song of benediction, or dithyramb, that welcomes the god to be the supreme form of speech. Significantly, Walsingham's song is a sort of dithyramb or hymn in praise of the goddess of death, plague; this is an incantation of sorts. Like Zarathustra's dithyramb, the song of Walsingham exalts the present eternity; it is a song of benediction that welcomes the plague. Moreover, Nietzsche's notion of the Dionysian man seems to fit perfectly Walsingham's philosophy of life: the Dionysian man, according to Nietzsche, affirms life in spite of suffering and finds pleasure in pain and strife; he transforms life into struggle, accepts the meaninglessness of life, and celebrates it; he is heroic. Likewise, Walsingham asserts the idea of welcoming whatever may come, confronting suffering and even death. His analogy between winter, which should be confronted with the fire of fireplaces, and plague is significant, for it brings to mind the idea of cycles and the eventual recurrence of seasons, or the natural alteration of life and death.

Significantly, in Nietzsche's philosophy, the Dionysian man is opposed to Christ (see his "The Two Types: Dionysus and the Crucified"). As opposed to Christ's reluctant acceptance of his suffering, the Dionysian man willfully accepts and exalts it. Pushkin anticipates this opposition between what Nietzsche calls a "religion of the weak" and the religion of the strong as a confrontation between Christian values, represented by the priest and Mary, on the one hand, and Walsingham, on the other. These contrasting attitudes are embodied most eloquently by Mary's and Walsingham's respective responses to death and suffering. Mary, who exemplifies a traditional Christian attitude, emblematized by the language and imagery that she uses (references to church, Sunday, God, prayers), advances traditional values that presuppose piety, humility, and acceptance of the inevitability of the natural evil and of the ways of God. In Mary's song, Jenny entreats her beloved, Edmond, not to kiss her plague-stricken lips, even though it may be painful for him to observe her death. Instead, as a true Christian he should accept her death and only later visit her "ashes." Walsingham, by contrast, displays a pagan Dionysian exaltation over death; he aspires to overcome mortality for the sake of affirming existence.

As opposed to Nietzsche, however, who boldly proclaimed that "God is dead," Pushkin as well as most romantics had not yet made the final choice. That is why the confrontation between the religion of the priest and the "religion" of Walsingham is not resolved. Tragedy is conceived not as a deviation from the norm but as the instability of the norm, as man's inability to determine "What is truth?" Comparison of the song of Mary with Walsingham's hymn to plague casts this sense of shifting values into sharp relief. Mary's song—an old Scottish song—depicts precisely a unifying system of values and clearly specifies norms of behavior, truth, and morality. This song is quickly dismissed, however, by Louisa as "out of fashion": "Such songs / Are out of fashion now" [Ne v mode / Teper' takie pesni!] (Pushkin 7: 178). Indeed, the values embodied in Mary's song seem no longer relevant to the revelers of Pushkin's play. The priest's sermons and his attempts to stop the feast fall on deaf ears because apparently his talk about "hell" ("He speaks of Hell as one who knows. / Be gone, old man, you've lost your way") sounds old-fashioned and anachronistic to the younger generation, or, in Nietzsche's terms, his sermons "depreciate" life. Walsingham advances a different set of values: instead of acceptance, rebellion; instead of fear of and reliance on God's providence, individualistic defiance and courage; instead of sorrow, joy; instead of love of God, a heroic love of life; instead of Christian immortality (and the promise of the other world), the Faustian immortality of the moment.

Thus, the sense of tragedy is conveyed in *The Little Tragedies* not so much by the deviation from the traditional set of values but rather by the collapse of these values, by a sense of their failure to speak to the "modern man." Tragedy arises from the uncertainty about the divine order and the unresolved tension between belief and unbelief that characterize the four protagonists of the plays.[44] That is why Pushkin's protagonists—similar to Dante's sinners—commit not only social and historical but also metaphysical crimes; all of them are "metaphysical rebels" of the sort later described by Camus. On the metaphysical level, the Baron's obsession with gold makes him a sinner against God,[45] while on the social plane, he commits a crime against his son by denying inheritance and continuity. Salieri's metaphysical rebellion takes the form of his rejection of God's justice; socially, it is manifested in the murder of his fellow musician. Don Juan's promiscuity is more than a social violation of contract, as his endless infidelity embodies an attempt to deny finalizability by asserting sexual omnipotence. He is not only an offender of women but also an offender of God. But although Pushkin's heroes lose confidence in God and immortality in the universe, they nevertheless cling to the traditional tenets of religion because they do not see and are unable to advance an alternative morality. Thus the Baron, for example, rebels against a natural order of things that presupposes filial inheritance ("and by what proper right?!" [a po kakomu pravu?]) but ironically relies on God's judgment: "O God of justice, sound thy thunder now!" [I grom eshche ne grianul, Bozhe pravyi!] (Pushkin 7: 119). Similarly, Salieri rebels against natural inequality and seems to reject God by claiming that there is "no truth above," but at the same time he sees himself as the scourge of heaven, doing God's will and claiming that he is "chosen to stop him" [ia izbran, chtob ego ostanovit'] (Pushkin 7: 128).[46]

The four plays clearly represent unity in diversity, for they overlap without duplicating each other. While emerging as a dominant "theme" in one play, the "passions" that Pushkin analyzes in *The Little Tragedies* are refracted and further developed in other plays of the cycle to produce a multifaceted picture of the modern self. Grounded as they are in the complex of ideas associated with romantic identity and selfhood, *The Little Tragedies* seek to present us with "studies" of the difficulties of modern selfhood: the pitfalls of the isolated and independent self, the tragedy of uncertainty, and the dangers of revolt.

Notes

1. Critics have frequently commented on the relevance of biographical material to Pushkin's conception of *The Little Tragedies.* Pushkin's financial litigation with his father may have triggered his interest in the problem of "miserliness"; his Don Juanesque guilt-ridden conscience on the eve of his marriage to Natalie Goncharova may have provided the inspiration for *The Stone Guest*; and finally, an epidemic of cholera that prevented him from joining his fiancée in Moscow may have heightened his awareness of his own mortality to compose *A Feast in Time of Plague.* A mere biographical explanation, however, one that links Pushkin's choice of his topics to his personal experiences, clearly simplifies Pushkin's project.

2. See Tomashevskii, "'Malen'kie tragedii' Pushkina i Mol'er."

3. See Gukovskii, *Pushkin i problemy realisticheskogo stilia.* Contradictions abound, however, as soon as we approach the plays and interpret their characters in terms of specific historical or cultural conflicts. If *The Covetous Knight* reveals the conflict between the era of chivalry and knighthood with its ideal of honor and the century of money (Gukovskii), then it is not clear why the chivalrous ideal is represented by the younger generation, that is, by Albert. No more convincing is an interpretation of *Mozart and Salieri* from the point of view of the conflict between classicism and romanticism. If Salieri seems to exhibit some of the classicist aesthetic principles, such as an emphasis on skill, labor, and reason, then as an individual he is truly romantic in his self-centeredness and his Cain-like rebellion against the injustice of the universe. Mozart may seem romantic in his free inspiration and interest in improvisation, but his playfulness and openness to the earthly delights are more akin to the Renaissance than to the age of romanticism. Pushkin's Salieri is no less modern than Mozart.

4. Scholars conclude that the events of the play could be placed in the sixteenth century because the Baron refers to an "old doubloon," while the production of doubloons was discontinued in the fifteenth century. While this is a valuable observation for a historian, it is unlikely that any reader of Pushkin's text was expected to take it as a clue to the historical period during which the events of the play take place. Pushkin was hardly trying to be an antiquarian in his depiction of *The Little Tragedies*' settings. This is precisely why references to time and place are extremely scarce.

5. Taylor, *Sources of the Self,* 393.

6. It is worthwhile to point out that with Byron the myth of Cain was transformed into a "splendid intellectual rebel." See Quinones, *The Changes of Cain,* 58; see also Thorslev, *The Byronic Hero,* 107. Explaining the historical causes that made the portrayal of Cain as a metaphysical rebel possible, Quinones specifically refers to the age of romanticism:

> Perhaps what is more important, looming behind these forces and reinforcing them are the ideals and experiences of an Age of Revolution. In the

> Christian presentation of the story, the authority of God the father and the justification of Abel went hand in hand. The role of each is integral: that of the sustaining father whose order will eventually make clear the mystery of the sacrifice of the son. [...] The French Revolution, in killing the King, killed off the father, God the father as well as the earthly one. [...] In the absence of fatherhood, brotherhood emerges as an extraordinary ideal, and with brotherhood we witness the emergence of the Cain-Abel story as its dire and shadowy counterpart, one reminding us of other possibilities, such as *la fraternité ou la mort*. (*The Changes of Cain*, 95)

Curiously, in his modern version of the story of Mozart and Salieri, Peter Shaffer also draws on the myth of Cain and Abel (in ibid., 167–72). A connection between the story of Mozart and Salieri as presented by Pushkin and the myth of Cain has been discussed by Vladimir Golstein in "Pushkin's *Mozart and Salieri*."

7. Watt, *Myths of Modern Individualism*, xii.

8. Rather than considering how one or another "theme" is treated in each of the four plays, I interpret the plays' major "passions" as constituents of the modern self, which is fully revealed in the cycle of *The Little Tragedies*. Pushkin presents these passions as interconnected, which is why the plays complement each other not only by providing various aspects of the modern self but also by exploring various manifestations of the same "passions" or aspects of that self.

9. Pushkin, *Eugene Onegin*, 188.

10. A full translation of this passage reads: "I wanted to depict this indifference to life and its joys, this premature aging of the soul, which became distinguishing traits of the nineteenth-century's youth."

11. Pushkin, *The Complete Works of Alexander Pushkin*, vol. 3, *Lyric Poems: 1826–1836*, 126.

12. Pushkin, *Eugene Onegin*, 70.

13. See Emerson, *Napoleon*, 34.

14. Pushkin, *Eugene Onegin*, 186.

15. Note that the highly ironic image of Napoleon as the cast-iron "doll," that is, literally as a "little Napoleon," represents a bridge to the portrayal of Hermann in *The Queen of Spades* as a "little Napoleon," or the type of the ambitious and calculative achiever. Consider the descriptions of Hermann: "[H]e was sitting on the windowsill with arms folded and brows fiercely knitted. In this pose he bore an amazing resemblance to Napoleon's portrait" [chernye glaza ego sverkali iz-pod shliapy; on sidel na okoshke, slozha ruki i grozno nakhmurias'. V etom polozhenii udivitel'no napominal on portret Napoleona] (Pushkin, *Complete Prose Fiction*, 227).

16. Cox, *In the Shadow of Romance*, 18.

17. Shelley, *"A Defence of Poetry" and "A Letter to Lord Ellenborough,"* no. 3, 45.

18. See Aikhenval'd, *Pushkin* (1916); and Kostalevskaia, "Aurum Vulgi."

19. Quoted in Murat, *Napoleon and the American Dream*, 224.

20. Rabinow, ed., *The Foucault Reader*, 294.

21. See Sergei Davydov's essay in this volume.
22. See the concluding lines of the Baron's monologue:

> If only from the grave
> I might return and, like a watchful shade,
> Secure my chests and from all living souls
> Protect my treasured gold as I do now! . . .
> [О, если б из могилы
> Прийти я мог, сторожевою тенью
> Сидеть на сундуке и от живых
> Сокровища мои хранить, как ныне! . .]
> (Pushkin 7: 113)

23. In discussing *The Little Tragedies*, Vladimir Alexandrov made the clever observation that Don Juan echoes the Baron in that he "collects" women just as the Baron collects gold ("Correlations," 184). One should point out, however, that their ways of "collecting" their treasures are entirely different. Although Don Juan adds one name after another to his list, he does not remain with the women he seduces, and he does not consider them his property; for that reason, he does not mind passing them to another. (He knows that Laura is unfaithful to him but does not protest.)

24. Unless otherwise specified here and in subsequent references to *The Tales of Belkin* and *The Queen of Spades*, I use Paul Debreczeny's translations of Pushkin's texts (see Pushkin, *Complete Prose Fiction*, 75).

25. Ibid., 226. Robert Louis Jackson demonstrated the significance of the type of "little Napoleon" for Russia and specifically discussed Pushkin's Hermann as "a physical and moral type" of a "little Napoleon" and "a nascent bourgeois type" in his essay "Napoleon in Russian Literature." Curiously, in his portrayal of Hermann, Pushkin follows the cultural myth of the Napoleonic man; that is, he endows Hermann with exactly the same features the popular press attributed to Napoleon. Consider, for example, a typical characterization of Napoleon by an anonymous author that appeared in *Vestnik Evropy* in 1815: "The same ardency of passions, same gloominess of character, same despotism, same contempt for religion, same predilection toward superstition, same desire to attribute one's actions to the influence of fate" [Ta zhe pylkost' strastei, ta zhe mrachnost' kharaktera, tot zhe despotizm, to zhe prezreniie k vere, ta zhe naklonnost' k sueveriiu, to zhe samoe zhelaniie pripisyvat' svoi deistviia vliianiiu sud'by] ("Sravnenie Takhmas Kuly-Khana i Bonaparta," *Vestnik Evropy*, nos. 5–9 [1815]: 142). Pushkin's portrayal of Hermann seems to follow this description almost word for word.

26. Pushkin, *Complete Prose Fiction*, 219.

27. Ibid., 218–19.

28. Ibid., 224.

29. Rather than using Falen's translation, I provide in this case my own word-for-word translation for the sake of accuracy. In Falen's translation this passage reads as follows:

And who would dare to say that proud Salieri
Could ever, like a snake, with envy crawl?
That, trampled underfoot, in mortal pain,
He'd gnaw with helpless rage the dirt and dust?
No man would dare! But I myself now say:
Salieri crawls! Yes, I, the great Salieri.

30. In fact, all four protagonists have an artistic nature, but they are unable to choose between God and Mammon (understood broadly as a search for earthly power through money, personal skill, sexuality, or even heroism) and are therefore locked in the "principle of self." For more about the poetic nature of Don Juan, see my introduction to this volume.

31. Parallels between Salieri and Silvio are numerous. Note, for example, almost identical phrases that the two characters use to describe their lives prior to their disruptive encounters with their rivals. Salieri: "I enjoyed with deep content / My labor, my success, my growing fame"; Silvio: "I was quietly (or not so quietly) enjoying my fame" (Pushkin, *Complete Prose Fiction*, 69).

32. Ibid., 70.

33. Ibid.

34. Ibid., 75.

35. Ibid., 224.

36. See Vsevolod Bagno's article on "gloomy" characters in Pushkin's texts ("Oppozitsiia 'guliaka prazdnyi' [Avel'] i 'ugriumets' [Kain] kak skvoznaia tema tvorchestva Pushkina").

37. Tocqueville, *Democracy in America*, 2: 232–34.

38. Moreover, Pushkin openly endorses the ideas of the author of this "great book" as he refers to him in his article "John Tanner" (1836; 7: 435).

39. Coleridge explains our fascination with Don Juan by our identification with his unique ability to captivate and enchant "the affections of the other sex" and to do so regardless of his moral flaws:

> To be so loved for my own self, that even with a distinct knowledge of my character, she yet died to save me! this, sir, takes hold of two sides of our nature, the better and the worse. [. . .] [I]t is among the mysteries, and abides in the dark groundwork of our nature, to crave an outward confirmation of that something within us, which is our very self, that something, not made up of our qualities and relations, but itself the supporter and substantial basis of all these. (Jackson, ed., *Samuel Taylor Coleridge*, 458)

40. Watt, *Myths of Modern Individualism*, 242.

41. Pushkin leaves these questions deliberately open to avoid the melodramatic conclusions of some of the romantic versions of the myth, which depict Don Juan's change in character and falling in love (cf. Prosper Mérimé's *Les Âmes du purgatoire* or José Zorilla y Moral's play *Don Juan Tenorio*).

42. Molière, *Don Juan*, 82.

43. The classical tragedy presupposes a unifying system of values, the violation of which results in tragedy. In the words of Jeffrey Cox, "The sense of cosmic disruption that we find in tragedy implies that, in fact, an absolute order exists to be disturbed—whether man can comprehend that order or not. Tragedy confronts chaos but is grounded in the vision of order. [. . .] The very fact that we can talk of tragic figures transgressing laws, violating limits, and overturning taboos suggests the importance to tragedy of a sense of law, limit, or taboo" (*In the Shadow of Romance*, 96).

44. For more about Pushkin's sense of tragedy as rooted in man's existential uncertainty and his identity crisis, see my introduction to this volume.

45. See Vladimir Golstein's discussion of Dante's usurers in this volume.

46. Similarly, although Don Juan acts as a convinced unbeliever, nowhere in the play—unlike, for example, in Molière's *Dom Juan*—does he actually openly profess to be an unbeliever. By inviting the statue of the Commander to his widow's house, Don Juan seems to deny the existence of the afterlife, yet the Commander figures in his imagination and his conversation as if alive. All four protagonists of *The Little Tragedies* rebel against God's order, but they implicitly affirm its existence by the very act of their rebellion.

Individual Readings

Time or Money

The Paradoxes of Aging in *The Covetous Knight*

Vladimir Golstein

Is Ben Franklin's "Time Is Money" a Good Guide to the World of *The Covetous Knight*?

The approaches to Pushkin's *Covetous Knight* can be roughly divided into two groups, both of which, however, share the same point of departure: money. As the well-known Soviet scholar Boris Gorodetskii puts it: "Gold reigns supreme in the tragedy. Its links are spread to all the characters of the play."[1] One group concentrates on the various literary subtexts of the play, exploring literary treatment of such money-related elements as gold, greed, misers, and usurers, Jewish in particular.[2] In his informative and still useful commentary in the Jubilee Academic edition of Pushkin, D. P. Iakubovich surveyed the literary sources of various characters, speeches, and attitudes, ranging from Plautus to Walter Scott and embracing such giants of world literature as Dante, Shakespeare, and Molière.[3]

Impressed by the wealth of the play's Western literary sources, Nikolai Minskii observed in 1909 that the play appears to be a translation not from English, as its subtitle claims, but rather from ... "European."[4]

Another approach can be called ideological: instead of literary subtexts, its proponents scrutinize various metaphysical, social, and economic themes generated by the play's fixation on money. The result of such an approach is a variety of readings that explore the metaphysical and religious dimensions of the Baron's avarice or concentrate on the social and economic issues connected with feudalism, capitalism, money, and power (more typical of Soviet scholars). Needless to say, these two approaches are also frequently used in conjunction with each other.

Yet the view of money as the source of various religious, social, or economic tensions in the play obscures an equally important but frequently ignored source of such tensions: the existence of a strong correlation between one's age and one's behavior, coupled with the willful and tragic desire of human beings to ignore such a correlation. Thus, while not arguing for a drastically new approach to the play, I would like to change the very subject of scholarly scrutiny: to recontextualize the play and to take as a point of departure the issue of time and its connection with religious, social, and natural duties. The play may indeed be a translation from "European," but not because it treats the age-old theme of greed and gold but because it explores an equally popular European theme: the mutual dependence of divine providence, time, and human conduct. It is this theme, articulated already in the Bible and explored by such great authors as Dante and Montaigne, that should provide the context for Pushkin's *Covetous Knight.*

Living in post–Benjamin Franklin America, one has very little reason to doubt that "time is money." Indeed, money seems to provide an equivalent and measure for everything, including such an abstract and intangible concept as time. Yet for those who inhabited less enlightened times and who happened to take their Bible seriously, the reverse was true. It was divine providence that allotted time for everything, and it was therefore the timing of a particular action that served as a criterion of various deeds and attitudes, including attitudes toward money. As the third chapter of Ecclesiastes reminded its readers: "To everything there is a season, and a time to every purpose under heaven [...] a time to mourn and a time to dance [...] a time to get, and a time to lose, a time to keep, and a time to cast away" (3: 1–6).

This attitude was clearly shared by Pushkin, a person who rarely considered any action, passion, or attitude outside the framework of time. Pushkin's propensity to historicize is summarized by his frequent appeal: "Let's view the tragedy [of historical events] through the eyes of Shakespeare" [no vzglianem na tragediiu vzgliadom Shekspira] (Pushkin 13: 259). Or, in the more vivid terms of his poetry: "[W]hat London needs now might be too early for Moscow" [chto nuzhno Londonu, to rano dlia Moskvy] (Pushkin 12, 1: 267). Ecclesiastes maintains the same even if it is put somewhat differently: "He [God] has made every thing beautiful in his time" (3: 11).

Yet Pushkin was also aware of the changes that such an outlook had undergone during previous centuries. Rejecting the traditional biblical wisdom, the Italian Renaissance philosopher Leon Battista Alberti confidently observed: "A man owns three things: his fortune, his body, and his time." By deliberately setting his play in premodern times, Pushkin uses it as a battlefield for the clash of two opposing outlooks: the more traditional and God-fearing wisdom of Ecclesiastes and the one that had begun to challenge it since the time of the Renaissance. The outcome of *The Covetous Knight* suggests that Pushkin clearly took issue with Alberti-like confidence: by the end of the play, the proud Baron owns neither his fortune, nor his body, nor his time.

I, therefore, contend that despite the characters' own fixation on money, it is time that reigns supreme in the universe of the play, and it is against the perspective of divine providence, which allotted time for every action, that the events of the play are measured. In the play, the Jew Solomon knows it only too well: "Our days are reckoned not by us." That the issues raised by Ecclesiastes are never far below the surface in Pushkin's play can be seen, for example, in the similarity between the Baron's musings on the fate of his money in the hands of his heir and the biblical text itself: "Yea, I hated all my labor which I had taken under the sun: because I should leave it unto the man that shall be after me. And who knows whether he shall be a wise man or a fool? Yet shall he have rule over all my labor wherein I have labored" (2: 18–19).

Dante as a Guide to Pushkin's Play

In order to reposition the center of the tragedy's gravity from money to time, let us consider the issue of usury and usurers, the issue that plays such an important role in *The Covetous Knight.* Until it was legitimized by the spirit of capitalism, the only way to evaluate usury was to approach it not from the perspective of, say, economy or morality (condemned as greed or exploitation) but from the perspective of the divine prohibition.

In the eyes of many, the Jewish rejection of Christ and Jewish money lending became two sides of the same coin, so it is hardly surprising that in medieval thought usury was condemned not so much for its connection with money, materialism, and greed but for its subversion of the most fundamental tenets of God and nature. As such, it was perceived as the equivalent of the most heinous crimes. In the writings of the great theologians, including Thomas Aquinas and Anselm of Canterbury, usury was compared to "theft, burglary, perjury, adultery, and homicide."[5]

Pushkin was familiar with medieval views of usury not only because the religious underpinnings of various attitudes persisted in Russia long after they ceased to exert their power in the West. (One can recall Dostoevsky's horror of usurers and bankers.) He must have known it also from such literary sources as Dante and Shakespeare. In fact, Pushkin explicitly connects the sin of usury or, rather, its punishment with the towering figure of Dante. I refer to Pushkin's cycle of two poems in which he utilizes *Inferno*'s metrical scheme, imagery, and themes. One of these poems, referred to usually by its first line, "I dale my poshli i strakh obnial menia" [And we went further, and fear overwhelmed me], contains a vivid description of an old usurer (of all possible sinners) who, in retribution for his sin, is being roasted on a grill.[6]

In his description of the moneylender's punishment, Pushkin obviously pushes Dante's concept of *contrapasso* (punishment fitting the crime) to its parodic limits. Dante's own punishment of usurers, while fiery, is much less comic than that of Pushkin. Yet regardless of its comic ramifications, Pushkin's poem ends on a rather solemn note: "[W]e *came down,* and I found myself in the *vault*" [soshli my vniz i ia uzrel sebia v podvale] (Pushkin 3, 1: 282, emphasis mine). This line takes us directly to the setting of *The Covetous Knight*, to the opening of the Baron's famous monologue, to be precise: "[S]o I / All day have marked the time till I might *come / Down* to my secret *vault.*" This similarity of place (vault) and action (descend) is hardly coincidental.

It is also quite striking that the usurer (*rostovshchik*) of Pushkin's poem and the Baron are presented in similar terms, and it is their similarity that provides clear proof that the Baron was in fact conceived by Pushkin as a usurer.[7]

As he explains the meaning of punishment to the narrator, Virgil (in Pushkin's poem) describes the usurer in terms that seem to describe the Baron as well: "[H]aving in mind only hoarding, this evil old man was sucking his debtors' fat and in his life roasted them mercilessly" [odno stiazhaniie imev vsegda v predmete, zhir dolzhnikov svoikh sosal sei zloi starik i ikh bezzhalostno krutil na vashem svete] (Pushkin 3, 1: 282). Both the usurer of the poem and the Baron are described as old, both torture their debtors, and both have only one purpose in life: "hoarding" (*stiazhaniie*). This passion for hoarding, as opposed to putting money into circulation, clearly highlights the peculiar similarity between the usurer of the poem and the Baron.

Since Dante's treatment of usurers appears to have such an impact on Pushkin's imagination, we have to go beyond Pushkin's parody of Dante and explore Dante's *Inferno* itself in the hope that it will shed some additional light on Pushkin's play.

According to M. N. Rozanov, 1829 marked the period of Pushkin's increased involvement with Dante.[8] Yet Pushkin's interest in Dante's treatment of usurers probably dates to a much earlier period. Most likely it was spurred by Voltaire, a writer whose dislike for Dante is well attested and who, in order to highlight Dante's shortcomings, translated canto 17 of *Inferno* (the one that describes the punishment of usurers) and included it in his essay on Dante for the *Dictionnaire philosophique portatif*.[9] Since Pushkin had the complete works of Voltaire in his library and kept on reading his writings throughout his life, we can presume that Pushkin was familiar with Dante's treatment of usurers long before he embarked on more serious study of Dante.

While there are several sins in *Inferno* that Dante associates with the abuse of money, it is the punishment of usurers that fits Pushkin's play better than any other. Canto 7, for example, describes the souls of both the miserly and the prodigal, who are doomed to an endless dueling with each other: "They struck against each other; at that point, each turned around and, wheeling back those weights, cried out: 'Why do you hoard? Why do you squander?' [...] Ill giving and ill keeping have robbed both of their fair world and set them to this fracas."[10] Curious as this subtext is, the punishment that Dante describes is evenhanded toward both the prodigal and the greedy. Such a punishment might correspond to the Duke's evenhanded condemnation of both the Baron and his son but not to Pushkin's asymmetrical conclusion of the play.

The very location of the usurers in Dante's *Inferno* strikes one as rather unconventional, since Dante places them in the seventh circle, the circle of violent sinners. Modern thought would hardly associate violence with either greed or usury, yet it is the violence against nature that, according to Dante, drives his usurers. The seventh circle, to which usurers belong, also contains two other unexpected groups of sinners: homosexuals and the sacrilegious. According to Virgil's explanation to the narrator, it is their violence against God and nature that unites these diverse groups: "One can be violent against the Godhead, one's heart denying and blaspheming Him, and scorning nature and the good in her; so with its sign the smallest ring is sealed, both Sodom and Cahors and all of those who speak in passionate contempt of God" (canto 11, ll. 46–51). Incidentally, the reference to the French city Cahors, known in medieval times as one of the most prominent banking centers, might explain Pushkin's choice of a French setting for his own play about usury.

The explanation of usurers' sin is provided in canto 11, while their actual punishment is depicted in canto 17. Such an unusual time delay parodies, in fact, the activity of moneylenders, since it is in and through time that they get their payoff. Aware that he proposes here a rather unusual concept, Dante allows his pilgrim to interrogate Virgil on the very issue of the usurers' transgressions: "Go back a little to that point [...] where you told me that usury offends divine goodness; unravel now that knot" (canto 11, ll. 94–96). Pressed by the pilgrim, Virgil reiterates:

> From these two, art and nature, it is fitting,
> If you recall how Genesis begins,
> For men to make their way, to gain their living;
> And since the usurer prefers another
> Pathway, he scorns both nature in herself,
> And art, her follower; his hope is elsewhere.
> (Canto 11, ll. 106–11)

When the narrator finally sees them, the usurers are sitting despondently on the sand, trying to protect themselves from the raging elements. The pilgrim fails to recognize any of these sinners, and Virgil explains: "[T]he undiscerning life that made them filthy, now renders them unrecognizable" (canto 17, l. 53). As they try to shake off the flames, the usurers remind the narrator of dogs, a comparison that invokes the numerous dog similes of Pushkin's play.

> This side, then that, their hands kept fending off,
> At times the flames, at times the burning soil,
> Not otherwise do dogs in summer. [. . .]
> I recognized no one, but I did notice that
> From the neck of each a purse was hung
> That had a special color and an emblem,
> And their eyes seemed to feast upon these pouches.
> (Canto 17, ll. 47–57)

As opposed to regular rain and fertile soil, both burning soil and fiery rain highlight "unproductiveness" and thus unnaturalness. Dante scholars explain the strange and unnatural climate conditions of this canto through its connection with the very activity of usurers, who make fertile what by nature is sterile (money).[11] It is this interaction between sterility and fertility that enables Dante to pair usurers and homosexuals, since, according to him, the latter make sterile what by nature is fertile.

Since both Dante's usurers and Pushkin's Baron operate in the area of the unnatural, it is hardly surprising that the texts of both canto 17 and *The Covetous Knight* are dominated by imagery that invokes the monstrous and the grotesque and tend to mix human and animal images. It is also quite telling that Dante's pilgrim is transported to and from the seventh circle on the back of the monster, Gerion, "that filthy effigy of fraud" who is described as having the features of man, snake, and lion: "The face he wore was that of a just man, so gracious was his features' outer semblance; and all his trunk, the body of a serpent, he had two paws, with hair up to the armpits" (canto 17, ll. 10–13). In its turn, Pushkin's text is filled with references to various animals (tiger cub, mouse, dog, snake, fawn, sharp-clawed beast), monsters (demon, witch, wretched rogue), and beastly acts ("Blood-spattered villainy itself will crawl"; "He's marked it with his claws! A monstrous son!").

Usury is based on growth in time, yet this is not an organic growth, like the growth that occurs in nature. It is curious that the Russian language retains the connection between usury and growth, since the word *rostovshchik* comes from the word *rost* (growth). In other words, a usurer (*rostovshchik*), in his activity of presiding over growth, becomes a rival of God, thus the connection with sacrilege, since, in the long run, a usurer challenges God's authority over times and seasons. From that perspective, the Jew's suggestion to poison the Baron: "But no, I thought . . . perhaps that you . . . I thought . . . / The Baron's time to die might well have come"—fits the image of the usurer perfectly. From tinkering with time one graduates into tinkering with somebody else's life. The Baron's desire to stifle his own son, his wish to stop the flow of time and preside over his money forever, amounts to the same thing. Monstrous professions suggest monstrous solutions.

Going against time, nature, and God amounts to the same thing in the world of Dante, since nature is the domain through which God operates. Dante's example of a sacrilegious sinner is Campaneous, a proud, strong, and irreverent warrior, punished for his sins by Jove's thunderbolt. In another curious connection with the text of Dante, the sacrilegious Baron, who in his blind self-righteousness appeals to God's thunderbolt to defend him against his son, immediately falls down, as if struck by lightning.

Dante's presence within Pushkin's text explains several of its key elements: its medieval setting; its almost mathematical, tripartite structure; its general preoccupation with triads (three scenes, three participants in the first and third scenes, three real sinners: the Baron, Albert, and the Jew); as well as Pushkin's very definition of the genre of his play (tragicomedy), which allows him to utilize the elements of both classical English tragedy and Dante's *Divine Comedy.* It is also worth noting that the three scenes of *The Covetous Knight* consist of approximately the same number of lines as any given three cantos of Dante, while the 118 lines of the Baron's monologue correspond to *Inferno*'s shortest cantos. (Canto 11, for example, the one that explains the sin of usurers, consists of 115 lines.) But first and foremost, Dante's presence highlights the play's tragic outcome and the very essence of the Baron's sins. The Baron's main crime is that of his fellow usurers: violence against nature and God. But the Baron manifests his violence, his challenge to God and nature, not only on some abstract metaphysical level but also as a father and a human being. It is there, in the domain of the family and everyday life, that his rebellion becomes most obvious and most destructive; it eventually results in his violent confrontation with his own son, a monstrous event that concludes Pushkin's play.

Montaigne as a Guide to Pushkin's Play

When considered from the perspective of his attack on God and nature, the Baron ceases to be a tragic or a comic miser and becomes a rebel instead: a blasphemous apostate, if considered from a religious perspective, and the epitome of imprudence, of failure to grow and modify one's behavior, if considered from a social one. The Baron persists in hoarding gold while perverting his key social obligations, both as a father and a knight. The Baron owes much to those who are below and above him on the feudal ladder; in the same way, he owes much to his ancestors and to his children. And it is the Baron's unscrupulous refusal to pay his dues that precipitates his tragic confrontations with both his son and the Duke. The Baron's rejection of his responsibilities and ties is witnessed already in the way he treats a widow with her three children, a primary object for knightly protection.

> I have an old doubloon ... it's this one here;
> Some widow brought it just this morn, but first
> She knelt for half the day outside my window,
> Three children at her side, and wailed aloud.
> [. . . . . . .]
> [...] I might
> Have driven her away, but something whispered
> That she had come to pay her husband's debt,
> Afraid that on the morrow she'd be jailed.

The Baron never questions the legality or morality of the situation, within which the widow must pay for her "husband's debt" [muzhnin dolg]. However, the Baron himself rejects the idea of a family debt and of family obligations. He somehow convinces himself that his own debts will be forgiven, even though he demands others to repay. The Baron's words, in fact, contain a direct mockery of the words of the Orthodox daily prayer to the divine Father: "Our Father, [...] forgive us our debts, as we forgive those who are indebted to us" [Otche nash (...) ostavi nam dolgi nasha, iakozhe i my ostavliaem dolznikom nashim]. The Baron's cavalier treatment of the issue of debt alerts us to a sacrilegious aspect of his behavior. Similar to Dante, Pushkin identifies religious connotations even in a simple social act.

Treating his son with the same cruelty and selfishness that he manifested in his treatment of the widow and her innocent children, the Baron reveals his failure to change from taking to giving, from caring for oneself to caring for future generations—a change that Pushkin viewed as the very basis of family and social life. It is worth recalling at this point that Pushkin's dramatic cycle was composed during a watershed year in Pushkin's development, at the time of the fundamental transition from being a son to being a father, from being a lover to being a husband, from being a reveler and rebel to being a pillar of society. On the eve of his marriage Pushkin remarked on the impending changes: "It used to be 'I,' but now it is 'we'" (14: 113). Sensitive as he is to the explosive and rebellious nature of youth (Albert's behavior is a case in point), Pushkin does not expect maturity from children. It is the plight of a father who fails to mature and who thereby keeps his child as if he were a "mouse / Begotten in a cellar" [mysh / Rozhdennuiu v podpol'e] that is the object of Pushkin's artistic exploration.[12]

Pushkin's ideal of any social relationship, including that of generations, is articulated by the poetic persona of his lyrical poem "Brozhu li ia vdol' ulits shumnykh" (When I wander through the noisy streets, 1829). It is against this ideal that one should measure the behavior of all Pushkin's grown-up characters. Pushkin's meditation on the subject of the changes that time brings features a speaker who views himself against youth, old age, and the eternal changes of nature and who formulates the following rule of behavior:

> Whether I am caressing a dear child
> I am already thinking, Farewell,
> I am vacating the place for you.
> It is now your time to blossom, mine to rot.
>
> Младенца ль милого ласкаю,
> Уже я думаю: прости!
> Тебе я место уступаю:
> Мне время тлеть, тебе цвести.
> (Pushkin 3, 1: 194)

Pushkin suggests that the best test of maturity and temporal wisdom is the attitude toward the younger generation. This insistence on temporal prudence has a rather obsessive character for Pushkin. Compare a famous line from *Eugene Onegin*: "The old Derzhavin had noticed us and on his way to a grave had given us his blessing" [Starik Derzhavin nas zametil i, v grob skhodia, blagoslovil] (Pushkin 6: 165). Instead of a blessing, the Baron, of course, prefers to humiliate his own son as well as the children of a widow.

Raised as he was in the spirit of classical wisdom and its preoccupation with the mystery of time, Pushkin did not remain a stranger to these preoccupations. In evaluating the behavior of his characters, Pushkin frequently assumed the biblical perspective of Montaigne's favorite maxim, "Every thing has its season" [Toutes choses ont leur saison]. This ideal attitude has been known since antiquity as the principle of *tempestivitas*, or seasonableness. Already Horace, in his *Ars Poetica,* observed: "We must always adhere to what is suitable to each age." Seneca, a recognized authority on the subject of old age, was quoted approvingly by Montaigne as saying: "Young man must store up, the old man must use." Dante, in his turn, insisted that the noble soul "exercises its acts in their times and ages" (*Il Convivio,* 4: xxiv, 8), since "certain ways are suitable and laudable at one age which are foul and blameworthy at another" (*Il Convivio,* 1: i, 17).[13] This classical view of *tempestivitas* must have been transmitted to Pushkin through a variety of classical sources, yet it appears that it was the writings of Michel Montaigne that played the crucial role in this transmission. Thus it is hardly a coincidence that "When I wander through the noisy streets," as well as a number of Pushkin's meditative lyrical poems, have easily identifiable subtexts in Montaigne.[14] Recently, Sergei Kibal'nik explored Montaigne's presence in Pushkin's *Feast in Time of Plague.*[15] Yet the literary connection between *The Covetous Knight* and Montaigne remains unexplored by Pushkin scholars.

All the pages of Pushkin's own four volumes of Montaigne were cut and obviously read. Pushkin's increased interest in Montaigne is connected by scholars to the year 1829, that is, the year of his heightened involvement with Dante. As in the case of Dante, Pushkin's interest did not abate until his death: in 1835, while in Mikhailovskoe, he would write to his wife requesting her to get Montaigne's volumes off the shelf of his favorite books and send them to him.

While Montaigne addresses the paradoxes of time in a number of his essays, I believe that it is his "De l'affection des pères aux enfants" (On fathers' affection to their children) that provides the most illuminating subtext to Pushkin's play. This essay not only discusses the debilitating effects of fathers' greed, but, more important, it also explores the shifting dynamics of family relationships while condemning the fathers who fail to act in accordance with their age and nature. Montaigne focuses specifically on fathers and on their obligations toward their families, in particular, the younger generation. He quotes approvingly Plato's Lawgiver, who rejects the desire of an old man to dispose of his money according to his fancy, thereby, according to Plato, echoing gods, and asserts, "Both your goods and you belong to your families, the past as well as the future. But both your family and the goods belong still more to the public. Wherefore, if some flatterer in your old age or in your sickness, or some passion should unseasonably urge you to make an unjust will, I will guard you against it."[16] This Lawgiver is obviously a precursor of Pushkin's Duke, to whom Albert appeals for help and who has to confront the Baron's unseasonable urge to hoard money.

Montaigne takes a very hostile position toward selfish, self-centered fathers. He views such behavior as unnatural, since, according to him, it is quite natural for "the begetter" to experience affection for his offspring. In Montaigne's view, fathers' stinginess toward their grown-up children is caused by generational conflict. In other words, fathers do not fail in their duties because they are greedy; instead, it is their jealousy and selfishness, their failure to become fathers, that turn them into misers: "Some are very liberal in providing toys for their childhood, who become very closefisted for the smallest necessary expense when they grow up. Indeed it looks as if the jealousy we feel at seeing them appearing in and enjoying the world when we are about to leave it renders us more niggardly and stingy towards them; *it vexes us that they tread upon our heels*, as if to urge us to depart. And if we had to fear that, since the *order of things* provides that they cannot [...] be or live but at the expense of our being and our life, *we should never meddle with being fathers*."[17] Montaigne recognizes here that money can serve as a weapon with which to strike back at the inevitable flow of time. Pushkin's Baron might claim purity and nobility for his quest for gold, suggesting that he finds in gold a source of disinterested interest, so to speak, something akin to a sublime or aesthetic experience. Yet Montaigne's perceptive analysis reveals that behind the hoarding of money lurks a fear of old age and death and an irrational desire to strike back at those who remind one of the inevitable. Montaigne, in fact, is rather explicit about the hidden causes of parental stinginess; they are malice and envy: "But a father, struck down by age and infirmities [...] wrongs himself and his family by uselessly brooding over a great pile of wealth. [...] It is right that he should leave the enjoyment of those things to [those to whom by the order of nature they belong.] [...] [O]therwise there is doubtless malice and envy present."[18] Montaigne's analysis suggests, therefore, that behind the Baron's desire to take his gold out of circulation lurks a rather cruel and cynical way of using it: to stifle his own son.

Yet according to Montaigne, "the order of things" precludes any hope for stasis. It is therefore highly significant that, regardless of his celebration of gold, his glorification of his divine power, and his experience of timeless joy, the Baron inevitably turn to his son:

> And all this mighty realm submits to me.
> My bliss is here, my honor and my glory!
> I rule the world! ... But who, when I have gone,
> Will reign in this domain? My wretched heir [*moi naslednik*]!
> A raving madman and a spendthrift youth,
> The comrade of licentious debauchees!

The Baron's train of thought reveals that it is Albert who lurks behind his fixation on money, while his hostile characterization of his son betrays his anger at Albert, who reminds him that his aspirations for timeless existence are doomed.

Montaigne's description of greedy fathers also explains the moral corruption that their stinginess generates. Montaigne's scenario is clearly reminiscent of Pushkin's play: "It is unjust that an old father, broken down and half dead, should enjoy alone in his chimney corner resources that would suffice for the advancement and maintenance of many children, and suffer them in the meantime to waste their best years for want of means to push themselves in public service and the knowledge of men. They are driven to the desperate plight of seeking by any means, however wrong, to provide for their needs, as I have seen in my time several young men of good family so addicted to stealing that no correction could turn them from it."[19]

Nonetheless, Montaigne's condemnation of fathers is balanced by his refusal to side with children: "Do we desire to be loved by our children? Do we remove from them all the occasion of desiring our death (though no occasion of so horrible a desire can be either right or excusable). [...] Let us reasonably furnish their lives with what is in our power."[20] Montaigne's balanced view prefigures the complex and balanced judgment of Pushkin's play. While not excusing Albert's patricidal desires, Pushkin points to the Baron's own significant contribution to the emergence of such desires.[21]

As to the question of the Baron, "And by what proper right" should his son come into possession of his money, Montaigne answers, "By the order of things," the answer that Pushkin with his passion for observing and articulating various laws of nature would surely second. The Baron himself inadvertently reveals the inevitable rhythm of nature: "But who, when I have gone, / Will reign in this domain? My [. . .] heir!" [No kto *vosled* za mnoi priimet vlast'?—*Naslednik*] (emphasis mine). By having the two concepts derived from the same root, the Russian language links inseparably the process of following and inheriting ("kto voSLED—naSLEDnik"). The language of the Baron points thus to the order of things as both Montaigne and Pushkin have recognized it, but the Baron has not. The younger generations follow and build upon the older ones. As Montaigne remarks on children: "[T]hey tread upon our heels." Such is the inevitable rhythm of the universe, the rhythm sustained by the flow of time.

The Baron's refusal to change with time makes him similar to a mythical figure, Kronos, the Greek god (Saturn in Roman mythology) who attempted to preserve his rule over time and space by consuming his own children. Ever since the Greeks the control of time and the destruction of one's progeny have been perceived as two sides of the same coin. It is worth noting in that respect that in classical iconography old age was frequently associated with both money and the figure of Kronos.[22] According to Erwin Panovsky, Saturn was sometimes depicted with a purse in order to convey the stinginess of old age.[23]

The principle of *tempestivitas*, invoked by Pushkin's literary allusions, reveals to us that it is the Baron's stubborn refusal to change, to obey the calls of time, that fuels his passion for money and his violent confrontation with his son. The Baron wants to stop time, which is the equivalent of getting rid of his heir, of killing his son, the best image and reminder of time's changes. The Baron's claim that his son harbors patricidal desires might correspond to reality, but he formulates it not on the basis of observation but as pure projection. It is the Baron who wants to have his son dead as he wants to stop the flow of time.

The comparisons with both Montaigne and Dante make it perfectly clear that the Baron's pursuit of money goes well beyond the traditionally conceived sin of avarice. Directed against his son, against the nature and flow of time, the Baron's fixation on gold is connected with his defiance of nature and ultimately of God. The Baron's sudden death allows Pushkin to hint at the forces that were instrumental in the Baron's downfall. In fact, the Baron himself invokes the powers that ultimately crush him. When Albert accuses his father of lying, the Baron, ironically, appeals to both nature and God for justice: "O God of justice, sound thy thunder now!" [I grom esche ne grianul, Bozhe pravyi!]. What happens immediately after that is emblematic of Pushkin's conception of his play: the Baron falls down as if stricken from above. The sequence of events suggests that the Baron's appeal has been heard and immediately answered: the culprit is struck by the righteous God. In other words, what appears to be a sudden heart attack or some sort of deus ex machina was long in the making. Pushkin carefully weaves the work of providence into his text. Having been exposed to the light of the day in the Duke's palace and revealing his total bankruptcy, the Baron is already destroyed. He has nothing left to do but to die clinging to the keys of his "trusty chests." The Baron is punished for trying to meddle with and reverse the process of the flow of time, a process that lies beyond human control. There is a natural order that, when violated too much, recoils.

Pushkin thus accomplishes a rather complicated feat in his play. He does not align himself directly in the conflict, something that a lesser artist would instantly do, siding (for obvious reasons of generational solidarity) with the young as did, for example, Pushkin's contemporary Alexander Griboedov in his play, *Woe from Wit.* Nor is Pushkin satisfied with the high moral position of the Duke that condemns both participants of the conflict: "O God in Heaven! / What dreadful times are these, what dreadful hearts!" The Duke's seemingly equal distribution of blame does not mesh with the play's asymmetrical outcome.

Pushkin, who declared very early in his life, "[W]hatever was the guilt, the punishment was terrifying" (14: 168), never wavered in his condemnation of vindictiveness and cruelty. The Baron, nevertheless, is punished right in front of our eyes. Pushkin thus creates a complex scheme in which he himself refuses to judge and allocate the guilt, yet, by the set of literary and thematic allusions and by the unfolding of the plot itself, he manages to suggest the presence of another judge, one who in fact pronounces and carries out his judgment.

The Covetous Knight and the Principle of *Tempestivitas*

Dante's and Montaigne's presence in the text of *The Covetous Knight* helps us to evaluate the Baron's passion from the perspective—obviously shared by Pushkin—that was central for these authors' understanding of religious and social relationships and duties. These literary subtexts clearly alert us to the source of Pushkin's values and his attitudes toward the issues of time, age, and duty. I would also argue that these values and attitudes form an integral part of Pushkin's play itself. In the concluding part of this essay, I would like to explore how Pushkin incorporated these views and values into the very fabric of his play so that the meaning of the play manifests itself on levels that go beyond literary allusion.

The short text of *The Covetous Knight* is saturated with references to time, age, children, parents, growth, and change. The terms for time and age (young, old, now, before, after, earlier, later, ten, twenty, twenty-five, thirty, fifty years) and for kinship and generations (father, grandfather, children, husband, friend, servant) are everywhere. The play closes, in fact, with a reference to time: "What dreadful times are these, what dreadful hearts!"

Furthermore, the theme of age and of corresponding conduct is declared loud and clear already in the first scene, when the Jew observes:

> Why, wealth at any age can serve us well;
> But youth, in wealth, seeks nothing more than slaves
> And, pitiless, dispatches them all round.
> Old age, in wealth, sees good and worthy friends
> And guards them like the apple of his eye.

Solomon's comment not only presupposes that the issue of money is inexorably connected with that of time and age but suggests also the precise relationship between the two. It is time and age that define the use of money and our attitude toward them, not the other way around.

Paradoxically, each character of the play, including the Baron, has something to say about the flow of time and the need to modify one's behavior accordingly. Thus, in the third and last scene of the play, both the Duke and the Baron exchange their opinions on the subject. Addressing the Duke, the Baron recollects:

you were—
A lively boy. The great deceaséd Duke
Would say: "Well, Philip, friend [...]
[. . . . . . .]
In twenty years or so, both you and I
Will be but dotards in this stripling's eyes...."

Yet, while recognizing the changing needs of generations and admitting to the Duke that the court is the place to be for the young ("I've grown too old, my liege. And here at court / What use am I? You're young and still delight / In tournaments and festive rounds. But I / Am little fit for such pursuits"), the Baron refuses to act upon this recognition. He boldly disregards his own observation as well as that of the Duke: "The court for you is dull, but for your son / Both age and rank do call him to our side." In fact, it is the Baron's pathetic attempts to weasel his way out of the trap that he sets for himself by connecting the court life with youth that provide the only comic relief of the play.

However, as the Baron's example shows, acknowledging the importance and power of time might be one thing, but actually hearing time call is something entirely different. The Baron's deafness to the calls of time does not deny but in fact underscores the centrality of time to the play's problematics. As if to stress the flow of time as the proper perspective from which to evaluate the seemingly timeless conflict between father and son or the equally timeless quest for gold, *The Covetous Knight* features the representatives of three and not just two generations. Old age is embodied by the Jew and the Baron (who as a friend of the Duke's grandfather has to be at least in his sixties); the Duke, who must be in his thirties, represents the age of maturity; while the twenty-year-old Albert stands for youth. Presenting the conflict between familial generations against the background of the ages of man (youth, maturity, and old age) suggests the perspective that Pushkin wants us to take when approaching the play.

Similar to the traditional division of human life into youth, maturity, and old age, the play has three scenes, each centering correspondingly on the young Albert, his old father, and the mature Duke. The action of each scene takes place in the habitat of its central protagonist, one that highlights the traditional connotations of its dweller's age. Thus the first scene takes place in Albert's tower, the second in the favorite place of the Baron—the vault, and the third in the ducal palace, depicting the Duke's failure to find a peaceful resolution of the conflict between the Baron and his son. This sequence of ages and scenery suggests an upwardly mobile youth, earthbound old age, and maturity, oriented toward the here and now.

There is something both puzzling and confusing in this sequence, however, since it violates the traditional direction in which the story of an age unfolds: youth, maturity, and old age. One can recall in this connection Pushkin's early meditation on the nature of time, his 1823 poem "Telega zhizni" (The cart of life), which presents ages in their traditional sequence: the morning of life, its noon, and its evening. Yet the plot of the play unfolds in a zigzag fashion. The play's spatial movement highlights these zigzag oscillations: tower, vault, palace, that is, above the surface, below the surface, on the surface.

The tension, if not the confusion, implied by the juxtaposition of the temporal and spatial norms with the actual unfolding of the plot is also conveyed by various other aspects of the text. Thus the first scene centers on the unnatural offer of the Jew to poison Albert's father. The Jew knows that "[o]ur days are reckoned not by us"; in fact, he directly connects the duration of the Baron's life with the will of God: "God will—he'll live for ten, / For twenty, twenty-five ... for thirty years." Having declared it to Albert, Solomon immediately invites him to assume the role of God by reckoning the days of his father. Likewise, the Baron's monologue, this paean to the divine powers of his gold, exhibits a similar confusion between God and man, real and potential, past, present, and future.

The play, in fact, is haunted by confusion, inconsistencies, unnatural actions, and oxymoronic imagery captured, for example, not only in the play's title and its genre (tragicomedy) but even by such expressions as the Baron's "deepest Heaven" [glubokie nebesa], which confuses high and low. The Jew, as Albert's greeting suggests, can be both "accurséd" and "most worthy." Both the Jew and the Baron acknowledge one truth but act upon another, while Albert and the Duke intend to do one thing but accomplish quite the opposite. Even the stroke with which Albert knocks down his rival at the tournament is caused not by skill or courage but by greed. Time is clearly out of joint in the world of *The Covetous Knight.*

To highlight the deliberate temporal confusion of Pushkin's play, I would like to compare its structure with Titian's famous painting, *An Allegory of Prudence* (figure 1). This painting also depicts the three ages of man by portraying three faces: two profiles turning to the right and left of the viewer and a face staring straight at the spectator. The three faces, staring as if toward the past, present, and future, belong correspondingly to an old, mature, and young man. The face of the youth is exposed to too much light, the old man is somewhat obscured by the shadows, and it is the central face of a mature man that stares at the present (and at us) and is the most visible and well drawn.

The play's temporal references and its three parts immediately suggest a norm, an underlying grit, captured in Titian's painting or in

Pushkin's own "cart of life," while the play's actual events and the organization of the scenes reveal the violation of the order, the deviation from the norm. As opposed to the norm conveyed in the painting, in which the mature man dominates the setting, the Duke ends up being overshadowed by both the father and the son, and his conduct proves ineffective against their murderous rivalry and hatred.

The Duke, the main protagonist of the third scene, first appears to embody prudence. He insists on some proprieties while requesting the father to send his son to court: "Assign him here to us, and do bestow / A maintenance upon him due his rank [*prilichnoe*]." The epitome of a prudent ruler, the Duke moves freely from past recollections (of himself as a child, of his father, of the young Baron) to Albert's future plans. The Duke's speech itself suggests an attempt to mediate between the past and the future in order to find a perfect solution for the present. This reasonable and prudent approach of the Duke proves extremely ineffective vis-à-vis the imprudent behavior of both the Baron and Albert. Their passions seem to corrupt and confuse even the neutral magistrates. Thus the Duke seems to suffer from the same affliction that haunts the rest of the characters: the discrepancy between his intentions and his actions (cf. both Albert's and the Jew's words and behavior in the first scene). For example, he promises to Albert: "I shall appeal, myself, / In private, gently [*bez shumu*], to your father's heart." Of course, in reality, he allows the son to overhear his conversation with the Baron, which results in a very noisy and public confrontation.

With the prudent Duke proving so ineffective, the person who dominates Pushkin's play is the Baron. Consequently, the Baron's monologue, this glorification of uncontrollable passion, occupies the central position within the play. Structurally, this monologue corresponds to Titian's portrayal of a mature, prudent man, yet, thematically and ideologically, the Baron's views are the very opposite of prudence.

In violation of the norms of old age as they were articulated by classical wisdom and depicted in Titian's painting, the Baron, instead of the past, is preoccupied with the present and the future. He opens his monologue, which constitutes the entire second scene, with references to intense waiting, to love pursuits and other activities of the young:

> The way a youthful rake awaits a tryst
> With some licentious harlot or, perhaps,
> Some foolish girl that he's seduced, so I

All day have marked the time till I might come
Down to my secret vault and trusty chests.

The Baron's interest in the future takes him to the time of his inevitable death and thus to the issue of inheritance: "I rule the world! . . . But who, when I have gone, / Will reign in this domain? My wretched heir!" It is precisely this following, this inevitable flow of time that the Baron dreams of preventing. In Shakespeare's *Richard II*, York warns the king:

take from Time
His charters and his customary rights;
Let not to-morrow then ensue to-day;
Be not thyself; for how art thou a king
But by fair sequence and succession?
(2.1.195–99)

The Baron is father and knight due to "fair sequence and succession." Yet by rejecting such a succession the Baron ceases to be himself, that is, a knight and a father, and becomes an impostor, a walking lie. The attentive audience, as opposed to the Baron, is hardly surprised when Albert states the obvious and responds to his father's outrage ("[You] dare [. . .] / To hurl at me, your father, such a word! . . . / [. . .] or am I knight no more!") with his cruel but ultimately fair characterization: "You lie!"

Pushkin's interest in the mystery of time and his decision to approach it within the larger framework of either natural rhythms or divine providence were hardly accidental. From an early age Pushkin was not only haunted by the paradoxes of time, he was also trying to approach it by articulating a set of guidelines or principles, a certain algorithm that would allow one to synchronize one's desires and deeds with one's age, thus his almost compulsive need to reiterate maxims related to the interdependence of one's age and behavior. In 1834, for example, he stressed the correlation between one's age and the need for home and companionship: "Youth has no need in home; the mature age is terrified by its loneliness. Blessed is the one who finds himself a partner, then he should retire to his home" (Pushkin 3, 2: 941), while in his 1836 essay on Alexander Radishchev he asserted: "Time changes man both physically and spiritually. Whether with a smile or a sign, a mature man rejects the dreams that agitated him in youth. There is always something uncanny and ridiculous in youthful thoughts, as well as in a youthful face. Only a fool does not change, since time does not bring him development, and the experience does not exist for him" (12: 34). Nineteen years earlier, Pushkin, who never forgot that "there is a time and season for everything" [vsemu pora, vsemu svoi mig] (1: 237), made a similar pronouncement, this time in his early poem "To Kaverin" (1817): "[T]he flighty old man and the solemn youth are equally ridiculous" (1: 237).

It is clear that we are dealing with a powerful topos here.[24] Yet this topos flourished into magnificent and complex art during the period when Pushkin was reaching the "nel mezzo del camin" (Dante, *Inferno*, canto 1, l. 1) of his own life. In 1830, Pushkin's fascination with time exploded into a burst of creativity as it found a powerful stimulation in the overlapping of two momentous circumstances: the encounter with the issues of maturity, marriage, and parenthood that began to loom so large in Pushkin's consciousness, and his embracing of such acknowledged authorities on the subject of time and the principle of *tempestivitas* as Dante and Montaigne. The superb mastery of *The Little Tragedies* is one of the great products of these fortuitous circumstances.

As *The Covetous Knight*, the first play of the cycle, sets the tone for the rest of the plays, its images, themes, and system of values are reiterated and relied upon in the rest of the cycle's plays. The principle of *tempestivitas*, which I have discussed here, clearly manifests itself throughout the cycle.[25] Equally significant is the presence of Dante. Not only is his name mentioned in the next play of the cycle, *Mozart and Salieri*, but the various aspects of *Inferno* are reworked within each of the plays so that in the last play, for example, the revelers are compared to the demons who administer punishment in hell: "I might have thought that fiends [*besy*] had come / To torture sinners' godless souls / And drag them, cackling, off to Hell."

Furthermore, Dante's presence in Pushkin's cycle is felt not only on the levels of themes (crime and punishment) and images (devil, demons, death, or torture) but also on the level of the plays' "stern" (*surovaia*) morality, to borrow Pushkin's favorite epithet for Dante. By "sternness" I mean Dante's ability to recognize sin behind the multitude of human actions and the sinner's desire to challenge God and divine providence behind the multitude of sins. In fact, it appears that the cycle of *The Little Tragedies* was created by Pushkin on the basis of what he valued so much in Dante: the latter's ability to combine exuberant imagination with the most symmetrical, logical, and mathematically perfect structure. Pushkin's praise of Dante (among others) applies to his own achievement in *The Little Tragedies* equally well: "[T]here is a higher audacity, the audacity of invention, of creation, in which creative thought thoroughly pervades a vast and all-encompassing plan" (9: 61).

Notes

1. Gorodetskii, *Dramaturgiia Pushkina*, 273–75.

2. Such is the focus of Tomashevskii, "'Malen'kie tragedii' Pushkina i Mol'er"; Arinshtein, "Pushkin i Shenston"; Dolinin, "Zametka k probleme 'Pushkin i Shekspir'"; Levin, "Metafora v 'Skupom rytsare'"; and Proskurin, "Chem pakhnut chervontsy?"

3. Iakubovich, "Skupoi rytsar'."

4. Minskii, "Skupoi rytsar'," 3: 108.

5. Quoted in Shatzmiller, *Shylock Reconsidered*, 45.

6. M. N. Rozanov viewed Pushkin's cycle of poems, sometimes called *Podrazhaniia Dante* (Imitations of Dante), as a bridge connecting Dante and *The Covetous Knight* ("Puskin i Dante," 35). The dating of this cycle, never published during Pushkin's lifetime, remains problematic. The editors of the Jubilee Academic edition attribute it to the period between June 1831 and the beginning of 1832 (Pushkin 3, 2: 1235), which puts it in direct proximity to *The Little Tragedies.*

7. The play features an obvious usurer, the Jew Solomon, yet it is the Baron's connection with the set of themes associated with usury that is the most interesting. Even though Pushkin's text does not describe the Baron as "a usurer" explicitly, it mentions, nevertheless, the Baron's activity as a debt collector. (Debt collection is, of course, the purpose of the Jew's first appearance in the play.) So it is lending and demanding a payback with interest that appears to be the most likely source of the Baron's wealth, since the text is deliberately silent about any other possible source of his income, such as rent collection, for example.

The Baron, in fact, shares several key features with the play's usurer, Solomon, the character who clearly functions as the Baron's foil and thus highlights the Baron's peculiar features. Solomon's similarity with the Baron is suggested first by Albert, who not only compares his father's wealth to that of a Jew but also compares both Solomon and his father to "dogs." The comparison of usurers with dogs occurs in Dante's own treatment of usurers in canto 17 of *Inferno* as well. Furthermore, the Jew also functions as a surrogate father to Albert, since it is the Jew and not Albert's own father who provides for Albert's knightly pursuits. As a dependent, Albert manifests a combination of fear and anger in his violent reactions to both of his father figures. Likewise, both the Jew and the Baron challenge time's natural flow: the Baron in his rejection of his son, the Jew in his suggestion to speed up the process of the Baron's death. One wants to stop time, another to speed it up, but both go against it.

One argument against viewing the Baron as a usurer is the claim that as a Christian and an aristocrat he was not supposed to be engaged in such an activity (see Bayley, *Pushkin*, 213–15; Anikin, "'Vse kupliu'—skazalo zlato," 114–18). Yet the circle in Dante's *Inferno* in which the usurers are punished is filled with aristocratic Christians, condemned for their usury.

8. Rozanov, "Puskin i Dante," 19–20.

9. See Vatsuro, "Pushkin i Dante," 236.

10. Dante, *Inferno*, canto 7, ll. 28–30, 55. Hereafter cited in text.

11. Mandelbaum and Oldcorn, eds., *Lectura Dantis*, 231–33.

12. One can include in this list of failed fathers not only the Baron but also Samson Vyrin of "Stationmaster" (1830) and even Tsar Dadon of "The Golden Cockerel" (1834). Stationmaster Vyrin persists in viewing his grown daughter as a little girl in need of his protection. Equally emblematic is Tsar Dadon, who forgets the death of his two sons once he meets the cause of their fratricide, a beautiful and seductive princess. Whether they love too much or too little, these characters do not change, do not modify their behavior according to the changing family circumstances.

13. The quotations from Horace and Dante can be found in Burrow, *The Ages of Man*, 195, 151, 135.

14. Scholars connect these poems with Montaigne's essays "To Philosophize Means to Learn How to Die" and "On Some Verses of Virgil." See Butakova, "Pushkin i Monten'," 208–9; Levkovich, "Vnov' ia posetil . . . ," 306–22; and Kibal'nik, "Tema smerti," 169–71. On Montaigne and his role in shaping the Renaissance concept of time, see Quinones, "Montaigne." On Montaigne and his reflections on old age, see Friedrich, *Montaigne*, 233–39.

15. See Kibal'nik, "Tema smerti," 164–69.

16. Montaigne, *Selected Essays*, 146.

17. Ibid., 132.

18. Ibid., 136.

19. Ibid.

20. Ibid., 134.

21. Years after Montaigne and Pushkin, Dostoevsky felt the need to revisit a similar theme. While subjecting it to artistic treatment in *The Brothers Karamazov*, he also contemplated it in his *Diary of a Writer* and his numerous letters. Thus in 1878 he wrote to one of his female correspondents: "Imagine that your child, grown up to the age of fifteen or sixteen, comes to you (influenced by bad friends in school, for example) and asks you or his father: 'Why should I love you and why should this be my duty?' Believe me: no knowledge of questions will help you there, nor would there be much sense in answering him. *And therefore*

you must make sure that he never comes to you with such a question" (Dostoevskii, *Polnoe sobranie sochinenii*, 30, 1: 17, emphasis mine).

22. On Pushkin's treatment of the image of Kronos/Saturn, see Murianov, "U istokov pushkinskoi filosofii vremeni," 158–68.

23. See Panovsky, "Father Time."

24. Pushkin's interest in the concept of time was so strong and pervasive that it informed most of his celebrated texts, including *Eugene Onegin* and *The Queen of Spades*. The characters that Pushkin finds wanting are those who fail to change, fail to come to terms with the shifting dynamics of human relationships. Hence, their lives, whether Onegin's or Hermann's, end in fiasco. On Hermann's crimes against time, see my "Sekrety 'Pikovoi damy.'"

25. In my essay on *Mozart and Salieri* ("Pushkin's *Mozart and Salieri* as the Parable of Salvation," I explore how this principle works in the second play of the cycle.

Feasting on Genius

Monika Greenleaf

It has often been remarked that the alternative titles Pushkin jotted down in his list of dramatic projects in 1826 sound like so many deadly sins or literary archetypes—*The Miser* (*Skupoi*), *Don Juan*, *Envy* (*Zavist'*)—for which *A Feast in Time of Plague* then provided a metaphysical summation or symposium.[1] Yet *Mozart and Salieri* differs from the other three *Little Tragedies* in being a subject drawn not from the timeless storehouse of traditional narratives but rather from a timely rumor. Whereas the title *Envy* would have turned the specific collision of its protagonists into a classical study of a universal passion, the pairing of the proper names Mozart and Salieri instantly brought to mind the current rumor that fatally bound the two composers. As he lay dying and only fitfully sane in a state sanatorium from 1823 to 1825, Antonio Salieri spent his last lucid moments trying to combat the dreadful accusation that threatened to convert his respectable page in the history of eighteenth-century music into a role to rival Iago's: Mozart's poisoner, envious destroyer of God's messenger of harmony.

Why, Katenin asked following the brief staging of *Mozart and Salieri* in 1832, had Pushkin joined his voice to the ignorant crowd's slander? It is often assumed that the note Pushkin wrote in his notebook, as if to himself, was an answer and a justification: "At the first performance of *Don Juan* [*Don Giovanni*], at the moment the whole theater full of amazed connoisseurs was wordlessly intoxicating itself with Mozart's harmony, a whistle sounded out. All turned with indignation, and the renowned Salieri walked out of the hall in a fury, devoured by envy. [. . .] Certain German newspapers said that on his deathbed he confessed to a horrible crime—the poisoning of the great Mozart. An envier who was capable of hissing *Don Juan* could have also poisoned its creator" (11: 218).[2] A difference of taste, Pushkin tells himself in the sententious tones of his own character, Salieri, is tantamount to murder. If Salieri was capable of hissing *Don Giovanni* when connoisseurs were being transfigured by its divine harmonies, then he was capable of any crime against humanity, and he deserved to be hissed forever in the black-and-white melodrama of public memory.

Critics have responded to this question of historical factuality in two ways. Some maintain that Pushkin's statement was an accurate representation of his knowledge or belief. Others insist that art creates the sole, higher, and poetic reality of its characters and need not bear reference to the facts at all.[3] And yet, in his comments to N. N. Raevskii about *Boris Godunov* (1829), Pushkin instructed his reader to collate his play with the last volume of Karamzin's *History of the Russian State*: "[I]t is filled with good jokes" [elle est remplie de bonnes plaisanteries] (14: 46). The latent meanings of his text would be activated only by the intertextual relation, the montage, in effect, of different representations drawn according to different criteria. The play *Boris Godunov* hangs suspended between the two poles of transmission actually represented in it: the divinely—or at least theocratically—sanctioned historiographical text of the monk Pimen' and the unruly proliferation of popular rumor.

It is worth noting what role Pushkin the author reserves for the character, his ancestor Gavrila Pushkin, in the play's denouement. The seventeenth-century Pushkin is depicted as the very soul of realpolitik: the first to inform Shuisky of a pretender's emergence, he is one of the first to cross over to "Tsarevich Dimitrii's" side, to witness the flimsiness of his leadership and his rout—and yet to act as "Dimitrii's" messenger to the Kremlin fully confident of "where our strength lies [. . .] in opinion; Yes! Popular opinion" [chem sil'ny my (. . .) mneniem; Da! mneniem narodnym] (Pushkin 7: 93). Note that the penultimate scene of *Boris Godunov* takes place "at the place of execution (crucifixion)" [na lobnom meste] and begins with the interesting stage direction: "Pushkin comes, surrounded by the people" [Pushkin idet, okruzhennyi narodom] (Pushkin 7: 95). It is, in fact, his speech that galvanizes "popular opinion" into a mob's descent on the Kremlin, where a moment later it is asked to corroborate the official cause of Boris's heirs' death: the people (*narod*) are to dismiss the evidence of their own ears, which have heard a violent murder take place behind the castle walls, and to believe a boyar's report of the heirs' self-poisoning, for "he has seen the dead bodies" (Pushkin 7: 98). At the end, then, the play has cycled back to its unstable point of departure: a tsarevich's dead body.

An interesting metatextual question presents itself: what is the relationship between Gavrila Pushkin, the expedient seventeenth-century messenger between the two sides of the civil war–torn nation, and Alexander Pushkin, the contemporary mediator between Russia and its past(s)? Implicit in the play's differentiation between the seen and officially reported, on the one hand, and the heard and orally transmitted, on the other, is an image of the poet as a secret hearer of voices excluded from history's visual monuments and textual documents. Among these illicit voices is the voice of rumor.

Among the topics Pushkin projected in 1826, *Mozart and Salieri* sticks out as perhaps the most incongruous choice—a product of print culture's rumor mill that turned artists' lives, as it had royal scandals, into food for an insatiable public's "right to know." What if Pushkin, fresh from his imaginative immersion in the rumor-bred world of the seventeenth-century Time of Troubles (Smuta), was fascinated by the engendering of this strange, retrospective myth about Mozart's death? Certainly we can discern quite explicit parallels: at the center of both fermenting worlds lies the dead body of the young, unjustly cut down bearer of the divine crown; with the passing years the absent body is read and reread as evidence of an unnatural crime, a myth that acquires an uncanny life of its own out of all proportion to the "facts." Still more specifically, the final rumor in *Boris Godunov* about the poisoning of the "Boris line" and the restoration of the mythical "Dimitrii" foreshadows the way Pushkin motivates the rumored poisoning of Mozart: by Salieri's need to arrest the senseless proliferation of Mozart's gift and to reincorporate the stilled body of his works back into the high dynastic line of musical evolution.

What accounts of the Mozart-Salieri story Pushkin read himself can only be a matter of informed conjecture. He almost certainly did not read German newspapers or musical publications (his library contained not a single work on music per se, insofar as my thorough perusal of Modzalevskii's *Biblioteka Pushkina* could ascertain), but he must have run across the French and English synopses of German news items: anything that purported to shed light on the twin mysteries of Mozart's death and genius was news.[4] In the next section I will review the specific contents of the rumor, together with the cultural import of Mozart and Salieri's biographical suturing as romanticism reached its philosophical peak. What need and what cultural truth were being expressed in this modern refabrication of the eighteenth-century past? Why, in 1826 and still more in 1830, was it as important to Pushkin as to "German newspapers," biographers, high-society gossips, and popular myth consumers all over Europe to tell and retell this particular lurid story?

At the end of his life Salieri was made to enact a profoundly disturbing spectacle before the eyes of Europe: the loss of control over his own legacy. It was a temptingly romantic, even Shakespearean scenario. As his mind took part in his body's disintegration, Salieri was said to have fallen under the spell of the rumors swirling around him, even to the extent of finally corroborating them in a melodramatic confession to a Jesuit priest. The European music-loving audience was thus presented with the classic problem of recognition: were these simply clinical symptoms of an organic dementia? Was the cracking of Salieri's (Enlightenment) reason allowing the real buried iniquities of the ancien régime to reemerge? Or was the once-powerful *Kapellmeister*'s mind now helplessly mirroring the print age's fantasies, poisoning itself—much as Pushkin's soliloquizing Boris had—with the internalized "bloody boys" [mal'chiki krovavye] of buzzing rumor (7: 27)?

The Salieri confession was always reported as a rumor, not a fact, that was already at the time regarded as a disturbing cultural phenomenon. Thus Beethoven, immured in his deafness and the romantic cult of his own genius, recorded his anxious interest in the affair in his conversation book entries for 25 January and 8 February 1824. When Schindler reported to Beethoven, "Salieri is very poorly again. He is completely deranged. He keeps fantasizing that he is to blame for Mozart's death and poisoned him," Beethoven called it slander, citing medical witnesses who could prove how Mozart died on the basis of his symptoms.[5] Yet Schindler noted the effect of all this discussion on Beethoven: "You are so somber again, illustrious master, what is wrong, what has happened to your happier mood lately? [...] Don't take it so to heart, such is generally the fate of great men!" He then adds, as if the poisoning were a mere technicality: "But [Salieri] must have damaged Mozart more with his criticism than Mozart affected him."[6] Indeed, the situation became so extreme that Salieri himself begged his student Moscheles to lay the rumor to rest and restore his good name: "Although this is my last illness, however I assure you in good faith that there is no truth in the absurd rumour; you know what I mean—that I poisoned Mozart. But no, dear Moscheles, tell the world that it is malice, pure malice; old Salieri, who will soon be dead, has told you this."[7] Accordingly, in August 1824, Salieri's old friend Giuseppe Carpari published a long defense of Salieri's character, together with an account of Mozart and Salieri's collegial relations and Mozart's doctors' dismissal of poisoning as the cause of death.

However Pushkin may have learned of the story, he is likely to have understood its broader implications as a parable of the possession of genius by the public. The very paradigm of this process was the romanticization of Mozart's death by a succession of nineteenth-century Mozart biographers.[8] Salieri was, in fact, introduced late in the biographical narrative, as the villain, as the Judas, as the necessary narrative solution to the mystery and perceived injustice of Mozart's death. As at the end of *Boris Godunov*, there was a dead body, a young and gifted body, to account for; and also as in *Boris Godunov*, there was no longer a single sacred authority to establish the meaning of its loss. The unnatural giftedness of the life was matched by the unnatural suddenness of the death and the inadequacy of the mourning rituals society extended to this sort of loss. (Beethoven's state funeral a generation later would promote the national composer to a new category.) Where the physical monument was lacking, texts accrued to fill the gap. In his study *The Mozart Myths,* William Stafford does a marvelous job of separating out the successive layerings of the biographical accounts; I will highlight certain features useful to my present analysis.

The narration of Mozart's death began already with the plentiful recording of his precocious young life and performances; numerous eyewitnesses testified that this supreme creation of Nature, the supernaturally gifted child, could not survive long—and several near-fatal brushes with illness seemed to bear them out. Mozart's life was perceived even at the time as a race with the ordinary clock of mortal maturation and achievement, a race with death. Interestingly, however, it was the budding national pride of Prague, the city that had given

Mozart's *Figaro* and *Don Giovanni* their first rapturous successes, that expressed itself in the writing of the most influential Mozart biographies. The earliest recorded reference to the murder was made by the Prague correspondent to a Berlin weekly one month after Mozart's death and vaguely alluded to the inimical role of "the Italians": "Mozart is—dead. [. . .] Because his body swelled up after death, some people believe that he was poisoned. [. . .] Now that he is dead the Viennese will at last realize what they have lost in him. In his life he was constantly the object of cabals, which he at times may well have provoked by his sans souci manner."[9] The Prague biographer Franz Xaver Niemetschek used his own meetings with Mozart and Mozart's associates to pen a characterization of Mozart's last decade in 1798. Clearly possessed by the idea that Prague was Mozart's ideal audience, he created the basic elements of the romantic biography: a superficial imperial Vienna, inimical to Mozart's genius; Joseph II's famous dismissal, "too beautiful for our ears"; a vicious and corrupt musical profession competing for imperial patronage, with the "jealous Italians" (jealous, that is, of Mozart's successful encroachment on their operatic territory) making their first melodramatic appearance; and the dramatic account of the mysterious commissioner of the Requiem and Mozart's complaint to Constanze that he had been poisoned. Although all subsequent accounts (Friedrich Rochlitz's anecdotes, the novelist Ignaz Ferdinand Cajetan Arnold's very popular *Mozarts Geist* [1803], Stendhal's derivative *Vies de Haydn, de Mozart et de Métastase* [1814], Constanze Mozart's second husband, Georg Nikolaus von Nissen's seven-hundred-page biography [1828]) repeatedly refuted the theory of Mozart's poisoning, they also kept it in circulation, together with the idea of an envious "Italian cabal" that had persistently blocked Mozart's successes in Vienna and gradually poisoned his very existence. From there, it was only a matter of dramatic economy to fuse the story of Mozart's poisoning with the spectacle of the former Viennese *Kapellmeister*, the Italian Salieri, driven mad by guilt.

Mozart died into the genius myth, the late eighteenth century's fusion of the classical and Christological myths of a sacrificial god. The Christological paradigm assigned a degree of guilt to the age that witnessed this divine life and death without recognizing their sacred import. Particularly guilty was the competitive professional world of imperial music, which treated brilliant composers and librettists as purveyors of stylish vehicles for the court's favorite performers and routinely elicited musical miracles while remaining deaf to them. Mozart's nineteenth-century biographers and their avid readers thus assigned themselves a dual role: as music lovers, even chief mourners, they received the message of divine harmony wasted on Mozart's own godless age; and as prosecutors, they sought to identify the guilty party. Mozart's death was the last crime of the ancien régime, and onto Salieri—a hard-working colleague and competitor of Mozart in the Viennese imperial opera—was eventually projected its perpetration. Underlying the persistent scapegoating of "the Italians" was a revulsion against the imperial culture that often subsidized professional foreign artists over native artists, who were consequently relegated to second-class status.[10] Thus the purging and vilification of the ever-successful Italians was a prelude to the vindication of "national genius." Indeed, as Mozart was reclaimed more and more explicitly as a German composer, part of the great continuum of German musical spirit (*Geist*), Salieri's role devolved onto ever more spectacular international conspiracies: in 1861, the Illuminati/Socialist God-men, headed by Karl Marx; in 1910, the Jews.[11] The enemy of natural, native genius was the cosmopolitan-demonic project to systematize the world.

Stendhal's *Life of Mozart* (1814) tells us a good deal about how the concept of "genius" was being reconstituted by and for the romantic generation. In contrast with the masterfully synthesizing mental and spiritual powers understood to distinguish "Génie" in Diderot and d'Alembert's *Encyclopédie*, for example, Stendhal's Mozart floats in the realm of the involuntary. He stands in the same relation to the other great eighteenth-century composers as the blessedly gifted boy Raphael did to the mature Renaissance masters. His childlike nature and exclusive hypersensitivity to music make him prey both to worldly patrons and schemers and to an obsessive preoccupation with his work, in which may be discerned "a type of madness similar to that which took possession of Torquato Tasso or Rousseau.... It may be that, without this exaltation of the nervous sensibility which borders close on madness, there can be no superior genius in those arts that require a most delicate susceptibility."[12] This is expressed above all in Mozart's fatalistic submission to the will of the strange messenger in the carriage who delivers the commission for the Requiem, a labor so consuming that the piece grows parasitically out of Mozart's waning strength until, "at the expiring of the agreed term, the stranger reappeared; but Mozart was no more."[13] While suggesting that both sociological (lack of intellectual property rights) and psychological factors played their part in Mozart's strange story, Stendhal concludes with a tantalizingly metaphysical invitation: "Mozart is even more remarkable taken as a subject for philosophical speculation."[14]

Such, indeed, was the treatment given to Mozart's music beginning with the performances of *Don Giovanni* in Moscow and Petersburg in 1826. Pushkin may have first heard of Mozart's posthumous dominance in the music world from an emphatic article by V. F. Odoevsky that used the occasion to denigrate the Russian passion for Rossini, a merely "timely" composer (and Pushkin's favorite), in contrast to Mozart's "eternal" and spiritually uplifting art.[15] There was a certain symmetry of replacement for Pushkin: the arbiters of refined taste required that his youthful love for Rossini's contagious libidinal "melodies," together with the whole "southern" erotic-elegiac poetics with which they were intertwined, be sacrificed to the more demanding spiritual "harmony" disclosed by German musical genius and aesthetic philosophy. Thus by 1830, Smirnova-Rossett recorded, Pushkin's beloved *Barber of Seville* had been replaced for the Petersburg elite by Saturdays devoted to "absolute music": Beethoven's symphonies, Haydn's *Creation*, Mozart's Requiem.[16]

Between the years 1826 and 1830, Pushkin's own life and art were subjected to teleological pressures similar to those that had mythicized Mozart's life and death. In this next section, I will sketch a picture of the force field Pushkin entered when he returned to Moscow after five years of exile in 1826. Then I will show how Pushkin transfigured the vulgar rumor of Mozart's poisoning by Salieri into—to borrow the poet's famous formulation from his poem "Geroi" (The hero)—"an elevating deception" [nas vozvyshaiushchii obman] (3, 1: 253), by whose light the Russian public could be taught to read Pushkin himself.

Pushkin returned to the Russian capital in 1826 armed with what he considered his first mature masterpiece and the awareness of having crossed over into a new relationship with Russia. One can thus read the poet's stage direction in *Boris Godunov* ("Pushkin comes, surrounded by the people") not only ironically but as a bold announcement of his new poetic vocation. Transfigured by the writing of his "national tragedy" into the national poet-prophet, he pictures his sudden charismatic relationship with the Russian people and locates it at "the place of sacrifice" [na lobnom meste]. It is likely that Pushkin was alluding to the Decembrist context and to the danger he courted by portraying a historical crisis of succession during the current Decembrist crisis of succession in ways that radically questioned Karamzin's statist-moralist insistence on the Romanov dynasty's "divine predestination." The stage direction bears an affinity with the poet's sacrificial destiny in *André Chenier*, also written in 1825. *André Chenier* portrays a dual sacrifice, in that the poet knowingly sacrifices his youthful (and safe) lyrical muse to the burden of a civic and revolutionary voice, only to be sacrificed in turn to the temporarily maddened popular will. Underlying both images is a clear Christological paradigm or, more generally, the archaic myth of a dying and fructifying god. Pushkin pointedly shows the transposition of the role of sacrificial god to the contemporary national poet, from whose word the amorphous, usually blind, and ungrateful mass derives its identity, the contours of its self-consciousness and being in time, as a "people."

But it is not the poet's written text that has this efficacy. In all his representations of the charismatic contact between poet and people, Pushkin marks the difference between the written text and the bodily and spiritually absorbed sound of the poet's orally repeated word: "Gather together to read my truthful scroll" [Sbiraites' inogda chitat' moi svitok vernyi] (2, 1: 399); "Pronounce [my name] in sorrow" [Proiznesi ego toskuia] (3, 1: 210). Such scenes of ideal aural reception replace the modes of concrete oral contact between poet and public that nineteenth-century culture still afforded. The most important, and the one on which Pushkin still pinned his hopes in 1825, was the national theater. Since the Renaissance, the equation of national poet and leading dramatist had held true; the culturally unifying function of the royal or heroic "sacrificial tragedy" that underlay European classical and then romantic historical dramaturgy has been well explored.[17] When *Boris Godunov* was banned from the Russian stage, Pushkin was denied access to the most powerful and immediate forms of vocalization and public ratification or controversy.

Yet far from disappearing from theatrical playbills, Pushkin's name was ubiquitous. It is a striking irony in Pushkin's relations with the Russian theater that, even while *Boris Godunov* languished offstage and out of print, imperial theaters were packing in audiences for spectacular (and royalty-free) adaptations of Pushkin's narrative poems. One can imagine Pushkin's initial thrill when his taut narrative poem *Kavkazskii plennik* (*The Prisoner of the Caucasus*) was inflated by the combined efforts of the Italian *Kapellmeister* of the Imperial Theaters Caterino Cavos and the court choreographer Didelot into (to quote the poster) "a huge, ancient, nationally pantomimic ballet in four acts, with a grandiose spectacle, costumed games, battles, marches, apparitions, etc."—and with the celebrated ballerina Istomina dancing the role of Cherkeshenka![18] The indefatigable Shakhovskoi did not hesitate to rework other Pushkinian texts—*Ruslan and Liudmilla, The Fountain of Bakhchisarai,* and *The Queen of Spades*—into similar multimedia spectacles and prophesied the blessed day when "music, united to a poem, will constitute a whole sublime creative work, belonging exclusively to our [Russian] theater" [muzyka, soedinennaia so stikhotvoreniem, sostavit tseloe vysokoe tvorenie, prinadlezhashchee iskliuchitel'no nashemu teatru].[19] What was funny and gratifying to the young poet riding the crest of his popularity must have been less so when the theater doors slammed in his face. Surely the revealing disagreement between Mozart and Salieri about the laughable or gravely offensive nature of popular renditions—"I cannot laugh—when some repellent clown / With parody dishonors Alighieri" [Mne ne smeshno, kogda figliar' prezrennyi / Parodiei beschestit Alig'ieri] (Pushkin 8: 126)—rests on Pushkin's wealth of experience in this area and on his own varying reactions.[20]

In fact, a second type of "oral/aural reception" was concurrently being enacted in the realm of popular song. Pushkin's poems sounded ubiquitously in the public's ear in the form of popular "gypsy" romances, subversive drinking songs, and, increasingly, serious "art songs" by Russian composers such as Glinka. Propelled by melody, songs such as "Kinzhal" (The dagger), "Chernaia shal'" (The black shawl), and "Staryi muzh, groznyi muzh" (Old husband, terrible husband) from *The Gypsies* traveled easily from army encampment to exclusive Petersburg salon to provincial "musicale" (*muzitsirovanie*), purveying a certain youthful effigy of Pushkin in their wake.[21] In all these cases, the poet's loss of control over his own legacy is manifest, even while some kind of influence, labeled as "Pushkinian," infiltrated literate and even illiterate society from top to bottom.

It is not difficult to identify the theme of the penetrating, unpredictable, and control-eluding "life of the song" in *The Little Tragedies.* Three of the four plays (the exception being *The Covetous Knight,* with its focus on hoarding and noncirculation) are organized around casually interpolated yet crucial popular songs. Thus, in *Mozart and Salieri* Mozart drags a blind street fiddler to perform "a bit of Mozart" before the snobbish Salieri. He thus opens a window of escape, of already uncontrollable contact with the public imagination that Salieri, for all his efforts to install Mozart in his purist edifice of classical music history, cannot contain again. Similarly, try as the king and Madrid society might, in *The Stone Guest*, to banish Don Juan's transgressive spirit to the outskirts of the country and capital, his songs, performed with contagious passion by the singer Laura before a crowd of her admirers, are the songs they make love and die to. Finally, in *A Feast in Time of Plague*, the girl from the conquered Scottish borderlands, Mary, sings an old song that raises forgotten ghosts of past cataclysms suffered by her people that have gone unrecorded in official history, thus creating a medium of popular contact and a continuum of tragic experience upon which the leader of the feast, Walsingham, draws in his final aria of apostasy.

A third form of immediate contact through voice and ear was the author's reading or performance of his new, unpublished, or banned works in the select company of an urban salon. In *Eugene Onegin* Pushkin humorously locates his first private performances of *Boris Godunov* in rural banishment, alternately trapping an unwary neighbor in a corner or frightening a flock of wild ducks into the open sky. Yet eyewitnesses of Pushkin's first reading of his banned tragedy in 1826 at the Venevitinovs', before the flower of Moscow's intellectual youth, recorded its enormous impact in well-nigh mystical terms.[22] Gomolicki's diary of Adam Mickiewicz's sojourn in Russia gives a fascinating glimpse of the Kireevsky-Pogodin circle, attended concurrently by both poets, which featured heady discussions and readings of ongoing creative work of this band of talented young men spared by the post-Decembrist dragnet. It was here, before this hand-picked audience, that Pushkin tested and was confirmed in his dramatic vocation, here that he excitedly announced his list of further dramatic projects, here also that he listened to Mickiewicz perform his Polish national-mystical dramas, including *Dziady* and *Konrad Wallenrod*, and heard himself and Mickiewicz hailed expectantly as Russia's and Poland's respective national geniuses. In the magic circle of this salon, talent erased political inequality in an atmosphere of healthy competition between national poets, each serving as the proving ground for the other in a joust delightful to all witnesses. Yet Mickiewicz so perfectly incarnated the romantic Walter Scott ideal of the charismatic bard that he left Pushkin, just released from his own romantic exile at the Russian Empire's periphery, now uncomfortably occupying the "center," confronted with the difficult task of redefining Russia's peculiar "genius" as a nation.

It was also in the Moscow circle of 1826 that Pushkin encountered a synergistic new form of author-audience contact, the public improvisation. Pushkin's fascination with the phenomenon is well attested—from his fervent reaction to Mickiewicz's gripping improvisations in French prose on themes chosen by lot from the "little scrolls of paper" offered by his Russian audience to Pushkin's much darker representation of the ritual before the quite different society of 1830s Petersburg in *Egyptian Nights.* It is useful to remind ourselves of the social and aesthetic function of the improvisational performance. It is rooted in three traditional practices: "inspired" religious and political oratory; the archaic tradition of oral epic performance, assumed to be preserved only in premodern cultures even as they are being taken over by modern imperial forces; and the "piano duel" or public musical improvisation on prescribed themes that differentiated the divinely inspired and inimitably inventive composer from the merely skillful and well-trained virtuoso. Eyewitness descriptions placed emphasis not so much on the qualities of the work but on the transfiguration of the genius's mortal body. Eagerly awaited and recorded were the visible signs of "the approach of God": first, the visible physical transformation that presaged the pouring of "harmonious sound" through the divine vessel; second, the contagious spiritual transfiguration of the audience as those sounds poured through them.

Two contrasting but complementary processes were similarly recorded during the poetic improvisation: the absolute differentiation of the immortal "genius" and his pulsing language from the witnessing audience, and the emotional unification of the audience as it responded involuntarily to his divine authority. Thus the improvisation provided the sacrament in which the transcendent idea of "nation" manifested itself, demonstrating the involuntary interfusion of the people's "national character" or "spirit" and the "national genius" who gave it phenomenal form. One can see why this charismatic experience was so highly valued in the period following the Decembrist Rebellion, when the officially imposed and policed ideological triad of Autocracy, Orthodoxy, and Nation was supposed to serve as the nation's credo. In the liberal intellectual salon, an alternative form of awed collective submission could be offered up to the artistic "genius" and the real "spirit of the nation" he was taken to voice.

So we can see that something else was happening in this Moscow salon of 1826: the audience was establishing certain identification and ratification criteria for "genius," and the improvisation served as a ritual ceremony for their public consecration. A decade later in *Egyptian Nights,* Pushkin would turn the Petersburg salon quite obviously into a "place of execution," where the foreign improviser was publicly sacrificed while the Russian poet chose to remain safely masked and poetically silent. In 1826 Moscow, Mickiewicz perfectly realized the new criteria for the national genius before Russian eyes. In its magnanimous reception of the Polish poet precisely in his national significance, his Russian audience manifested its own liberal and all-embracing cultural identity as well.

"What am I before him?" Pushkin is known to have exclaimed with characteristic warmth and graciousness after one of Mickiewicz's performances. But a different question lurks under the compliment: what should I be, how should I perform the Russian poet now that Mickiewicz has reset the "horizon of expectation"? *Boris Godunov,* because it ventriloquized rich and audible speech from a thinly documented, virtually unrecoverable past, met the criteria for inspired improvisation and "popular spirit" (*narodnost'*) even if its portrayal of Russian history was ambiguous and not heroically exemplary. The ten dramatic projects Pushkin announced to the company almost as proof of his abundant and varied creative flow were, however, mostly topics from international history and legend: "The Miser; Romulus and Remus; Mozart and Salieri; Don Juan; Jesus; Berald of Savoy; Paul I; an enamored devil; Dmitry and Marina; Kurbsky." In their seemingly random diversity they resemble the topics on separate "little scrolls of paper" that an audience might offer up for the artist's imaginative transformation. In essence, Pushkin was taking over the audience's role himself, adjusting the "horizon of expectation" back to an imperially cosmopolitan and unpredictably self-willed standard and rejecting the romantic nationalist compulsion. The ritual public improvisation of genius gives a concrete justification for linking Pushkin's random list of topics with the polemical 1829 poem on the autonomy of inspiration that would eventually be recast as the Italian improviser's first performance in *Egyptian Nights*:

> The poet approaches: his orbs are open,
> But he sees no one;
> Yet meanwhile, by the edge of his garment,
> A passerby tugs at him . . .
> "Say, why do you wander without aim?
> You've scarce attained the heights,
> And you already lower your gaze
> And rush to descend.
> At the harmonious world you look distraughtly;
> A fruitless fever torments you;
> Some trivial object every minute
> Disturbs and seduces you.
> A genius must strive toward the heavens,
> A true poet is obliged
> To choose an elevated subject
> For his inspired songs."
>
> [Поэт идет]: открыты вежды,
> Но он не видит никого;
> А между тем за край одежды
> Прохожий дергает его...
> «Скажи: зачем без цели бродишь?
> Едва достиг ты высоты,
> И вот уж долу взор низводишь
> И низойти стремишься ты.
> На стройный мир ты смотришь смутно;
> Бесплодный жар тебя томит;
> Предмет ничтожный поминутно
> Тебя тревожит и манит.
> Стремиться к небу должен гений,
> Обязан истинный поэт
> Для вдохновенных песнопений
> Избрать возвышенный предмет.»
> (Pushkin 8, 1: 269)

When the public tries to dictate the proper elevated concerns of genius, the poet retorts:

And asking no one's leave
Like Desdemona he chooses
An idol for his heart.

не спросясь ни у кого,
Как Дездемона избирает
Кумир для сердца своего.
(Pushkin 8, 1: 269)

In this, as in many other works of the late 1820s, Pushkin seems to balk at his own induction into the high and burdensome rank of "national genius" as nineteenth-century European and Russian culture needed it to be defined—and performed on demand.[23]

The Little Tragedies can be seen as Pushkin's last variation on the public ritual of improvisation. As if by dictation (the dates of completion, their well-nigh miraculous speed were recorded in his manuscript), Pushkin performs a set of intensely condensed improvisations on a series of timeless, migrating, and not intrinsically "high" European subjects. If the dramas offered a strange "feast of the imagination" to which the already doubting public of 1830 was invited to bear witness, *Mozart and Salieri* provided the model for its ingestion, for here Pushkin pictures the two polarized "circuits" of transmission parallel to those we found in *Boris Godunov*. On the one hand, Mozart's genius is shown to seep down into popular culture, which deforms it and yet endows it with a tenacious underground life. On the other hand, for the aesthetic elite Mozart's unruly creative flow must be sacrificed in order to be reborn as a sublime national heritage ("narodnoe dostoianie").

Having examined the related cultural phenomena of the Mozart-Salieri rumor, on the one hand, and the production of "national genius," on the other, we are in a position to appreciate how original Pushkin's variation on this theme really is. Pushkin's characterization of Salieri is unprecedented: it draws not on past or contemporary portrayals of the man but on a penetrating insight into the cultural dynamics that had surfaced in the Mozart and Salieri story. Pushkin's first radical transformation is to make Salieri head priest of the cult of music. Extracting the two composers from the hectic imperial musical profession of eighteenth-century Vienna, Pushkin imagines a relationship between a young, instinctive genius and a purist aesthete, self-appointed historian and lawmaker of the musical realm. Although many critics have called Pushkin's Salieri a scholastic "classicist" compared to Mozart's spontaneous melodist, Salieri really talks like a romantic aesthetic philosopher, wedded to high notions of *Geistesgeschichte* and the metaphysical evolution of music. Mozart brings his improvisations to Salieri for ratification and repeatedly receives from Salieri's lips the title of "genius" and "god" ("You, Mozart, are a god and know it not. / But I, I know" [Ty, Motsart, bog, i sam togo ne znaesh; / Ia znaiu, ia]) without realizing that his own casual repartee ("You do? Well, maybe so . . . / But now this little god is slightly famished" [Ba! pravo? mozhet byt'... / No bozhestvo moe progolodalos']) has put his life on trial as its unworthy, corruptible vehicle. In Pushkin's play it is Salieri who takes up Stendhal's challenge and treats Mozart as "a subject for philosophical speculation" even while he lives, creating the fatal distinction between the unconscious, essentially subjectless "god" and the aesthetic worshiper who "knows"—"But I, I know"—his posthumous public value. Salieri performs the metaphysical surgery of releasing "Mozart's spirit," the completed oeuvre of Mozart's music, from its erring mortal and social body. Like an impatient necrologist or biographer, he is eager to commence the work of mourning and cultural systematization.

In response to the teleological and meaning-seeking pressures being exerted on his life and art between 1826 and 1830, Pushkin made a preemptive strike: he starkly dramatized the institutional thinking by which—to use his favorite phrase—"inexplicable art" [neiz"iasnimoe iskusstvo] would be reprocessed into readily legible genius and national heritage. By uniting in Salieri the high priest of art and the poisoner, Pushkin fashioned a warning effigy of any Pushkin cult, present or future, that pretended to speak in his name. This is not to deny the tragic complexity of Salieri's internal motivations. As the deepest analysts of *Mozart and Salieri* have shown,[24] Salieri's divided, sadistically self-tormenting consciousness attains an Oedipal grandeur and horror precisely in its drive to unriddle, cleave, and autopsy the music he loves for the sake of a usable human knowledge. Yet while listening to Mozart's Requiem he is as helplessly and blissfully in music's thrall at the end of a lifetime's study as at the beginning and as far from mastery. *Mozart and Salieri* is, among other things, a "little tragedy" of unrequited love turned to poison.

Like that of Oedipus, Salieri's pursuit of the truth he thinks he desires leads to the sudden unearthing of unwanted knowledge. A moment too late, Salieri recognizes that his desire to penetrate the originary, bliss-suffused body of *muzyka* and his twin desire to kill the father who held exclusive access to its potency have merged him not with immortal genius, inside the temple of art, but merely with the sordid history of human rumor and error, forever locked outside:

> But could he be right . . .
> Am I no genius? Villainy and genius
> Sit ill together. Surely this is wrong:
> Take Michelangelo. Or is it only
> A tale the dull and witless tell—and he,
> The Vatican's creator, did no murder?
>
> но ужель он прав,
> И я не гений? Гений и злодейство
> Две вещи несовместные. Неправда:
> А Бонаротти? или это сказка
> Тупой, бессмысленной толпы—и не был
> Убийцею создатель Ватикана?
> (Pushkin 8: 133–34)

Counterpointing Salieri's self-pitying tale of his own self-sacrifice, then, Pushkin presents Mozart as the unconscious victim of a peculiarly modern prosecution and ritual sacrifice. If "big tragedy" traditionally offered the audience a cathartic illumination by forcing it to contemplate the sacrificial destinies of kings, their overreaching and fated self-punishment, Pushkin's "little tragedy," with an incisiveness that much anticipates Freud's, identifies the genre's modern substitute. The elevation to divine authority of the artistically gifted must lead inexorably to his sacrifice, as over and over the human community reconsecrates itself through the ritual of patricide, blood bonding, and the equalized "brotherhood" conferred by shared guilt.[25] One of the motifs that unites *The Little Tragedies*, it has often been noted, is the feast, a sacramental last supper at which the one marked out for more-than-human attainment is sacrificed to the dark laws of the human psyche and social organism. In the collectively crafted nineteenth-century myth of Mozart's sacrificial murder, Pushkin recognized culture's cannibalistic imperative to feast on genius, digesting its inexplicability into public value. Dismissed from the national stage, he would use the theater of his own existence in Petersburg to enact his dark allegory.

Notes

1. For cogent structural analyses and/or rich contextualization of the *Little Tragedies*, see Ardens, *Dramaturgiia i teatr*, esp. "Pushkin i drama," 218–48; Eiges, *Muzyka v zhizni i tvorchestve Pushkina*; Tomashevskii, "'Malen'kie tragedii' Pushkina i Mol'er"; Alexandrov, "Correlations in Pushkin's *Malen'kie tragedii*"; Brun-Zejmis, "*Malen'kie tragedii* and *Povesti Belkina*"; Brown, *A History of Russian Literature of the Romantic Period*; and the excellent essay on the metonymic structure of the *Little Tragedies* in Shapiro and Shapiro, *Figuration in Verbal Art*. For the most incisive and wide-ranging interpretations of *Mozart and Salieri*, see Alekseev, "Kommentarii k 'Motsartu i Sal'eri'"; Reid, *Pushkin's Mozart and Salieri*; and Nepomniashchii, ed., *"Motsart i Sal'eri," tragediia Pushkina*; see, in particular, articles by Gershenzon, Bliumenfeld, Gukasova, Nepomniashchii, Blagoi, Fedorov, Retsepter, and Kostalevskaia.

2. See Gukasova's similar analysis in Nepomniashchii, ed., *"Motsart i Sal'eri," tragediia Pushkina*, 295. The translation of all Pushkin texts, with the exception of *The Little Tragedies*, which are given in James Falen's translation, are my own.

3. For an eloquent formulation of this argument, see Evdokimova, *Pushkin's Historical Imagination*. My essay refutes D. Granin's enthusiastic assumption that Pushkin's choice of Mozart "out of the gallery of mankind's geniuses" [iz vsei gallerei geniev chelovechestva] was uncannily prophetic of Mozart's future fame (in Nepomniashchii, ed., *"Motsart i Sal'eri," tragediia Pushkina*, 377).

4. My basic sources for the following pages are Stafford, *The Mozart Myths*; Braunbehrens, *Maligned Master*; and Eiges, *Muzyka v zhizni i tvorchestve Pushkina*. According to Stafford, C. F. Cramer's 1801 *Anecdotes sur Mozart* is translated from F. Rochlitz, while T. F. Winckler's "Notice sur Mozart" in *Magasin encyclopédique* (1801) is plagiarized from Cramer and Schlichtegroll and Stendhal's *Vie de Mozart* (1814) primarily from Winckler.

5. Stafford, *The Mozart Myths*, 33.

6. Braunbehrens, *Maligned Master*, 229.

7. Stafford, *The Mozart Myths*, 43.

8. My basic sources are ibid. and Eiges, *Muzyka v zhizni i tvorchestve Pushkina*.

9. Stafford, *The Mozart Myths*, 31. "A Prague correspondent in a Berlin weekly,"

quoted by Stafford from Otto Erich Deutsch, *Mozart: A Documentary Biography* (London, 1966), 432; and Cliff Eisen, *New Mozart Documents: A Supplement to Otto Erich Deutsch's "Mozart: Die Dokumente seines Lebens"* (London, 1991), no. 113.

10. Taruskin, *Defining Russia Musically*, 186–235.

11. Stafford, *The Mozart Myths*, 35.

12. Stendhal, *The Lives of Haydn, Mozart, and Metastasio*, 194.

13. Ibid., 200.

14. Ibid., 206.

15. Odoevskii, *Muzykal'no-literaturnoe nasledie*: "Ital'ianskii teatr. Don Zhuan-opera Motsarta, 31 ianvaria; benefis gospozhi Anti" (92–95), "Antikritika. Otvet G-na U.U. g-nu P" (102–5), and "Nemetskii teatr. Don Zhuan opera Motsarta, predstavelennaia na Aleksandriiskom teatre 22-go oktiabria, v benefis g-zhi Karl" (11–12).

16. Several scholars, among them Tomashevskii, Ardens, and, most convincingly, Eiges, have studied the concert and opera repertoires of Petersburg, Moscow, and Odessa in order to determine when Pushkin might have been exposed to Mozart's music and under what circumstances. See also Shik, *Odesskii Pushkin*; "Ob operakh u raznykh narodov (Okonchanie)," *Vestnik Evropy* 16 (August 1823): 251–70; "Iz Tygodnika muzycznego," *Vestnik Evropy* 16 (August 1823): 129–30; and Vol'f's extraordinarily informative *Khronika Peterburgskikh teatrov s kontsa 1826 do nachala 1855 goda*, chap. 1.

17. Greenberg, *Subjectivity and Subjection*.

18. Ardens, *Dramaturgiia i teatr*, 198.

19. Ibid., 202.

20. The direct stimulus is usually considered to be Faddei Bulgarin's (known as "Figliarin") plagiarism of Pushkin's Dmitri Samozvanets theme.

21. See Eiges for a comprehensive catalog of adaptations of Pushkin's works into songs, musicals, and ballets as well as Debreczeny's analysis of popular adaptations for specific societal strata in *Social Functions of Literature*, 79–95, 162–77.

22. Gomolicki, *Dziennik pobytu Adama Mickiewicza w Rosji*. See also Czapska, *Szkice Mickiewiczowskie*.

23. I include Anna Akhmatova's and Robert L. Jackson's classic essays, together with the above-mentioned more recent articles in Nepomniashchii's volume.

24. See Nancy Anderson's theory that Salieri intends to drink a suicidal Bruderschaft with Mozart and thus merge amorously with him in death ("Betrayal of a Calling: *Mozart and Salieri*," in Pushkin, *The Little Tragedies*, 131–55).

25. Freud, "Dostoevsky and Parricide."

Moral-Philosophical Subtext in *The Stone Guest*

Robert Louis Jackson

Who is it that can tell me who I am?
—King Lear

A Question of Identity

"The beginning is always decisive," German novelist Theodor Fontane observed well over a hundred years ago. "If one hits it off right, then what follows succeeds through a kind of inner necessity."[1] One may add that that necessity very often carries with it the gist of the artistic matter. That is eminently so in the case of the beginning of *The Stone Guest* (*Kamennyi gost'*), one where Pushkin projects a major concern of his play: the question of Don Juan's identity.

The four opening lines of *The Stone Guest*, in contrast to the opening lines of Pushkin's *Mozart and Salieri*, seem disappointingly plain. But plainness in Pushkin always masks complexity. Nothing in Pushkin ever disappoints. He had the uncanny art of making simple words, speeches, gestures, and actions laden with meanings and resonances inside and outside the text. The opening lines of *The Stone Guest* are remarkable in the way they intimate in their camouflaged way the tragic direction of the action and a basic issue of the play. On the surface the lines introduce a tale and hero as familiar to the audience as was the story of Oedipus to the ancient Greeks.

Let's wait for night here. Ah, finally
We've reached the gates of Madrid! Soon
I'll fly through familiar streets,

My moustache covered with a cloak, my brows with a hat.
What do you think? Could I ever be recognized?[2]

Дождемся ночи здесь. Ах, наконец
Достигли мы ворот Мадрита! скоро
Я полечу по улицам знакомым,
Усы плащом закрыв, а брови шляпой.
Как думаешь? Узнать меня нельзя?

The ineluctable fate of Don Juan, the dark fatality of the play's action, is prefigured in the words "night," "finally," "gates," "soon" (*noch',* *nakonets, vorot, skoro*). The first two lines subtly foreshadow the fate of Don Juan at the gates of hell, suggesting, too, that he is "flying" toward that fate, that is, freely accepting and motivating his own fatality; this fact is made explicit in his last words at the end of the play: "I called you, and I am glad to see you" [Ia zval tebia i rad, chto vizhu]. The last two phrases of the opening lines signal with equal subtlety Pushkin's conscious and unconventional quest in his Don Juan play: the deconstruction of the standard or popular image of Don Juan and its replacement with a morally and psychologically complex figure.

Don Juan, attired in cape and hat that half-masks his face yet at the same time flaunting his conventional signature identity; this familiar Don Juan, ready to fly along "familiar streets," asks lightheartedly: "What do you think? Could I ever be recognized?" Don Juan here puts the question of the entire play: Who *is* Don Juan? Will the reader "recognize" Pushkin's Don Juan? What is the nature of his identity? Not accidentally do the words "know," "recognize" (*znat',* *uznat',* *priznat'*) recur in the text.

To the popular audience, the dashing cavalier that appears at the beginning of *The Stone Guest* is as recognizable as the "familiar streets" through which he flies. But the question of Don Juan's identity is put, almost mockingly, to the audience: "What do you think? Could I ever be recognized?" The answer will come, slowly but surely, in the course of the play. The audience will ultimately be confronted with a Don Juan who defies conventional romantic or preromantic monological labeling; they will find a man, like Odysseus, of many turns, a man of complex and elusive identity, a polyphonic and ultimately tragic Don Juan. The image that Pushkin creates for his reader is that of a man who specializes in masks but who, at the last moment, is unable or unwilling to put on a new disguise, unless it be his own face.

This man of many faces is not apparent to the good-hearted but limited Leporello, a person who in fact stands closest to the audience in his monological perception of Don Juan. Leporello takes the mask or myth for the man; loyal to the traditional two-dimensional image of Don Juan, he is certain that his master will be easily recognized. With irony Leporello replies to Don Juan's question, "Could I ever be recognized?"

> Oh yes! It's hard to recognize Don Juan!
> There's a mass of people like him!
>
> Да! Дон Гуана мудрено признать!
> Таких, как он, такая бездна!

Don Juan, carefree but reluctant to be tagged, retorts:

> You're joking?
> Now who will recognize me?
>
> Шутишь?
> Да кто ж меня узнает?

Leporello proceeds to name the people who will recognize him:

> The first watchman,
> Gypsy, or drunken musician,
> Or one of your own kind, some insolent knight
> In a cape with sword under arm.
>
> Первый сторож,
> Гитана или пьяный музыкант,
> Иль свой же брат, нахальный кавалер,
> Со шпагою под мышкой и в плаще.

Leporello's Don Juan is the cliché, the familiar Don Juan, the stock image that will be recognized by people of his class or by people who share similar traits with him. Yielding to a fatalism that will characterize him throughout the play, Don Juan gives up the argument with the remark: "Well, what matter, what if I'm recognized" [Chto za beda, khot' i uznaiut]. Pushkin, however, does not give up the matter. He has just begun his play, one in which a complex Don Juan will defy the expectations of the audience and, indeed, if we are to believe Don Juan's final revelations to Dona Anna, perhaps Don Juan's own image of himself.

Don Juan's encounters with Dona Anna in scenes 3 and 4 witness a dramatic process of unmasking. Confronted by Dona Anna's persistent questioning, he declares at last: "I am Don Juan [and] I killed your husband"; "I am Don Juan and I love you" [Ia Don Guan (. . .) Ia ubil supruga tvoego; Ia Don Juan, i ia tebia liubliu]. Don Juan's strange, seemingly reluctant, yet inwardly driven unmasking of himself leads Dona Anna to respond with amazement: "So this is Don Juan . . ." [Tak eto Don Guan...]. Yet even *this* "Don Juan," the supposedly rock-bottom one, does not strike the reader as the ultimate Don Juan. The removal of one mask after another leaves a gallery of masks. The reader is left to wonder, Is the Don Juan who declares, "I am Don Juan," just one more mask, or is he the sum of all the masks that he has worn?

The image Don Juan seeks to present to Dona Anna in the final moment of their encounter before the appearance of the knight-commander is that of a man reborn to virtue and humility. Yet even in confession, Don Juan has difficulty (one might say a constitutional one) in expressing, indeed, in feeling, a direct sense of guilt or remorse for his actions. At first he flatly and defiantly declares to Dona Anna that he has killed her husband, that he "doesn't regret it," and that "there's no repentance" in him ("Ia ubil / Supruga tvoego i ne zhaleiu / O tom—i net raskaian'ia vo mne"). Yet in response to Dona Anna's "So this is Don Juan . . ." he is driven to a strange, even hobbled confession, one in which he speaks of himself, as it were, at a remove:

> True, is it not, *he's been described to you*
> A villain, a monster.—O Dona Anna,
> Rumor, *perhaps*, is not quite mistaken,
> On my tired conscience much evil
> Weighs, perhaps. Thus for long I have been
> An earnest student of debauchery. [Emphasis mine]

> [Не правда ли, он был описан вам
> Злодеем, извергом.—О Дона Анна,—

Молва, быть может, не совсем неправа,
На совести усталой много зла,
Быть может, тяготеет. Так, разврата
Я долго был покорный ученик.]

Don Juan is certain only of his earnest attention to "debauchery." Not without reason does the reader (to say nothing of Dona Anna) react with a certain suspicion to the affirmation of rebirth that follows Don Juan's reference to his "tired conscience":

But from the time I first saw you,
It *seems to me* that I have been completely reborn.
Loving you, I love virtue
And for the first time humbly
Bend my trembling knees before it. [Emphasis mine]

[Но с той поры, как вас увидел я,
Мне кажется, я весь переродился.
Вас полюбя, люблю я добродетель
И в первый раз смиренно перед ней
Дрожащие колена преклоняю.]

Don Juan is at least consistent in indicating, most surely naively, the fact that he relates to issues of good and evil in a very vague way. His conscience, it would seem, is "tired" not so much through stress as inactivity.

Does Don Juan really have knowledge of himself when he speaks of being reborn? Is there a perceptive shift toward "virtue" in him? Or does it just *seem* so to him? Is not the supposedly unmasked face he turns to Dona Anna in these last moments even more of a mask than his other disguises? Everything in Don Juan's moral nature at this last moment is in the realm of "perhaps," a realm of flux. What is certain is that his sensitivity to moral problems at this point is not above that of the child-adult (in this Don Juan is emblematic, like Dostoevsky's Dmitry Karamazov, of the broad human condition) struggling with the names or notions of "good" and "evil," awkwardly trying to relate them to the confused reality of his own inner feelings and strivings. The concept of a "tired conscience" best describes the deepest stratum of his moral personality at this fatal turning point in his life.

The near-final image we have of Don Juan as he confronts the "stone guest," the statue of the knight-commander, whom he has summoned, is that of an untrembling and unrepentant figure boldly and gladly accepting his fate. Yet even this picture of a defiant Don Juan is not the final picture of Don Juan that Pushkin leaves us.

"Who knows you?" [Kto znaet vas?], that is, who can make you out, Dona Anna wonders. Her "Who knows you?" is, of course, the obverse side of Don Juan's "It seems to me." Don Juan does not fully know himself, and Dona Anna, like the reader, is baffled by appearances. In any case, the figurative meaning of "Who knows you?" masks the practical question of recognition, for Dona Anna accompanies her words, "Who knows you?" with an obvious concern that Don Juan, in coming to her, risks being recognized:

> But how could you come here.
> You could be recognized,
> And your death would be inevitable.
>
> [Но как могли прийти
> Сюда вы; здесь узнать могли бы вас,
> И ваша смерть была бы неизбежна.]

With this practical question we have come full circle to the beginning of the play, where the literal question of Don Juan's recognition, and of his safety in Madrid, masks the figurative question of his identity: will anybody recognize the real, complex, enigmatic Don Juan? The implications of being recognized are spelled out in Dona Anna's concern that recognition of Don Juan would lead ineluctably to his death.

Death, however, will come not from the king of Spain but from the statue of the knight-commander, from the implacable stone guest, an embodiment of a fate that Don Juan has been inviting from the opening lines of the play: "I have come at your call," says the commander. "I called you, and I am glad to see you," replies Don Juan.

Don Juan's question at the opening of the play, "Could I ever be recognized?" has now become moot. He has long discarded the familiar cape and disguise that popularly define him and that are the signs of carefree erotic triumphs. He has made himself vulnerable and disclosed his complexity. He recognizes both his fatality and his free choice of that fatality. All that remains, it would seem, is a proud confrontation with death. Yet here, too, Don Juan defies expectations.

Don Juan's behavior in the last act and in his last moments casts his fate in a tragic light. To the knight-commander's peremptory "Give me your hand" [Dai ruku], Juan answers, "Here it is . . ." [Vot ona...]. Pushkin's suspension points suggest hesitation on the part of Don Juan. *Ona* ("it" when the Russian noun is of the feminine gender but also "she") refers to Don Juan's hand, but it might also refer to the commander's hand, the death-bearing "right hand" (*desnitsa*) of retribution: "Here it is . . . oh, it's heavy / The grip of his stony hand!" [Vot ona... o, tiazhelo / Pozhat'e kamennoi ego desnitsy!], that is, the hand of death.

The same kind of ambiguity a few moments earlier in the text characterizes Dona Anna's "Here it is" [Vot on] when Don Juan begs a kiss. *On* ("it" when the Russian noun is of masculine gender but also "he") refers to the kiss—a masculine noun in Russian—Dona Anna gives Don Juan. "Vot on" may also refer, however, to the arrival of the knight-commander, the "stone guest" whose knocking is heard simultaneously with Don Juan's kiss; thus, "Here he is."

In remarkable play with the simplest elements of the Russian language and with the simplest gestures, Pushkin accents at the end of his play the complex and dramatic linkages of love and death in the relationship of Don Juan and Dona Anna.

The phrase "Vot ona" (that is, "Here it is," here is my hand) might also refer in the subtext to the presence of Dona Anna, who, at the appearance of the commander, "falls" (*padaet*). Thus, along with "Here it is" (Don Juan's hand or the right hand of the knight-commander), the same Russian phrase might also read "Here she is" [Vot ona], that is, here is Anna lying on the ground. Such an association between *ona* (she, it) and "Anna" is strengthened by the fact that *ona* and "Anna" are similar-sounding words in Russian, differentiated orally only by differences in stress.

Don Juan's "Vot ona" at the end of the play echoes his use of this phrase at the *beginning* of scene 3. Immediately after his evasive but still hubristic description of how he killed Dona Anna's husband, Don Juan sees Dona Anna and remarks: "Ah! Here she is" [A! vot ona]. At this point, Pushkin notes: "Dona Anna enters." When one considers the intimate associations in the play between Dona Anna and death, one may say that Don Juan, seeing Dona Anna for the first time immediately after having described his murder of Dona Anna's husband, sees not merely the woman who will arouse a storm of passion in him but his nemesis, that is, "death"—but without recognizing it.

The allusion to Anna at the end of the play ("Vot ona") suggests Don Juan's human concern for Dona Anna. Thus, "Vot ona"—"Here it is" or "Here she is"—preludes both approaching death (the death-bearing hand) and Don Juan's despairing invocation of Anna's name at the end of the play: "O Dona Anna!"—last words that now, poignantly and unambiguously, attest to his attachment not so much to himself as to Dona Anna.

The movement, then, in the development or disclosure of Don Juan's character is bracketed by two signposts, one at the beginning of scene 3 and the other at the end of scene 4: "Vot ona," "Vot ona." Though identical, each pair of words testifies to very different attitudes toward Dona Anna: in the first instance Don Juan sees Anna as an object, in the second case as a subject, a shift that hints at a change of consciousness in Don Juan—at least "momentarily." But the moment of change is the moment of death. Death puts an end to the individual's ever-present freedom, a freedom that in Don Juan's case has been systematically abused. It is death, and only death, that makes it possible to invoke the ancient Heraclitian law that "a man's character is his fate."

Actions have consequences, Tolstoy observed in connection with his novel *Anna Karenina.* Pushkin's *Stone Guest* is about many things, but it is also about consequences. Don Juan invites the knight-commander to his tryst with Dona Anna. However, his resoluteness, his almost buoyant defiance of a moment earlier—"I called you, and I am glad to see you"—deserts him. His final appeal to the "stone guest"—"Leave me alone, let go, let go my hand" [Ostav' menia, pusti—pusti mne ruku...]—and his last words—"I'm perishing—it's the end—O Dona Anna" [Ja gibnu—koncheno—O, Dona Anna!]—no longer reflect a resolute acceptance of fate.

Don Juan's last words, however, reflect not repentance but regret and concern for Dona Anna. As such, they also undercut any last attempt on the part of the reader to reset the portrait of Don Juan in any of the old conventional moral-didactic frames. Pushkin is never the prescriptive moralist; he is a writer, in this case, a tragedian. The final image we have of the doomed Don Juan is that of a man liberated from literary convention; though a transgressor of higher law (on this point Pushkin remains firm), his Don Juan is far from a mere deceiver or villain.[3] He is psychologically complex, multidimensional; he is strangely appealing; at the same time, he is enigmatic and disturbing in the way anarchy combines in him with a beguiling aspect of innocence. Don Juan is, ultimately, a tragic figure.

The play's conclusion, one that presents Don Juan disappearing or descending (*provalivaiutsia*) into some netherworld, brings the reader back to the opening lines of the play: "Let's wait for night here. Ah, finally / We've reached the gates." These lines, as we have suggested, signify the fact of Don Juan's arrival, "finally," at the gates of Madrid; they also anticipate his final arrival at the gates of hell.

A Question of Higher Law

> Alas! My God! he said, I have killed my old master, my friend, my brother-in-law. I am the best man in the world, and just look, I have already killed three men; and of these three, two were priests. [Hélas! Mon Dieu! dit-il, j'ai tué mon ancien maître, mon ami, mon beau frère; je suis le meilleur homme du monde, et voilà, déja trois hommes que je tue; et dans des trois il y a deux prêtres.]
>
> Voltaire, *Candide ou l'optimisme*, 15: 179

Scene 3 of *The Stone Guest* opens with a brief monologue by Don Juan. As the Russian scholar Dmitrii D. Blagoi observed, the monologues in Pushkin's *Little Tragedies* serve the function of psychological self-disclosure. With respect to Don Juan's monologue, however, Blagoi maintains that it has "not so much a psychological as an informational character, leading [us] on into the subsequent course of action."[4] I argue to the contrary that whatever its informational function this monologue, indeed, its opening phrase, goes to the heart of Don Juan's complicated psychology and raises the fundamental moral-philosophical issues that underlie Pushkin's whole play. These issues involve, finally, Pushkin's complex response to the Renaissance and the Enlightenment.

"All's for the best; having accidentally killed Don Carlos" [Vse k luchshemu: nechaianno ubiv Don Karlosa] are Don Juan's opening words in his brief monologue. The accidental, unintentional, unexpected killing of Don Carlos (this is Don Juan's view of the matter) has annoying consequences: Don Juan is obliged to mask himself as a hermit in a monastery.

However, there are compensations: he is now in a position to cast his eyes on the charming Dona Anna. In short, "All's for the best."

The phrase "All's for the best" resonates with meaning. It recalls the social-philosophical, indeed, cosmological, euphoria of the early-eighteenth-century Enlightenment, Voltaire's lethal counterattack in *Candide ou l'optimisme* (1759), and the unforgettable Dr. Pangloss, who in the face of every misfortune insists that "all's for the best" [tout est au mieux] "in this best of all possible worlds" [dans le meilleurs des mondes possibles].[5]

Voltaire is satirizing Leibnitz's philosophy as distilled in Christian Wolff and others, one that posits a divinely preestablished harmony in which everything has its place and purpose, and everything is directed toward a beneficent end. Moral evil and suffering ultimately dissolve in the universal harmony. "But Pangloss consoled them by the assurance that things could not be otherwise than they are; for, said he, all this must necessarily be for the best. As this volcano is at Lisbon, it could not be elsewhere; as it is impossible that things should not be what they are; as all is good."[6] Optimism here is but the obverse side of fatalism: "All Chance, Direction which thou canst not see," as Pope put it in his *Essay on Man.*

With fatalism, of course, goes the rejection of the notion of responsibility or accountability. Such a fantastic and shallow outlook is quite congenial to Pushkin's Don Juan: this buoyant and blithe gallant, this happy libertine, this childlike lover who appears to live beyond good and evil. But is this outlook Pushkin's? Pushkin's approach to the question of responsibility lies at the center of his "little tragedies."

"All's for the best; having accidentally killed": Don Juan's evasion of the question of responsibility is implied in the juxtaposition of these two phrases. The problem of responsibility dissipates in the realm of a larger beneficent purpose. Juan's monologue closes as it opens: with a characteristic evasion of the question of responsibility.

> When hard by the Escurial we met,
> He stumbled upon my sword and expired.
> Just like a dragonfly upon a pin.

> [Когда за Эскурьялом мы сошлись,
> Наткнулся мне на шпагу он и замер,
> Как на булавке стрекоза.]

Don Juan does not consider himself responsible for killing Dona Anna's husband; rather, he views his opponent as at fault for stumbling upon his, Juan's, sword! Juan further distances himself from the moral significance of his act by comparing his opponent to an insect.

The theme of arbitrary self-will (*volia*) is raised obliquely at the play's beginning in Leporello's reference to Don Juan's decision to return to Madrid. "Don Juan has returned from exile and turned up in Madrid on his own authority" [Don Guan iz ssylki samovol'no v Madride iavilsia].

Don Juan's hubris—his declaration of moral independence—echoes again in the subtext of Leporello's answer to the monk's question: "Who are you? The servants of Dona Anna?" [Kto zdes'? ne liudi l' Dony Anny?]. "No, we are our own masters, / We are out for a stroll" [Net, sami po sebe my gospoda, / My zdes' guliaem]. Yet as Pushkin demonstrates in his play, no man is master in this world, and life is not a stroll.

Scene 2 is decisive in establishing the moral-philosophical context of Don Juan's strange psychology. The theme of guilt and responsibility is introduced at first, indirectly, by Laura, a character who in large measure shares the optimistic and carefree nature of Juan but who nonetheless is not oblivious of moral questions. When Don Carlos objects to Laura's uttering the name of Don Juan, she retorts: "Am I to blame if every moment / That man's name is on my tongue?" [A vinovata l' ia, chto pominutno, / Mne na iazyk prikhodit eto imia?]. What is spontaneous, happenstance, unpremeditated, Laura seems to suggest, is not subject to moral accountability or censure. This outlook is implicit in Don Juan's behavior and actions.

The theme of the accidental, the unintentional, the unexpected is a major one in scene 2. When Don Juan arrives in Laura's apartment he finds Don Carlos there and exclaims: "What an unexpected meeting! / Tomorrow I'm at your service" [Vot nechaiannaia vstrecha! / Ia zavtra ves' k tvoim uslugam]. But the encounter and its consequences can be viewed only partly as unexpected or accidental. Don Juan, on setting forth to Laura's house unannounced, remarks: "I'll go straight in the door—and if somebody's with her, / I'll suggest that he jump out the window" [K nei priamo v dver'—a esli kto-nibud' / U nee—proshu v okno prygnut']. Don Juan comes looking for trouble. Characteristically, after killing Don Carlos, he puts all the blame for the event on the Spanish grandee: "What's to be done? / He asked for it himself" [Chto delat'? / On sam togo khotel]. "And it is difficult to come up with any rebuttal to this [fact]," Blagoi remarks at this point in his analysis of *The Stone Guest.*[7] The matter is not at all that simple, however. There is much to object to in Don Juan's remark, "He asked for it himself." We have here a typical attempt on his part to sidestep any personal responsibility for killing Don Carlos.[8]

Laura grasps the issue more subtly than does Blagoi. To Juan's "he asked for it himself," she replies with irony:

> Ah, Don Juan,
> It's really most vexing. Your eternal tricks—
> And yet you're never to blame . . . Where have you come from now?
> Have you been here for long?
>
> [Эх, Дон Гуан,
> Досадно, право. Вечные проказы—
> А все не виноват . . . Откуда ты?
> Давно ли здесь?]

Laura's words go to the heart of the problem of the capricious child-adult, Don Juan: eternal tricks, pranks, spontaneous actions, gambling with love and death—and yet never guilty! Laura brings to the foreground Don Juan's unexpressed assumptions: chance is supposedly at fault. Yet the childish prank committed by an adult is often a stepping outside of law and limits. One may recall, too, in this connection that "tricks" (*prokazy*) are usually mischievous, even malicious. Of significance here is that the Russian word for trick (*prokaza*) also means leprosy.

We, too, may ask Don Juan, as Laura does, Where have you come from now? Have you been here for long? That is, from what world or realm comes this man who places himself consciously or unconsciously above all accountability and law? Does Don Juan, variously called "devil," "a real demon," arrive with his "eternal tricks" like some fallen angel from exile? "I've just arrived, / And on the sly—for I've really not been pardoned" [Ia tol'ko chto priekhal / I to tikhon'ko—ia ved' ne proshchen]. Precisely. Neither king nor God has pardoned this charming but devilish Juan.

Laura's remarks inadvertently bring out the moral dimension of Juan's tricks. She quickly drops the matter but in a manner that recalls Juan's "All's for the best." She goes on:

And you immediately remembered your Laura?
Well and good. But come now,
I don't believe [it]. You were passing by accidentally
And saw the house.

[И вспомнил тотчас о своей Лауре?
Что хорошо, то хорошо. Да полно,
Не верю я. Ты мимо шел случайно
И дом увидел.]

"Chto khorosho, to khorosho," "Well and good," literally, "What's good is good." In other words, whatever happened, the end is good. What is good for us, what brings pleasure, however, is not always ethically good. In the hierarchy of things good, aesthetic good does not take precedence over ethical good. "What's good is good" does not address the issue of the corpse on the floor, of murder, although in Dr. Pangloss's philosophy "it is demonstrable that things cannot be otherwise than they are, for all things having been made for some end, everything must necessarily be for the best end."[9] Not in Pushkin's view, however. Indeed, in his play the notion that "all is good" [tout est bien], "all's for the best" [tout est au mieux], or that man is what he is and ought to be is not the end of the matter but the beginning of the problem.

In Pushkin's dynamic subtext, Laura's "I don't believe [it]" tells us more than the fact that she doesn't believe Don Juan intentionally came to see her. In moral-religious terms neither Laura nor Don Juan believes firmly in anything, except themselves; certainly, they do not "believe" in the religious sense of the word. In any case, they do not strongly believe in a world in which one is accountable for one's acts.

Scene 2 ends with a mutual confession of infidelity. Juan asks Laura how many times she has been unfaithful to him. "What about you?" she asks in return. "Tell me . . . No, we'll talk it over later" [Skazhi. . . Net, posle peregovorim], Juan replies as the scene concludes. What Don Juan wants, feels, desires comes first; other matters come later, if at all. In the presence of the dead Don Carlos both Don Juan and Laura make love. Significantly, the words "We'll talk it over later" are immediately followed by the phrase that opens scene 3: "All's for the best." That notion is the underpinning of all of Don Juan's actions and behavior.

Of course, Don Juan is not beyond good and evil, either objectively or subjectively, as the play's conclusion makes clear. Nor is the "improviser of a love song"—one of Don Juan's redeeming disguises—always an improviser. In his monologue at the beginning of scene 3 he wonders how to address Dona Anna but then decides:

> Whatever comes into my head
> That's what I'll say without preparation,
> Like the improviser of a love song.
>
> [Что в голову придет,
> То и скажу, без предуготовленья,
> Импровизатором любовной песни.]

All the ambiguity of Juan's character is present in this remark: he is an improviser by nature, an impromptu musician of love who bends to the winds of chance. Yet the improvisation can also be a calculated one. With Don Juan sincerity and guile go hand in hand: "I'll strike up a conversation with her; it's time" [Vpushchusia v razgovory s nei; pora]. Time for what? Time to entangle, time to seduce, time to love.[10]

"All's for the best," then, is pivotal in the play: it defines Don Juan's underlying amoral outlook; it inaugurates the final movement toward catastrophe in scenes 3 and 4 of *The Stone Guest,* episodes in which Don Juan challenges the statue of the knight-commander and makes his last gamble with love and death, his final and fatal play for unlimited freedom.

It is clear, however, that Pushkin, like E. T. A. Hoffmann in his novella *Don Juan,* breaks decisively with the traditional perception of Don Juan as mere libertine, a cynical and godless bon vivant. Like Hoffmann, Pushkin posits a complex psychology in Don Juan, a person in whom the sensual and spiritual elements are strangely contiguous with one another. But while sharing Hoffmann's deeper perception of Don Juan's nature, Pushkin generally dispenses with the romantic idealization of Juan as (in Hoffmann's words) a superior being hoping to "still through love the [higher] longing that tore at his heart."[11] Pushkin replaces the suggestive but still flimsy romantic and melodramatic paraphernalia with a profound and quite realistic examination of Juan as a complex moral-psychological and cultural type.

What if Dona Anna had been destined by Heaven to let Don Juan recognize the divine nature in him? asks Hoffmann, and he answers, "Too late."[12] But does the tragedy of Pushkin's Don Juan consist in the fact that he was snatched away at the very moment he was reborn, that is, when he was on the threshold of a new life? There is no question that Pushkin's Don Juan *feels* reborn in his encounter with Dona Anna, that he experiences "the value of momentary life" [tsenu mgnovennoi zhizni]—precisely momentary, however. His tragedy is not that he meets a potential savior, Dona Anna (his "angel," his "goddess," his "heavenly beatitude") when it is too late;[13] this puts the matter back into that realm of accident and contingency that is so congenial to Juan. The tragedy of Don Juan is that he *is* Don Juan, that he cannot escape himself. He is forever moving in and out of his multiple disguises and identities; forever gambling, challenging limits, laws, conventions, death itself, in the pursuit of a limitless and chimerical freedom; forever experiencing the deceptive self-renewal of the gambler in his momentary triumphs.

What the English critic D. S. Savage has said of the gambler in Dostoevsky's novel *The Gambler* may be said of Don Juan as well: "The seduction which draws his soul is that of an ultimate irrational and groundless freedom which, containing equally within itself every possibility, is devoid of the power to actualize any of these possibilities and can give birth only to an ineluctable necessity."[14] Challenging the ultimate necessity, death, Don Juan brings death to himself; positing a fatalistic universe ("all's for the best"), Juan in the end succumbs to fate, to the grip of the "stony right hand" of the knight-commander. Don Juan recognizes that fate had something other in store for him than beatitude: "Fate decreed something else for me" [Sud'ba sulila mne inoe]. But Juan, obsessed with death, "relentlessly courting his own death,"[15] has freely brought about that fate through his own actions. His tragedy is that he cannot escape his nature. That nature has much that redeems it. Yet the very elements that redeem it condemn it to immaturity and, ultimately, to a tragic end.

The ideal of a life without constraints or limits is emotional and moral utopia: the womb, the paradise of the child, the happy world of the playground. Here, indeed, is the "best of all possible worlds," a world seemingly without beginning or end, outside of time, and free, at least ideally, of any perception of causality or consequences. Noteworthy in this connection is Don Juan's response to Dona Anna's willingness to meet with him again: "I am happy! . . . [. . .] I am happy as a child! [. . .] I am happy! / I am ready to sing, I am ready joyfully to embrace the whole world" [Ia schastliv!.. (. . .) Ia schastliv, kak rebenok! (. . .) Ia schastliv / Ia pet' gotov, ia rad ves' mir obniat']. The child-lover Don Juan is ready to embrace Dona Anna as he would embrace the world. Yet Juan's childlike happiness is a regressive and impossible dream; it can never be realized in lasting love; or, if realized momentarily in passive childlike adoration and reverence, it will be quickly replaced by the old restless and domineering quest for new conquests and stronger satisfactions.

Yet for all the regressive elements that mark Don Juan's passion for Dona Anna, one cannot deny the intensity of his feelings for her in the last scene of the play, that is, in that last encounter when his passion for Dona Anna, one that is manifestly physical as well as platonic, leads him to confession. Pushkin calls into question not so much Don Juan's feelings of the moment, however, but the permanence of the change he experiences within him.

Dona Anna is the apotheosis of Don Juan's quest, one in which love and death are intertwined. "Well? What? What do you want?" Dona Anna asks Don Juan early in their acquaintance. "Death," he replies. "Oh, let me die at your feet" [Nu? Chto? Chego vy trebuete? / Smerti. / O pust' umru seichas u vashikh nog]. Don Juan utters a romantic cliché, yet it gives expression to a nature that finds congenial the contiguity of love and death. If we are to speak of a permanent change in Don Juan's inner life, then it is only in the sense of the phrase *death and transfiguration.* The dynamics of Don Juan's nature allow for no other denouement. Don Juan's change can only be anchored in death: here is his final metamorphosis; here is where the true unmasking of Don Juan takes place.

"Poor Inéz," Don Juan remarks in scene 1 of a woman who in her "strange" beauty, her contiguity with death, anticipates Dona Anna. "Well, there were others after her," says Leporello. "That's the truth," replies Don Juan. "And if we go on living, there will be others," remarks Leporello. "That too," Juan replies. Don Juan's "truth" here is not only bravado; it is, in Pushkin's conception, an intuition of his own true nature. "If we go on living." Pushkin's own attitude toward Don Juan is ambivalent. He is drawn to the "improviser of love," the charming, direct, ebullient man of the Renaissance, the life-loving rebel who stands up against the stony, life-destroying prescription morality of the Middle Ages; the adult-child whose god is freedom and who recognizes no laws except those of his own nature. Yet precisely here the other side of Pushkin's Don Juan emerges: the man of the Enlightenment, the confused child of nature who took the philosophes at their word when they made a cult of Nature; the gambler who stakes his own life upon chance and therefore has no qualms about sacrificing others; the man for whom life is a series of chance encounters and "eternal tricks"; the hero for whom chance is fate.

On the narrative historical plane of Pushkin's play, Don Juan is a man of the Renaissance; but he is also a hero of his time, a product of the Enlightenment in his moral-philosophical make-up. Pushkin's attitude, as tragedian, toward Don Juan is one of fascination and apprehension, affection and gloom. His Don Juan is in part a joyous and liberating answer to a restrictive and constrictive past; like the Enlightenment, however, Juan embodies the confused answers of the age to the questions raised; he is unable to distinguish between the demands of liberated individual consciousness and those of the community, between the legitimate rights of personality and the demands of morality. Pushkin's *Stone Guest* was an attempt to maintain a middle ground while at the same time a recognition that for the Don Juans no such middle ground existed.

Pushkin's complex attitude toward his Don Juan might be summed up in two lines of Dona Anna at the end of the tragedy, lines that embody affection and understanding and, at the same time, a recognition of ineluctable necessity. Responding to Juan's astonished question, "So there's no hatred in your heavenly soul, Dona Anna?" Dona Anna responds: "Ah, would that I could hate you! / Nonetheless, we must part" [Akh, esli by vas mogla ia nenavidet' / Odnako zhe nabodno rasstat'sia nam].

Notes

1. "Der Anfang ist immer das Entscheidende. Hat man's darin gut getroffen, so muss der Rest mit einer Art von innerer Notwendigkeit gelingen." See Fontane, *Briefe*, 3: 190, letter of 6 March 1879 to Matthilde von Rehr.

2. All translations of *The Stone Guest* are mine.

3. Of relevance here is Pushkin's remark in a letter to Prince P. A. Vyazemsky about the crowd's attitude toward Byron: "It is delighted at the discovery of any

kind of nastiness. *He is petty, as we are, he is nasty, as we are!* You lie, scoundrels. He is both petty and nasty—not like you,—but in a different way!" (Bogoslovsky, ed., *Pushkin o literature,* 85).

4. Blagoi, *Tvorcheskii put' Pushkina* (1967), 648.

5. Voltaire, *Candide,* 1: 146.

6. "[M]ais Pangloss les consola, en les assurant que les choses ne pouvaient être autrement; car, dit-il, tout ceci est ce qu'il y a de mieux; car, s'il y a un volcan à Lisbonne, il ne pouvait être ailleurs; car il est impossible que les choses ne soient pas où elles sont; car tout est bien" (ibid., 5: 157).

7. Blagoi, *Tvorcheskii put' Pushkina* (1967), 647.

8. Another typical instance of Don Juan's moral evasiveness is his response toward the end of scene 4 to Dona Anna's question: "How many poor girls did you ruin?" Don Juan replies: "I did not love a single one of them till now"—as though not loving these girls justified his ruining their lives!

9. "Il est démontré, disait il, que les choses ne peuvent être autrement; car, tout étant fait pour une fin, tout est nécessairement pour la meilleure fin" (Voltaire, *Candide,* 1: 146).

10. In his psychological make-up Pushkin's Don Juan anticipates elements in Lermontov's Pechorin in *Geroi nashego vremeni* (A hero of our time).

11. "Here on earth there is really nothing that so elevates man in his innermost nature as love. [. . .] Little wonder, then, that Don Juan hoped to still through love the [higher] longing that tore at his heart and that the devil here flung the noose around his neck" [Es gibt hier auf Erden wohl nichts, was den Menschen in seiner innigsten Natur so hinaufsteigert, als die Liebe. (. . .) Was Wunder also, daß Don Juan in der Liebe die Sehnsucht, die seine Brust zerreißt, zu stillen hoffte, und daß der Teufel hier ihm die Schlinge über den Hals warf?] (Hoffman, "Don Juan," 75).

12. Ibid., 77.

13. The Russian poet Anna Akhmatova held this view. She writes: "Don Juan's last exclamation [. . .] 'I'm perishing—it's the end—Oh, Dona Anna' convinces us that he really has been reborn at the time of his meeting with Dona Anna; the whole tragedy consists in the fact that at this moment he loves and is happy, but instead of salvation that is within an arm's reach he is struck down [*gibel' prishla*]" ("*Kamennyi gost'* Pushkina," 190).

14. See Savage, "The Idea of *The Gambler,*" 120.

15. See Monter, "Love and Death," 210.

Literary Connections—Before and After

"A Higher Audacity"

How to Read Pushkin's Dialogue with Shakespeare in *The Stone Guest*

David M. Bethea

The literary historian and poet Stepan Shevyrev was the first to identify what is doubtless a resonant intertextual echo of Shakespeare in Pushkin's *The Stone Guest.* Writing in the *Moskvitianin* in 1841, Shevyrev stated:

> The scenes with Don Juan and Dona Anna strongly recall the scene in *Richard III* with Gloucester (Richard III) and Lady Anne, the widow of Edward, Prince of Wales, right down to the detail of the dagger that Don Juan, like Gloucester, uses as a clever means for the coup de grace [*dlia doversheniia pobedy*]. The situation is precisely the same. It is not surprising that Pushkin, without imitating, without prodding his memory, coincided inadvertently [*soshelsia nechaianno*] in several traits with the world's leading dramatic genius.[1]

Since Shevyrev, a number of prominent Pushkinists, among them M. P. Alekseev, Iu. D. Levin, and, most recently, L. S. Ospovat have commented on the plot similarities between Juan's wooing of Dona Anna and the dizzyingly rapid turn of events in act 1, scene 2 of Shakespeare's play.[2] As for the differences within the parallelisms, that is, how Pushkin presumably used Shakespeare in order to distinguish himself from him and to say something new about his erotically charged encounter, both Levin and Ospovat offer insightful points of reference. First Levin:

> But, while in large part following Shakespeare, Pushkin altered the situation, intensifying its psychological verisimilitude. The scene in *Richard III*, though very effective in a dramatic sense, is deprived of psychological plausibility. [. . .] In Pushkin the seduction takes place gradually, in two scenes; what is more, Don Juan reveals his true name only at the end, when Dona Anna is already, in effect, won over by him. On the other hand, Richard the seducer, in the process of realizing his selfish ends, remains an evil-doer and hypocrite over the course of the entire scene—his influence on Lady Anne is one-sided. Don Juan, in the act of seducing Dona Anna, falls in love himself—the impact of the protagonists on each other is mutual.[3]

Then Ospovat: "In Shakespeare there is a duel of two powerful natures in which victory is won by the more powerful and perfidious side. In Pushkin there is, in essence, no duel at all: Dona Anna does not try to resist the love-blind [*osleplennyi liubov'iu*] Don Juan but rather goes forth to meet him—surreptitiously, she conquers the man while leaving him to think that he himself is the conqueror."[4]

Given the importance of "Our Father Shakespeare" to Pushkin (11: 66), I would like to probe beyond the essentially plot-based parallelisms asserted by earlier scholars in order to understand more fully what was at stake for the Russian poet, in terms of the psychology of creativity, by invoking act 1, scene 2 of *Richard III.* For to claim that Pushkin "coincided inadvertently" with Shakespeare in several particulars, or that his aim in invoking Shakespeare was to point up his own greater commitment to "plausibility" (*pravdopodobie*), or that Dona Anna is actually the more aggressive voice in this dialogue is, on the face of it, not very convincing. The essence of the intertextual challenge is not to isolate a "reminiscence" (*reministsentsiia*) in the chronologically younger text but to demonstrate why that echo is there and how it continues to generate meaning in dialogue with the older text. In this respect, what joins the erotic duels in Shakespeare and Pushkin seems more than "inadvertent"; what inspired Pushkin at this point to turn to Shakespeare was not "believability" per se, at least not in the sense of a normativity or typicality he felt he could improve on;[5] and what attracts Pushkin's Don Juan to his Dona Anna cannot be sufficiently contained in a description that underscores her "human ordinariness, even her commonplace quality."[6] In other words, in order to understand how Pushkin is conversing with Shakespeare in *The Stone*

Guest we need to know what Anne signifies to Gloucester/Richard and why he feels compelled to woo her in this way, what Dona Anna signifies to Don Juan and why he needs to woo her the way he does, and, most important, what the *differences* between these two acts of seduction could have meant for the Pushkin of the Boldino autumn in the context of the other *Little Tragedies*.

But first, the context of *The Little Tragedies*. As various commentators have pointed out, there is a richly interwoven unity to these four "dramatic sketches" that would have to be borne in mind while making statements about any one of them.[7] To cite only the most obvious parallels, all four works center on the interplay of Eros and Thanatos (perhaps the pivotal concern of the Boldino autumn); they involve a single powerful desire (which is also a desire *for power*) whose excessive expression leads to what, in the Christian worldview, is mortal sin (greed, envy, lust/adultery, despair); they show characters (the Baron, Salieri, Juan, and the Master of Revels) who are very near to experiencing a kind of consummation/climax (the erotic link is always there) but then are thwarted at the last possible moment by a higher authority; they repeat certain themes (retribution from beyond the grave, murder as a deadly sin, poison as inverted love potion, feasting as symposium–cum–death wish) that are then progressively "embodied"—made more and more literal; and they challenge the notion of a *giftedness or good fortune bestowed beforehand* (Albert's claim on his father's estate, Mozart's inborn artistic genius, Don Alvar's prior rights as husband to Dona Anna, the sanctity/gift of life itself) that does not seem "fair" under the circumstances. For our purposes, it is important that the theme of love, so crucial to Pushkin at this turning point in his life, is placed *after* the themes of wealth and art and *before* the theme of life itself; in other words, Pushkin is a "Renaissance man" and a "Shakespearean" in this regard as well, that in these four plays where the embodiment of desire becomes more and more pronounced, the dialogue does not stop at issues of personal aggrandizement (the Baron's gold) or chosenness (Mozart's musical genius) but spreads out into areas of greater and greater interpersonal and, finally, group risk.[8] Juan's ultimate incarnation and self-definition ("Mne kazhetsia, ia ves' pererodilsia") is *through a living other* (Dona Anna)—his essence cannot be captured by itself, as can the Baron's, through his treasure chests, or even Mozart's, through his splendid Requiem. It is little wonder that *The Stone Guest* is the longest of these plays and the one most dependent on dialogue and least dependent on monologue or soliloquy (cf., e.g., the long monologues of the Baron and Salieri). Likewise, but even more so, *A Feast in Time of Plague* is the most impersonal and the most indeterminate of the plays because its point of departure is Wilson's "another's words" [chuzhie slova] and because the notion of personal happiness and "ego gratification" has become so patently absurd in this situation. In these plays too, written at a time when Pushkin couldn't tell whether he or his fiancée would survive the cholera epidemic and be reunited across the quarantines, the author's trajectory recalls the Shakespeare who, in the words of a recent biographer, went to his grave "not knowing, and possibly not caring, whether *Macbeth* or the *Tempest* or *Anthony and Cleopatra* ever achieved the permanence of print."[9] It is not art as self-affirming perfection—what we might call the transcendence of the self through the recorded act of authorship—that Pushkin, perhaps the most technically refined of all poets, is concerned with here.

Which brings us to the role of Shakespeare in *The Little Tragedies* and in Pushkin's "life creation" as he contemplated marriage, turned increasingly from poetry to prose, and entered into the 1830s and his period of maturity. Pushkin made numerous references to Shakespeare in his correspondence and in publicistic articles and notes. Of these references, which make for fascinating reading in their own right, several stand out for the quality of their formulations: drafts of two letters to N. N. Raevskii *fils*, one of 1825, the other of 1829; "Materialy k 'Otryvkam iz pisem, mysliam i zamechaniiam'" (Materials relating to "Excerpts from letters, thoughts, and notes," 1827); "Pis'mo k izdateliu 'Moskovskogo vestnika'" (Letter to the editor of the *Moscow News*, 1828); "Nabroski predisloviia k 'Borisu Godunovu'" (Drafts of the preface to *Boris Godunov*, 1830); "O narodnoi drame i drame 'Marfa Posadnitsa'" (On popular drama and the drama *Martha the Governor/ Posadnitsa*, 1830); and "Table-Talk" (1830s).[10] Perhaps not surprisingly, 1830, the year of the first Boldino autumn, was also a time when Pushkin was returning repeatedly to thoughts of Shakespeare and to the latter's indwelling ways of knowing. *Boris Godunov*, written during the Mikhailovskoe exile, had finally passed the censorship and was due to be published at the end of that year.[11] Add to this the fact that *The Merchant of Venice* has been universally recognized as a key source for *The Covetous Knight* (i.e., Shylock's character has become split between that of the Baron and that of the Jew) and that there appears to be something very Iago-like in the remorseless plotting and deeply offended amour propre of Salieri, and we begin to sense how Shakespeare was a guest, and not at all an inadvertent one, at Pushkin's magnificent autumnal feast.

Pushkin's statements about Shakespeare tell us a great deal about his own view of literary tradition on Russian soil and about how he saw himself in that tradition. What Pushkin perceived in Shakespeare was, above all, a verbal daring, a willingness to break the rules of polite or civilized (read: French) discourse, beginning with the unities of neoclassical drama, in the name of a higher form of creativity and closeness to the life source. Pushkin also sensed this daring in Derzhavin, but perhaps because Derzhavin was his (Pushkin's) own chief precursor and because Derzhavin's very Russian, very un-Gallic excesses were better known to him,[12] it fell to Pushkin to become "Russia's Shakespeare," as Mickiewicz, Baratynskii, and others intimated was his role.[13] If Pushkin could praise Derzhavin for the vividness of his imagery—say, the diamond-studded mountain turned upside-down and falling from its heights that opens "Vodopad" (The waterfall, 1791–94; Pushkin 11: 60)—then he could just as easily, if the forum permitted it,[14] criticize the older poet for lacking "style or harmony" and for not knowing the "rules of versification."[15] "Here is what is in him [Derzhavin]," wrote Pushkin in a letter to Del'vig, "*thoughts, pictures, and movements which are truly poetic*; in reading him you seem to be reading a bad, free translation of some marvelous original. By God, his genius thought in Tatar—and he did not know the Russian ABC's from lack of leisure."[16] Why was this so, why was Pushkin more demanding of Derzhavin, less willing to admit his breaking of the "rules" (the Russian ABC's)? Because Derzhavin belonged to *his* tradition, the one in which he was trying to establish himself as the central figure, while Shakespeare was an "other" he could never completely master linguistically and thus could more freely "project upon." Or, to put it another way, the universality, the ability to transcend his "Englishness," that was Shakespeare's was not, in Pushkin's opinion, Derzhavin's. In this same essay , for example, Pushkin singles out those authors whose "bold locutions [...] powerfully and uncommonly convey to us a clear thought and poetic pictures" (11: 60–61); not fortuitously, Derzhavin heads the list of native writers, while Shakespeare heads the list of foreign ones. "There is," says Pushkin, "a higher audacity, an audacity of invention, creativity [*smelost' izobreteniia, sozdaniia*], in which the broad scheme [plan] is subsumed by creative thought." And it is this higher audacity, argues Pushkin further, that the French, too constrained by issues of taste and the rules of individual word usage ("le bon mot"), totally lack.[17] The problem for Pushkin here, of course, especially the Pushkin who is contemplating setting off in new generic directions, is that his roots are much closer to French *bon goût* and restraint than he would like, and he knows it. As he acknowledged to his friend Prince Viazemskii back in December 1823, "I hate to see in our primitive language traces of European affectation and French refinement. Rudeness and simplicity are more becoming to it. I preach from internal conviction, but as is my custom I write otherwise."[18] Now, in 1830, the poet was once again returning, inter alia, to the dramatic form and trying to realize that "higher audacity" that he linked both with the overcoming of his past and with the establishment of a living literary tradition. He was, we might say, trying to practice the "internal conviction" that he preached.

We can sense how much Pushkin saw himself as "Russia's Shakespeare" by the way those close to him, and particularly those whose aesthetic judgments he respected, ascribed that role to him. For example, Baratynskii, responding to news that Pushkin had completed *Boris Godunov*, wrote the following in a letter of December 1825:

> Don't think that I am such a marquis that I can't feel the heights of romantic tragedy! I love Shakespeare's heroes, almost always natural, always engaging, in the genuine attire of their time and with sharply featured countenances. I prefer them to the heroes of Racine; at the same time, I must give the great talent of the French tragedian its due. I will say more: I am almost certain that the French cannot possess a true romantic tragedy. It's not the rules of Aristotle that shackle them—from them [the rules] one can easily be freed—but [the fact that] they are deprived of the most crucial means of success: an elegant popular language. I respect the French classicists; they knew their language, they practiced the kinds of poetry that were characteristic to them, and they produced much that was wonderful. [But] their newest romantic writers are pathetic to me: it seems they have bitten off more than they can chew [*mne kazhetsia, oni sadiatsia v chuzhie sani*].
>
> I'm dying to learn [*zhazhdu imet' poniatie*] about your Godunov. Our marvelous language is capable of everything—I sense this, although I can't myself make this happen [*ne mogu privesti v ispolnenie*]. This

> language is created for Pushkin, as Pushkin is for it. I am certain that your tragedy is filled with moments of extraordinary beauty [*ispolnena krasot neobyknovennykh*]. Go forth, complete what has been begun—you, in whom genius resides. Raise up Russian poetry to that level among the poetic works [literally, "poetries" (*poezii*)] of all peoples, just as Peter the Great raised up Russia among the nations [literally, "powers" (*derzhavy*)]. Complete on your own what he did on his own. Our business will be to stand by in recognition and wonder [*a nashe delo—priznatel'nost' i udivlenie*]. (Pushkin 13: 253)

Here we can see a friend and literary comrade in arms comparing Pushkin to the two giants—Shakespeare as the great master of popular, living language and the *auteur barbare* (La Harpe) most clearly embodying a *civilisation du Nord* (Guizot), and Peter as the great ruler of another "northern" people and the one responsible for leading his rough subjects onto the path of "European" consciousness—who hover at the edges of the poet's mature thinking as competing exemplars and challenges (linguistic versus political power). Baratynskii is challenging his friend to become through poetic words what Peter became through legendary tsarist deeds. That he makes these statements on the very eve of the epoch-defining Decembrist Rebellion could only have appeared foreordained to the letter's superstitious recipient.

The Stone Guest versus *Richard III*: The Meaning of Love

How exactly did the "higher audacity" I cited above manifest itself in Shakespeare or, more accurately, in the Shakespeare Pushkin believed he had discovered and endeavored to internalize? What the example of Shakespeare seems to have given Pushkin was, first and foremost, the *unpredictability* of personality, the ability to step out of a role assigned to a dramatic persona by the "unity of character." "In Molière," writes Pushkin in "Table-Talk," "the Miser is miserly, and that's it. In Shakespeare, [on the other hand,] Shylock is miserly, sharp, vengeful, fond of his children, witty. In Molière the Hypocrite chases after the wife of his benefactor by acting the hypocrite. In Shakespeare [. . .] Angelo is a hypocrite because all his public actions contradict his secret passions! What depth there is in this character!" (12: 160). Hence in Shakespeare Pushkin first came face to face with a humanity capable of remaking itself at any moment, of shedding behavioral codes (stereotypes) imposed by convention, of genuinely *becoming* in a language fully appropriate to a history imagined as open-ended, as once existing in the present. This is where the boldness came in, for such a humanity—regardless of the role it played onstage—had less to lose, since it was by definition closer to the "people" and the raucous spectacle of the "square" (*ploshchad'*) and farther from the "court" with its aristocratic emphasis on "servility" (*podobostrastie*) and a strict rule-centered hierarchy.[19] Moreover, such unpredictability with regard to language and character was especially cherished by Pushkin for the reason that, as we know from his 1830 review of Polevoi's *Istoriia russkogo naroda* (History of the Russian people), the poet associated randomness, "chance"-ness (*sluchainost'*) with a Russian past too dominated by European versions of causality and specifically by *French* romantic historiography (Guizot, Thierry, Barante).[20] In other words, Shakespeare's linguistic consciousness was a happy example of that same unpredictability *as it applied to another people's history* that Pushkin was trying to capture for Russia in his novelistic and historiographic experiments of the 1830s (*The Captain's Daughter*, *The History of Pugachev*).

But let us now turn to *Richard III* and *The Stone Guest.* I begin again by reformulating the parallelisms between the two erotic duels, except now I focus on their internal contrasts, for it is here that Pushkin (consciously or no) *creates meaning.* First, both Gloucester and Juan tell why, either implicitly or explicitly, they are bent on wooing these women. At the same time, the "how," "when," and "to whom" they reveal their motivations are much different. Likewise different is the dramatic conceit underlying each case of disclosure. Gloucester addresses himself to the audience (who chance to "overhear" his private thoughts) in the optical illusion of the soliloquy:

> Was ever woman in this humour wooed?
> Was ever woman in this humour won?
> I'll have her, but I will not keep her long.
> What! I that killed her husband and his father
> To take her in her heart's extremest hate,
> With curses in her mouth, tears in her eyes,
> The bleeding witness of my hatred by,
> Having God, her conscience, and these bars against me,

And I no friends to back my suit at all
But the plain devil and dissembling looks?
And yet to win her! All the world to nothing!
Ha!
(1.2.227–38)

But Juan states his intentions to his servant Leporello *in a dialogue*:

DON JUAN:
I didn't see a thing
Beneath those somber widow's weeds—just glimpsed
A bit of slender ankle as she passed.
LEPORELLO:
Oh, that'll do. Your keen imagination
Will picture you the rest, I have no doubt;
It's defter than a painter's brush, I swear.
And never has it mattered where you start—
With forehead or with foot, it's all the same.
DON JUAN:
O Leporello, you can be assured,
I'll know the lady soon.[21]

More to the point, Juan says this in the play's opening pages, *before* the scenes where he progressively "exposes" himself to Dona Anna, while Gloucester's soliloquy comes at the end of scene 2, *after* he was won over Anne. And it is Leporello, Juan's interlocutor from the "people," and not simply his imagination that eggs him on, arouses him. That Juan is never "alone with himself" the way Gloucester is is crucial. Similarly, the urge that in Shakespeare is premeditated, malicious, and retaliatory ("All the world to nothing!") and that comes into focus only after the fact is in Pushkin purely erotic and spontaneous to begin with (the "narrow heel" whose "chance" sighting draws the *improvisatore* of love into the future and the hope of further embodiment). Or, to rephrase the opposition, Gloucester wants to "take" Anne in "her extremest hate"; Juan wants at some level *to be taken*—to feel the change in the other, from hate to love, that can, somehow, change him. Indeed, the way these two protagonists come at the challenge of winning the beautiful and faithful widow who has every right to hate her tormentor is strikingly different: Gloucester's intent is no more and no less than to vanquish the world through the power and magnetism of his (variously understood) "deformity"; Juan has no other ulterior goal than to sleep with this woman who should be, by all the rules of society and religion, inaccessible. In the one Eros is clearly the tool of power, politics, public display; in the other there is no power on earth greater than Eros itself.

Second, both Gloucester and Juan are referred to repeatedly as *devils* and their female counterparts as *angels*, and one has to assume that these appellations are not mere figures of speech, metaphors *tout court.* In other words, the two heroes begin their wooings from positions *beyond* the laws of God and man. However, it is the righteously indignant Anne who changes in Shakespeare (she of course mistakenly thinks that Gloucester has committed his misdeeds out of love for her), while it is the supposedly damned Juan who changes (or who comes to believe he has changed—"Mne kazhetsia, ia ves' pererodilsia") in Pushkin. That Dona Anna eventually yields to Juan can be viewed either as a lack of fidelity on her part (a betrayal of her dead husband) *or* as a sacrifice of her "angelic" purity for the sake of this "demon" ("Vy sushchii demon") who needs her love in order to be "reborn." But even here there is a way to parse Dona Anna's behavior that stresses her essential difference (as opposed to her "ordinariness"). To repeat, Gloucester's soliloquy comes *after* Anne has been won, revealing all and removing any hint of risk or vulnerability in his prior words of love. Juan, on the other hand, has another dialogue with Leporello in scene 3, immediately after his first extended exchange with Dona Anna but *before* their ultimate meeting, this time in the presence of *the statue that nods.* In other words, Juan goes to his tryst with the wife of the dead husband–cum–statue in a real way knowing the risk, the sense that this is his personified doom coming for him, involved. And such an understanding would have to alter the dynamics of that tryst, making it maximally "open" and dangerous for both sides. In this respect, we could say that it is Anne who fails/"falls" in her reading of Gloucester (she is merely a pawn), but it is Juan who succeeds/"rises" in his reading of Dona Anna (he bets everything on the intercession of this "guardian angel"). The problem is that in Pushkin seduction (carnal love) is experienced simultaneously, *through dialogue,* as potential redemption (spiritual transfiguration) *and* damnation (judgment from beyond). Juan's carnality cannot be separated out from his need to be saved from his prior self and to change. It is not the hero's unworthiness (the story in Shakespeare) but the heroine's transformative beauty (the story in Pushkin) that is the issue. This is one of those indeterminacies typical of the mature Pushkin and often revolving around the theme of superstitious dread and the natural/supernatural opposition, where there is nothing internal to the text to help the critic solve the moral tensions of the situation.

Third, the most striking parallelism between the two seduction sequences is, as Shevyrev originally noted, the hero's presentation to the heroine of a weapon (a sword in Shakespeare, a dagger in Pushkin) by which she is invited to kill the speaker, who simultaneously acknowledges being the killer of her husband (and, in Anne's case, her father-in-law, the king). But this most glaring likeness carries with it an equally glaring difference: in Shakespeare, the revelation comes as no surprise, since Anne knows already with whom she is dealing; in Pushkin, however, this is a genuine revelation—Dona Anna has no idea that this man to whom she is attracted and who has already gone through one transformation in her eyes—from modest "monk" to passionate "Don Diego"—is indeed the diabolical Don Juan until this moment. At the time the respective weapons are unsheathed, the women are invited, or challenged, to kill not enemies per se but enemies changed into men in love. How this argument is smuggled into the two wooing scenes is telling. Gloucester explains that it was Anne's beauty that provoked him to kill ("I did kill King Henry— / But 't was thy beauty that provokéd me" [1.2.179–80]), whereas in Juan's case it is Dona Anna's beauty that, supposedly, saves him from his past:

For all too many years
I've been the most devoted slave of lust;
But ever since the day I saw your face
I've been reborn, returned once more to life.[22]

Thus, the revelation in Shakespeare is the exculpatory "why" of his crimes (they were committed "out of love"), while the revelation in Pushkin is the "who":

I'm not Don Diego . . . I'm Don Juan.
[. . . . . .]
I killed your husband—and regret it not;
I feel no true repentance in my soul.[23]

Juan takes full responsibility for the crimes before his chief victim, and he does so *in the incarnation of the criminal.* Then he, in effect, through the act of seduction (or love—we cannot tell the difference!), asks the victim to see him as someone other or better.

This is an extraordinary gambit on Pushkin's part, despite his greater commitment to so-called plausibility (*pravdopodobie*), and one worth pausing on for a moment. Recall that Shakespeare's character can use his stable identity as villain to break down Anne's defenses and make her see (even if this is duplicity) her part in his past crimes. Juan, on the other hand, has no equivalent rationale to fall back on. He, and he alone, is the author of his past. The moment at which he finally discloses himself to Dona Anna is also, and not fortuitously, the moment at which he transgresses the boundaries of verbal intimacy:

DON JUAN:
And what if you [*vy*] should chance
To meet Don Juan?
DONA ANNA:
Why then I'd thrust a dagger
Inside the villain's heart.
DON JUAN:
O Dona Anna!
Then thrust your [*tvoi*] dagger here![24]

The hero's statement of maximal honesty ("This is who I am!") is, once again, inextricable from a highly eroticized *cognitio* when he "takes" Dona Anna not only unawares but, as it were, emotionally *naked.* She is caught in the act of desiring the unspeakable: it is as though he pierces her psychological armor with the phallic dagger of his words in a manner that is more than figurative. "I am not Diego, I'm Juan" is, following immediately on the first usage of *tvoi,* not so much a disrobing of himself but of the chaste widow who has allowed herself to come this far.

How different this moment is from that in *Richard III* when Anne, in essence, backs down from Gloucester, refraining to strike him because she wants to believe he is telling the truth:

ANNE:
Arise, dissembler; though I wish thy death

I will not be thy executioner.

GLOUCESTER:

Then bid me kill myself, and I will do it.

ANNE:

I have already.

GLOUCESTER:

That was in thy rage.
Speak it again, and even with the word
This hand, which for thy love did kill thy love,
Shall for thy love kill a far truer love;
To both their deaths shalt thou be accessory.

ANNE:

I would I knew thy heart.

GLOUCESTER:

'Tis figured in my tongue.

ANNE:

I fear me both are false.

GLOUCESTER:

Then never was man true.

ANNE:

Well, well, put up your sword.
(1.2.184–96)

Anne yields ("put up your sword"), won over by Gloucester's staged eloquence yet still fearing he is not telling the truth. If one might put it this way, it is not so much her desire *for Gloucester* that has been "pricked" as it is her wish (however ambiguous and self-incriminating) to be the cause (inspiration) of his actions and therefore the power behind him. Here Anne, though her motivations are not so clearly drawn out and she is much more the victim, seems closer in her "desiring" to Lady Macbeth and, analogously, to Pushkin's Marina Mniszek. Eros for these Renaissance women cannot be separated out from the power and status their men possess. But Dona Anna is not attracted to Juan, in any of his incarnations, for his worldly power and prestige; quite the opposite, in fact. In her, and in the way her being as a desiring woman has been awakened by this "demon" who has no right to "possess" her, Eros has become a free, open, and powerfully dialogic signifier: it is this process that is the "last word" and nothing outside it.

Which brings me to my final point about the Shakespearean lesson of the Boldino autumn. The unpredictability of human personality and the ability of genuine "romantic" drama to step outside the neoclassical unities and create a situation much closer to the "people" and to life "as such" are very much on Pushkin's mind as he considers all the possibilities at the dénouement of *The Stone Guest.* Here is a Don Juan who, finally and fully revealed, can be reborn into something other than a "pure demon" of Eros; here is a Dona Anna who, starting out modest and faithful, can still experience desire and can therefore become other than her role as grieving widow; and here is a stone husband who, even in death, refuses to remain fixed in place and to play the role of unwitting cuckold. The "higher audacity" of this play consists precisely in these changes we cannot separate out from their dialogism (their always "triangulated" desire, as we might say today, after Girard) but understand nonetheless to be irreversible (the "tragic" quality). The Pushkin of the Boldino autumn and of *The Stone Guest* specifically is concerned above all with the *unlikely in love.* This is what he, the aging bridegroom and great-grandson of Peter's jealous blackamoor, needs. Despite the carping of critics, a young and impressionable Mariia can fall in love with a grizzled Mazepa (*Poltava*), just as a Desdemona can fall in love with an Othello. All this Pushkin not only understood at some level but took as an article of faith (again, he *needed* to), as he discusses in another contemporaneous Boldino text, "Oproverzhenie na kritiki" (Refutations of criticisms) (Pushkin 11: 158, September–October 1830). Yet there is one more strange metamorphosis of feeling, this one involving Ovid's Pygmalion, which is also mentioned by the poet in the same section of "Refutations" and which, I would argue, was crucial to his thinking about statues and Eros in *The Stone Guest.* Here we find a "classical" text, and one that Shakespeare himself was possibly engaging in *The Winter's Tale,* that takes the element of unpredictability in love to another, mythopoetic or "Promethean" level bound to appeal to Pushkin in this most anxious and creative of all autumns.

Pygmalion, we recall, was the legendary king of Cyprus who, unhappy in love, created a statue of such beauty that he became enamored of it and prayed to Aphrodite to give him a wife resembling his creation. Aphrodite not only heeded the supplicant but gave Pygmalion precisely *his own statue* come to life. It is my argument, developed at greater length elsewhere, that *The Stone Guest* is a reworking of this myth, with the following important differences: the statue come to life out of love (the "tranquille indifférence" of Natal'ia Goncharova that is figured in the play in the cool, "marble" beauty of Dona Anna) is tragically counterbalanced in this season of dread by the statue of death (the humiliated husband come to take the miscreant down to hell for his past crimes).[25] That the living statue is the poet's own, so to speak, is made clear in the other plot of love and marital fidelity being completed that fall: the concluding chapter 8 (originally 9) of *Eugene Onegin*, in which the village maiden, Tat'iana, undergoes a "miraculous" metamorphosis to comme il faut high-society princess *and* muse (the poet's "creation"), so that her graceful presence now outshines even that of the legendary Nina Voronskaia, *with her marble beauty* (Pushkin 6: 172).[26] In this reversal of the plot of *The Stone Guest*, Pushkin places the husband (the general), now neither dead nor cuckolded, in the virtuous and departing wife's boudoir at the climactic moment when the failed hero freezes on the spot: "She [Tat'iana] leaves. There stands Evgenii / As though thunderstruck."[27]

Thus, in the erotic space of the Boldino autumn, as the poet contemplates being given Aphrodite's gift of his beautiful statue/muse come to life, he also imagines the full weight of his past crimes. Indeed, these crimes seem to be replayed when Juan, who being himself cannot help but enjoy an opportunity for male rivalry, *brings the other statue to life as well* by having Leporello invite it to take up its humiliatingly "erect" post and then refer to it, following the gender of *statuia*, as *ona* ("she")—the ultimate putdown. In this sense, the one statue ("female" grace) cannot exist without the other statue ("male" retribution)—hence the tragedy. As the ecstatic Juan says to this woman who has fallen for him despite his past,

> No doubt you've often heard the man described
> As villain or as fiend. O Dona Anna . . .
> Such ill repute may well in part be true:
> My weary conscience bears a heavy load
> Of evil deeds.[28]

I am suggesting that the Pushkin of *The Stone Guest* is *both* the Juan hoping to be reborn *and* the husband (his new role) protecting what is his by right. And his dialogic counterpart, that through which he experiences his own new incarnation? She is *both* the pagan living statue that comes to know passion (Ovid) *and* the spiritualized Christian beauty that confers grace through compassion/mercy (Dona Anna become Madonna).[29] When the recently married Pushkin wrote to Pletnev that "[t]his state [marriage] is so new to me that it seems I have been reborn [*chto kazhetsia, ia pererodilsia*]" (14: 154–55),[30] he was repeating, with the same joyous surprise, the sentiments of his hero.

The question of how Pushkin creatively adapted the principles of Shakespearean dramaturgy to his own tradition is only just being posed, despite all the excellent philological work done in the past on this topic. One is emboldened to assert this because the psychic mechanisms underwriting the works of the mature Pushkin lie somewhere between the Bloomian notion of influence ("strong," Oedipally challenged poets finding ways to say something new outside the shades/shadows of great precursors) and the depersonalized notion of intertext (a borrowing that is purely linguistic and exists in the absence of poetic fears, resentments, and "dodgings"). My guess is that Shakespeare, as the "barbaric northerner" whose magnificent language could never be fully absorbed by the "Gallically" restrained and elegant Pushkin, gave the poet the example he needed to transcend his own, and his immediate tradition's, past. As Akhmatova first insisted, Don Juan is not only a poet of love, he is also a poet in the more literal sense.[31] Thus as Pushkin, in that exceptional Boldino autumn, passed from poet to prose writer, illicit paramour to lawful husband, man who dreamed of muses to man who had to live daily with a muselike beauty come to life, he had as his "best man" the Bard whose shadowy biography, as opposed to Byron's, did not and could not stand athwart his path. Shakespeare more than any other writer, foreign or domestic, gave Pushkin this "higher audacity" he needed. How Pushkin took up this challenge is especially evident in *The Stone Guest*—in the way Dona Anna is different, more fully a dialogic partner, from Anne; in the way Juan wants to be desired by this woman more than he wants the "power" that is the token of her submission; and in the language, so eroticized in its constant need to draw in and on the other, yet at the same time so pregnant with its own fatal "ontological rhymes" and with its implicit knowledge that the statue has its rights too and it *will* come.

Notes

1. *Moskvitianin* 9 (1841): 246.

2. Alekseev, "A. S. Pushkin"; Levin, "Pushkin"; Ospovat, "'Kamennyi gost'' kak opyt dialogizatsii tvorcheskogo soznaniia."

3. Levin, "Pushkin," 54.

4. Ospovat, "'Kamennyi gost'' kak opyt dialogizatsii tvorcheskogo soznaniia," 56.

5. Recall Pushkin's July 1825 letter to N. N. Raevskii *fils*, in which he states: "Read Sh[akespeare] [. . .] he never fears compromising his hero/character; he has him speak with all the naturalness of life because he is certain that at the appropriate time and place he can make that hero find a language consistent with his character" (13: 198, original in French).

6. Ospovat, "'Kamennyi gost'' kak opyt dialogizatsii tvorcheskogo soznaniia," 50. Here Ospovat is to some extent following Akhmatova, who tetchily dismissed Dona Anna as a "very coquettish, curious, faint-hearted woman full of false piety—a typical Catholic devotee" (*O Pushkine. Stat'i i zametki*, 163).

7. My discussion in the following paragraph owes much to Sergei Davydov's essay on the unity of the *Little Tragedies* included in this volume.

8. The structural progression I speak of here is borne out by the dates of composition during the Boldino autumn: *The Covetous Knight* (*Skupoi rytsar'*) was completed on 23 October, *Mozart and Salieri* (*Motsart i Sal'eri*) on 26 October, *The Stone Guest* on 4 November, and *A Feast in Time of Plague* (*Pir vo vremia chumy*) on 6 November.

9. Schoenbaum, *William Shakespeare*, 174.

10. See Pushkin 13: 196–98, 14: 46–48, 11: 59–61, 66–69, 140–42, 177–83, 12: 159–61. The dates signify approximate or unconfirmed times of composition. The language in the 1825 and 1829 draft letters to Raevskii *fils* was used again in the 1830 draft preface to *Boris Godunov*.

11. *Boris Godunov* indeed appeared for the first time in print in St. Petersburg at the end of 1830, although the date of publication is recorded in the text as 1831.

12. Shakespeare's dense Renaissance English would always be difficult for Pushkin, and it is hard to say how much he actually apprehended, either in the original or in a French translation.

13. See Bethea, *Realizing Metaphors*, 137–234; and Cornwell, ed., "Aleksandr Pushkin: From Byron to Shakespeare." Mickiewicz wrote in his Paris lectures, for example, "Et tu [Pushkin] Shakespeare eris, si fata sinant!" [And you (Pushkin) too would have been Shakespeare, if the fates had permitted!] (*Dziela*, 5: 301). The Baratynskii reference (from a December 1825 letter to Pushkin) is cited below in the text.

14. That is, a personal letter to a close friend like Del'vig. Pushkin's public statements about Derzhavin were much more guarded and respectful.

15. Pushkin, *The Letters*, 225, original in Pushkin 13: 182. The letter to Del'vig was written in the first days of June 1825.

16. Ibid.

17. Citing examples of individual usage taken for "boldness" by the French in

the language of Racine and Delille, Pushkin remarks sarcastically, "This is a wretched literature, that would obey such petty and capricious criticism" (11: 61).

18. Pushkin, *The Letters*, 146; original in Pushkin 13: 80.

19. See Pushkin 11: 178–79, where these terms are glossed. It is here, for example, that Pushkin explains the difference between the "popular tragedy of Shakespeare" [tragediia narodnaia, Shekspirova] and the "court-sponsored drama of Racine" [drama pridvornaia, Rasinova].

20. For more on this topic, see the fine recent discussion in Evdokimova, *Pushkin's Historical Imagination*, esp. chap. 1, "The Impediments of Russian History," and chap. 2, "Chance and Historical Necessity."

21. "[Don Juan:] Ee sovsem ne vidno / Pod etim vdov'im chernym pokryvalom, / Chut' uzen'kuiu piatku ia zametil. [Leporello:] Dovol'no s vas. U vas voobrazhen'e / V minutu dorisuet ostal'noe; / Ono u vas provornei zhivopistsa, / Vam vse ravno, s chego by ni nachat', / S brovei li, s nog li. [Don Juan:] Slushai, Leporello, / Ia s neiu poznakomlius'" (Pushkin 7: 143).

22. "Tak, Razvrata / Ia dolgo byl pokornyi uchenik, / No s toi pory kak vas uvidel ia, / Mne kazhetsia, ia ves' pererodilsia" (Pushkin 7: 168).

23. "Ia ne Diego, ia Juan [...] Ia ubil / Supruga tvoego; i ne zhaleiu / O tom— i net raskaian'ia vo mne" (Pushkin 7: 167).

24. "[Don Juan:] Chto esli b Don Juana / Vy vstretili? [Dona Anna:] Togda by ia zlodeiu / Kinzhal vonzila v serdtse. [Don Juan:] Dona Anna, / Gde tvoi kinzhal? vot grud' moia" (Pushkin 7: 166–67).

25. See Pushkin's letter to his future mother-in-law of 5 April 1830, in which he refers to his fiancée's beauty in potentially "statuesque" terms ("the calm indifference of her heart") and claims that he has "nothing with which to please her" [je n'ai rien pour lui plaire] (14: 76). See the discussion in Bethea, *Realizing Metaphors*, 109–11.

26. Further corroboration that Pushkin had the Pygmalion myth squarely in mind as he "mused" about the source of erotic love is found in the first four stanzas of chapter 4 of *Eugene Onegin*, which were excluded (presumably for personal reasons) from the completed editions of the novel-in-verse but were still published separately as "Zhenshchiny. Otryvok iz 'Evgeniia Onegina'" (Women: An excerpt from *Evgenii Onegin*) in the *Moskovskii vestnik* in 1827. The second of these stanzas ends with the lines: "To vdrug ia mramor videl v nei (v zhenshchine), / Pered mol'boi Pigmaliona / Eshche kholodnyi i nemoi, / No vskore zharkii i zhivoi" (Pushkin 6: 592).

27. "Ona ushla. Stoit Evgenii, / Kak budto gromom porazhen" (Pushkin 6: 189).

28. "Ne pravda li—on byl opisan vam / Zlodeem, izvergom—o Dona Anna— / Molva, byt' mozhet, ne sovsem neprava, / Na sovesti ustaloi mnogo zla, / Byt' mozhet, tiagoteet" (Pushkin 7: 168).

29. One thinks here of the "Marian" theme in poems such as "Zhil na svete rytsar' bednyi" (1829) and "Madona" (1830), Pushkin's lyric portrait of his fiancée.

30. Cited in Akhmatova, "*Kamennyi gost'* Pushkina," 2: 268.

31. Ibid., 2: 260.

The Weight of Human Tears

The Covetous Knight and *A Raw Youth*

Susanne Fusso

In the preparatory notes for his 1875 novel *A Raw Youth* (*Podrostok*), Dostoevsky sets himself a high stylistic benchmark: "The confession [should be] unusually concise (learn from Pushkin)" [Ispoved' neobychaino szhata (uchit'sia u Pushkina)]; "Form, form! (simple narration à la Pushkin)" [Forma, forma! (prostoi rasskaz à la Pushkin)]; "Write more tersely. (Imitate Pushkin.)" [Koroche pisat'. (Podrazhat' Pushkinu.)].[1] As D. D. Blagoi and others have pointed out, in the finished novel Dostoevsky fell far short of this rather quixotic goal: nothing could be further from Pushkin's stylistic economy and elegance than the sprawling, incoherent narrative of *A Raw Youth.*[2] Nevertheless, Pushkin's works do play a vital, central role in *A Raw Youth*, a novel in which Dostoevsky engages in dialogue with his own earlier literary self. Each of the three parts of *A Raw Youth* involves two major subtexts: a Pushkin text that is openly labeled as such and an earlier Dostoevsky text that is tacitly evoked through verbal cues or plot parallels. Part 1 is involved with Pushkin's *The Covetous Knight* and Dostoevsky's *Crime and Punishment* (1866); part 2 with Pushkin's *Queen of Spades* and Dostoevsky's *The Gambler* (1866); and part 3 with Pushkin's "Table-Talk" aphorism "Othello was not jealous by nature, he was trusting" and Dostoevsky's *Idiot* (1868). Since Dostoevsky most often uses the narrator of *A Raw Youth* to replay his melodramas and tragedies of the 1860s in a lighter, almost anticlimactic mode, one could read the title *A Raw Youth* as referring to the younger Dostoevsky and the breathless first-person narrative as a parody of Dostoevsky's own earlier narrative style. Pushkin's texts, with their drier, more ironic texture, enable Dostoevsky to reread his own earlier work in a mode of self-awareness, self-criticism, and self-parody.

When we turn from such general questions of tone and style to the more specific use of individual texts, the problems of interpretation become more complex. The present essay investigates the triangular relationship among *The Covetous Knight*, *Crime and Punishment*, and *A Raw Youth*. In *A Raw Youth* Dostoevsky advances the argument against capitalism that is present in *Crime and Punishment* in a vague, inchoate form. In doing so, he moves closer to the creation of *The Brothers Karamazov*, which no longer thematically foregrounds the coming of capitalism to Russia but maintains the vision of loss, disintegration, and moral interdependence that is established in *A Raw Youth*.

In *A Raw Youth* Dostoevsky depicts a world in which the disintegrative force of capitalism has shaken all firm foundations and disrupted all traditional relationships. He chooses as his narrator a callow nineteen year old, Arkadii Dolgorukii, the illegitimate son of the nobleman Versilov. Dolgorukii seems not at all up to the task of managing a large-scale narrative; the novel is maddeningly chaotic and unreadable. In his study of the bildungsroman in European culture, *The Way of the World*, Franco Moretti could be speaking of Dolgorukii when he says of Balzac that "he never grants the satisfaction of a well-closed narrative sequence, of a clear and stable meaning: there are always other plots that knock on the door, loose threads everywhere, divergent viewpoints to take into account."[3] Moretti links this type of narrative to the historical moment: the "interdependent and indecipherable" world of capitalism creates "a consuming desire for the new *as such*," "a need for sheer narration—without beginning or end."[4]

A key character in *A Raw Youth* is Stebel'kov, whom Dostoevsky based on the real-life obstetrician and forger of railway shares Kolosov.[5] Stebel'kov represents the novel's two great themes: the growing influence of capital, speculation, and fraud and the disintegration of the Russian family and the Russian nobility (he is the stepfather of Vasin, "who was an orphan under his care for a long time" [Dostoevskii 13: 119], and he involves the young Prince Sokol'skii in his railway-share fraud, causing the prince's imprisonment and ultimate death). But Stebel'kov also exemplifies the apparent link in Dostoevsky's scheme of things between capitalism and linguistic incoherence.

Arkadii's first conversation with him is a mind-boggling muddle in which the words "money," "purchaser," and especially "soundness" (*osnovatel'nost'*, in this context "financial soundness") are blended in a Gogolian discourse that only mimics logical coherence—Dolinin calls it "tongue-tied, absurd chatter" [kosnoiazychnaia nelepaia boltovnia].[6] The conversation ends with Arkadii's surrender: "'Excuse me, but it's very difficult for me to follow you.' 'Difficult?' 'Yes, you're exhausting me'" (Dostoevskii 13: 120). The reader could say the same to Arkadii, whose discourse is very nearly as "tongue-tied" and "absurd" as Stebel'kov's at times.

For this and other reasons, Arkadii seems at first glance to be very much a man of his era. In part 1 of *A Raw Youth* he announces his plan to achieve supreme power in the capitalist world, a goal he somewhat anachronistically formulates as "becoming a Rothschild." Although Arkadii repeatedly expresses his scorn for "literary beauties," his cherished idea has been inspired by one of the most beautiful texts in world literature, the Baron's act 2 monologue in Pushkin's *The Covetous Knight*, which Arkadii learned by heart as a child and quotes repeatedly during his narration. In 1936 A. L. Bem noted the originality of Dostoevsky's use of this subtext: while both Pushkin's and Dostoevsky's works are centrally concerned with father-son conflicts (and in both cases an autobiographical element may be present), Arkadii the son identifies with the *father* in the earlier text.[7] Arkadii plans to save money fanatically, amassing a fabulous fortune by hoarding kopecks and denying himself all physical comforts, while his father plays the role of spendthrift, the role assigned by the Baron to his son, Albert. Arkadii tells us that his father has already gone through three inheritances in his life (Dostoevskii 13: 17)—he is the Baron's nightmare of an irresponsible heir.

The use of the subtext yields even more surprising connections when we consider the nature of the Baron's fortune and precisely what kind of economic model Arkadii has set himself. References in the Baron's monologue to the debts owed to him by the widow and Thibault seem to indicate that he has accumulated his fortune through usury, not a normal or Church-sanctioned activity for a French nobleman.[8] Although Arkadii tells us that he doesn't at all resemble "a Jew or a buyer of second-hand goods" and that he does not plan to become a "pawnbroker" (*zakladchik*) or a "usurer" (*protsentshchik*), by identifying with the Baron and with Rothschild he becomes both a usurer and a Jew (Dostoevskii 13: 38, 69).[9] Moreover, in choosing the Baron as his model he identifies with the hereditary nobility to which his father belongs, despite his repeated claims to have rejected that world. In short, Arkadii is confused about whether he is father or son, nobleman or illegitimate upstart, Jew or Christian, feudal usurer or capitalist entrepreneur. As Dostoevsky points out in *Notes from the Dead House*, a folk etymology for the loan word *kapital* is to derive it from *kopit'* (to accumulate) (Dostoevskii 4: 110). Arkadii thinks he is becoming a capitalist by engaging, like the Baron, in "accumulation" (*nakoplenie*), but in fact he explicitly rejects a major element of capitalist entrepreneurship: risk. He compares himself to a hunchback who rented out his hump as a desk for Parisians frantically signing up for shares in a bubble company. "And who came out the winner? Only the hunchback, precisely because he took not shares but louis d'or in cash. Well, sir, I happen to be that very hunchback!" (Dostoevskii 13: 71).

A man who prefers actual gold pieces to shares of stock is not really getting into the spirit of nineteenth-century capitalism. The confusion between old and new, tradition and innovation, is also reflected in Arkadii's narrative. He claims to have rejected traditional literary form, but, faced with the inadequacy of his own verbal resources, he continually has recourse to Pushkin's highly formalized lines of verse. As he begins to describe his "idea" of becoming a Rothschild, Arkadii predicts failure: "I am experiencing an insurmountable difficulty in recounting this 'thought.'" After having described it, he admits failure: "Now what have I expressed? I haven't expressed even a hundredth part of it; I feel that it came out trivial, crude, superficial, and even younger than my years" (Dostoevskii 13: 65, 71). These two lines make up a small percentage of the space Arkadii devotes to apologizing for his verbal inadequacy. The deficiency of his prose is, however, made up for by Pushkin's poetry. The essence of Arkadii's idea is made clear to us by Pushkin's words, especially the phrase Arkadii repeats obsessively: "[J]ust the consciousness of it is enough for me" [s menia dovol'no / Sego soznan'ia].

This phrase is a touchstone for Arkadii. He is enthralled by the Baron's discourse of pure potential, his satisfaction with the *idea* of power and renunciation of the need to *wield* power. In his *Philosophy of Money*, in the section entitled "Greed and Avarice," Georg Simmel links the avaricious hoarding of money to power in a very Pushkinian way:

> Where the character of money as a means makes its appearance as the abstract form of enjoyment which, none the less, is not enjoyed, the individual's appreciation of ownership—to the extent that it is preserved intact—has a touch of objectivity about it. [...] In avarice [...] money, as the *absolute* means, provides unlimited possibilities for enjoyment, while at the same time, as the absolute *means*, it leaves enjoyment as yet completely untouched during the stage of its unused ownership. In this respect the significance of money coincides with that of power; money, like power, is a mere potentiality which stores up a merely subjectively anticipatable future in the form of an objectively existing present.[10]

In a study of the alchemical subtexts to *The Covetous Knight*, Marina Kostalevskaia has pointed out that the Baron is obsessed not with money as a means of exchange but with gold, the actual substance.[11] In identifying with the Baron, Arkadii partakes of this archaic, premodern economic attitude. As we see from his obsessive quotation of Pushkin, he is similarly drawn to the weighty, self-valuable poetic word, the literary word that, as Foucault says, "has nothing to say but itself, nothing to do but shine in the brightness of its being."[12] Nevertheless, he pretends to be a poetry-despising child of his time: "In a word, I cannot express my impressions because it's all fantasy, finally it's poetry, and therefore nonsense" (Dostoevskii 13: 113).

Although Arkadii claims to have memorized the Baron's monologue, he seems not to have *read* it very carefully. There is one theme in that text, and one theme of modern capitalism, that Arkadii does not mention when expounding his "idea": the theme of human suffering. The Baron's gold is heavy indeed, but its weight is measured in tears:

> of how many human cares,
> Deceptions, tears, prayers, and curses,
> Is it the heavily weighted representative!

> скольких человеческих забот,
> Обманов, слез, молений и проклятий
> Оно тяжеловесный представитель![13]

In an 1861 work on political economy, *Unto This Last*, John Ruskin independently echoed Pushkin's insight about the weight added to money by the human tears shed in the making of it:

> It is impossible to conclude, of any given mass of acquired wealth, merely by the fact of its existence, whether it signifies good or evil to the nation in the midst of which it exists. Its real value depends on the moral sign attached to it, just as sternly as that of a mathematical quantity depends on the algebraical sign attached to it. Any given accumulation of commercial wealth may be indicative, on the one hand, of faithful industries, progressive energies, and productive ingenuities; or, on the other, it may be indicative of mortal luxury, merciless tyranny, ruinous chicane. *Some treasures are heavy with human tears, as an ill-stored harvest with untimely rain*; and some gold is brighter in sunshine than it is in substance. And these are not, observe, merely moral or pathetic attributes of riches, which the seeker of riches may, if he chooses, despise; they are literally and sternly, material attributes of riches, depreciating or exalting, incalculably, the monetary signification of the sum in question.[14]

In Ruskin's system, the Baron's gold actually depreciates in value (at least, in its value "to the nation in the midst of which it exists") because of the human pain it has caused. As he speaks of his "idea," Arkadii seems to close his eyes to this aspect of the model he has chosen for himself.[15] Robert L. Jackson has pointed out the flaw in Arkadii's plan: "The solitary consciousness of strength, self-isolation, the hoarding of wealth, and the craving for power, as Dostoevsky illustrates throughout his work, lead to self-destructive impotence."[16] It becomes clear as the novel proceeds that Arkadii really is not the kind of person who can "become a Rothschild" by cutting himself off from his fellows or by ignoring the cost in human suffering. In this he recalls not only Albert, who gives his last bottle of wine to an ailing blacksmith, but also an earlier *Dostoevskian* hero, Raskol'nikov, whose tragic act of murder is evoked in the text of *A Raw Youth* by specific verbal cues. By bringing *Crime and Punishment* into dialogue with Arkadii's story, Dostoevsky manages to highlight the very same aspect of Pushkin's text that Arkadii suppresses (or represses).

Arkadii's first venture into the capitalist marketplace is his visit to an auction of the "moveable property" of a certain Mrs. Lebrecht (Dostoevskii 13: 36). Arkadii labels this visit with two words he emphasizes with quotation marks: "step" (*shag*) and "trial" (*proba*). Arkadii has a fondness for quotation marks, but in this case he really is quoting—quoting Dostoevsky. The two words *shag* and *proba* are also marked in the beginning of *Crime and Punishment*, *proba* always in italics (Dostoevskii 6: 6, 7, 50, 51). They refer to Raskol'nikov's plan to "step across" by murdering an old female pawnbroker. The *proba* is his trial run visit to her apartment, the first event narrated in the novel.

At the auction Arkadii again quotes *Crime and Punishment.* As he inspects the objects for sale, he compares his feelings to those of a gambler before staking a card: "But indecision soon begins to weigh on you, and you somehow go blind: you stretch out your hand, take a card, but mechanically [*mashinal'no*], almost against your will, as if your hand were being directed by someone else; finally you've decided and you place a bet—immediately you have a completely different sensation, a huge sensation. I'm not writing about auctions, I'm only writing about myself: who else could feel their heart beat faster at an auction?" (Dostoevskii 13: 37). These last words seem to indicate that Arkadii is aware of what he's quoting and is embarrassed by the incommensurability of the two texts. For when he says, "You take a card, but mechanically, almost against your will," he invokes the devastating moment at which Raskol'nikov first swings the axe: "He took the axe completely out, wielded it with both hands, hardly conscious of himself, and, almost without effort, almost mechanically [*mashinal'no*], he brought the butt of it down on her head" (Dostoevskii 6: 63).

When compared to Raskol'nikov's crime, Arkadii's act is farcically insignificant. He buys a "domestic album" in a damaged ivory case for two rubles five kopecks and then immediately sells it for ten rubles to a man whose interest in the seemingly worthless object is never explained. Here Arkadii is imitating not Raskol'nikov but the pawnbroker: he is profiting from the value added to objects by personal associations and human emotions. The first two objects Raskol'nikov pawns are "his father's old silver watch and a little gold ring with three tiny red stones of some sort, which had been given to him by his sister upon parting, as a keepsake" (Dostoevskii 6: 53). The pawnbroker profits from the discrepancy between the priceless human value the objects have for Raskol'nikov and their low market value: "'You come to me with trifles, my dear sir; they're hardly worth anything. Last time I gave you two bills for the ring, but you can buy one new at the jeweler's for a ruble and a half'" (Dostoevskii 6: 9). There is a similar discrepancy between the apparent market value of the damaged family album Arkadii buys and the price he sells it for. *A Raw Youth* is a novel that leaves many loose ends hanging, and one of them is the reason why a man would pay ten rubles for what Arkadii calls "the most worthless thing in the world" [samaia driannaia veshch' v mire]. But we can surmise that the added value is made up of human love, pain, or grief (Dostoevskii 13: 38).[17]

Yet another verbal echo of *Crime and Punishment* occurs a bit later in part 1, when Arkadii's father, Versilov, visits his room for the first time. Raskol'nikov's tiny room is called many things in the early part of the novel: "garret" (*kamorka*), "closet" (*shkaf*), "ship's cabin" (*morskaia kaiuta*). It is his mother, though, who after the murder gives it the most meaningful label: "What a bad apartment you have, Rodia, it's like a coffin" [Kakaia u tebia durnaia kvartira, Rodia, tochno grob] (Dostoevskii 6: 178). The word *grob* takes on its deepest significance when Sonia reads Raskol'nikov the story of the resurrection of Lazarus: "[H]e already stinks; for it is *four* days that he has been in the grave [same word as "coffin" in Russian]" [uzhe smerdit; ibo *chetyre* dni, kak on vo grobe] (Dostoevskii 6: 251, emphasis in original). Raskol'nikov's spiritual death and resurrection are encapsulated in this tiny word.

Just as Raskol'nikov's momentous act of killing the pawnbroker is evoked in Arkadii's narration of his trivial auction transaction, the scene in which Raskol'nikov's mother labels his room a *grob* is replayed in *A Raw Youth* but without the moral and religious resonance of the earlier scene. Here it is the male parent who pronounces the word. Versilov visits Arkadii in his room for the first time: "Merci, my friend, I haven't crawled in here even once, not even when I was renting the apartment. I had a feeling what it would be like, but even so I didn't expect such a kennel. [. . .] But it's a coffin, a perfect coffin! [*grob, sovershennyi grob*]" (Dostoevskii 13: 101). Unlike Raskol'nikov, Arkadii has not symbolically killed himself by committing a terrible crime. There is no symbolic reason for him to be living in a coffin. The major reason for the epithet seems to be to add to the complex of verbal references to *Crime and Punishment.*

Arkadii's double quotation—the open quotation of *The Covetous Knight* and the hidden quotation of *Crime and Punishment*—prompts us to investigate the links between his two sources. The most obvious link is that *The Covetous Knight* hints at a possible murder, while *Crime and Punishment* depicts a murder carried out. When the Jew Solomon offers Albert poison, he is, as many critics have said, only responding to Albert's secret and unacknowledged desire to kill his father. The gender shift in *Crime and Punishment* is significant, for Raskol'nikov's father is already dead as the novel begins, and in killing the female usurer he is perhaps symbolically killing the parent who does appear in the novel, his mother (who ultimately dies as a result of his act).[18]

There are many links between the Baron and the pawnbroker: they both live by lending money to the desperate; her keys and the gold objects in her chest (*sunduk*) are mentioned during the *proba* and the murder scene; her apartment is even assimilated into the Baron's "cellar" (*podval*): "[A]ll her windows were closed, despite the stuffiness" (Dostoevskii 6: 9, 63, 64, 62). Just as the Baron is implicitly identified with the Jew Solomon, the pawnbroker is said to be "rich as a Jew" [bogata, kak zhid] (Dostoevskii 6: 53). One of the epithets the Baron uses for his conscience is "uninvited guest" [nezvanyi gost']; Raskol'nikov, who can be seen as an avenging visitation on the evil old woman, gets the same label: "The old woman was about to look at the pledge, but she immediately fixed her eyes directly into the eyes of the uninvited guest" (Dostoevskii 6: 62). After killing the pawnbroker, Raskol'nikov takes over her position as a stand-in for the Baron. Like the Baron, he renounces the use of the wealth he has appropriated and buries it in the ground: "The investigators and judges were very surprised, by the way, at the fact that he hid the purse and the objects under a stone without making use of them. [...] In particular, the circumstance that he never once opened the purse and didn't even know precisely how much money was in it seemed improbable" (Dostoevskii 6: 410). Of course, the money buried by Raskol'nikov is a sign not of preserved power but of "self-destructive impotence," the sheer uselessness of his terrible act.

If Pushkin's Baron is present in *Crime and Punishment*, it is yet another case of the premodern usurer displaced into the world of nineteenth-century capitalism. For although capitalism is not placed as squarely at the center of attention in *Crime and Punishment* as it is in *A Raw Youth*, the word *kapital* occurs with emphatic frequency, most strikingly in a dialogue between Raskol'nikov and the maid Nastas'ia before the murder. She asks why he no longer goes out to tutor children, and he replies that he doesn't want to work for kopecks. She asks, "And do you want all the capital at once?" After a moment's thought he firmly replies, "Yes, all the capital" [Da, ves' kapital] (Dostoevskii 6: 27). Killing the pawnbroker is supposed to be the first move in the game of acquiring "ves' kapital."

By the time of *A Raw Youth*, Dostoevsky is interested in illuminating the human costs of capitalism more obliquely. Arkadii does not directly commit a murder. Instead, through some cavalier words he utters to a desperate young woman named Olia, he contributes to a situation that leads to her suicide. This "crime" is more in keeping with the "interdependent and indecipherable" world of nineteenth-century capitalism, in which humans are caught in a web of interrelationships that complicate and obscure moral obligations. It is a step along the path that leads from Raskol'nikov to the infinitely more disturbing cases of Ivan and Dmitrii Karamazov, as responsibility becomes more diffuse and shared and less easily assigned to one person.

At the end of part 1, Arkadii is plagued by guilt over his flippant words to Olia, but he hopes to expiate his crime:

> But then, on that morning, although I was already starting to torment myself, all the same it seemed to me to be nonsense: "Hey, this whole situation began to 'burn and boil' without me"—I would repeat from time to time—"Hey, it's nothing, it'll pass! I'll fix my mistake! I'll make up for it somehow [...] with some kind of good deed. [...] I have fifty years ahead of me!" (Dostoevskii 13: 162)

The plan to make up for a crime with a "good deed" recalls the justification offered for Raskol'nikov's crime by the student in the tavern: "Kill her and take her money, in order with its help then to dedicate yourself to the service of all humanity and the common goal: what do you think, wouldn't one teeny, little bitty crime [*odno, kroshechnoe prestuplen'itse*] be mitigated by a thousand good deeds?" (Dostoevskii 6: 54). As we have seen, Arkadii typically replays Raskol'nikov's weighty tragedy in a tonality of anticlimactic farce, and the same is true in this case: Arkadii has not committed murder, so his hope of expiation is not unfounded. The suicides of Olia and, the night before, of Arkadii's acquaintance Kraft have made him newly sensitive to the fact that he is not the Baron—he cannot silence the voice of human sympathy within him.

The development of Arkadii's character is reflected in the text of *A Raw Youth* by a change in his Pushkin references (and in his unconscious Dostoevsky references). In part 2 he moves from the Rothschild idea to the idea of gambling as his salvation. In doing so, he trades one Pushkin hero for another, the Baron for Germann, the hero of *The Queen of Spades* (*Pikovaia dama*). He also trades his subterranean references to *Crime and Punishment* for secret quotation of *The Gambler*. On a certain level, the level on which Dostoevsky the author is in dialogue with his own earlier self, *The Covetous Knight* has been overcome. Raskol'nikov has killed the Baron—and the dream of heartlessly accumulated wealth—on Arkadii's behalf.

On the first page of *A Raw Youth*, Arkadii says, "I am just noting down events, avoiding everything superfluous with all my might, and especially avoiding literary beauties; a writer [*literator*] writes for thirty years and in the end doesn't know at all why he wrote for all those years [*dlia chego on pisal stol'ko let*]" (Dostoevskii 13: 5). If we take extratextual evidence into account, we can read the implied author Dostoevsky as speaking along with Arkadii in the second part of this sentence. Those "thirty years" mark the span between Dostoevsky's literary debut in 1846 and the publication of *A Raw Youth* as a separate edition in 1876. In *A Raw Youth* the callow, incompetent narrator is helping the writer to figure out "why he wrote for all those years."

Here an insight of Nathan Rosen, that by writing *A Raw Youth* Dostoevsky was regenerating himself, can be of use.[19] Lawrence Lipking has studied the life of the poet in terms of how the poet defines himself at crucial moments of his career through particular types of works that Lipking labels "initiation," "harmonium," and "tombeau."[20] As I have noted elsewhere, the "initiation," in which the poet refreshes and deepens his work by rereading his own earlier works, is apposite to Dostoevsky's task in writing *A Raw Youth.*[21] (Although Lipking restricts himself to poets, I see no reason why the life of the novelist should not follow a similar path.) The young Arkadii, breathless and seemingly incompetent as a writer, is deeply engaged in the retrospective and prospective projects of the mature author Dostoevsky. In *A Raw Youth*, to use Lipking's phrase, Dostoevsky "learned to read his own early work." In part 1 of *A Raw Youth* we see him reading *Crime and Punishment* through the prism of *The Covetous Knight*, thus accenting the murderous force of capitalism that Arkadii muffles in his admiring interpretation of the Baron's monologue. Arkadii's unwitting quotation of *Crime and Punishment* in turn serves to ironize and parody the lurid melodrama of Raskol'nikov's story. Although melodrama returns in *The Brothers Karamazov*, it is inevitably accompanied by the parodistic humor and the more complicated awareness of collective, shared guilt that permeate *A Raw Youth*.

Notes

I would like to thank Robert T. Conn, Priscilla Meyer, and Gil Skillman for their comments on this essay.

1. Dostoevskii, *Polnoe sobranie sochinenii*, 16: 47, 122, 172. All citations are from this edition, which is hereafter cited in the text. All translations are mine.

2. Blagoi, "Dostoevskii i Pushkin," 513.

3. Moretti, *The Way of the World*, 146. Compare Dostoevsky's description of his own stylistic deficiencies in a letter to N. N. Strakhov: "To this day I do not at all know how (have not learned how) to control my resources. A multitude of separate novels and stories squeeze together into one, so that there's neither measure nor harmony" (cited in Blagoi, "Dostoevskii i Pushkin," 513). For a thorough discussion of entropy and decomposition in *A Raw Youth*, see Knapp, *The Annihilation of Inertia*, 131–71. As her title implies, Knapp highlights the metaphysical rather than the socioeconomic implications of the theme.

4. Moretti, *The Way of the World*, 143, 146.

5. See Dolinin, *Poslednie romany Dostoevskogo*, 142–50.

6. Ibid., 146.

7. Bem, "'Skupoi rytsar' v tvorchestve Dostoevskogo," 107–8. See also Blagoi, "Dostoevskii i Pushkin," 482–97, for a general discussion of Dostoevsky's use of *The Covetous Knight*. Carl R. Proffer's interpretation of *The Covetous Knight* as depicting a sexual rivalry between father and son is also relevant to the plot of *A Raw Youth*: "At the conscious, explicit level, the rivalry between Albert and the Baron is over the money in the locked chests. But unconsciously it is a sexual conflict" ("Pushkin and Parricide," 349). The underlying sexual rivalry between Arkadii and his father, Versilov, is also often masked by difficulties over money.

8. See Shapiro, "Journey to the Metonymic Pole," 177, on usury as one of the three crimes present in the text of *The Covetous Knight*. Shapiro's essay is full of important insights about the interrelationships among *The Little Tragedies*.

9. There is not room here to discuss all the ramifications of the "Rothschild" theme in *A Raw Youth*, but I would like to briefly outline the salient issues: (1) Arkadii's focus on the importance of privileged information to the building of the Rothschilds' wealth, which nicely dovetails with his own obsessive trading in secret "documents"; (2) the importance to the Rothschilds of strong family ties of the kind that are seemingly absent in Arkadii's Russia; and (3) the relation of

Dostoevsky's anti-Semitism to his critique of capitalism. It is also worth noting that Arkadii focuses precisely on James Rothschild, the head of the Paris branch of the family, who serves as the model for Nucingen in several novels by Dostoevsky's master, Balzac. See the recent magisterial treatment of the history of the Rothschild family by Ferguson, *The House of Rothschild.* I would like to thank Elizabeth K. Beaujour for alerting me to the deeper significance of Dostoevsky's use of the Rothschild name.

10. Simmel, *The Philosophy of Money,* 242.

11. Kostalevskaia, "Aurum Vulgi." See also Sergei Davydov's essay in this volume. Nusinov takes a somewhat different approach: "Gold is not a goal but a means. It is the means of defense against servility, dependence, humiliation. [...] Since from the very beginning gold for the Baron is not a goal but merely a means for realizing a noble human striving for independence, the Baron has preserved all the human passions" ("Tragediia skuposti," 453). Nusinov's point is well taken, but it does not account for the sensual pleasure the Baron takes in his carefully accumulated piles of gold (see Proffer, "Pushkin and Parricide," 350). I would like to thank Omry Ronen for bringing Nusinov's essay to my attention.

12. Foucault, *The Order of Things,* 300.

13. Pushkin 7: 111. All translations are mine.

14. Ruskin, *Unto This Last,* 56–57, emphasis added. The Ruskin passage was brought to my attention by Christina Crosby's unpublished paper, "Faith and Flesh in Ruskin's Political Economy."

15. Nusinov explains Arkadii's lack of concern for the victims of capitalism by the fact that Arkadii, unlike the Baron, has committed no crime and therefore is not tormented by pangs of conscience ("Tragediia skuposti," 463). This does not, however, explain why he would ignore the explicit discussion of those victims in the very text he so obsessively quotes.

16. Jackson, "The Temptation and the Transaction," 249.

17. See Moretti's discussion of an auction scene in Flaubert's *Sentimental Education*:

> Flaubert invites us to observe those by now familiar objects (the worktable, the shelves of *Industrial Art,* the two firescreens, the blue rug with camellias) through two simultaneous and opposite perspectives. First of all through the eyes of Frédéric, who associates with each of them a memory, an emotion, perhaps still a promise. For him these objects are not things: they are *symbols*—vehicles of meaning, of *the* meaning of his life. They are, in other words, objects which through subjectivity increase in value: to the point of being overrated. But next to Frédéric's, there are the eyes of the countless anonymous buyers: the eyes of the market. For this profane but lucid gaze the Arnoux's [*sic*] possessions have no "meaning," only a price. They are not symbols, but *commodities* (shoddy ones, like the piano—"*her* piano!"—which no one wants). (*The Way of the World,* 168)

18. For an interesting discussion of Raskol'nikov's relationship with both his parents as reflected in his dream of the horse, see Curtis, "Raskol'nikov's Sexuality."

19. Rosen, "Breaking Out of the Underground," 236, 238–39.

20. Lipking, *The Life of the Poet.*

21. Fusso, "Dostoevsky's Comely Boy," 595–96.

Pleasures of the Plague

Pushkin and Camus

Sofya Khagi

Although it has become a commonplace of Camus studies to point out the French existentialist's interest in the classical Russian writers (with Dostoevsky reasonably in the lead), Pushkin is not considered in this context.[1] This strikes me as a critical oversight.

It is clear that Camus was interested in Pushkin from an early age. A few telling biographical points: in 1937 the Algerian House of Culture (of which Camus was named secretary-general) held a Pushkin gala with a special Pushkin evening on 24 March featuring a lecture by Professor Jacques Heurgon, reprinted later in *Jeune Mediterranée*, the House of Culture organ; a piano recital; and a performance of Pushkin's *The Stone Guest*. Camus played Don Juan, and the play was performed by an amateur theater group, Théâtre du Travail, which he himself launched in 1935. The same play was given for the society Les Amis de l'USSR on May Day and on 5 May under the joint sponsorship of the House of Culture and the Union Franco-Musulmane. At the end of the performance a huge portrait of Pushkin was carried onto the stage. It is highly likely that Camus, being at the center of all the activities of the House of Culture as well as of the Théâtre du Travail, was in fact the one to inspire and organize the gala in connection with the centennial of the poet's death. Many years later, in 1959, Camus was occupied with the Festival of Mers-el-Kebir, near Oran, dedicated to Don Juan that year. Given a choice of productions, he decided on Molière, Tirso de Molina, Pushkin, Lope de Vega, and Corneille.

What is arresting in this biographical information is not that it proves Camus's acquaintance with Pushkin's oeuvre but that it shows Camus being introduced to *The Little Tragedies*, a cycle of plays that remains little known to Western readers. It is reasonable to conclude, therefore, that Pushkin figured quite prominently in Camus's imagination and that both Camus's knowledge of the Russian poet's heritage and the interest he took in Pushkin were considerable.

As *The Myth of Sisyphus* (*Le Mythe de Sisyphe*) demonstrates, Camus continued to be under the influence of *The Stone Guest* as he matured. Don Juan, remember, is one of the five representative absurd characters in *The Myth of Sisyphus*. It is apparent that Camus's interpretation of the figure is closer to that of Pushkin than to the classical renditions of Don Juan by Tirso de Molina, Molière, and Da Ponte as well as to the romantic reinterpretation of the character by Hoffmann. Rejecting both the traditional notion of Don Juan as a wicked libertine and the romantic conception of a tormented idealist, Camus offers instead a vision of the hero as a frankly hedonistic but nevertheless appealing character.[2] Evidently keeping in mind Pushkin's innovative portrayal of the hero as one whose love is always sincere, Camus argues that Don Juan loves all his women "with the same passion and each time with his whole self."[3] Similarly, like Pushkin, Camus emphasizes the character's defiant attitude to fate, focusing on the theme of the ontological rebellion in his contemplation of "Don Juanism."[4]

In fact, Camus's links to Pushkin go beyond the Don Juan motif. Of great interest are the connections *The Plague* (*La Peste*) reveals to another of Pushkin's *Little Tragedies, A Feast in Time of Plague*. Thus my task in this essay is to juxtapose Pushkin's play and Camus's novel and to show that bringing together *The Plague* and *A Feast in Time of Plague* reveals affinities between the two works that go way beyond the obvious similarities expected from narratives treating a common subject.

As René Girard pointed out in "The Plague in Literature and Myth," although "it would be exaggerated to say that plague narratives are all alike, the similarities may well be more intriguing than individual variations."[5] According to Girard, these similarities consist of an employment of the plague as a metaphor for a social crisis that involves "a spreading of mimetic violence" and "scapegoat rituals."[6] To support his thesis, Girard analyzes Raskolnikov's dream at the end of Dostoevsky's *Crime and Punishment*, Shakespeare's *Troilus and Cressida*, Sophocles'

Oedipus the King, and a few other plague tales. Neither Pushkin's *Feast in Time of Plague* nor Camus's *Plague* are discussed by Girard. These works clearly do not fit his argument, for they do not constitute examples of plague narratives in which the plague becomes a metaphor for social violence. Instead, as I am going to show, *A Feast in Time of Plague* and *The Plague* share a central preoccupation—that of "a life riddled with contradictions."[7] It is known that Pushkin's drama was one of the works Camus read as he researched literature on the disease.[8] No attempt, however, has been made to consider Pushkin's play and Camus's novel side by side—a comparison that will illuminate *The Plague*'s interest in the paradoxical. Camus's work has been read as an allegory of the French Resistance, of the Holocaust, and of World War II; more generally, as a parable of struggle against any type of totalitarianism; and still more sweepingly, as a tale of the human fight against "natural evil" in the absurd world.[9] No matter what the proposed level of generalization, however, the novel has been seen predominantly as a discovery that "men and women are not alone," through which knowledge "they gain the strength to resist, if not transform, the world."[10] Staging a dialogue between Pushkin's play and Camus's novel allows me to examine the latter from a different angle—as a speculation on the law of the paradoxical, with the phenomenology of "divorces within reality" orchestrated on both the formal and the narrative planes in the work.[11] If *A Feast in Time of Plague* could be termed "a study in oxymoron," Camus's novel may be envisioned as "an oxymoronic panorama."

Let me start with Pushkin's *Feast in Time of Plague*, which is, as is widely known, a partial translation of a portion of act 1, scene 4 from John Wilson's *The City of the Plague*. Roman Jakobson pointed out the oxymoronic nature of the title *The Stone Guest*.[12] An examination of the interplay between form and content in *The Little Tragedies* shows that all four plays are, among other things, exercises in oxymoron.[13] Three out of four titles of the individual pieces (*The Covetous Knight, The Stone Guest, A Feast in Time of Plague*) present somewhat ironically tinged, self-contradictory combinations of words. *Mozart and Salieri*, although not a formal oxymoron, expresses the idea more subtly: Mozart and Salieri represent conflicting artistic essences. Oxymoronic titles on the level of rhetoric correspond to paradoxical themes on the level of content: a knight serving gold (*The Covetous Knight*); a genius who is "a foolish idler," "not worthy of himself" (*Mozart and Salieri*); Don Juan finding his real(?) love (*The Stone Guest*); and, finally, a celebration before the face of death (*A Feast in Time of Plague*). The last piece, thus, in keeping with the overall strategy of the cycle, enacts, among other things, a paradoxical, seemingly absurd idea of "pestilent delights."

Pushkin's deviations from Wilson illuminate his project well.[14] On the level of language, we find a proliferation of oxymorons, a few of which are faithfully translated from *The City of the Plague* but most of which are Pushkin's own. A couple of examples: "amusing solemnity" [vazhnosti zabavnoi] (Pushkin 7: 175) replaces Wilson's "solemn gravity," which is not an oxymoron; "with a wild perfection" [s dikim sovershenstvom] (Pushkin 7: 176) stands for Wilson's "and wildly to thy native melodies can tune its flute-like breath"; "winter heat" [zimnii zhar] (Pushkin 7: 180) is employed by Pushkin's Walsingham in his hymn and finds no analogue in Wilson. Similarly, Wilson's straightforward words, "go, for mercy's sake, leave me to my despair,"[15] are transformed by Pushkin into another ironic paradox—Walsingham's last statement, "father, for God's sake, leave me" [otets moi, radi Boga, ostav' menia] (Pushkin 7: 184), a request to leave him "godless," "for God's sake."[16] In terms of the plot, we meet with the inconceivable and the irrational—a party of young men and women feasting on a plague-ridden London street, with the Master of Revels singing a hymn to the plague.

The addition of numerous oxymorons, presented above, comprises one way in which Pushkin transforms Wilson's original material. Regarding larger modifications, Pushkin first completely rewrites Mary's and Walsingham's songs and second stops translating almost a hundred lines before the end of the scene he selected. Views widely diverge as to his motivations with respect to shortening the scene. Donald Loewen and Victor Terras, for example, propose that Pushkin sought to subdue Wilson's anticlerical message by omitting the young man's diatribe against the Church.[17] N. Iakovlev, on the other hand, suggests that this is done not to detract attention from the basic theme—the fear of death.[18] While agreeing with Iakovlev, I believe that the theme to be highlighted is not the fear of death but a study in contradiction—an intense enjoyment of life against the "limiting situation." The very same contradiction will be explored in Camus's *The Plague*.

At this point, we come to Pushkin's original material—the major transformations of Mary's and Walsingham's songs, which have traditionally been the locus of critical attention in the play. Walsingham's celebrated hymn is preceded by Louise's fainting fit and the young man asking the Master of Revels to

> sing a rash and lively song,
> No tune composed of Scottish grief—
> But reckless, bacchanalian song,
> One fit for friends and flaming cups!

> спеть
> Нам песню вольную, живую песню,
> Не грустию шотландской вдохновенну,
> А буйную, вакхическую песнь,
> Рожденную за чашею кипящей.
> (Pushkin 7: 179)

The young man's request highlights the opposition the play builds between Mary's and Walsingham's songs as expressive of two approaches to the plague and, by extension, of two contesting worldviews; furthermore, it identifies the background against which the hymn should be considered—a bacchanalian song. The genre is not new to Pushkin—in 1825 he composed the peculiar "Vakkhicheskaia pesnia" (Bacchanalian song) in which he praised, along with wine and "tender maidens," "the immortal sun of reason":

> Why, revelry's voice, are you still?
> Ring out, songs of Bacchus, our patron!
> Long life to you, maiden and matron,
> Ye fair ones who gave your love with a will!
> Drink, friend, drink with gusto and relish!
> As I do in mine,
> In your glass of wine
> Fling lightly the ring that you cherish!
> Come, let's clink our glasses and high let us raise them!
> Hail, muses! Hail, reason! In song let us praise them!
> Thou, bright sun of genius, shine on!

Like this ancient lamp that grows dimmer
And fades with the coming of dawn,
So the false wisdom pales at the first tiny glimmer
Of true wisdom's ne'er-fading light . . .
Live, radiant day! Perish, darkness and night![19]

Что смолкнул веселия глас?
Раздайтесь, вакхальны припевы!
Да здравствуют нежные девы
И юные жены, любившие нас!
Полнее стакан наливайте!
На звонкое дно
В густое вино
Заветные кольца бросайте!
Подымем стаканы, содвинем их разом!
Да здравствуют музы, да здравствует разум!
Ты, солнце святое, гори!
Как зта лампада бледнеет
Пред ясным восходом зари,
Так ложная мудрость мерцает и тлеет
Пред солнцем бессмертным ума.
Да здравствует солнце, да скроется тьма!
(Pushkin 2: 420)

The poem is no less paradoxical than a feast in time of plague. From the title we expect a paean to Bacchus, the god of wine, and, as such, a praise of the ecstatic, orgiastic, and irrational elements of life; yet our expectations are thwarted, and we find a celebration of reason and mind, the antithetical sphere of the rational and the light. In other words, in Nietzschean terms, a hymn to Dionysus turns out to be a praise of the solar-diurnal ("before mind's eternal sun") Apollo.[20] In *A Feast in Time of Plague* we encounter a similar subversion of the reader's expectations: instead of celebrating the pleasures of life, Walsingham offers something that at first appears to be a praise of death, a tribute to the plague. Or is it? Walsingham's hymn presents a number of complexities. For one thing, it follows Wilson in developing a tension between two responses to the plague: underscoring the plague's "deadly grandeur" versus its trivialization as the inevitable evil (Wilson), and hiding from pestilence in revelry versus defiance and valorization of mortal danger (Pushkin). Starting with conventional declarations in the "carpe diem" spirit, the hymn moves on to celebrate heroic grace under pressure. Still, it must be noted that, in Walsingham's hymn, the motif of active confrontation overpowers the theme of escaping the horror by "locking oneself up" and "drowning gaily minds." Whereas the "seize the day" psychological response is touched upon in a single stanza, three powerful final stanzas are devoted to the "irrational" delights of confronting death. Moreover, the first scene and character descriptions expressly state that the heroes are feasting in the street ("A street; a table, laid for a feast"; "Several men and women celebrants" [Pushkin 7: 175]), making open confrontation the play's leitmotif from its very start.[21] Similarly, both psychological insights (hiding in revelry and defiance) will be explored in *The Plague.*

Even more importantly, the theme of "inexpressible delights" [neiz'iasnimy naslazhden'ia] is itself ambiguous. How are we to interpret the depicted emotions? One possibility would be to read the lines as an intimation of the death wish. To support such a view, one could quote the poet himself, who once confessed that he wanted to express in verse "the incomprehensible desire of a man, standing on a height, to throw himself down."[22] The problem with this explanation, however, has to do with Walsingham's focus not on death as such but on the fascination with life through confronting extinction. It is more fruitful to interpret "inexpressible delights" as a Nietzschean delight in one's power that finds its ultimate expression in daring the greatest of enemies.[23] In this context, the line "perhaps, a token of immortality" [bessmert'ia, mozhet byt', zalog] (Pushkin 7: 180) must be understood not in the traditional Christian sense, that is, in Terras's words, as "a subconscious awareness that death is a bridge to eternal life,"[24] but as Mikhail Gershenzon, N. Iakovlev, and Nikolai Beliak and Mariia Virolainen, among others, understood it—in the sense of rising above death by spurning it.[25]

The third (and, to my mind, most productive) perspective on this enigmatic pronouncement would be to read it as a reaffirmation of the zeal for happiness and life, shown in the hymn to be inseparable from and, in fact, dependent on the cognizance of despair and death. "All, all that threatens to destroy" [vse, vse, chto gibel'iu grozit] (Pushkin 7: 180) delights us not only as an opportunity to rise above ourselves (the greater the challenge, the greater the glory) but also as an enlightening experience of a mortal realizing the preciousness of existence against the certainty of annihilation. In this respect, Walsingham's announcement that he does not know a bacchanalian song but will sing a hymn in honor of the plague can be seen as bringing forth the paradoxical intermingling of the joy of *Existenz* and the horror of mortality.[26] The idea, to be sure, is one of *The Plague*'s underlying themes. As a number of critics have pointed out, Mary's song is momentous in the narrative, since it provides a competing Christian attitude to the disaster.[27] For my purposes, it is also important that the story of the plague that ravaged a small Scottish village is framed by Walsingham's remarks before and after it as an artistic piece. It is stressed that Mary's song, albeit on a tragic subject, serves to entertain:

> So sing us, Mary, something sad,
> That we may then more madly still
> To mirth return, like one who wakes
> From some dark dream to earth again.
>
> Спой, Мери, нам уныло и протяжно,
> Чтоб мы потом к веселью обратились
> Безумнее, как тот, кто от земли
> Был отлучен каким-нибудь виденьем.
> (Pushkin 7: 176)

Walsingham questions the appropriateness of turning a tale of suffering into art:

> And now that dreadful year that took
> So many brave and noble souls
> Has only left the barest trace
> In this your simple, rustic song,
> So touching and so sad.
>
> И мрачный год, в который пало столько
> Отважных, добрых и прекрасных жертв,
> Едва оставил память о себе
> В какой-нибудь простой пастушьей песне,
> Унылой и приятной.
> (Pushkin 7: 177)

These bitter and ironic words, emphasizing the rift between the graveness of the story and the trivial uses to which it is put, touch upon an ethical problem that will be explored in *The Plague* in great depth.

The conclusion of Pushkin's play has also generated a variety of readings, from interpreting the ending as Walsingham's total victory over the priest to understanding the finale as his no-less-than-total defeat. Thus, at one end of the spectrum we have the hymn expressing "the triumph of a lofty human spirit over death" and, at the opposite end, "a self-deceived protagonist eloquently claiming to enjoy a happiness which proves to be transient and false" and "a would-be 'superman' unmasked as a mere pretender."[28] Critics also argue that the way Pushkin translates Wilson reveals "moving from the portrayal of Walsingham as a defiant, perhaps victorious figure in Wilson's scene, to a portrayal as a tragic figure."[29] It may be objected that the new hymn that introduces the theme of "inexpressible delights" makes Pushkin's Walsingham appear more rebellious than Wilson's Master of Revels; besides, Pushkin's Walsingham, as opposed to Wilson's, does not admit to "hatred and deep contempt of his own worthless self" or to being "sunk in utter wretchedness."[30] Nor does Pushkin's hero confess to despair when the priest leaves but instead remains "sunk in deep contemplation" [pogruzhen v glubokuiu zadumchivost'] (7: 184). As the closing remark indicates, the end is open: Pushkin's Master of Revels is neither victorious nor beaten but deliberating the dilemma.[31] The possibility that the opponents may offer complementary rather than mutually exclusive truths is hinted at on the level of language by an interplay of reverberations in Walsingham's and the priest's speeches. Walsingham's "more madly" [bezumnee], "stormy darkness" [burnoi t'my], and "grim abyss" [bezdny mrachnoi] are echoed in the priest's "godless madmen" [bezbozhnye bezumtsy], "pitch dark" [t'mu kromeshnuiu], and "over grim silence" [nad mrachnoi tishinoi] (Pushkin 7: 176–81). Conversely, the priest's "frantic songs" [beshenye pesni] and "pale faces" [blednykh lits] echo in Walsingham's "frantic gaiety" [beshenykh veselii] and "with a pale hand" [blednoiu rukoiu] (Pushkin 7: 181–82). Extreme situations may be conducive to the reconciliation of the opponents.

These insights are echoed in Camus. At the conclusion of *The Plague*, with Oran liberated from the disease and Tarrou dead, the narrator, Dr. Rieux, muses about his friend: "Tarrou, denying as he did the right to condemn anyone whomsoever—though he knew well that no one can help condemning and that it befalls even the victim sometimes to turn executioner—Tarrou lived a *life riddled with contradictions* and had never known hope's solace" (263, emphasis added). *The Plague* shares a number of narrative parallels with *A Feast in Time of Plague*. Thus, Rieux and Rambert (two of the three major protagonists of the novel), like Walsingham, find themselves separated from their loved ones by the epidemic.[32] Walsingham's Mathilda is killed by the disease. Rieux's wife dies from the "white plague" in a tuberculosis sanatorium while he battles pestilence in Oran. Rambert, caught by the plague in the quarantined city, desperately tries to obtain a certificate that will permit him to return to Paris to his lover. *A Feast in Time of Plague* makes it clear that for Walsingham the loss of Mathilda is the most terrible consequence of the plague. Likewise, Camus's narrator stresses that the plight of separation from loved ones in the quarantined city is the most painful effect of the disaster: "[O]nce the town gates were shut [. . .] a feeling normally as individual as the ache of separation from those one loves suddenly became a feeling in which all shared alike and—together with fear—the greatest affliction of the long period of exile that lay ahead" (61).[33] In addition, *The Plague*, like Pushkin's play, juxtaposes characters who espouse an attitude of proud defiance to the disaster to personages epitomizing self-effacing, meek qualities. If Rieux, Tarrou, and Rambert (the three main characters of *The Plague*) correspond to Walsingham and his friends, Rieux's mother represents Camus's analogue of Mary. Significantly, Tarrou's last entry into his diary is about Rieux's mother. The entry tells us about Mme Rieux's "self-effacement" and "kindness" and stresses that, "dim and silent though she was, she quailed before no light, even the garish light of the plague" (248). Rieux-Tarrou-Rambert and Mme Rieux, like Walsingham and Mary, serve as complementary truths, two types of defiance against the plague. Finally, just as Pushkin's Walsingham is confronted by the priest, Camus's heroes are opposed by Father Paneloux, who initially praises the plague as "the scourge of God," sent "to humble the proud of heart and lay low those who hardened themselves against Him" (81). Like Pushkin's Priest, he calls people to submit to a "higher will" but later, shaken by the horrors of the epidemic, joins the voluntary brigades. The possibility for reconciliation hinted at by Pushkin is realized here. Importantly, it is the "godless" Rieux, rather than Father Paneloux, who has matured enough to discern that they are comrades, fighting destruction together, so that "God himself can't part them now" (197).

Camus's narrator commences the tale by expressing his desire that the chronicle be about the shared feelings of the populace as it was affected by the epidemic. Stressing the plague's leveling effect, making individual emotions communal, the narrator begins each of the five parts with an overview of the psychological consequences of the disease in the populace.[34] It is vis-à-vis these generalizations that Pushkin's insights with respect to the disaster's emotional impact on the people become particularly relevant: "In the early days, when they thought this epidemic was much like other epidemics, religion held its ground. But once these people realized their instant peril, they gave their thoughts to pleasure. And all the hideous fears that stamp their faces in the daytime are transformed in the fiery, dusty nightfall into a sort of hectic exultation, an unkempt freedom fevering their blood" (111). Accordingly, the citizens of Oran "seem determined to counteract the plague by a lavish display of luxury" (111). As dusk sets, they "stream down into the open, drug themselves with talking, start arguing or love-making, and in the last glow of sunset the town, freighted with lovers two by two and loud with voices, drifts like a helmless ship into the throbbing darkness. In vain a zealous evangelist with a felt hat and flowing tie threads his way through the crowd, crying without cease: 'God is great and good. Come unto him'" (111). Like Pushkin's revelers, who, disregarding danger, celebrate on the street, Oran's populace "stream[s] down into the open," talking, arguing, and making love. Just as Pushkin's priest cannot dissuade young men and women, Camus's preachers vainly try to bring the citizens to their senses. Notably, Camus manages to communicate precisely the same mental state of the populace, with all its subtleties and contradictions, that is played out in Walsingham's hymn. Is it defiance ("stream down into the open")? An escape (intoxication is emphasized—"drown gaily minds" in Pushkin, "drug themselves" in Camus)? A valiant desire to assert their superiority over the all-powerful plague/death ("an unkempt freedom fevering their blood")? A general psychosis ("all the hideous fears [...] hectic exultation")? A defense mechanism? All these? Regardless of the preferred answer, the book reconstructs faithfully the whole spectrum of conflicting sentiments and motivations arising in connection with the plague explored by Pushkin, all of which are rarely heeded by critics taken chiefly with the solidarity and resistance motif of Camus's novel.

Structurally, the work is divided into five parts, of which the first details the onset of the disease, the second depicts its rise, the third its apogee, and the last two its fall. Thus the novel's organization corresponds to that of Pushkin's play, which is divided by Mary's and Walsingham's songs into five tiny sections. Hence Camus's novel and Pushkin's play follow the five-act division used in classical tragedy.[35] *The Plague*'s playlike features have been noticed by Sophie Picon, who, however, assumed that they were not intentional and criticized Camus: "The dialogues are troublesome. [...] It is plain that their 'register' is one of intellectual stylization. The voices answer one another like voices in a play reading, when, unmindful of decor and characters, we are attentive only to the alternating brilliance of the language. But Camus seems suddenly to remember that his characters are not eloquent abstractions. [...] He then separates the voices and introduces moments of dramatic orchestration into these short sentences."[36] It is likely that *The Plague*'s dramatic "feel" is not accidental. Indeed, as a consideration of the novel's plot plainly shows, Camus's work does not simply conform to the conventional five-act structure but, rather, closely replicates the five phases of the dramatic conflict as prescribed in the canon: part 1, introduction/protasis (presenting the setting, the characters, and the problem); part 2, rising action/epitasis (escalation of the disease); part 3, climax (the plague's peak); part 4, falling action/catastasis (the plague slowly subsiding); part 5, catastrophe (Tarrou's death, the death of Rieux's wife).[37] From this perspective *The Plague* presents itself as a novel-play or, to be more exact, a modern novel–ancient tragedy.[38]

A Feast in Time of Plague's two supreme incompatibilities, love and death, are invoked by Camus's narrator in the very beginning as he provides a short depiction of his native town:[39] "Perhaps the easiest way of making a town's acquaintance is to ascertain how the people in it work, how they love, and how they die. In our little town [...] all three are done on much the same lines, with the same feverish yet casual air. The truth is that everyone is bored, and devotes himself to cultivating habits. For lack of time and thinking, people have to love one another without knowing much about it" (4–5). The words "without knowing much about it" are crucial: the citizens of this typical modern town lead superficial, dull existences, unaware of possibilities for a deeper, fuller, and more intense sense of love and being. Boredom implies waste of life and time, of which little was "squeezed out" (137). Appropriately enough, Tarrou, perhaps the most insightful character of the novel, has a humorous contemplation on "how to contrive not to waste one's time" as one of the first entries in his diary (24). In a paradoxical twist, intimated in Pushkin, it is the plague that awakens the citizens to the realization that it is blissful merely to exist, just as it is the death sentence that thrusts Meursault, another of Camus's heroes, out of his sleepy state into a fierce infatuation with "being." In a sense, the whole of Oran becomes "Meursaults," condemned to death by the epidemic and expressive of the frenzy for life that is brought about by an immense disaster. *A Feast in Time of Plague*'s leitmotif, affirmation of "being" through a cognizance of "nothingness," is played out on an epic scale in Camus's work.

Rieux, Tarrou, and Rambert form a triangle that constitutes the center of resistance to the epidemic. Dr. Bernard Rieux is a dedicated physician who puts up a fight against the fatal disease, selflessly and unflinchingly attending to the sick while his wife is dying in a sanatorium far away. Jean Tarrou is a wealthy, mysterious tourist who befriends Rieux and joins him in the fight. Raymond Rambert is a journalist, trapped in Oran by the quarantine, eventually "enlisting in the ranks." Joseph Grand, a petty clerk and the "unheroic" hero of the struggle, and Father Paneloux are two other important characters. The trio Rieux-Tarrou-Rambert comprises Camus's analogue of Pushkin's Walsingham and his young friends. It is equally possible to consider them as an analogue of Walsingham alone, for they are presented in the novel in such a way as to suggest that they are reflections of one another. The physical depictions of the three personages emphasize their likeness: the men are of average height, square shouldered, powerfully built, rather coarse looking but manly.[40] The portrayals accentuate virility, intellect, and determination. None of the three major protagonists believes in God, yet they display a propensity for astounding devotion and self-sacrifice. Rieux, Tarrou, and Rambert merge into a single figure—that of "the rebel" [l'homme revolté], who, like Walsingham, rallies against "natural evil" but, unlike Pushkin's hero, turns to help his peers at the time of calamity. This is precisely Camus's point, his response to *A Feast in Time of Plague*, and the novel's central paradox—that of the "atheist-saint" who proclaims happiness as life's highest goal, devoid of any vestige of hope or faith and yet ready to die himself because "he's never managed to get used to seeing people die" (117).

The Plague's principal paradox is voiced by Tarrou during the scene of the last long discussion between him and Rieux, followed by their swim, which comprises the philosophical crux of the novel:

> "It comes to this," Tarrou said almost casually; "what interests me is learning how to become a saint."
>
> "But you don't believe in God."
>
> "Exactly! Can one be a saint without God?—that's the problem, in fact the only problem, I'm up against today." (230–31)

The Plague stages the seemingly incomprehensible: holiness without heaven and hell or, more exactly, holiness with "hell-being" and nothingness afterward. It is usually accepted that Camus aims at proving the possibility of "secular sainthood" and that "true saintliness has little to do with belief in God."[41] In fact, he goes further than that, hinting that true saintliness has everything to do with disbelief in God, for this purest kind of grace "by caprice" does not depend on the notions of punishment or reward. In a powerful critique of Christian mores, Camus completely reverses the orthodox understanding of the relation between faith and virtue. (Here Camus clearly takes issue with Dostoevsky.) "Can one be a saint without God?" gets transformed into "Can one be a saint with God?" The text presents a series of statements that seem paradoxical at first but that, upon deeper contemplation, reveal their discernment to the reader: "Rambert savored that bitter sense of freedom which comes of total deprivation" (101); "God does not exist, since otherwise there would be no need for priests" (108); "I lived with the idea of my innocence, that is to say, with no idea at all" (222); and "he was one of those rare people who have the courage of their good feelings" (43). Numerous insights like these build up to the central divulgence—that of the atheist sainthood.

In the course of their discussion, Rieux and Tarrou come up with another incongruity. Rieux remarks: "'You know, I feel more fellowship with the defeated than with saints. Heroism and sanctity don't really appeal to me, I imagine. What interests me is being a man.'" Tarrou's response is "'Yes, we're both after the same thing, but I'm less ambitious'" (231). Clearly, living by an ideal provides exultation and is therefore easier than living humbly with common decency. Hence the next oxymoron—"unheroic hero"—in the person of Joseph Grand, a petty government employee with strong Gogolian traits whose wife left him many years ago and who is consumed by a ludicrous passion for writing and rewriting the opening sentence of a novel: "If it is a fact that people like to have examples given them, men of the type they call heroic, and if it is absolutely necessary that this narrative should include a 'hero,' the narrator commends to his readers, with, to his thinking, perfect justice, this insignificant and obscure hero who had to his credit only a little goodness of heart and a seemingly absurd ideal" (126).

The "unheroic hero" is also interesting to us as a means of illuminating the dilemma of transforming "plague" into "art." Pushkin's play, one remembers, calls our attention to the trivial uses to which the story of the ravaged village in Mary's song is put. Paradoxically, this trifle, in no way doing justice to the tragedy, is the only way in which the memory of it will survive. Three complex issues are thus intimated here: art as a memorial to the wiped out, art as an inadequate expression of the tragedy, and art's trivial uses. All three questions are explored in great subtlety in Camus's novel. Since space does not permit me to go into details here, I shall merely draw attention to the fact that Rieux insists that his narrative be looked at as "bearing witness in favor of those plague-stricken people, so that *some* memorial of the injustice and outrage done them might endure," and to Grand's request when ill to burn his numerous "slim young horsewomen" (278, emphasis added).[42] It has been pointed out that the horsewoman, with her apocalyptic overtones, presents an "aestheticized" image of the plague; accordingly, Grand's request that his manuscript be burned should be understood along the same lines as Walsingham's observation on turning tragedy into art in Mary's song.[43]

As demonstrated above, the general populace's psychological condition seems to correspond largely to the one depicted in the third stanza of Walsingham's hymn. The major protagonists of *The Plague* (Rieux and Tarrou in particular), on the other hand, relate to the hymn's second half. Tarrou, with his confession that "death means nothing to men like him" for "it's the event that proves them right" (112) and his heroic stance, comes closer than any other character to the Nietzschean reading of Walsingham's song. Neither for him, nor even less for Rieux, however, do the pleasures of "living dangerously" have primary significance. What is of paramount importance is that the plague brings "knowing," and knowing means "a living warmth, and a picture of death" (263), the former thrown by the latter into relief. Just as Walsingham's hymn can be viewed as a reaffirmation of life, inseparable from the horror of extinction, Rieux and Tarrou come to grasp the paradoxical interplay of "feast" and "plague." The climactic scene of the night swim, with its rich sensual pleasure and the joy of friendship deepened by the plague-ridden city in the background, expresses exactly that: the preciousness of "being" against the certainty of "nothingness."

Critics have customarily stressed the evolution of Camus's thought from a stance of individual revolt (*The Stranger*, *The Myth of Sisyphus*) to that of communal responsibility and solidarity (*The Plague*, *The Rebel*). *The Plague* was considered chiefly in terms of "the values of justice, loyalty and courage appearing on the absurd's frontiers."[44] *The Plague*'s preoccupation with paradoxes, highlighted through the novel's dialogue with *A Feast in Time of Plague*, shifts accents from the challengers back to the challenged, for this preoccupation leads us straight to the notion of the principal "divorce within reality" or the absurd, conceptualized in existentialist thinking as the contradiction between man's longing for eternity and the inevitability of death. The nobility of the protagonists (from "an innocent murderer" in *The Stranger* to "atheist saints" in *The Plague*), if anything, intensifies the feeling of the absurd; the chasm grows still more vast between the ignominy of reality and human grandeur. The heroes' defeat after, in Camus's words, "the last disastrous battle that ends a war and makes peace itself an ill beyond all remedy" becomes all the more tragic.

Remarkably, it was Pushkin's miniplay, created more than a century before Camus wrote *The Plague*, that anticipated in numerous respects the treatment of poignant existential dilemmas in one of the greatest novels of the twentieth century.

Notes

I want to express my deep gratitude to Svetlana Evdokimova for her helpful comments on this essay.

1. Both *The Myth of Sisyphus* and *The Rebel* discuss Dostoevsky's works. *The Fall* draws on *Notes from Underground*. See a recent book-length investigation of the subject by Davison, *Camus*.

2. As compared to Tirso de Molina's violent and deceitful hero, Molière's trickster-hypocrite, and Da Ponte's unscrupulous Don Juan, Pushkin's Juan is much more positively portrayed. At the same time, *The Stone Guest* questions Juan's conversion from a libertine into an idealistic lover.

3. Camus, *The Myth of Sisyphus*, 68.

4. In contrast to Tirso's Don Juan and to Molière's hero, Pushkin's character remains defiant until the very last moment of the drama. Likewise, Camus claims that Don Juan "has but one reply to divine wrath, and that is human honor" (ibid., 71).

5. Girard, "The Plague in Literature and Myth," 155.

6. Ibid., 158–60.

7. Camus, *The Plague*, 263. Hereafter cited in text.

8. Brée, *Albert Camus*, 263. The other pieces are Boccaccio's *Decameron*, Defoe's *A Journal of the Plague Year*, and Kleist's and Manzoni's stories (ibid., 33). It is often pointed out that Defoe's work influenced Camus. In this context, it may be recalled that Pushkin's play also has a link to Defoe. Wilson's *The City of the Plague* drew on *A Journal of the Plague Year*. However, this drama treats the plague in a way that has little, if anything, in common with Defoe's account. Correspondingly, Pushkin's play, based on an excerpt from Wilson's work, has very little to do with Defoe. For comparisons of Camus and Defoe, see Stephanson, "The Plague Narratives of Defoe and Camus"; and Rocks, "Camus Reads Defoe."

9. Thody explains why bubonic plague as an illness is particularly fitting as a representation of "natural evil": "It is not an illness which human beings either cause or make worse by their own unwise or immoral conduct. It can be explained, if at all, only by saying that the universe makes no sense whatsoever if you look at it in terms of human ideas of right and wrong" (*Albert Camus*, 47).

10. Rhein, *Albert Camus*, 35.

11. In existentialist philosophy the expression "divorces within reality" refers to paradoxes.

12. See Jakobson, "The Statue in Pushkin's Poetic Mythology." Lotman, "Opyt rekonstruktsii pushkinskogo siuzheta ob Iisuse," also remarks on Pushkin's propensity for coining "sharp-dull" titles.

13. Monter notices that Walsingham's hymn "is an extended oxymoron epitomizing the paradox [. . .] of the 'inexplicable pleasures' in a dark love" ("Love and Death," 212). Similarly, Shapiro mentions oxymoron in his discussion of *The Little Tragedies* but believes that "the four plays were governed in structure by an overarching formal principle—that of metonymy" ("Journey to the Metonymic Pole," 181, 182). I consider the employment of oxymoron as not limited in *A Feast in Time of Plague* to a contemplation of "inexplicable pleasures" but, rather, functioning as the play's overarching principle, implemented on both the thematic and the formal levels.

14. A widely discussed question is how close (or distant) *A Feast in Time of Plague* is to *The City of the Plague* or, at least, to the translated scene. Although most critics seem to favor "the distant view" (for the opposite argument, see, for example, Terras, "Pushkin's 'Feast during the Plague' and Its Original"; Karpiak, "Pushkin's *Little Tragedies*"), opinions are divided as to how precisely the translation departs from the original. Indeed, the state of matters is such that almost any argument on the subject can be easily matched with its antithesis in another article. For examples of "theses antitheses," see Iakovlev, "Pir vo vremia chumy,"

608, and Loewen, "Disguised as Translation," 46–49; Terras, "Pushkin's 'Feast during the Plague' and Its Original," 218, and Beliak and Virolainen, "'Malen'kie tragedii' kak kul'turnyi epos novoevropeiskoi istorii," 83; Monter, "Love and Death," 212, and Kibal'nik, *Khudozhestvennaia filosofiia Pushkina*, 166.

15. Wilson, *Oxford Prize Poems*, 44, 45, 57.

16. I use James E. Falen's translation of *A Feast in Time of Plague* except when literal translations are required for the purposes of my argument. The omission of "to my despair," along with a few details discussed elsewhere, weakens Loewen's suggestion that the translation trajectory "indicates a movement from the portrayal of Walsingham as a defiant, perhaps victorious figure in Wilson's scene, to a portrayal as a tragic figure closely identified with Jenny and Edmond" ("Disguised as Translation," 54).

17. See Terras, "Pushkin's 'Feast during the Plague' and Its Original," 211; Loewen, "Disguised as Translation," 55. The Young Man's "godless" speech, in fact, is more than counterbalanced in Wilson by the Master of Revels's "Fool! hold thy peace! / Thou in thy heart hast said there is no God. Yet knowest thyself—liar" (*Oxford Prize Poems*, 58). Consequently, Wilson's Walsingham occupies a more (and not less, as Loewen claims) dutiful position in religious matters than Pushkin's Master of Revels.

18. Iakovlev, "Pir vo vremia chumy," 608.

19. Pushkin, *The Complete Works*, vol. 2, *Lyric Poems: 1820–26*, 161–62.

20. The poem received particular attention during the Silver Age. However, Russian philosophical critics did not seem to appreciate the rift between the form and the content. Thus, Merezhkovsky reads it as "a hymn to Bacchus's health, to the eternal sun, golden measure of things—beauty" (Gal'tseva, ed., *Pushkin v russkoi filosofskoi kritike*, 103).

21. This contradicts a recent assertion that the heroes "are totally preoccupied with their own personal fear and desire to seize any distraction from that fear" (Anderson, "Essays on Pushkin's 'Little Tragedies,'" in Pushkin, *The Little Tragedies*, 193). As Monter justly points out, Pushkin's characters, unlike the storytellers of the *Decameron*, another famous plague story, "do not attempt to move themselves from the plague and create a pleasant life outside of it" ("Love and Death," 212).

22. Bartenev, *Rasskazy o Pushkine*, 44.

23. Pushkin and Nietzsche have been discussed in detail in Svetlana Evdokimova's lectures on *A Feast in Time of Plague*.

24. Terras, "Pushkin's 'Feast during the Plague' and Its Original," 214.

25. Compare to Kirillov's death in Dostoevsky's *The Devils*.

26. The disease, rather than being a metaphor for social ills, functions in Pushkin's drama as a representation of nature's destructive forces. Analogously, Camus's novel turns the plague into a symbol of the absurd. Neither the crisis of contagious violence nor the transference of responsibility for the crisis on a scapegoat (see above on Girard's *The Plague in Literature and Myth*) takes place in the works.

27. The song's major purpose is hardly that of establishing a connection

between Walsingham and Edmond in order to show that "Walsingham's revelry is really a betrayal of Matil'da's memory" (Loewen, "Disguised as Translation," 51). There seems no need for additional explications—the reader perceives the dilemma as soon as "a woman's voice" announces, "He raves about his buried wife" [on bredit o zhene pokhoronennoi] (Pushkin 7: 183). Furthermore, Jenny's request to Edmond "to leave behind their stricken village and find some place apart where these torments may be lightened" [i potom ostav' selen'e, uhodi kuda-nibud', gde b ty mog dushi muchen'e usladit' i otdohnut'] (Pushkin 7: 177) pushes him in the direction of a path that is none too admirable.

28. Blagoi, *Tvorcheskii put' Pushkina* (1967), 666; Gregg, "The Eudaemonic Theme," 190; Terras, "Pushkin's 'Feast during the Plague' and Its Original," 217.

29. Loewen, "Disguised as Translation," 54.

30. Wilson, *Oxford Prize Poems*, 589, 590.

31. Lotman and Rassadin support the open-endedness interpretation. See Lotman, "Opyt rekonstruktsii," 316; Rassadin, *Dramaturg Pushkin*, 357.

32. An interesting biographical parallel: Pushkin wrote *A Feast in Time of Plague* in Boldino, separated from his fiancée by an epidemic of cholera; Camus composed *The Plague* estranged from his wife, Francine, by war (Rizzuto, *Camus*, 67).

33. According to Girard, the plague "is universally presented as a process of undifferentiation, a destruction of specificities." Girard links this "process of undifferentiation" to a spreading of imitative violence and, ultimately, to a total social collapse ("The Plague in Literature and Myth," 155, cf. 156–62). In Camus's novel, by contrast, the leveling of differences brought about by the epidemic plays a positive role. The "destruction of specificities" unites the Oran populace against the common enemy.

34. See ibid., no. 32.

35. See Bronner, *Camus*, 64. The critic mentions that *The Plague* follows the five-act division but does not consider its implications.

36. Picon quoted in Brée, ed., *Camus*, 148.

37. Tarrou's death presents an example of the sacrificial theme in a plague narrative that, however, does not at all conform to Girard's interpretation of the sacrificial theme as a scapegoat process. According to Girard, a scapegoat ritual implies finding a supposed wrongdoer, upon whom the community transfers the responsibility for the crisis. Such a wrongdoer is the "right victim" in the sense that everyone can unite against him ("The Plague in Literature and Myth," 164). By contrast, Tarrou is the "right victim" in the sense that his death is particularly fit to dramatize the absurd: Tarrou is stricken by the plague when the epidemic has all but ended.

38. Similar observations have been made by Viacheslav Ivanov about Dostoevsky's novels.

39. Monter, "Love and Death," 206.

40. Compare the three portrayals: Rambert—"short, square-shouldered, with a determined-looking face and keen, intelligent eyes, he gave the impression of someone who could keep his end up in any circumstances"; Tarrou—"a stocky,

youngish man, with a big, deeply furrowed face and bushy eyebrows"; Rieux—"moderate height. Broad shoulders. Almost rectangular face. Dark, steady eyes, but prominent jaws. A biggish, well-modeled nose. [. . .] A curving mouth with thick, usually tight-set lips" (Camus, *The Plague*, 23, 24, 25).

41. Oxenhandler, *Looking for Heroes in Postwar France*, 54.

42. See Leavy, *To Blight with Plague*, 199–205; Fitch, *The Narcissistic Text*, 15. The latter argues that "the real subject of *The Plague* is none other than the text in all its various forms."

43. For instance, see Leavy, *To Blight with Plague*, 200–201: "The seemingly contrasting picture of Grand's young horsewoman among the flowers of a Paris garden is transformed by the author's impending demise into an aestheticized image of the plague."

44. Brée, ed., *Camus*, 62.

The Little Tragedies in Film and Opera

Little Tragedies, Little Operas

Caryl Emerson

In January 1999 in the Russian city of Perm on the Siberian frontier, the Pushkin Bicentennial year was set into motion with an unusual musical event. The Perm Academic Theater of Opera and Ballet premiered an ambitious project that had been two years in the making: a cycle of five operas in three nights entitled *Operatic Pushkiniana.* It featured Musorgsky's initial (1869, chamber-sized) version of *Boris Godunov* and then, performed back to back, the four chamber operas created by four Russian composers out of Pushkin's *Little Tragedies: The Covetous Knight, Mozart and Salieri, The Stone Guest,* and *A Feast in Time of Plague.*[1]

The Perm musicians had debated at length the unity of Pushkin's dramatic cycle. Was it a laboratory in which the poet had experimented with minimalist dramatic form? A concise encyclopedia of human passions and vices? A window into Pushkin's own anxieties circa 1830 (miserly fathers, professional jealousies, the pleasures of love becoming the horror of cuckoldry, the capriciousness of cholera)? Were these miniature plays meant to be "pocket metatheater," with the Baron, Don Juan, Salieri, and Walsingham each representing a static eternal type—or do the heroes undergo genuine dramatic development, a moral change or moment of conversion that makes their stories more akin to the dramatized parables of didactic theater? And then there was the usual anxiety that flares up whenever Russia's perfect poet is transposed to opera. Is it not a sort of blasphemy to dilute Pushkin's lines by adding actors and music?

One thing was clear: however one assessed the cohesiveness of Pushkin's dramatic cycle, there was no easy or ready unity among the musical works created out of it. The "little operas" had been composed by various hands, variously gifted, between 1869 and 1906. Each of the composers—Alexander Dargomyzhsky, Nikolai Rimsky-Korsakov, César Cui, Sergei Rachmaninoff—took advantage of the remarkable verbal compression of the plays, their already "librettistic" quality, and each set Pushkin's text essentially intact, making the occasional tiny cut but neither supplementing nor rearranging the poet's words. Thus these transpositions have been spared the charge of "grossly violating Pushkin" that is routinely leveled against Musorgsky and, even more, against Tchaikovsky. Those two titans in the world of opera sinned and achieved on a grand scale. Since their source texts were not in singable (or actable) form, they were obliged to adapt and compress, producing out of Pushkin very fine, very free, and inevitably "unfaithful" full-length operas that today proudly coexist in the canon as independent creations. None of the chamber operas built off *The Little Tragedies* possesses the range or complex vision that governs the operatic *Boris Godunov, Eugene Onegin,* or *The Queen of Spades.*

In fact, the problem presented by these four little musical works is unusual in the annals of nineteenth-century opera, which adapted full-length plays, novels, epics, and national legends with great inventiveness and aplomb. The plays in Pushkin's dramatic cycle required almost no reworking. The astonished librettist is confronted with that most rare thing: a source text that, as it stands, is not too long. Thus absolute fidelity to the poet's words becomes a real possibility—and another problem presents itself to the composer: what precisely should a musicalization accomplish? Why is music needed at all? Is there such a thing as overrealizing an emotional gesture or psychological moment, already perfectly pitched? The task bears some resemblance to song writing. With a miraculous confluence of talents, a perfect lyric poem can be set as a perfect song. But vocal settings that strive to be faithful to a larger verbal-dramatic whole, where so much depends on dialogue and on the precise timing of encounters and scenes, are always vulnerable to that curious blend of inflation and flattening that full-scale opera knows so well. As one recent American translator of Pushkin's plays has remarked, "[E]ach of the 'Little Tragedies' starts, so to speak, at the beginning of the fifth act, at the moment when a preexisting unstable situation is at the point of becoming a crisis, and moves swiftly and inexorably to its catastrophic climax."[2] Recast for chamber performance, these "fifth acts" come to resemble more closely a heightened dialogic fragment—the explosive end moment of recognition and catastrophe—than they do authentic drama. There is no time for musical motifs to develop, for actions to ripen, or for heroes to mature. Unsurprisingly, each little opera in its own era was welcomed as a curiosity but received mixed reviews.

With the exception of Rimsky-Korsakov's *Mozart and Salieri* (and that only barely), none of the four entered standard repertory. They are recalled to performance most often as an extension of Pushkin's legacy, linked to one of his jubilees, rather than recognized as musical achievements central to their composers' creative evolution. (Significantly, the operas in piano-vocal score were reissued in 1999, as a Pushkin Bicentennial tribute, in a single glossy four-volume series, with brief introductory essays in Russian and English and an [uncredited] English translation of Pushkin's play at the end.[3] Cui's effort would otherwise never have merited such prolonged life or distinguished musical company.) In 1999 the Perm Opera Company billed its three-night extravaganza as the "Russian *Ring*," but such a Wagnerian promotion tactic was a considerable liberty. Was there any musically valid rationale for linking, in a single performance cycle, these four works of uncertain genre by four different composers? Can the glistening thread of Pushkin's word provide sufficient unity? In terms of musical style or technical excellence, certainly not. As part of the history of nineteenth-century Russian music (a history as dense, self-referential, and replete with genius as its literary counterpart), very possibly so. This essay will briefly review the birth of each little opera and speculate on their collective contribution to the larger canvas of Pushkin and music.

Four Premieres, Four Disappointments

In February 1872, three years after the death of its creator, Alexander Dargomyzhsky (1813–69), *The Stone Guest* premiered in St. Petersburg's Mariinskii Theater.[4] It soon faded from repertory, making a brief revival only thirty years later in a fresh orchestration by Rimsky-Korsakov for the Pushkin Centennial. This delicate chamber work has had a curious fate. Everywhere cited as pathbreaking (the first Russian "dialogue opera") and admired for its scrupulous word-for-word realization of a lyric text, the opera is nevertheless rarely performed. Without a doubt, its purely musical appeal has been obscured by the strident polemics surrounding its birth. Dargomyzhsky was a disciple of Mikhail Glinka and elder patron of the so-called Balakirev Circle of composers in St. Petersburg. This group of very young, intensely gifted "amateurs" eschewed the conservatory, with its Germanic professoriat, that had just been founded (1862) across town; instead, they trained around the keyboard, analyzing in four-hand piano reduction the latest major European compositions and experimenting with Russian variants on these genres. During the final year of his life, invalided by heart disease, Dargomyzhsky was seized with a passion for expressing "truth" in music. The values to which he pledged to be true were the intonational contours and dramatic impulse of Pushkin's speech—and the crowning work of his career, that which most perfectly honors this principle, is his *Stone Guest* (the composer died with all but a few bars complete). Dargomyzhsky was Russia's first thoroughgoing disciple of Gluck.[5] He studiously avoided the devices by which mainstream opera composers of his day subdued a vocal line and subordinated it to music: division into numbers, strict definition between aria and recitative, strophic repetition, the rounded set song, syncopation that was incompatible with the stress and accent of uttered speech, melisma or exaggerated pitch intervals. But unlike his fellow reformer Richard Wagner, who also sought to liberate music drama from conventional operatic structure, Dargomyzhsky did not rely on a symphonic principle to give melodic and rhythmic unity to the whole. He insisted that the orchestra serve the voice.

Dargomyzhsky did not understand voice in a naturalistic sense, however, that is, as a prosaic, crude, street-smart sound. In the mid-1860s the only member of the Circle with such radical aspirations was Modest Musorgsky, who created deliberately harsh "sung conversation" in his setting of Gogol's prose farce *Marriage*. (Musorgsky nevertheless dedicated his exercise in declamation to the older composer.) Pushkin's graceful poetic text hardly invited such abrasive treatment. And in any event, Dargomyzhsky's goal was more conventional: a texture that was part parlando and part song, where music would enhance the expressiveness of the words but not drag the words into its own rhythmic wake, not engulf them with too much intricately patterned sound or exploit them as mere carriers for virtuoso vocal effects. With a single exception, the composer does not develop leitmotifs musically. (That exception is the Commandore's ominous "signature," five ascending and then descending degrees of the whole-tone scale, variously harmonized, and embellished with the conventional horrific diminished seventh when the statue appears at the door.) Overall, leitmotifs remain mere character tags announcing the approach of a person or an idea. Taking his cue from Pushkin's play, Dargomyzhsky presents Don Juan as neither farcical nor evil but as earnest, romantic, amoral, bold, a passionate and impetuous improviser who is wholly committed to realizing appetites in the present. To transmit this impulse, the play is set (in Richard Taruskin's apt formulation) as "a gargantuan, kaleidoscopically varied, through-composed 'romance.'"[6] Although more of a realist than the romantics before him, Dargomyzhsky never disavowed his simple and robust gift for song.

The Balakirev Circle would soon become known to history as the *Moguchaia kuchka,* or "mighty handful," of nationalist composers: Milii Balakirev, Modest Musorgsky, Alexander Borodin, Nikolai Rimsky-Korsakov, and César Cui. *The Stone Guest* was created literally under the eyes and ears of these "mighty-handful-ists" (*kuchkisty*), who educated themselves through musical scores and sustained themselves through charismatic personal example. They followed Dargomyzhsky's every gesture with reverence. Especially impressed was the young fortifications engineer, composer, and prolific music critic César Cui, who several decades later (and with much less skill) would set *A Feast in Time of Plague.* In 1868, when the musicalization of *The Stone Guest* was not yet half finished, Cui published an essay extolling Dargomyzhsky's approach as the perfect realization of Pushkin's original.[7] It is rare, he remarked, to find a single artistic nature endowed equally with literary and musical talent. Librettists are usually giftless, and musicians—especially great ones—are accustomed to running roughshod over literary texts. Thus was Dargomyzhsky's experiment so extraordinary. He recognized Pushkin's play as an "ideal opera text" and was setting it "without changing a single word," guided by a passion to enhance, not engulf, the existing poetry. (Implicit in Cui's argument is a summons to rethink, perhaps even to reconcile, the ancient polemic between music and words—and to do so, one might add, in the spirit of Pushkin himself, who in 1823 had written to Vyazemsky that he disapproved of the latter's collaboration with Griboedov on a comic libretto: "What has come into your head, to write an opera and subordinate the poet to the musician? Observe precedent properly!")[8] Dargomyzhsky's *Stone Guest,* Cui predicted, would become "the index by which Russian vocal composers will make corrections [in their own work] regarding accuracy of declamation and accurate transmission of the phrases of a text; this is dramatic truth, carried to its highest expression and united with intelligence, experience, knowledge of the matter and in many places [even] musical beauty."[9] There are no numbers or set pieces and no autonomous musical development; with the exception of Laura's two interpolated songs, the unfolding of the opera is identical to Pushkin's play. It was, Cui wrote, a "contemporary opera-drama without the slightest concession" and as such a great forward-looking work.

With this first little opera, then, a principle was established that became a standard for the remaining three musical settings, two of which were undertaken by Dargomyzhsky's *kuchkist* friends in the twilight of their careers. This principle, common to much musical realism, is in fact a negation, the undoing of a criterion that has long distinguished spoken drama from operatic dramaturgy.[10] In contrast to staged plays, opera has traditionally insisted that the action taking place onstage (external, motivated by visible deeds, socially coherent, communicated through public recitative, responsive to the tangible world) is fundamentally separable from the inner life of the actors (which constitutes its own integral whole, answers to another logic, unfolds on its own, and is often transmitted solely through music). Thanks to this separation, musical forms can achieve independent development within the dynamic processes of operatic drama without being sensed as a distortion or a psychological untruth. A libretto is formally segmented into arias, ensembles, recitative in order to make provision for this unfolding of purely musical structure. And, judged by this traditional standard, Dargomyzhsky's *Stone Guest*—for all its musicality and inserted songs and for all that Pushkin took the epigraph for his own play from the Da Ponte–Mozart *Don Giovanni*—can be said to contain only singing lines, not a libretto. Thus it is not an opera, and the effort spent realizing it is not at base a musical one.

Such precisely was the polemic, irritable and protracted, mounted by Pyotr Tchaikovsky, Ivan Turgenev, and other aesthetic conservatives of the 1870s and 1880s against Dargomyzhsky's quest for "accuracy and truth" in music. Among themselves these men ridiculed Cui's passionate defense of the *kuchkist* position. In the history of Western music, the debate is a familiar one. What is curious about its reflection on Russian soil, however, is the dual role played by Russia's greatest poet. In the crude polarization of critics during and after the Reform Era (radical anti-aesthetes such as Chernyshevsky and Pisarev against the conservative "defenders of Pushkin"—Annenkov, Druzhinin, Katkov), those parties who revered Dargomyzhsky's *Stone Guest* were musical radicals, hostile to received forms and rebels against the rule mongering of the conservatory. But their radicalism was deployed to preserve and honor Pushkin's word, not to bury it. Their opponents in the Turgenev-Tchaikovsky camp, also worshipers of Pushkin, were not persuaded by these efforts. To them, this clarion call to "be true to the source text" was worse than misplaced fidelity; it was mistaken identity, a failure to understand fundamental rules of musical genre and the musician's role in creating synthetic, aggregate works of art. If a play or any other complex literary narrative "goes in to music" without resistance and without adjustment, it could only suggest that the original was imperfect or inadequate. An "accurate" musical hybrid would not be homage to Pushkin but quite the opposite.

Great transposed art, the conservatives reasoned, was always less timid. The literary text should work on the musician the way Pushkin's *Eugene Onegin* or *The Queen of Spades* worked on Tchaikovsky or, to borrow Leporello's formulation, the way Dona Anna's delicate shrouded heel worked on the imagination of Don Juan. For a true and original poet, one glimpse at a single part of a living whole is sufficient to trigger a creative response powerful enough to inspire a new, free work of art. Most of Don Juan's appalling erotic success in this play, and a good part of his valor in the face of death, is "improvisational" in just this inspired way, a product of his absolute trust that the needs and demands of this very minute will be satisfied and that the spirit of the whole has been grasped. There is no prior script, no score, and thus no place for bookish fidelity or regrets. He has the perfect courage of the present. As Laura, Don Juan's female counterpart, explains this dynamic in scene 2 of Pushkin's play, all successful performance art must submit freely to inspiration in its own medium and on the spot, without relying on "words born slavishly and by rote" [Slova lilis', kak budto ikh rozhdala / Ne pamiat' rabskaia, no serdtse] (Pushkin 7: 144). It appeared to the detractors of the operatic *Stone Guest* that Dargomyzhsky had not been free in this way. And thus, paradoxically, in his attempt to cherish Pushkin and to realize accurately the musical potential of the poet's lines, the composer stood accused of diminishing him.

In August 1898 in his St. Petersburg quarters, Rimsky-Korsakov (1844–1908) held a run-through of his just completed chamber opera, *Mozart and Salieri.* A gifted young bass from the provinces, Fyodor Chaliapin, sang both vocal parts; Sergei Rachmaninoff was at the keyboard. In November of that year, Savva Mamontov's Private Russian Opera Company premiered the work, which launched Chaliapin's spectacular career. But reception was overall lukewarm—and the composer's own voice was among the most ambivalent. In his habitually restrained tone, Rimsky noted in his memoirs that during the summer of 1897 he had set one scene from Pushkin's play and was pleased. "My recitatives were flowing freely, like the melodies of my latest songs," he wrote. "I had the feeling that I was entering upon a new period." In three weeks the work was done, "in the form of two operatic scenes in recitative-arioso style," which for Rimsky was new. He dedicated the opera to the memory of Dargomyzhsky. But in fact his own work is far less tuneful than his mentor's. Indeed, the sparse, arrhythmic, discontinuous orchestral texture, at times no more than chords that mimic the contours of a prior, unaccompanied vocal line (usually Salieri's), recalled the experiments in musically enhanced speech undertaken by the Balakirev Circle's most radical member, Musorgsky. "Although it approached the manner of Dargomyzhsky in his *Stone Guest,*" Rimsky remarked guardedly, "the form and modulatory scheme of *Mozart and Salieri* were not quite so much of an accident."[11]

This bland reportage and cautious double-voiced tribute to his *kuchkist* past conceal what is perhaps a more dramatic story. Of all *The Little Tragedies,* this one has most to do with music; of the four composers who set Pushkin's texts, Rimsky has the creative biography most relevant to its famous plot of innocent genius versus professional discipline and the schoolmaster's rod. By the late 1890s, Rimsky's relationship to the Balakirev Circle of his youth had changed profoundly. The painful early stages of this weaning were compassionately described by Pyotr Tchaikovsky in a letter to his patroness, Nadezhda von Meck, in December 1877. "All the new Petersburg composers are a very talented lot," he wrote,

> but they are all infected to the core with the most terrible conceit and the purely amateurish conviction that they are superior to the rest

> of the musical world. The sole exception recently has been Rimsky-Korsakov. Like the others, he is self-taught, but he has undergone an abrupt transformation. [. . .] As a very young man he fell in with a group of people who, first, assured him he was a genius, and second convinced him that there was no need *to study*, that schooling destroys inspiration, dries up creative power, etc. At first he believed it [. . .] [, but five years ago] he discovered that the ideas preached by his circle had no sound basis, that their contempt of schooling, of classical music, their hatred of authority and precedents was nothing but ignorance. [And how much time had been wasted!] He was in despair [and asked me what to do.] [. . .] Obviously he had to study. And he began to study with such zeal that academic technique soon became indispensable to him. In a single summer he wrote an incredible number of contrapuntal exercises and sixty-four fugues. [. . .] From contempt for the schools, he went over abruptly to a cult of musical technique. [His recent symphony and quartet] are crammed full of tricks but, as you so justly observe, bear the stamp of dry pedantry. At present he appears to be passing through a crisis, and it is hard to say how it will end. Either he will emerge a great master, or he will get totally bogged down in contrapuntal intricacies.[12]

In 1897, twenty-five years after that crisis summer, Rimsky (by now a great master and revered teacher) was again immersed in the study of fugues by Bach and Mozart. As he turned to Pushkin's "little tragedy" with the intention of commemorating his own past through two different paths to music, how uncannily resonant the poet's warning must have seemed.

Much attention has been given to Pushkin's self-image in this famous dichotomy. Did the poet identify with Mozart (so easy for Pushkin's infatuated readers to assume today) or, as some of the most acute Pushkinists have insisted, with the nervous, neurotic, plodding craftsman Salieri? All creative work partakes of both moments, certainly, but it is relevant to Rimsky's setting of the play to consider the nature of Salieri's envy. Two matters are crucial to grasp in Salieri's opening monologue. First, Salieri is envious not of Mozart's fame—at the time, Salieri was more famous than Mozart—but of his incommensurability, his natural authoritativeness, what Salieri calls in an unguarded moment Mozart's "divinity." Salieri is sufficiently gifted as a *receptor* of art to know that fame and glory are worth very little, being only as trustworthy as their immediate audience. And second,

Salieri is envious not so much of the man and not of the music (he worships the music and has no problem elsewhere in his life with gratitude or discipleship). His envy is mounted on behalf of the dignity of disciplined work. In Pushkin's "little tragedy," this imperative of work—of Salieri's sort: dry, pedantic, overscrutinized, promising the toiler accountability and control—is foregrounded and obsessively replayed in his lengthy, crabby monologues. Mozart is the briefer role, the opposite case, almost a hallucination, the spirit of pure music that analyzes itself only with difficulty and that in public would prefer to laugh and play.

In Rimsky-Korsakov's setting, Mozart moves to the fore. Like Dargomyzhsky before him, Rimsky chose not to tamper with Pushkin's words (except for one seven-line cut in Salieri's second monologue).[13] He thus had two options for altering the balance between the protagonists: he could realize their two lines differently, giving Mozart a more vigorous melodic, harmonic, and rhythmic profile, or he could "fill in" Pushkin's stage directions with real music, perhaps even with the real music composed by these two historical figures. Rimsky does both. It has often been noted that the two protagonists "are" their compositional styles: they sing onstage as they wrote. Salieri's part recalls *The Stone Guest* in the choppy, restricted melodic development of its recitative; although verbally passionate, it is musically quite meek and inert, taking its genres from a pre-Mozart era (for example, the species counterpoint of the opening monologue). In an intriguing variant on recitative, conventionally a "public" communicating genre, Salieri's meditations are not set as utterances—which they are not—but as thoughts, with a steady pulse and with the stress of spoken intonation unnaturally effaced, almost as if in "mental speech."[14] At no point is Salieri allowed to lose himself in song. And when he "speaks," it is not primarily to his interlocutor onstage (to the immediately present Mozart) or as a stage aside (to the audience) but to himself. His battle is wholly an inner one. Only two measures of the historical Salieri's actual music (his *Tarare*) are quoted, and those are sung affectionately by Mozart.

In contrast, Mozartian music—prototypical or authentic—is abundant. When Mozart breaks in on his friend's morose monologue, he brings his music with him. Throughout, Mozart's vocal line is lyrically and rhythmically rounded. The blind fiddler plays eight bars of Zerlina's aria from *Don Giovanni*; the fortepiano improvisation or "fantasia" that Mozart performs for Salieri at the keyboard is a stylization by Rimsky in the manner of Mozart's Piano Sonata in c minor. This fantasia, in two parts, contains themes that recur at appropriate psychological moments for Mozart: a limpid, lyrical section radiating harmonious good nature, followed by a dissonant ominous passage that comes to dominate in the second act as Mozart's thoughts turn darkly to the visit of the "man in black." The closer we approach the end, the more real Mozart's music becomes.

In keeping with Pushkin's stage direction and following his performance of the fantasia earlier, Mozart in his final moments sits down at the piano to play a portion of his Requiem for Salieri. But, as Peter Rabinowitz has pointed out, this last quotation is already performance of another sort.[15] What we hear are the opening sixteen bars of Mozart's Requiem, not imitated or stylized but pasted, with a piano overlay added and tiny adjustments in orchestration, directly into Rimsky's score. Since these opening measures call for the staggered entrance of a four-part chorus, those voices must resound backstage; in some productions of the opera, a Requiem is simply piped in. Either way, Mozart could not possibly be producing at the keyboard everything that the audience (both internal onstage and external in the hall) now hear. Salieri alone possesses sufficient musical competence to realize the majesty of the whole as it is being composed. If we in the hall hear the full-score Requiem, this is because we come later, with all the benefits of Mozart's fame and canonization; Salieri hears it through his gift.

At this point in the opera, Rimsky-Korsakov disappears, and the Mozart-Salieri unit remains the sole musical presence. One sketches out a work of musical genius, the other perceives it in full. The historical Mozart, of course, never heard his Requiem at all, for he died before this final masterpiece was performed. Rimsky's own surrounding music pales by comparison. It is the later composer's complex tribute to the creators, listeners, admirers, even the fatal enviers of very great music that Mozart is more present during this Requiem—and more in possession of his own immortal legacy—than he had been as a living self. And arguably, this fully realized musical quotation within the opera (a device available only to Rimsky-Korsakov, not to Pushkin) is a more memorable moment than the melodrama of the end.

The enhanced musical presence of Mozart in Rimsky-Korsakov's little opera hints at the complexity of this dialogue within the history of Russian music. As part of the musicalization of Pushkin's *Little*

Tragedies, this second work, with its focus on Mozart, evokes that great composer's own involvement with the theme of *Don Giovanni*/Don Juan/*The Stone Guest*. Much as Pushkin had transfigured the literary forms bequeathed to him, so the three great operas that Mozart wrote with Lorenzo Da Ponte changed the potential of operatic genres for all of Europe. Servants no longer had to be frivolous or farcical. The classical alternation between recitative and aria could be replaced by continuous, expressive musical storytelling. And musical drama at last became fully dramatic and responsive to the intricate wit of Italian speech without ceasing to be music of the genius class. Rimsky's attitude toward this legacy in the development of Russian music (and in his own evolution as a composer) could only be ambivalent. Foreign (mostly Italian) opera had reigned supreme in the Russian capitals for the past 150 years, subsidized by the court and handsomely compensated. Only with the end of the imperial monopoly on theaters in 1883 did it become possible for wealthy private citizens (like Savva Mamontov, whose company premiered *Mozart and Salieri*) to mount Russian operas without state sponsorship or bureaucratic interference. Dargomyzhsky and the feisty band of autodidacts in the *Moguchaia kuchka* had been pioneers in "de-Italianization" during a much more difficult era. What did Rimsky owe this period of his own youth, now seen as misguided, and how does his little opera reflect that debt?

In a letter to his occasional librettist V. I. Belsky, Rimsky spoke candidly about his *Mozart and Salieri*. "This type of music (or opera) is an exclusive sort, and in most respects not a desirable one; I have little sympathy with it. I wrote this thing out of a desire to learn [. . .] to find out how difficult it is [. . . but] can it be that recitative-arioso à la *The Stone Guest* is more desirable than real, free music?"[16] One might argue that to utilize Pushkin's little text as a "learning exercise" en route to an ugly but necessary product is already in the spirit of Salieri. But in fact the opera is a more successful fusion of these two approaches to creation, these two personalities, than the intensely self-critical Rimsky-Korsakov allowed. The gradual usurpation of self-pity by genius and the replacement of Salieri's bitter monologues by ever purer stretches of Mozart's music (and Salieri's appreciation of it) are accompanied in the score by an increasingly dense interweaving of the two composers' motifs—and thus of their fates. Of course, Pushkin knew both realities: inspiration that is bestowed like grace and the thankless task of calculation and revision. What ultimately marks Pushkin as a Mozart in the world of creators is not any childlike cheerfulness (his Mozart also suffers from insomnia and grim visions), not considerations of cosmic injustice, not details of personal behavior but simply that Mozart's (and Pushkin's) art is great enough to transcend the costs of its genesis and the complaints of its creator, whereas Salieri's is not.

In this opera, Rimsky-Korsakov—one of Russia's most indefatigable servants of music and a benefactor to his more chaotic, disorganized musical friends—pays tribute to Dargomyzhsky's achievement and yet at the same time would transcend it. As with *The Stone Guest,* the public's appreciation was muted. César Cui, the final *kuchkist* who would take on a "little tragedy" and a stern, capricious critic of his own circle, was among those least impressed by his friend Rimsky's effort. In his review of the premiere in March 1899, he again praised the rare, brave librettist who bestowed equal rights on music and words. He recalled the daring of Dargomyzhsky, who in his time had resisted the temptation to modify Pushkin's text—even though the poet's *Stone Guest* "lacked several important musical elements: ensembles, choruses, and everywhere one meets ordinary rational speech, inappropriate for musical transmission."[17] But this second attempt to set one of Pushkin's *Little Tragedies* was "considerably less successful." Cui's rebuke to Rimsky-Korsakov referred not to the "technical side" of the opera, which, given the composer's great gifts in orchestration and tone, was "almost above perfection"; what was deficient, according to Cui, was its "*melodic* recitative."[18] In his opinion, the dryness of the first scene was a lamentable decline from Dargomyzhsky, who had imparted musical vigor to his Don Juan from the first phrase. Apparently, Rimsky's decision to make Salieri as stiff and sterile as his music had achieved its purpose.

A Feast in Time of Plague, subtitled *Dramatic Scenes by A. S. Pushkin with Music by César Cui,* premiered in Moscow in November 1901. Fyodor Chaliapin performed in the role of the priest. It is a weak work by the weakest of the *kuchkist* composers; in addition, its source text, a fragment translated by Pushkin from John Wilson's play and featuring a collective protagonist, is the most diffuse and puzzling of *The Little Tragedies.* Yet this musical exercise too has a place in the sequence and its own lesson to impart. César Cui (1835–1918) was highly regarded as a professor of military fortifications (by 1901 he had retired from state service) and as tutor in military studies to the imperial grand dukes. Although a prolific composer, he was better known for his peremptory and trenchantly self-confident music criticism, which stretched over forty years. Curiously, the militant realism and radicalism of his journalistic writings (he began propagandizing for his fellow *kuchkisty* in the early 1860s) is not reflected in his own creative work, which is timid, mannered, elegant in its details, and easily forgettable.[19] (Russian commentators kindly call Cui a "traditionalist," a composer whose music is "heavily influenced by the high-society 'salon' culture of the nineteenth century," with "well-rounded vocal motifs" that impart a "rather static effect" to the whole.)[20] Cui composed in all genres: choruses, quartets, piano music, vocal romances. Of his ten operas, seven were based on Western European literature (French and German); his three Russian-based operas draw exclusively on the cosmopolitan Pushkin.[21] A handful of Cui's operas were familiar to the theater-going public of nineteenth-century Petersburg. But today, with the exception of several exquisite songs, all has slipped away with hardly a trace.

History has proved Cui more durable in his words and musical judgments than in his musical deeds. On one point, however, he was categorically consistent throughout his career, in both his musical practice and his journalism. When words and music are combined in a single composition, Cui believed, each have equal rights—but the words must be written first. The opera or song composer who desires to be both emotionally moving and psychologically precise must begin with the text of a great poet. Only such highly condensed, efficient verbal material can discipline the composer, who, in the process of applying to words the richer, more flexible vocabulary of musical form, always runs the risk of dilution or vagueness of expression. Working the other way around, Cui felt, was unreliable. Since musical moods are so polyvalent, transient, and inexpressible, a well-structured musical line might call forth the most clumsy and inarticulate prose or even no image at all. Least likely to emerge would be eloquent verse. Cui was not sympathetic to the familiar argument that great art songs are more safely built off second-rate poetry, because (so the argument goes) only deficient poetry stands to gain rather than to lose when alien music and rhythms are added to it, even though the history of lieder writing in the Western world knows dozens of happy examples. Little wonder that Cui's quest for the perfectly focused Russian text led him invariably to Pushkin. Unfortunately, in contrast to his fellow *kuchkist* composers, Cui was not equipped to set recitative with anything like the depth and originality that he admired in Dargomyzhsky.

Again, Tchaikovsky provides a portrait. He never understood why Cui, a miniaturist and devotee of light French music, should ever have associated himself with the nonaesthetic iconoclasts of the *kuchka.* All that united Cui with them, it seemed to Tchaikovsky, was dilettantism and disdain of professional schools. In the same 1878 letter to Madame von Meck in which Rimsky-Korsakov's crisis is so movingly described, Tchaikovsky wrote: "Cui is a talented amateur. His music lacks originality, but is graceful and elegant. It is too flirtatious and, as it were, too sleek, so you like it at first but then it quickly satiates. [. . .] When he hits upon some pretty little idea, he fusses over it for a long time, redoes this or that, decorates it, adds all sorts of finishing touches, and all of this at very great length. [. . .] Still, he undoubtedly has talent—and at least he has taste and flair."[22] Are grace, sleekness, and refined taste required for *A Feast in Time of Plague*? Cui in 1900 was apprehensive about the success of his *Feast* project—all the more so because he had been considering the idea for almost four decades.[23]

Cui was first attracted to the librettistic potential of Pushkin's *Feast* in 1858. Nothing came of the project at the time; thirty years later, however, he composed "Walsingham's Hymn" (1889) and soon after "Mary's Song," the only two portions of the tragedy that are Pushkin's original poetry, that is, not a translation of Wilson's tragedy. Both were performed in the Mariinskii Theater a decade later, in April 1899, at a Pushkin Centennial soirée. Success during that evening doubtless spurred Cui to wrap an opera around the two pieces. Thus in the evolution of this work we witness the reverse of *The Stone Guest,* where Dargomyzhsky inserted into his musicalization two songs of his own invention that Pushkin had indicated solely in stage directions. In *Feast,* the two pivotally important, nearly autonomous songs—Mary's submissive lament on the plague and Walsingham's defiant challenge to it—condense the musical virtues of the whole and in fact preexisted that whole by a decade.

Perhaps properly for this tableaulike heroless play, Cui provides only two leitmotifs, both employed rather statically. The first is a boisterous "feast" theme; the second, a motif for "burying the dead." The latter is of special interest, for it is an *ascending* chromatic progression.[24] More common as a musical marker for dread and death, of course, is a descending scale. But Pushkin's plague-stricken, feasting Londoners resist on precisely this point: they will eventually die (of that there is no doubt), but until such time they are resolved to orient themselves upward in spirit. Beyond these two nondeveloping motifs and the two structurally simple songs, there is a thinness to the orchestration and a blandness to the recitative that strike one as incongruous in so desperate an environment.

But paradoxically, the overly sweet and predictable quality of Cui's music, its static texture, lends a certain plausibility to the macabre frame around the two central songs. Their melodies hover over the dialogic exchanges. "Mary's Song," a balladlike composition in g minor, has a limpid, exhausted quality quite in keeping with its call for renunciation and the keeping of prudent distance, even (or especially) between lovers. In contrast, Walsingham's hymn resembles less a pious tribute than a crudely hewn march in syncopated rhythm, a demonic challenge,[25] with its stanzas alternating abruptly between major and minor key and ending on a high, affirmative, fortissimo command: "We'll sip the rosy maiden wine / And kiss the lips where plague may lie!" The old priest interrupts this blasphemy with his bass recitative in somber rebuke to the Master of Revels; in turn, the priest's lines evoke a choral evaluation from the feasters: "He speaks of Hell as one who knows. " At this point in the opera we realize, more powerfully than is possible through the printed page, that all these various options—Mary's gentle resignation, Walsingham's defiance (demonic and increasingly unhinged), the priest's fire and brimstone—are literally onstage. Each option is being performed, each invites a response from the audience, and none can alter the final truth. The feast is then revealed for what it has in fact become, under pressure of musical realization: a singing contest, with all the rich mythological resonances of that event.

It qualifies as a cultural universal. A public competition is held in which songs are performed in the face of, and in defiance of, death. The singer would win back life, for himself or his beloved, whereas death stands mortally offended by music, that most temporal of arts, and would put an end to it forever. (The same opposition is at the base of Salieri's attempt—futile, as he knows full well—to nullify Mozart's music with something as trivial as poison.) In a paradox surely not intended by the earnest César Cui, the very thinness and stasis of the operatic *Feast in Time of Plague* serve to balance these two forces, music against death, and make of the contest a more terrible draw.

By generation and musical training, Sergei Rachmaninoff (1873–1943) lies outside the three composers so far considered. His *Covetous Knight* had its premiere at the Bolshoi Theater in 1906 under the composer's own direction, and its intersection with the earlier little operas is biographical and solely coincidental. In August 1898 Rachmaninoff had been the pianist at a play-through of Rimsky's *Mozart and Salieri* for the benefit of Savva Mamontov, in whose Russian Private Opera he was then working as conductor; the young Chaliapin, who performed Salieri in the premiere, was the operatic artist whom Rachmaninoff envisaged for the all-important role of the miserly Baron in this new work. The sin examined here was greed, but the duty of fathers to sons was a vital supplementary theme. It is very possible that Rachmaninoff's father, who had squandered the family's wealth and left his newly married son struggling as a freelance professional musician, was the immediate stimulus for the opera project, just as Pushkin's own parsimonious father might well have been a pretext for the poet. In keeping with his predecessors who had composed little operas, Rachmaninoff chose to set Pushkin's text almost without change (only forty lines are omitted from the Baron's very lengthy monologue and two words added to the Duke). But with that the similarities end. The most significant focus of difference between these two generations of musicians was their attitude toward Richard Wagner.

For members of the *Moguchaia kuchka*, a distrust of Wagner and rejection of the "symphonic principle" as a route to operatic reform was an article of faith. Again, César Cui might serve as spokesman, for his position is by now a familiar one. In 1899, as part of the Pushkin Jubilee, Cui summed up four decades of polemics with an article, "The Influence of Pushkin on Our Composers and on Their Vocal Style."[26] He noted that to date thirty operas had been written to Pushkin's texts, and he attributed this remarkably high number to the clarity, simplicity, and conciseness of Pushkin's language.[27] According to Cui, the appeal of Pushkin to artists working in other mediums yielded a double benefit: since composers were reluctant to deform such perfect verse into a routine libretto, many strove to realize Pushkin's line without tampering with it—and this practice, with its scrupulous attention to the poetic word, inevitably refined their own skills in musical expression. Pushkin had become the cautionary standard.

So Russians were now masters at accurate declaration and true voice setting. But Russian word-and-music dramas were different from

Western European opera, even the most revolutionary. "In Wagner," Cui wrote, "the music does indeed illustrate the verbal text, but this illustration is located in the orchestra, to which the text hands over all major ideas; against this rich background the singer might declaim properly, but he declaims non-meaningful, often contentless musical phrases. Such a system is at base false."[28] Orchestral music could amplify the verbal line but should never overwhelm it, according to Cui. Formal unity achieved by way of symphonic development was an impurity. By design or by default, large-scale Wagnerian innovations had been kept out of the first three little operas. Such was not the case with the fourth.

In the summer of 1902 Rachmaninoff, already opera conductor in Mamontov's company for several years and soon to take over at the Bolshoi, extended his European honeymoon to include a visit to Bayreuth, where he heard *Parsifal* and *The Ring.* As the themes, leitmotifs, and orchestral texture of his own subsequent opera make clear, he was powerfully influenced by this concept of music drama. Not only will gold lust be linked with Eros and death; it will destroy whole families and peoples. During two intense weeks in August 1903 Rachmaninoff created a *Covetous Knight* that was a blend of Wagnerian symphonism, the text-setting principles of his revered Tchaikovsky, and Russian mastery at declamation (Musorgsky's methods in *Boris Godunov* are especially prominent, receiving several direct quotations)—all under the aegis of mythologically heightened greed. Such heterogeneous metaphysical texture was a harbinger of things to come. This was no longer the realist 1860s, when one argued over the relative value of Pushkin's genius versus a pair of warm boots; this was the symbolist era.

In obvious ways, Pushkin's *Covetous Knight* is not a grateful operatic text. There are no overtly musical episodes such as abound in Don Juan's Madrid, Mozart's Vienna, and even among the feasting, singing Londoners during a plague. Female characters are wholly absent. There is only the sinuousness of gold itself, which, as the Baron's great scene 2 monologue testifies in exhaustive detail, takes the place of everything: companionship, kindness, power, the sexual act, murder by the knife (which, like turning the key in a chest full of money, is "excitement . . . / And horror all at once"). But as with Salieri's envy, the Baron's greed is not a simple thing. What mortifies the miser about his heir, Albert, is not only that he will squander the content of the chests—wealth that the son did not earn and thus has no right to spend—but that he will remember his father as a man without passion, one who did not know "immortal longings," whose conscience never sounded, and whose "heart was all o'ergrown with moss." In this bitterness there is, of course, both miserly greed and knightly pride.

Rachmaninoff attended carefully to all these aspects of Pushkin's complex hero. But both Fyodor Chaliapin, who for unknown reasons declined to sing the Baron on opening night, and Rimsky Korsakov, whose magisterial opinion carried great weight, felt that the balance achieved was not the proper one. "The orchestra swallows almost all the artistic interest," Rimsky remarked, "and the vocal part, deprived of the orchestra, is unconvincing."[29] The overture establishes all important aspects of the conflict before any words are uttered. It introduces the three major motifs of gold (a descending chromatic figure, with a glittering tremolo effect), power (in heavy ascending lines), and a complicated, more dissonant motif of human woe; all three motifs hover continually over the Baron. The other actors in the drama are quite unidimensional. The drama opens on the awfulness of poverty because, in this play about the proper balance between matter (money) and spirit (honor), perversely it is poverty that ties us to matter, denies us rights to inspired movement and generosity, flattens us out. Thus Albert's character, while natively high-minded and generous, is nervous, impulsive, marked with broad melodic leaps, a man who wants to be anywhere but where he now is with the niggardly resources he now possesses. The Jewish moneylender and the Duke are portrayed, respectively, as an undulating caricature of deceitful flattery and as the Shakespearean ideal of serene, mediating justice. Everything dynamic and conflicted, musically as well as emotionally, is in those chests.

For such is the peculiar structure of Pushkin's play. Two fast-paced dueling grounds, complete with jousting and injured honor, are separated by an underground vault of static dead-weighted wealth. That vault, the site of the Baron's long and conflicted monologue, is where Rachmaninoff gives free rein to his Wagnerian "symphonism." Orchestral complexity is much less in evidence in the two flanking scenes, Albert's bargaining with the moneylender and the final confrontation between father, son, and ruler that triggers a duel and that ends, unexpectedly, with a "natural" death. In those two fast-paced dialogue scenes, Rachmaninoff muffles his sonorous orchestra, sets it whirling in repetitive patterns, and brings vocal declamation to the fore to service the swift action onstage. The exchanges between Solomon and

Albert, and between Albert and the Duke, are forward-moving and in their own way trustworthy, for they serve coherent deeds in the world of men. Each man announces his own single-minded principle and then stands by it: Albert the need to spend, Solomon the need to barter profitably, the Duke his need to reconcile his subjects justly. The Baron, however, is no longer in that pragmatic world. His is a fantasy kingdom, both burdensome and liberating, that has become completely real for him but is unreadable (of this he is certain) by anyone else. His motifs no longer communicate to others horizontally but relate only to himself. Themes drop into him, thicken, and swell up. The haunting, viscous quality of Wagnerian motivic development is perfect for this high gravitational pull of the Baron's field. And here music, which is movement incarnate, can contribute something significant to the theme of miserly accumulation.

To protect his fantasy kingdom the Baron must ensure, above all else, that nothing circulate. Albert is correct in his remark to Solomon that money, for his father, is neither a servant nor a friend but a master whom *he* must serve. Wealth for the Baron is reliable only when it is locked away. When it moves it threatens to speak up, take on its own tasks, become subject to someone else's market pressures, disobey. The task of standing guard over it and preventing any centrifugal outward flows of energy absorbs huge resources; indeed, for the Baron it replaces all other life. Thus the musical realization of the Baron is one cauldron of superimposed, intricately developed contradictory motifs. They are dependent upon the orchestra for their organization and subordination because they have no exit from within the Baron's own arguments. In vain does Albert request, at the end of scene 1, that his father treat him "as a son . . . and not a mouse / Begotten in a cellar." But such open-ended treatment is impossible, because that noncirculating cellar, an underground of thoroughly Dostoevskian pathology, understands only how to draw things in and cause them to stop.

In his operatic setting of this little tragedy, then, Rachmaninoff created a miniature music drama on a timelessly mythic theme with a web of orchestral language at its core: the Baron's scene 2 monologue. The composer's tribute to the time-bound, word-bound, action-bound present tense of debts and duels is parceled out to the wings, to the first and last scenes. There, in these more declamatory appendages that recall their *kuchkist* predecessors and Cui's "words-first" ideal, real dialogue is uttered, and unexpected confrontations happen. But drama, and especially tragic drama, is not only events. It can also be served by the more Wagnerian principle that musical texture, "chromatic alteration," and a constant postponement of the tonal goal are themselves forms of poetic knowledge. In Rachmaninoff's setting, Pushkin's Baron—realized through a fusion of harmony, counterpoint, and orchestration—is, in the sense that Wagner used the term, a genuinely polyphonic hero.

Concluding Comments: The Casket of Gold and the Feast of Music

Among the debates that divided the Perm musicians while they prepared for their Pushkin *Ring* was the optimal sequence of the "little operas."[30] *Boris Godunov* opened the cycle, but from that point on there was no imperative to observe Pushkin's order of plays. It was eventually decided that *A Feast in Time of Plague* would usher in the tetralogy, followed by *The Stone Guest, The Covetous Knight,* and finally *Mozart and Salieri.* The order of the little operas became one of increasing musical excellence but also one in which national collapse gave way gradually to the spirit of music. The interpretations of all four little operas were modernist and highly stylized. (The curtain went up the first night on a huge computer monitor projected on the stage that displayed a list of writers, among whom was Pushkin. According to one eyewitness, the audience sighed in disappointment. All day they had looked at screens. Could they never escape cyberspace, even on a night at the opera with their greatest poet?) As far as one can tell, all of Pushkin's cold intelligence and wit was intact in these four productions, but little of his lyricism, hope, and tenderness.

After the three-day event, members of the audience were asked to comment on the success of the cycle. The responses published in *Muzykal'naia akademiia* were overall appreciative but tended to be pessimistic and dark. Many referred to the topical importance of the operas for post-Soviet Russia and its recurring times of trouble. It was noted by several that Salieri washed his hands, like Pontius Pilate, after his murderous deed. An eleventh grader from Perm's Diagilev High School, E. Tamarchenko, submitted an essay in a deeply noncarnival spirit that began: "In my view, the entire plot pivots around the idea of the feast, an idea found at the very sources of world culture. . . . A feast presumes a special third world, one that is opposed to the highest moral values of the human being." From the feast of the plague, she notes, no one can escape. The feast of love in *The Stone Guest* is absolutely tragic. *The Covetous Knight* knows only the feast of power. *Mozart and Salieri* is a feast of creativity, but a poisoned one . . .

There was one published response, however, that moved against this general pessimistic grain, although still ambiguously.[31] It was evidence that even in these musicked versions, the metaphysical core of Pushkin's "little tragedies" could be turned to courage in the blink of an eye, kaleidoscopically. The author was commenting on *Mozart and Salieri,* the fact that the two protagonists in this production had been presented like parts of a single person, with their traits intermixed and dependent upon accidents of perception, envy, cowardice (Salieri was powerful and persuasive, Mozart petty and unattractive). "But they all possessed a priceless gift, the ability to create," she added, now including Pushkin in her purview. She concluded her internal dialogue on a question:

> Priceless because it cannot be paid for by anything except that utter trifle, life.
>
> *Ars longa, vita brevis.*
>
> A little tragedy?

The Perm audience's ambivalence toward these musicalized versions of Pushkin's *Little Tragedies* has its echo in Pushkin's own attitude toward the blending of music and word. On the one hand, there was that 1823 letter to Vyazemsky about respecting "proper precedent." On the other, Pushkin's lyrics and longer poems were exceptionally popular with transposers and adapters for both song and stage; and, as Thomas Hodge remarks in his study of the nineteenth-century art song, "Pushkin's apparent disdain for the musical appropriation of verse is mitigated by the character of his relationships with composer-contemporaries."[32] He enjoyed working with these composers, there was often an element of inspired impro-visation in it; and he did not disdain this boost in circulation of his name and words. He was also not one to doubt the endurance of his own work on its own terms. Musicalized hybrids need not enter into fatal competition with their poetic originals. Pushkin would have been curious about the Perm cycle. The conceptually bold and innovative Mozart in him always transcended the cautious, law-abiding Salieri, although both, he knew, were indispensible to creativity.

Notes

1. For a sympathetic report of the Perm opera project by its director that includes formal and informal reviews by members of the audience, see Isaakian, "Russkoe 'Kol'tso."

2. Anderson, "Introduction," in Pushkin, *The Little Tragedies*, 6.

3. Pushkin, *Malen'kie tragedii. Opery russkikh kompozitorov.* These popular, useful, bilingual volumes are not scholarly efforts, although there are some helpful inclusions (for example, the interscene "Intermezzo-fughetto" that Rimsky-Korsakov wrote for his *Mozart and Salieri* and then destroyed but that was discovered in a piano four-hand arrangement among his posthumous papers is included as an appendix to that volume).

4. The most thorough account of this opera and its significance for staged art in the 1860s remains Taruskin, *Opera and Drama*, chap. 5, "*The Stone Guest* and Its Progeny." Taruskin's thesis (here as everywhere) is strongly argued and invites dispute. I gratefully draw on it for my summary comments.

5. For a brief discussion in English, see Maloff, "Pushkin's Dramas in Russian Music," 137–39.

6. Taruskin, *Opera and Drama*, 269.

7. "Muzykal'nye zametki," slightly abridged in Kiui, *Izbrannye stat'i*, 143–47, hereafter cited in text. Cui's comments on *The Stone Guest* are translated in full in Taruskin, *Opera and Drama*, 298–300.

8. Pushkin to Prince Pyotr Vyazemsky, from Odessa to Moscow, 4 November 1823. Pushkin's comment about words versus music is followed by another remark on genre even more famous: "I wouldn't budge even for Rossini. As for what I'm doing, I am writing, not a novel but a novel in verse—a devil of a difference" (Pushkin, *The Letters*, 141).

9. Kiui, *Izbrannye stat'i*, 147.

10. I owe the initial formulation of this idea to Taruskin, *Opera and Drama*, 249–50, although he is not responsible for my extension of it here. Dargomyzhsky's "realism of dramaturgical technique and psychological penetration" permitted far more flexibility in the setting of character than did conventional operatic practice.

11. Rimsky-Korsakov, *My Musical Life*, 366–67, translation slightly adjusted.

12. Piotr Tchaikovsky to Nadezhda von Meck from San Remo, 24 December 1877–5 January 1978, quoted from Garden and Gotteri, eds., *To My Best Friend*, 120, translation adjusted.

13. Rimsky wrote music for the entire second monologue but then omitted seven lines (following the first mention of Izora's poison) when he published the score.

14. This point is suggested by Mikhail Mishchenko in his prefatory note to the 1999 piano-vocal score of Rimsky-Korsakov's *Mozart i Salieri* (see note 3). I am also indebted to Professor Simon Morrison of Princeton University's Department of Music for his prescient ideas on this little opera (1999).

15. Rabinowitz, "Rimskii and Salieri." In this contribution to his larger study of musical "listening acts," Rabinowitz draws two pairs of distinctions: between "technical" and "attributive" (or associative) listening and between primary music and imitative music (60–62). A subcategory of the imitative is "fictional music" (which imitates not some extramusical object but other music or some other musical performance); to this category the quotation from the Requiem belongs. The fact that Salieri can realize its majesty from Mozart's bare-bones piano rendition onstage is indication, in Rabinowitz's opinion, of Salieri's musical superiority, both to his own contemporaries and to us, who need the aural prompt of the full score. Even if Rimsky-Korsakov the composer suspected "Salierism" in himself (and such moments are documented), then he shared with Salieri a highly gifted listener's appreciation of genius, as his handling of the Requiem quotation demonstrates (64). Mozart was correct to value this friend.

16. Cited in Taruskin, *Opera and Drama,* 326. Taruskin is rather negative on the success of Rimsky's opera, seeing it as a corrosion of Dargomyzhsky's more thoroughgoing, pathbreaking experiment. "Rimsky cut the opéra dialogué adrift from its aesthetic moorings," Taruskin writes and then tries to recuperate by casting "much of the music in an academically tinctured distillate of eighteenth-century style. [. . .] The result is a kind of superficially 'neoclassical' resurrection of the Mozartean recitative [. . .] which impoverished the genre to the point of futility." Taruskin clearly is not persuaded that Salieri's "retrograde" music was in fact a deliberate character statement.

17. Kiui, "Moskovskaia Chastnaia Russkaia Opera," cited in Kiui, *Izbrannye stat'i,* 494–97.

18. Ibid., 496, 497.

19. For a thorough overview of Cui's several careers and considerable importance, see Taruskin, *Opera and Drama,* chap. 6, "'Kuchkism' in Practice: Two Operas by Cesar Cui." The two operas are *William Ratcliffe* (after Heine) and *Angelo* (after Victor Hugo). In the paragraphs that follow, I am indebted to Taruskin's summary of Cui's aesthetics.

20. These phrases are from Mikhail Mishchenko's prefatory note to the piano-vocal score of Cui's *Pir vo vremia chumy* (1999).

21. The other two are *Kavkazskii plennik* (1881) and *Kapitanskaia dochka* (1911), neither of which is in repertory.

22. See Taruskin, *Opera and Drama,* 121, translation slightly adjusted.

23. For a good capsule history of the opera's genesis, predictably published in a Pushkin journal, see Neff, "César Cui's Opera *Feast in Time of Plague.*"

24. The chapter on Cui's *Feast* in Maloff, "Pushkin's Dramas in Russian Music" (pt. 8, pp. 220–32), is valuable for bringing together what little is known about this work, its aftermath, and its feeble or ill-starred successors. The twelve-year-old

Prokofiev also tried his hand at Pushkin's *Feast,* three years after Cui's premiere; in the 1930s, the émigré composer Arthur Lourie in Paris set this final little tragedy as a ballet, but the Nazi invasion occasioned the cancellation of the premiere.

25. For a reading of Walsingham's nocturnal hymn as a document in Pushkin's demonology, designed as specific and ecstatic blasphemy, see Raskol'nikov, "'Pir vo vremia chumy' v svete problemy demonizma u Pushkina."

26. Kiui, "Vliianie Pushkina na nashikh kompozitorov i na ikh vokal'nyi stil'," in Kiui, *Izbrannye stat'i,* 501–5.

27. Ibid., 502.

28. Ibid., 503.

29. Ossovskii, "S. V. Rakhmaninov," cited in Tsuker, "K kontseptsii 'Skupogo rytsaria,'" 93. Tsuker attempts to rehabilitate the opera from its traditionalist, Russian Old School detractors, claiming that although a symphonic principle is indeed at work, this "symphonism" does not manifest itself in autonomously unfolding structures but becomes a highly efficient, descriptive, psychologically astute tool tailored to individual personalities.

30. Isaakian, "Russkoe 'Kol'tso,'" 24. Tamarchenko's comments on the cycle are on p. 27.

31. N. Chernysheva, a graduate student at Perm State University, in ibid., 26–27.

32. Hodge, *A Double Garland,* 168. Pushkin's friendship with the composers of his time is discussed on 165–82, although references to specific transpositions are densely scattered throughout the volume.

The Little Tragedies on Film

Cinematic Realism and Embodied Inspiration

Stephanie Sandler

All Pushkin films attempt to bridge the huge gap that separates modern audiences from the early nineteenth century, and most of them use the conventions of verisimilitude to create the illusion that we in the movie house or in front of our television screens are witnessing a re-creation of Pushkin's world. Biographical films seduce us into thinking that we watch Pushkin himself or at least his contemporaries, as in *Posledniaia doroga* (The last road, 1986), which leaves Pushkin out of the story while showing his friends' responses to his death. Films about Pushkin's lifetime present famous actors in tony versions of a daily life bound to strike Soviet (and post-Soviet) viewers as unbearably luxurious. There are, in fact, more films inspired by Pushkin's life than versions of his works.[1]

In Mikhail Shveitser's 1979 version of *The Little Tragedies* (*Malen'kie tragedii*), the life looms large, an odd emphasis, given that this is largely a screen adaptation. Nonetheless, two issues central to biographical films—how to convey a sense of Pushkin's world and how to capture on the screen a moment of Pushkinian inspiration—are as important to the director as the careful re-creation of the four little plays Pushkin wrote in 1830. This admixture of the biographical diminishes the film's more realist aspirations in favor of dramatic and allegorical representations of creative work. Shveitser's interpretation of Pushkin's writings (he includes other texts beyond the four tragedies as framing and interpolated material) is often innovative, and his unusual cinematic decisions challenge conventional ideas about Pushkin, artistic inspiration, and the creative process.

Director Mikhail Shveitser is little known outside the former Soviet Union. Born in 1920, he lived in Moscow until his death in 2000. He graduated from the prestigious VGIK film institute in 1944, where he studied with Sergei Eisenstein. He became an established and successful Soviet filmmaker whose works include a number of adaptations of literary texts by Tendriakov, Tolstoy, Kataev, Il'f and Petrov, Chekhov, Leonov, and Gogol.[2] He grew especially famous in post-Soviet Russia when his popular 1968 film, *Zolotoi telenok* (The golden calf), was rereleased. His work is often praised for its gentle humor and strong pathos, and his habit of mixing comedy with serious drama makes his films more human than many other period films. Shveitser resisted the temptation to make his historical work into allegorical commentary, although some measure of self-reference is always present in films that show moments of creative invention, like *The Little Tragedies*; still, he is principally interested in the historical material itself.[3] In filming Pushkin's *Little Tragedies*, for example, he immersed himself in the worlds that Pushkin created in his tragedies and in Pushkin's own world as well.

We deal, then, not with the monumental turn to Pushkin by an auteur filmmaker who purports to offer us an authentic, commanding version of his chosen text, which is one way to describe films like Sergei Bondarchuk's 1986 *Boris Godunov* or Alexander Proshin's 1999 *Russkii bunt* (Russian uprising), based on *Kapitanskaia dochka* (The captain's daughter, 1836). Rather, *The Little Tragedies* is the work of a director whose reputation has long been made by filming literary classics. In *The Little Tragedies*, Shveitser faced material that was itself already a form of adaptation. His creative imagination was liberated by the example of Pushkin's having turned others' ideas into four idiosyncratic and wonderfully shaped little plays. Thus it is no accident that we find in *The Little Tragedies* not a straightforward adaptation of the four plays from theater into filmed format but rather an interpretation of the four plays that emerges through the director's framing them with other Pushkinian texts, his use of music and cinematography, his sequencing the plays in a very deliberate way, and his transposition or cutting of material to intensify his view of the plays and of Pushkin more generally. I take his view to be tragic, even catastrophic, with a focus on the saving grace of artistic inspiration despite social, historical, and psychological pressures on the artist that nearly stifle his creativity.

Shveitser made *The Little Tragedies* for television. First shown in 1980, it was presented as a commemoration of the 150th anniversary of Pushkin's Boldino autumn, and it bears the reverential attitude toward Pushkin of all Soviet commemorative activities. *The Little Tragedies* feels like a late Soviet film in its extremely slow pacing (it is 227 minutes long), although, because it was intended for television screenings over three evenings, our perception of the film's pacing when we now watch it in one sitting is a little misleading. Shveitser takes advantage of the intimacy of television viewing in one's own home and the intervals inherent in a screening across several evenings, and he luxuriates in the scenic details, audible silences, and slow changes of impression that mark long films generally. The self-conscious references to Pushkin's "greatness," however, do not flow from the form so much as from the subject matter, and they are familiar from even such otherwise idiosyncratic Pushkin films as Andrei Khrzhanovskii's animated Pushkin film *Liubimoe moe vremia* (My favorite time, 1987). (Vladimir Semerchuk has observed that Pushkin films made in the Soviet period were dominated by a "jubilee-ideological" principle.)[4] In *The Little Tragedies*, these celebrations of Pushkin include an anniversary dedication, inscribed onscreen as the film begins, and a portrait of Pushkin with a candle burning before it used as transition between the plays. Pushkin's death mask also appears, issuing as if supernaturally from an open sky over the sea.

That seascape is the setting for Pushkin's "Stsena iz Fausta" (Scene from *Faust*, 1825), which opens the film (it is the first of several frames Shveitser creates for the four tragedies). Two costumed actors speak the poem's lines as if they were in conversation. One critic has observed that they seem almost to be in rehearsal, despite the seaside setting,[5] and this comment seems apt to me, particularly since the "Stsena iz Fausta" itself will rehearse some of the film's themes and technical devices for establishing those themes. It works as a practice session for the film's theme of performance, which recurs in each of the otherwise different segments that follow, and its Faustian motifs of temptation, self-aggrandizement, greed, and regret are all powerfully heard in the "little tragedies" themselves.

Next come two scenes from Pushkin's *Egipetskie nochi* (Egyptian nights, 1836).[6] The improviser from *Egipetskie nochi* "performs" three of the four "little tragedies" after he also re-creates one of Pushkin's late lyrics for Charskii's benefit; the first of the four tragedies, *Mozart and Salieri*, is presented as if Charskii imagines it, suggesting that he feels for the improviser something like the envy Salieri felt for Mozart.[7] This elaborate lead-in provides a plausible cinematic motivation for the plays, but it may also suggest an uncertainty about whether the "little tragedies" could stand alone (an anxiety we also find in the critical literature, where attempts to see them as a unified enterprise have often foundered). The framing scenes reveal Shveitser's boldness in shaping a relationship among the four plays. He has said that he wished to find an external equivalent for the internal thematic and philosophical links among the plays, and he also hoped implicitly to explain their preoccupation with evil.[8] Thus, the Mephistophelian will to destroy a ship full of people (in "Stsena iz Fausta") forewarns the murderous impulse to end the lives of Mozart, the Baron, Don Juan, and all who die in the plague. And it is a will that has the capacity to kill Pushkin himself, another reason why the death mask looms over the horizon at the end of the scene from *Faust*.

The use of *Egipetskie nochi* as a frame mechanism reveals Shveitser's impulse to provide psychological realism and plausibility.[9] In his framing of the plays, the tragedies' dramatic shifts in style, locale, and scope are amply motivated by Charskii's and the Improviser's ambitions. Additional inserted material from Pushkin's prose fragments "Gosti s"ezzhalis' na dachu" (The guests gathered at the *dacha*, 1828–30), "Na uglu malen'koi ploshchadi" (At the corner of a small square, 1829–31), and "My provodili vecher na dache" (We were spending the evening at the *dacha*, 1835) adds depth to the characters in the audience and creates parallels between one member of the audience, Zinaida Vol'skaia, and Cleopatra, the subject of improvisations. Since Pushkin himself included material from the last of these three fragments in *Egipetskie nochi*, Shveitser is in a sense merely following his lead.

Before these salon scenes, we witness the Improviser's private performance for Charskii of the poem "Poet idet, otkryty vezhdy" (The poet walks with open eyes), a selection that focuses our attention on the film's theme of artistic inspiration and the mysteries of the creative process. When told that he should seek loftier themes for poetic inspiration, the poet answers with a series of metaphors for the seeming caprice of his choice of material.

—Why does the wind swirl in a ravine,
Raise the leaf and carry off dust,
When a ship in motionless water
Greedily awaits the push of its breath?
Why does the eagle, heavy and fearsome,
Fly down from the mountains and past towers,
Onto a desiccated stump? Ask him.
Why is the Moor loved
By young Desdemona
As the moon loves the darkness of night?
Because no law rules wind or eagle
Or the heart of a maiden.
The poet is the same: like the cold wind of Aquilon,
He carries aloft what he chooses.
Like the eagle, he flies
And, asking no one,
He, like Desdemona, selects
An idol for his heart.

—Зачем крутится ветр в овраге,
Подъемлет лист и пыль несет,
Когда корабль в недвижной влаге
Его дыханья жадно ждет?
Зачем от гор и мимо башен
Летит орел, тяжел и страшен,
На чахлый пень? Спроси его.
Зачем арапа своего
Младая любит Дездемона,
Как месяц любит ночи мглу?
Затем, что ветру и орлу
И сердцу девы нет закона.
Таков поэт: как Аквилон,
Что хочет, то и носит он—
Орлу подобно, он летает
И, не спросясь ни у кого,
Как Дездемона избирает
Кумир для сердца своего.
(Pushkin 8, 1: 269)

Pushkin meant these lines as an aesthetic manifesto in his *Egipetskie nochi*, and Shveitser similarly presents this prominent "polemic against the idealists' elevated view of the poet" in defense of "so-called low subjects," as one scholar has put it.[10] Shveitser has his own mix of high and low in *The Little Tragedies*, but his film also develops a more emotional theme implicit in the figures of speech that here stand in for the poet's activities. The poet is described by three metaphors: a bitter winter wind, bearing off anything in its path; an eagle flying where he chooses; and the passionate Desdemona, deciding for herself whom to love. All three images emphasize the poet's freedom to choose things with which he will associate or those whom he will love, and the energy motivating each choice is enormous. Pushkin's metaphors all involve passionate choices, and Shveitser, in directing the actor who plays the Improviser, Sergei Iurskii, also stresses the emotional intensity of the creative act. Iurskii's voice rises precipitously in reciting these lines, not with the several images of lofty flight, as we might expect, but with the claim that the eagle will *ask no one* where to fly. In addition to this romantic image of creativity, *Egipetskie nochi* elsewhere presents an idea of the artistic product as a commodity, particularly in the Improviser's calculations of how much money he will earn. Monika Greenleaf has noted the tale's image of the "poet as circus performer, and of his poetic product and even process as commodity."[11] One could argue that Shveitser, too, recognizes the commodification of films in Soviet Russia, especially films about national myths such as Pushkin's legacy, and that this view grounds the film's more apocalyptic aspects. Especially in such a context, Shveitser repeats Pushkin's insistence on artistic freedom.

Thus the director urges us to share his astonishment at the mystery of the creative act. He was clearly fascinated by Pushkin's burst of creative energy in the Boldino autumn of 1830, the period during which *The Little Tragedies* were written; he worked on the film in part to understand how the achievements of that autumn were possible. At an early stage in planning the film, he intended to include a scene showing Pushkin writing at his desk, the camera peering through a window.[12] Perhaps it is a relief that the film swerved away from this particular form of realism, substituting the creative acts of others, each with its own idea of inspiration and genius. In fact, the poem "Poet idet, otkryty vezhdy" commences with an image of a poet walking wide-eyed but seeing nothing because he is too absorbed by the ideas of his own imagination. That sightlessness might suggest that the creative act occurs in isolation, without the stimulation of others, but nothing could be further from Pushkin's view of creativity or Mikhail Shveitser's. In the poem, an audience quickly intrudes on this poet: a passerby tugs at his coat and speaks at length about his own observations and aesthetic philosophies (it is the poet's answer that I have quoted above). The views of another person stimulate the poet's introspective meditation on his art, and substitution and exchange will more generally structure the film's representations of creative work. Shveitser also wants to show us that the moment of creation is never private, even in this intensely focused lyric poem, and even in the solitude of Pushkin's Boldino autumn, where his *Little Tragedies* were composed.[13]

The other thing worth noting about this segment of the film is the way the actor playing the Improviser, Sergei Iurskii, uses his body to create the spectacle of poetic invention—his body itself seems to find the words of his poem, his hand reaching up as if to pull them into his mind from the air above him.[14] I will return to the question of embodiment in the film at the end of this essay, not least because it complicates any principle of realism inherent in a filmed performance of the plays. But the cinematic apparatus is important here too, and its presence (obviously) marks the film as distinct from any live theatrical performance. The camera work and editing focus our attention on Iurskii's hands, for example, as he reaches up toward the ceiling or on his feet as he taps his foot to gather the momentum of poetic inspiration. His performance has its own audience, however, in the person of Charskii, and his face is shown several times during the speech, always a face rapt with attention, almost blinded by the light of what it beholds. The watching face is not unlike the passerby who tugs at the poet's coat in the poem itself, so that the structure of the performance mimics that of the text performed. But Charskii's presence also includes a note of evaluation—he is meant to tell the film's audiences how we should react to the performance on the screen. This stunned response is a single word, *udivitel'no* (amazing). His benumbed pleasure forewarns that of another audience shown later in the film, the ecstatic faces of male admirers who listen to Laura's songs in *The Stone Guest.* Audiences appear often in the film, in fact, always seeming both to enable the spectacles they witness and to provide cues to the film's audiences about how to react to what is seen: the Improviser will perform in a salon; in *A Feast in Time of Plague* feasting revelers will listen to Mary's song, and she, in turn, will listen to the Master of Revels when he intones the play's last song. Both these scenes show larger and more diverse audiences, some enchanted by what they see, some lost in their own feelings of boredom or frightened confusion.

No one, then, is immune to the visual inspection of the camera or other actors, which means that no one is imagined not to be involved in some sort of performance. In one sense, this proliferation of audiences in the film compensates for the absence of the theatrical audience that Pushkin's *Little Tragedies* would seem to require. No live audience was there to encourage, applaud, laugh, or weep at the actors' work, so the director amplifies the one obvious audience for actors in a film, himself, to include many other actors.[15] The layers of performance also balance the film's realist inclinations, making it impossible for us to interpret the film as invisibly catching or recording a spectacle or event. Neither the creative work of filmmaking nor the decisions that go into poetic creativity are meant to be effaced here.

The Little Tragedies thus goes on to show us many instances of creative performance, beyond the improvisations that effect transitions from one play to the next.[16] Some performances are musical (Laura's and Mary's songs), to melodies provided by the composer Alfred Schnittke, famous for his re-creations of musical styles. His melodies are so haunting that they dominate one's memory of the film. The music also unifies the film: a fragment of the melody for Laura's rendition of "Zhil na svete rytsar' bednyi" (Once there lived a poor knight, 1829) is strummed earlier by the Improviser in his private performance for Charskii; the organ music heard at the end of the Baron's soliloquy in *The Covetous Knight* recurs in *A Feast in Time of Plague.*

All these performances, in varying degrees, share two features: an intense moment of anticipatory buildup, just as art is about to be invented before our eyes; and clever camera cross-cutting between performer and audience, suggesting that the absorption of the performance is also a creative act. Shveitser reminds us that reception has its own elements of inspiration. But there is nothing fatuous about his self-reference. Salieri listening to Mozart, desperately and demonically, is a frightening measure of the director's filmmaking, even in the exceptionally generous and complex performance of Salieri given by Innokentii Smoktunovskii. But it's *all* frightening in this film—the deadly willingness of an artist to kill his model in order to better represent a dying body, an exile's surreptitious return to his native city and unexpected wooing of a widow whose husband he killed, and a young man's readiness to send a ship full of people to their death to allay his own boredom.

Shveitser concludes his film with *A Feast in Time of Plague*, pushing this terrible association of art with the ecstasy of death to its limit. He moves the famous hymn to the plague to the end of the play, which gives his film an apocalyptic conclusion: the spectacle of a terrifying, terrified man speaking words of fear but also pleasure and rage. We quickly lose sight of any watching faces that might give meaning to his hymn. As deeply introspective as the Baron's soliloquy, this song is heard as speech and as melody, a hoarse and diminished melody that is more terrible than the spoken word.[17] The Master of Revels is played by Aleksandr Trofimov, an actor famous at the time for his work at Moscow's Taganka Theater, where he was Raskol'nikov in *Crime and Punishment* (*Prestuplenie i nakazanie*) and Ieshua in *Master and Margarita* (*Master i Margarita*). His association with these roles intensifies his stage presence as the Master of Revels, absorbing into it their defiance, meekness, passion, and compassion. It has been said of Smoktunovskii's performances as Salieri and as the Baron that he embodied contradictory modes of being,[18] and the same is certainly true of Trofimov.

So I return, in conclusion, to the idea of embodiment, which offers a new angle on Shveitser's sense of his own film. He chose to have several actors appear in more than one role in *The Little Tragedies*, perhaps none so stunningly as Smoktunovskii.[19] These repetitions reveal unexpected similarities between characters, and they unify the film and make it more like a theater performance. It seems the work of a company of actors long familiar with one another rather than an unrelated group of trained professionals who disperse when the film is over. To say the same thing in the language of performance theory: the actors embody themselves at the same time that their bodies are meant as vessels for another imagined life.[20] They are, ironically, at once themselves and someone else, and that doubling itself allegorizes the relationship of the performance as a whole to the text on which it is based: "[P]erformance reconstitutes the text," as W. B. Worthen has observed,[21] and Mikhail Shveitser's particular reconstitution of the "little tragedies" is a reconstitution by means of addition, amplification, and at times daring rearrangement. It is not self-effacing—in this sense, it is furthest from realism, for we constantly sense the director's immense intellectual and creative work in his film. Its nervousness about realism permeates as well the style of acting, which is excessive, even melodramatic for some of the actors (Smoktunovskii as the Baron, for example, Vysotskii in his final scenes in *The Stone Guest*).

Pushkin's "little tragedies" also point us toward a different drama of embodiment, for in their tales of sensual passion, avarice, envy, murder, and the pleasure of creating art, they face up to the dangers inherent in these tantalizing experiences, showing the body ever at risk of insult, attack, illness, and exposure. Pushkin's plays, in this Dostoevskian version, contain a very different notion of lived experience from that of the Enlightenment (and, I would say, Soviet) idea of inspiration as a disembodied, spiritual ideal. *The Little Tragedies*, to be sure, includes this notion of pure inspiration with its ever-present candles. The flame that burns before a portrait of the poet in the end, however, is the same fire that lights the Baron's demented tour of his cellars, the Master of Revels's song praising the ecstasy of coming close to death, Don Juan's walk through a cemetery at night, and Laura's songs of sensual pleasure and knightly honor. Pushkin's creativity, too, seems in equal measure ecstasy and suffering, yet as the last camera frame freezes the image of the candle flame, it remains enigmatic as well, neither extinguished nor entirely understood.

The Little Tragedies does not, then, seek to delude us that we witness Pushkin's lived experiences or even the world in which he lived (the scenes of high society watching an Improviser are the closest that the film comes to this ambition, but these moments are richly layered as performances within performances and do not work as mere background or sources of historical information). Pushkin's creative work is itself shown to be a kind of performance, an activity for which he had to imagine or internalize an audience, as film must also do, but absorption and theatricality are not mutually exclusive. The film lets actors play roles from Pushkin's plays and stories and also play themselves acting; the motivations for enacting dramas of high emotion and complex ethics are explored in stylized but psychologically compelling ways. As such, Shveitser's film has an ambition we recognize from Pushkin's *Little Tragedies*: to take viewers into distant worlds with few illusions about the demands that distance will make on us; to offer spectacles of creative activity in which material that has already passed through other hands is fully reworked; and to suggest that creativity absorbs untold energy from the work of others. It occurs in a rich context of influences, examples, and imagined audiences no matter how solitary the creative artist may appear to have been.

Notes

1. The encyclopedia of Pushkin films now makes possible a much fuller appreciation for the dozens of films based on his works and his life. See *Pushkinskii kinoslovar'*.

2. Among Shveitser's films are versions of Tolstoy's novel *Voskresenie* (Resurrection, 1960) and Gogol's *Mertvye dushi* (Dead souls, 1984). For a full listing, see *Kino: Entsiklopedicheskii slovar'*, 497, where it is also noted that Shveitser worked on other films as a writer or cowriter of the scenario.

3. This is not to say that his adaptations are entirely removed from the concerns of the contemporary world or that his filmmaking decisions are reached outside the context of what is permissible and what will be noticed by those who judge Soviet and post-Soviet films. One scholar has noted that Shveitser's 1987 film *Kreitserova sonata* (The Kreutzer sonata) took advantage of early Glasnost's looser restrictions on sexual expression in cinema. See Gillespie, "New Versions of Old Classics," 118.

4. Semerchuk, "Mezhdu poetikoi i ideologiei," 246. He goes on to praise Shveitser's *Little Tragedies* as "brilliant" (252), especially notable in an essay that otherwise disparages Soviet Pushkin films.

5. Varshavskii, "Est' upoenie v boiu...," 57.

6. Into one of these scenes a portion of Pushkin's short story "Grobovshchik" (The coffinmaker, 1830) is also interpolated.

7. I know of one other dramatic performance of *The Little Tragedies* that used a similar framing device, where the plays were "told" by someone: the performance opened with *Pir vo vremia chumy*, broken up as if it were the *Decameron*, with feasting revelers "telling" each of the other three plays. Iurii Liubimov directed the production, which was shown in various spots; I saw it in Purchase, New York, in the late 1980s.

8. Rybak, *Kak rozhdalis' fil'my Mikhaila Shveitsera*, 135–41.

9. The scenes from *Egyptian Nights* also explore a social ethic as a basis for individual identity and self-worth. For a valuable reassessment of the ethics of community inherent in realist literary poetics, see Allen, *Beyond Realism*, esp. 18–34.

10. O'Bell, *Pushkin's "Egyptian Nights,"* 104; she in turn refers her readers to the solid treatment of this topic in Ginzburg, "Pushkin i liricheskii geroi russkogo romantizma."

11. Greenleaf, *Pushkin and Romantic Fashion*, 209.

12. Rybak, *Kak rozhdalis' fil'my Mikhaila Shveitsera*, 145.

13. The film also abounds in moments of intense seclusion, for example, the Baron underground, Don Juan and Dona Anna in her extraordinary chambers, the Master of Revels and Mary at the end of *A Feast in Time of Plague*. The paradox of solitude and observation is maintained even in these scenes, perhaps most powerfully in the Baron's soliloquies, which are so self-consciously and disturbingly addressed to the camera.

14. The camera's fascination with the Improviser's body and the wonderful suppleness of the actor Iurskii's body as he moves through this role urge us to focus on a different aspect of embodiment in Iurskii's performance—the gentle but splendid eroticism of the body as it performs before us. Compare the comments about Colin Firth's performance as Darcy in the 1995 BBC version of *Pride and Prejudice* in Sonnet, "From *Emma* to *Clueless*," 58.

15. On audiences within film, see Manvell, *Theater and Film*, 53.

16. These include the songs Laura sings in *The Stone Guest* (Shveitser supplies the words from Pushkin's poetry, "Ia zdes', Inezil'ia" and "Zhil na svete rytsar' bednyi") as well as those that Mary and Walsingham sing in *A Feast in Time of Plague*, the declaration of love Juan utters to Dona Anna, Mozart playing his Requiem for Salieri and supervising other performances for his benefit, and the extraordinary soliloquies uttered by the Baron in *The Covetous Knight*.

17. Compare an observation that Shveitser, the brother of Tsvetaeva's biographer Viktoria Shveitser, would certainly have known: "What does *A Feast in Time of Plague* leave us (in our ears and souls)? Two songs—Mary's and Walsingham's. A love-song and a plague-song" (Tsvetaeva, "Iskusstvo pri svete sovesti," 5: 349).

18. Varshavskii, "Est' upoenie v boiu...," 58.

19. We also see Nikolai Kochegarov as Faust, a reveler in Laura's admiring band and again around the feast table in *A Feast in Time of Plague*, Danilova as Zinaida Vol'skaia and also in the group scenes in *A Feast in Time of Plague*, and Ivars Kalnyn'sh as Faust and as Don Carlos, for example. For a full listing of the actors, technical team, and a summary of the film, see *Pushkinskii kinoslovar'*, 57–59.

20. See Hodgdon, "Replicating Richard," and Worthen, "Drama, Performativity, Performance." Both essays are about Shakespeare performances, itself a theme tied to the performance of Pushkin in the Russian context well worth further exploration.

21. Worthen, "Drama, Performativity, Performance," 1097.

Translations

The Covetous Knight

Translated by James E. Falen

Scenes from Shenstone's tragicomedy, *The Covetous Knight.*

SCENE I

A tower

ALBERT and JEAN

ALBERT:
Whatever be the cost, I must appear
At tournament. Let's see my helmet, Jean.
(Jean brings him his helmet.)
It's pierced all through, quite useless. Not a chance
Of wearing it. I'll needs obtain another.
A mighty stroke! That curséd Count Delorge!

JEAN:
But you requited him right well, my lord.
And after you had dropped him from his horse,
He lay like death all day and night—I doubt
He's well.

ALBERT:
And yet he suffered no great loss;
His fine Venetian breastplate's still intact;
His breast's his own—it cost him not a farthing,
Nor will he need to buy himself another.
I should have stripped his helmet where he lay!

And would have done, had I not been ashamed
Before the Duke and ladies. Curséd Count!
Far better had he gored my skull instead.
I need new raiment too. Last time the knights
Were all in satin and in velvet clad;
While I alone, among the ducal guests,
Sat clothed in coat-of-mail. I made excuse,
By claiming that I'd happened there by chance.
But what shall I say now? This wretched state!
How poverty humiliates the heart!
When that Delorge with his full-weighted lance
Did run my helmet through and gallop past,
And I, with all-uncovered head, did spur
My steed, Emir, and like a whirlwind rushed
Upon the Count and hurled him like a page
Full twenty steps; when all the ladies then
Uprose them from their chairs; when fair Clotilda,
Her eyelids closed, unknowingly cried out,
And all the heralds praised my mighty blow—
Oh, none of them had inkling of the cause,
The reason for my courage and my strength!
I went berserk to see my helmet crushed—
The parent to my deed was paltry meanness.
Oh yes, that foul disease attaches quick
When one resides beneath my father's roof!
How fares my poor Emir?

JEAN:

Still lame, I fear.
You'll not be riding him for some good time.

ALBERT:

There's nothing to be done; I'll buy the bay.
The asking price, at least, is nothing much.

JEAN:

Not much, perhaps, but money have we none.

ALBERT:

What says that worthless scoundrel Solomon?

JEAN:

He says that he no longer can afford
To lend you any funds without a pledge.

ALBERT:

A pledge! And what am I to pledge, the devil?

JEAN:

I told him that.

ALBERT:

What then?

JEAN:

He groaned and shrugged.

ALBERT:

You should have told him that my father's rich
And like a Jew himself; that soon or late
His wealth will pass to me.

JEAN:

I told him so.

ALBERT:

And then?

JEAN:

He shrugged and groaned.

ALBERT:

What wretched luck!

JEAN:

He said he'd come himself.

ALBERT:

Thank God for that.
I'll have a ransom ere I let him go.
(A knock at the door.)
Who's there?
(A Jew enters.)

JEW:

Your humble servant.

ALBERT:

Ah, my friend!
Accurséd Jew, most worthy Solomon,
Come in, come in! What's this they tell me, friend:
That you mistrust a debt?

JEW:

O noble knight,
I swear to you . . . I'd gladly . . . but I can't.
I have no funds. I've made myself a bankrupt

By slavishly assisting all you knights,
For no one pays me back. I came to ask
If you could pay at least some part . . .

ALBERT:

You thief!
If I myself had funds, do you believe
I'd have the slightest intercourse with you?
Be not so obdurate, friend Solomon.
Release your gold. A hundred you can spare.
I'll have you searched.

JEW:

A hundred, did you say!
Oh, when have I had such a sum!

ALBERT:

Take care . . .
You ought to be ashamed that you refuse
To aid a friend.

JEW:

I swear to you . . .

ALBERT:

Enough.
You want a pledge? What sort of rant is this!
What kind of pledge? A boar skin, would you say?
Had I the merest trifle I could pledge,
I'd sold it long ere this. A knight's good word
Is not enough for you, you dog?

JEW:

Your word,
While you're alive, is worth a great, great deal.
It's like a talisman that can unlock,
For you, the chests of all the Flemish rich.
But if you then transfer that word to me,
A wretched Jew, and if you chance to die
(Which God forbid!), then in these hands of mine,
'Twould be no use . . . or like a key that fits
Some casket at the bottom of the sea.

ALBERT:

You think it true, my father will outlive me?

JEW:

Who knows? Our days are reckoned not by us;
The youth who bloomed last night today lies dead,
And four old men, on bent and burdened shoulders,
Now bear him in his coffin to the grave.
The Baron's hale. God will—he'll live for ten,
For twenty, twenty-five . . . for thirty years.

ALBERT:

You lie, you wretched Jew: in thirty years—
I'll be nigh fifty then! What use will wealth
Avail me at that age?

JEW:

What use, you ask?
Why, wealth at any age can serve us well;
But youth, in wealth, seeks nothing more than slaves
And, pitiless, dispatches them all round.
Old age, in wealth, sees good and worthy friends
And guards them like the apple of his eye.

ALBERT:

My father sees in wealth nor slaves, nor friends;
He only sees the master whom he serves.
And how he serves! Like some Egyptian slave
Or chainéd dog. In his unheated kennel
He lives on water and on crusts of bread;
He never sleeps but runs about and howls
While all his gold rests peacefully in chests.
Be silent, Jew! The day will surely come
When it will rest no more but service me.

JEW:

The funeral of the Baron will unleash
A great deal more of money than of tears.
God grant you your inheritance ere long.

ALBERT:

Amen!

JEW:

Perhaps . . .

ALBERT:

What now?

JEW:

I had a thought,
That maybe there's a way . . .

ALBERT:

What way?

JEW:

Well, then—
I have a friend, a little agéd fellow,
A Jew, a poor apothecary . . .

ALBERT:

Ha!
A usurer like you. Or is he honest?

JEW:

No, knight, Tobias deals a different trade.
He mixes potions . . . and his drops, in truth,
Work wondrous well.

ALBERT:

And what are they to me?

JEW:

Three drops is all—into a glass of water;
They have no taste, no color do they show;
And he who drinks will have no writhing gut,
No nausea, no pain . . . and yet will die.

ALBERT:

Your agéd friend in poison trades.

JEW:

Ah, yes,
In poison.

ALBERT:

So? Instead of lending cash,
You offer me two hundred venomed vials,
A vial for a coin? Is that your game?

JEW:

You choose to laugh at me, my noble knight—
But no, I thought . . . perhaps that you . . . I thought . . .
The Baron's time to die might well have come.

ALBERT:

What's that! . . . a son . . . give poison to his father!

Arrest him, Jean! How dare you think that I! . . .
Do you not know, you Jewish thing, you dog,
You serpent, you! that I can hang you now
Upon these gateposts here!

JEW:

I did you wrong!
Have mercy, I but jested.

ALBERT:

Jean, the rope!

JEW:

A jest . . . a jest . . . I have the money . . . here!

ALBERT:

Away, you dog!
(The Jew leaves.)
Thus low have I been brought
By this my father's greed! See what the Jew
Has dared suggest! Bring me a glass of wine . . .
I'm all distraught . . . And yet . . . the money, Jean—
I need it! Follow that accurséd Jew
And take his gold away. And bring me then
A pot of ink. I'll give the wretched rogue
A full receipt. But don't admit the man,
That Judas soul . . . But stay you, Jean . . . I fear
His gold will reek of poison evermore,
As did that silver of his ancestor . . .
I asked for wine.

JEAN:

We haven't, sir, alas,
A drop of wine.

ALBERT:

But what about the crate
That Raymond sent me, as a gift, from Spain?

JEAN:

Just yesterday I took the ailing smith
Our final bottle.

ALBERT:

Yes, I do recall . . .
Well, pour me water then. This curséd life!

The die is cast. I'll get me to the Duke
And seek redress: let father be compelled
To treat me as a son . . . and not a mouse
Begotten in a cellar.

SCENE II

A cellar vault

BARON:

The way a youthful rake awaits a tryst
With some licentious harlot or, perhaps,
Some foolish girl that he's seduced, so I
All day have marked the time till I might come
Down to my secret vault and trusty chests.
O happy day! This evening can I pour
In coffer number six (as yet unfilled)
Another gathered handful of my gold.
Not much, perhaps, but by such tiny drops
Do mighty treasures grow. I read somewhere
That once a king commanded all his troops
To gather dirt by handfuls in a heap,
And thus, in time, a mighty hill arose—
And from that summit could the king with joy
Survey his valleys, decked in gleaming tents,
And watch his great armada ply the sea.
Thus I, by offering in tiny bits
My customary tribute to this vault,
Have raised my hill as well—and from its height
I too survey the reach of my domain.
And who shall set its bounds? Like some great demon,
From here I can control and rule the world.
I need but wish—and palaces will rise;
And in my splendid gardens will appear
A throng of nymphs to caper and to sport;
The muses too will offer me their tribute,
And freedom-loving genius be my slave;
And virtue too, and unremitting labor,

Will humbly wait on me for their reward.
I need but whistle low—and, bowing, scraping,
Blood-spattered villainy itself will crawl
To lick my hand and look into my eyes
To read therein the sign of my desire.
All things submit to me, and I—to none;
I stand above all longings and all cares;
I know my might, and in this knowledge find
Enough reward . . .
(He looks at his gold.)
It hardly seems like much,
But oh, what human woes, what bitter tears,
Deceptions, orisons, and imprecations
This heavy-weighted gold is token of!
I have an old doubloon . . . it's this one here;
Some widow brought it just this morn, but first
She knelt for half the day outside my window,
Three children at her side, and wailed aloud.
It rained and rained, then stopped, then rained again,
And still that hypocrite stayed on; I might
Have driven her away, but something whispered
That she had come to pay her husband's debt,
Afraid that on the morrow she'd be jailed.
And this one here was brought me by Thibault—
A lazy cheat who got it God knows where!
He lifted it, no doubt; or else outside,
Upon the high road, late at night, in woods . . .
Ah yes! If all the tears, the blood and sweat
That men have shed for such a hoard as this
Should suddenly gush forth from out the earth,
There'd be a second flood!—and I'd be drowned
Inside my trusty vaults. But now it's time.
(He starts to unlock the chest.)
Each time I come to open up a chest,
I fall into a fever and I shudder.
It isn't fear (for whom have I to dread?
I have my saber by; its trusty steel
Will answer for my gold), but all the same
Some strange and eerie feeling grips my heart . . .

Physicians claim that there are certain men
Who find a pleasure in the act of murder.
When I insert my key inside the lock,
I feel what murderers themselves must feel
As they plunge dagger into flesh: excitement . . .
And horror all at once.
(He opens the chest.)
My ecstasy!
(He slowly pours in his coins.)
Go home—you've roamed the world quite long enough
In service to the needs and lusts of men.
Sleep well in here—the sleep of peace and power,
The sleep the gods in deepest Heaven sleep . . .
I will arrange tonight a solemn feast:
Before each chest I'll light a candlestick,
And all of them I'll open wide, and I
Will gaze in rapture at my dazzling hoard.
(He lights the candles and, one after the other,
opens all the chests.)
I rule the world! . . . What magical refulgence!
And all this mighty realm submits to me.
My bliss is here, my honor and my glory!
I rule the world! . . . But who, when I have gone,
Will reign in this domain? My wretched heir!
A raving madman and a spendthrift youth,
The comrade of licentious debauchees!
Before I'm cold, he'll come! He'll hurry down,
With all his crew of greedy sycophants,
To enter these serene and silent vaults.
He'll rob my corpse and, when he has the keys,
He'll cackle as he opens all the chests.
And all my treasured gold will quickly flow
To pockets satin lined and full of holes.
He'll desecrate and smash these hallowed vessels,
He'll feed the regal balm to dirt and dust—
He'll squander all! . . . And by what proper right?!
Have I, indeed, attained all this by naught?
Or through a game, as if I were a gambler
Who rattles dice and rakes the booty in?

Who knows how many bitter deprivations,
How many bridled passions, heavy thoughts,
Unceasing cares, and sleepless nights I've paid?
Or will my callous son assert aloud
That my poor heart was all o'ergrown with moss,
That never did I know immortal longings,
That conscience never gnawed me, mighty conscience,
The sharp-clawed beast that rakes the heart, O conscience,
That uninvited guest, that dull companion,
That churlish creditor, that horrid witch
Upon whose call the moon grows dark and tombs
Explode . . . and send their dead to roam abroad? . . .
No! Suffer first! and earn the wealth you crave,
And then we'll see if you'd allow some wretch
To squander all the treasure got by blood.
If only I could hide this sacred vault
From worthless eyes! If only from the grave
I might return and, like a watchful shade,
Secure my chests and from all living souls
Protect my treasured gold as I do now! . . .

SCENE III

At the palace

ALBERT: and THE DUKE

ALBERT:
Believe me, sovereign liege, I've long endured
The shame of bitter want. Were not my plight
Extreme indeed, you had not heard my plaint.

DUKE:
I well believe you, sir: a noble knight,
A man like you, would not accuse his father
Except in deep distress. Such knaves are few . . .
So rest your mind; I shall appeal, myself,
In private, gently, to your father's heart.
I wait him now. It's long since last we met.

He was my grandsire's friend. I well recall—
When I was still a boy, your father oft
Would seat me on his stallion and, in jest,
Would place his heavy helm upon my head
As if it were a bell.
(He looks out the window.)
Who comes here now?
Your father?

ALBERT:

He, my liege.

DUKE:

Then get you hence.
I'll summon you when all's arranged.
(Albert leaves; the Baron enters.)
Well, Baron,
I'm pleased to see you, and so hale and hearty.

BARON:

I'm overjoyed, my liege, to have the strength
To come to court once more at your command.

DUKE:

It's quite some time since last we parted, Baron.
Do you remember me?

BARON:

Remember, lord?
I see you even now as once you were—
A lively boy. The great deceaséd Duke
Would say: "Well, Philip, friend" (he called me that;
'Twas always Philip then), "what say you, eh?
In twenty years or so, both you and I
Will be but dotards in this stripling's eyes . . ."
In yours, that is to say.

DUKE:

Well, let's renew
Our friendship now. You've quite forgot my court.

BARON:

I've grown too old, my liege. And here at court
What use am I? You're young and still delight
In tournaments and festive rounds. But I
Am little fit for such pursuits. If God

Should send us war, then I'd remain prepared
To mount, if groaningly, my horse once more.
I'd find the strength, although my hand might tremble,
To draw my ancient sword in your behalf.

DUKE:

Your valor, Baron, is well known to us;
You were my grandsire's friend; my father too
Respected you. And I have ever found you
A brave and worthy knight . . . But come, we'll sit.
You've children, Baron, yes?

BARON:

An only son.

DUKE:

Why is it that he hides from our regard?
The court for you is dull, but for your son
Both age and rank do call him to our side.

BARON:

My son dislikes the bustling, courtly life.
He has a shy and gloomy cast of mind—
All round the castle wood he ever roams
As if he were a fawn.

DUKE:

It bodes no good
To shun the light. We'll soon accustom him
To festive rounds, to tournaments and balls.
Assign him here to us, and do bestow
A maintenance upon him due his rank.
I see you frown—your journey, I much fear,
Has laid you low.

BARON:

I am not weary, liege,
But you have much confused me. I would fain
Not make confession to Your Grace . . . but now,
You force me to be frank about my son,
To tell you what I'd rather keep well hid.
My sovereign liege: my son, alas, deserves
No mark of your good favor or regard.
He wastes away his youth in brute excess,
In basest vice . . .

DUKE:

The cause may be, good Baron,
That he's too much alone. Great solitude
And idleness prove ruinous to youth.
Appoint him then to us, and he'll forget
Those habits that forsakenness doth breed.

BARON:

Forgive me, sovereign liege, but I protest;
I cannot give consent to such a course.

DUKE:

But, Baron, why?

BARON:

Release a poor old man . . .

DUKE:

I must insist, old friend, that you reveal
The cause of your refusal.

BARON:

Anger, liege,
Against my son.

DUKE:

For what?

BARON:

A wicked crime.

DUKE:

But tell me, knight, in what does it consist?

BARON:

Release me, Duke, I pray.

DUKE:

'Tis passing strange . . .
Or feel you shame on his account?

BARON:

Yes . . . shame . . .

DUKE:

What was it, though, he did?

BARON:

He tried . . . he sought
To murder me.

DUKE:

To murder you! See here,
I'll have the wretched villain bound to court.

BARON:

I cannot offer proof, although I know
He greatly thirsts indeed to see me dead;
And well I know that he had dark intent
To . . .

DUKE:

What?

BARON:

To rob me.
(Albert rushes into the room.)

ALBERT:

Baron, that's a lie!

DUKE (to the son):

How dare you, sir! . . .

BARON:

You here! And dare to speak,
To hurl at me, your father, such a word! . . .
To say—I lie! Before our noble Duke! . . .
To me . . . or am I knight no more?

ALBERT:

You lie!

BARON:

O God of justice, sound thy thunder now!
Pick up my gauntlet—let the sword decide!
(He throws down his glove; his son promptly picks it up.)

ALBERT:

My gratitude. Your first paternal gift.

DUKE:

What's this I see? Before my very eyes?
A son takes up an agéd father's dare!
Oh, woeful times are these that I should wear
The ducal crown! Be silent, madman, you.
And you, you tiger cub, enough.
(To the son.)

Have done;
Relinquish me that glove.
(He takes it away.)

ALBERT (aside):
A pity that.

DUKE:
He's marked it with his claws! A monstrous son!
Begone; and keep thee, sirrah, from my sight
Until such time as I, upon the need,
May summon you.
(Albert leaves.)
And you, unhappy wretch,
Have you no shame?...

BARON:
Forgive me, noble liege ...
I feel unwell ... my knees have turned to water ...
I'm choking! ... choking! ... air! ... the keys? The keys!
I want my keys! ...

DUKE:
He's dead. O God in Heaven!
What dreadful times are these, what dreadful hearts!

Mozart and Salieri

Translated by James E. Falen

SCENE I

A room

SALIERI:

Men say there is no justice here on earth.
I say there's none on high as well. To me
This seems as patent as a simple scale.
I came into this world in love with art;
While still a boy I listened and was thrilled
When in our ancient church the organ sang,
And deep within my soul the music swelled
As sweet unbidden tears poured down my cheeks.
I early turned away from idle pleasures;
All studies far from music I despised;
And, scorning them with chill and stubborn pride,
In music I invested all my hopes.
First steps to any goal are always hard,
And arduous and long the path ahead.
But all my early trials I o'ercame,
And craft I made the basis of my art.
A craftsman I became: I made my fingers
The servants who would race to do my will;

My ear I trained: subduing potent sounds,
I disassembled music like a corpse,
Put harmony to algebraic test,
And only then, well steeped in practiced craft,
Did I embrace the lure of true creation.
I set to work . . . but secretly, alone,
Not daring yet to dream of future fame;
Oh, many times, inside my silent cell,
Not having slept or fed for days on end
And having tasted inspiration's tears,
I burnt my work . . . and watched, aloof and cold,
My thoughts and sounds, those children of my soul,
Take flame . . . and vanish in a wisp of smoke.
Oh, more than this! When mighty Gluck appeared
And showed the world the secrets he had found
(Great captivating harmonies of sound),
Did I not then abandon all I knew,
All things I'd loved and ardently believed,
To follow bravely on the track he laid,
Without complaint, like one who'd lost his way
And from some fellow traveler learned the path?
Through constancy of deep intense endeavor,
In time I proved successful and attained
The limitless and lofty realms of art,
And fame at last presented me its kiss.
My work had found a place in people's hearts,
And, happy, I enjoyed with deep content
My labor, my success, my growing fame.
I prized no less the triumphs of my friends,
My comrades in the vineyards of the arts.
And never did I feel a jealous pang!
Not even when Piccini with his charm
Quite captured fickle Paris for a day,
Not even when I heard with bated breath
The overture from *Iphigenia* soar.
And who would dare to say that proud Salieri
Could ever, like a snake, with envy crawl?
That, trampled underfoot, in mortal pain,
He'd gnaw with helpless rage the dirt and dust?

No man would dare! But I myself now say:
Salieri crawls! Yes, I, the great Salieri,
Am tortured by the sting of jealous love.
O Heaven! Where is justice to be found?!
When genius, that immortal sacred gift,
Is granted not to love and self-denial,
To labor and to striving and to prayer—
But casts its light upon a madman's head,
A foolish idler's brow? . . . O Mozart, Mozart!
(Mozart enters.)

MOZART:
Aha! You've seen me then! And here I'd hoped
To treat you to an unexpected jest.

SALIERI:
How long have you been here!

MOZART:
I came just now.
I'd started out to show you some new piece;
And on the way, while passing by the inn,
I heard a fiddle play . . . O good Salieri!
In all your days you've never heard, I swear,
A droller sound . . . A blind old fiddler there
Was scraping out "Voi che sapete." Bliss!
I couldn't wait—and brought the fellow here
To treat you to the pleasure of his art.
Come in!
(A blind old man with a fiddle enters.)

MOZART:
A bit of Mozart, if you will!
(The old man plays an aria from *Don Juan.* Mozart roars with laughter.)

SALIERI:
And you can laugh at this?

MOZART:
Salieri, come!
Are you not laughing too, my friend?

SALIERI:
Oh no!
I cannot laugh—when some benighted hack

Besmirches Raphael and his Madonna;
I cannot laugh—when some repellent clown
With parody dishonors Alighieri.
Begone, old man.

MOZART:

Here, wait ... take this, my friend,
And drink my health.
(The old man leaves.)

MOZART:

I see, my good Salieri,
You're out of sorts today. I'll call again
Some other time.

SALIERI:

What was it that you brought me?

MOZART:

Indeed, it's nothing much. For some nights past,
As sleeplessness tormented me again,
A phrase or two kept running through my mind.
I wrote them down this morning—and I'd come
To ask for your opinion ... but I see ...
You're not quite in the mood.

SALIERI:

O Mozart, Mozart!
Not in the mood for you? Oh, come, sit down,
I'll hear you play.

MOZART (at the fortepiano):

Now picture ... let me see? ...
Well, ... *me,* let's say—a somewhat younger version,
In love—not overmuch, but lightly so;
I'm with a lady ... or a friend ... say, *you;*
I'm cheerful ... then ... some vision from the grave ...
A darkness comes ... or something of the kind ...
Now listen ...
(He plays.)

SALIERI:

You were bringing *this* to me!
And yet could loiter at a wretched inn
To hear some blind old fiddler play! O God!
O Mozart, you're unworthy of yourself.

MOZART:
You think it good?

SALIERI:
What richness and what depth!
What boldness of design and grace of form!
You, Mozart, are a god and know it not.
But I, I know.

MOZART:
You do? Well, maybe so . . .
But now this little god is slightly famished.

SALIERI:
I tell you what: let's dine together then,
The tavern at the Golden Lion Inn.

MOZART:
How nice. But let me first drop in at home
To tell my wife I won't be there for supper.
(He leaves.)

SALIERI:
I'll meet you there. I'll wait. Don't fail me, Mozart.
No more! No more can I resist my fate:
This night shall his undoing bring . . . and I
Must be the cause! Or else we all are lost!
Not I alone, with my dim spot of fame,
But all who worship and who serve our art.
What good if Mozart live? Or if indeed
He soar to such a height as none before?
Will he, by this, exalt the realm of art?
Not so! For fall it must when he departs,
And no successor will he leave behind.
What profit then his life? Like some great angel
He brought immortal music from the skies
To stir within poor creatures of the dust
Unwingéd dreams . . . and then—to fly away!
Go now, Mozart! You are too good for earth.
This poison was a gift from my Isora;
I've had it with me now for eighteen years.
How often since she left have I known pain;
How often have I feasted with some foe
Who little knew how close to death he sat;

Yet never have I yielded to temptation.
No cowardice has kept me from the deed,
Nor is it that I take offenses lightly,
Nor do I hold for life a high regard.
Yet I delayed. Some last resolve I lacked.
Whenever dreams of death beset my soul,
I thought upon the gifts that life might bring:
Of joys unknown, abandoned ere they came;
Of night's creative bliss, and inspiration;
Of how another Haydn might compose
Great masterworks whose depths I then could plumb . . .
When dining with some loathsome fellow creature,
I've often thought that one day I would meet
My mortal foe; or else some rank offense
Would fall upon my head from haughty heights—
And then Isora's gift would do its work.
And I was right! The enemy I sought
Is in my hands at last! Another Haydn—
Who ravished me with ecstasies of sound!
The time has come! O thou prophetic gift,
Get thee tonight . . . into friendship's cup!

SCENE II

A private room at an inn; a fortepiano

MOZART and SALIERI at a table

SALIERI:
You seem in blackish mood tonight.

MOZART:
Not so.

SALIERI:
But something, Mozart, troubles you, I fear.
A splendid meal . . . a wine beyond compare,
Yet you sit dark and mute.

MOZART:

I must confess,
My Requiem is on my mind.

SALIERI:

Aha!
You're working on a requiem . . . How long?

MOZART:

Three weeks or so. The circumstance was strange . . .
I haven't told you?

SALIERI:

No.

MOZART:

I'll tell you now:
Three weeks ago, I happened to come home
Quite late and learned that while I'd been away
A man had called. I don't know why myself,
But all that night I wondered who he was
And why he'd come. Next day he reappeared
But found me once again away from home.
Next afternoon, while romping with my son
About the floor, I heard my name called out.
I went below. A man, all dressed in black,
With solemn bow, commissioned from my hand
A requiem and disappeared. At once
I set to work—but ever since that day,
My visitor in black has not returned,
Which suits me fine, for though my work is done,
I'm loath to give it up. And yet . . .

SALIERI:

Go on.

MOZART:

I'm quite ashamed to tell you this . . .

SALIERI:

What is it?

MOZART:

All day and night, my caller dressed in black
Looms heavy in my mind and haunts my peace.

He follows like a shadow where I go,
And even now, I sense him near . . . a third . . .
Who dines with us tonight.

SALIERI:

What childish fears!
Dispel such empty thoughts. Old Beaumarchais
Quite often used to tell me: "Good Salieri,
Whenever morbid thoughts invade your mind,
Uncork a sparkling bottle of champagne,
Or else, go read my *Figaro* again."

MOZART:

Yes, you and Beaumarchais were friends, I know;
You put his play *Tarare* into song . . .
A splendid thing. There's one motif of yours
I love to sing . . . when in a happy mood . . .
La-la la-la . . . But is it true, Salieri,
That Beaumarchais gave poison to a friend?

SALIERI:

I doubt it's true—he seemed too droll a man
For such a crafty deed.

MOZART:

He was a genius,
Like you and me. And villainy and genius,
As you'll agree, my friend, sit ill together.

SALIERI:

You think it so?
(He pours the poison into Mozart's drink.)
Come, Mozart, drink.

MOZART:

Your health,
Good friend, and to the deep and lasting bonds
That link forever Mozart and Salieri,
Two sons of blesséd harmony.
(He drinks.)

SALIERI:

No, wait!
You've drunk it down! . . . and could not wait for me?

MOZART (throwing his napkin onto the table):

I've had enough.

(He goes to the fortepiano.)
I'll play you now, Salieri,
My Requiem.
(He plays.)
You weep?

SALIERI:
I've never shed
Such tears before: I feel both pain and joy,
As if I'd just fulfilled some heavy debt,
As if a healing knife had just cut off
An aching limb! Dear Mozart, pay no mind
To these my tears. Don't stop, play on . . . play on,
And fill my soul once more with magic sound . . .

MOZART:
If only men could feel as you, Salieri,
The power of the music! Ah . . . but then
The world itself would crumble into dust,
For all would seek the freedom to create,
And none would care a fig for petty needs.
We are but few . . . a happy, chosen few
Who hold in scorn the vulgar path of use,
Who worship only beauty . . . nothing else.
Is that not so? But here . . . I feel unwell,
Some heaviness upon me sits. I'll sleep.
Good night.

SALIERI:
Farewell, my friend.
(Alone.)
You'll fall asleep
Forever, Mozart! But could he be right . . .
Am I no genius? "Villainy and genius
Sit ill together." Surely this is wrong:
Take Michelangelo. Or is it only
A tale the dull and witless tell—and he,
The Vatican's creator, did no murder?

The Stone Guest

Translated by James E. Falen

LEPORELLO: O statua gentilissima
Del gran' Commendatore! . . .
. . . Ah, Padrone!
—Don Giovanni

SCENE I

DON JUAN and LEPORELLO

DON JUAN:
We'll wait for nightfall here. And so at last
We've reached the very gates of old Madrid!
I'll soon be racing down familiar streets,
My face behind a cloak, my hat pulled down.
What think you—am I well disguised or no?

LEPORELLO:
Oh, surely none will recognize Don Juan!
One sees such figures all about!

DON JUAN:
You laugh?
But who would know it's I?

LEPORELLO:
Why, any watchman,
Or gypsy that you meet, or drunken fiddler,
Or one like you—some brazen cavalier
With sword beneath his cloak and black as night.

DON JUAN:
What matter then if I be seen? Of course,

The King himself I'd best avoid. But come,
I fear no other man in all Madrid.

LEPORELLO:

By morning, though, the King will surely learn
That once again Don Juan is in Madrid,
Returned from banishment upon his own.
What then will be your fate?

DON JUAN:

He'll send me back.
I greatly doubt, old man, he'll take my head,
For after all, I'm guilty of no treason.
The King dispatched me hence with kind intent,
To gain me safety from the vengeful kin
Of one I killed . . .

LEPORELLO:

Indeed he did! Just so!
And safe you should have stayed and not returned.

DON JUAN:

Your humble servant! God, I all but died
Of boredom there. I never saw such folk!
And what a land! The sky . . . a pall of smoke.
Their women . . . Ha! Why, I would never trade,
I'll have you know, my foolish Leporello,
The lowest peasant girl in Andalusia
For all their proudest beauties, I do swear.
At first I rather liked them, I'll admit—
Their deep blue eyes, the whiteness of their skin,
Their modest ways . . . and most of all, their novelty.
But thank the Lord, I quickly saw the light
And shunned all further contact with their sort.
They have no spark, they're all but waxen dolls;
While women here! . . . But look you, Leporello,
We've seen this place before; it seems familiar.

LEPORELLO:

It is. The convent of Saint Anthony.
You used to come here late at night, while I . . .
I watched the horses in this very grove—
A wretched task, I have to say. But you,
You had a grand old time . . . far more than I,

As I can well attest.

DON JUAN (pensively):

My poor Inéz!
She's dead and gone! And how I loved her then!

LEPORELLO:

Inéz . . . the dark-eyed one . . . Oh, I recall!
Three months or so you courted her in vain,
Then won her, with the devil's help, at last.

DON JUAN:

July it was . . . at night. I always found
A strange attraction in her mournful eyes
And pallid lips. How strange it is, how strange.
You never thought her beautiful, I know,
And yes, it's true—she wasn't what you'd call
A dazzling beauty. But those eyes of hers,
Those eyes . . . her searching look. I've never known
So beautiful a gaze. And then her voice—
As soft and weak as some poor invalid's . . .
Her husband was a hard and vicious brute,
As I soon after learned . . . My poor Inéz! . . .

LEPORELLO:

No matter, though, for others followed.

DON JUAN:

True.

LEPORELLO:

And while we live, still others will there be.

DON JUAN:

Indeed.

LEPORELLO:

Which lady now in all Madrid
Do we intend to seek?

DON JUAN:

Why, Laura, fool!
I'm off to her this very night.

LEPORELLO:

Of course.

DON JUAN:

I'll straightway to her room—and if, perchance,
A man is there, I'll speed him out the window.

LEPORELLO:

Quite so. And see how greatly cheered we are.
The dead need not disturb us overlong.
But someone comes.
(A monk enters.)

MONK:

She'll be here any moment.
And who are you? From Dona Anna's house?

LEPORELLO:

Why, no, we're honest gentlemen ourselves,
Just come to see the sights.

DON JUAN:

And you're expecting?

MONK:

The pious Dona Anna shortly comes
To look upon her husband's grave.

DON JUAN:

De Solva?
The slain Commander's widow, Dona Anna?
Though slain by whom I can't recall.

MONK:

That foul,
Depraved, and godless reprobate, Don Juan.

LEPORELLO:

Aha! The reputation of Don Juan
Has penetrated even convent walls,
And anchorites now sing his praises too.

MONK:

You know the man?

LEPORELLO:

Oh, not at all, not we.
But where's the fellow now?

MONK:

No longer here,
But banished far away.

LEPORELLO:

Thank God for that.
Let's hope it's far indeed. I'd have these rakes
All bound in chains and thrown into the sea.

DON JUAN:
What drivel's this?
LEPORELLO:
Be quiet, I'm attempting . . .
DON JUAN:
So this is where they buried the Commander?
MONK:
Indeed. His wife put up a monument
And comes here every evening without fail
To pray to God for his departed soul
And weep.
DON JUAN:
A strange, uncommon widow this!
And pretty too?
MONK:
We anchorites forbid
A woman's beauty to affect our souls;
But falsehood is a sin, and I admit:
A saint himself could see her wondrous charms.
DON JUAN:
Then he who was her husband had good cause
To be so jealous that he kept her hid,
For none of us did ever see her face.
I'd like to see her now and have a chat.
MONK:
Oh, Dona Anna never speaks with men.
DON JUAN:
And does she, holy father, speak with you?
MONK:
That's quite a different matter; I'm a monk.
But here she comes.
(Dona Anna enters.)
DONA ANNA:
Unlock the gates, good father.
MONK:
At once. I've been expecting you, Señora.
(Dona Anna follows the monk.)
LEPORELLO:
So, how's she look?

DON JUAN:

I didn't see a thing
Beneath those somber widow's weeds—just glimpsed
A bit of slender ankle as she passed.

LEPORELLO:

Oh, that'll do. Your keen imagination
Will picture you the rest, I have no doubt;
It's defter than a painter's brush, I swear.
And never has it mattered where you start—
With forehead or with foot, it's all the same.

DON JUAN:

O Leporello, you can be assured,
I'll know the lady soon.

LEPORELLO (to himself):

Oh, not again!
That's all we need! The husband he dispatched
And now would see the grieving widow's tears.
The shameless wretch!

DON JUAN:

But look, the darkness falls.
And so, before the moon ascends her throne
And turns this inky black to glowing night,
We'll see Madrid.

(He leaves.)

LEPORELLO:

The Spanish grandee, thieflike,
Awaits the night yet fears the moon. O God!
This cursèd life. How long must I endure
This madman's ways? I lack the strength, I swear.

SCENE II

A room; supper at Laura's

FIRST GUEST:

I tell you, Laura, never in your life
Have you with such perfection played a role.
You grasped the very essence of the part.

SECOND GUEST:

You played it to the hilt! With such emotion!

THIRD GUEST:

Such artistry you showed!

LAURA:

Ah yes, tonight
My every gesture, every word . . . was perfect.
I totally succumbed to inspiration;
The words poured forth—not lines I'd dryly learned,
But from my very soul itself . . .

FIRST GUEST:

How true.
And even now your eyes retain their glow,
Your cheeks their flame; the passion in your heart
Has not yet passed. Don't let it die, my dear,
Or fruitless waste away. Come, Laura, sing,
We beg you, sing.

LAURA:

Then hand me my guitar.

(She sings.)

ALL:

Oh, brava, brava! Marvelous! Divine!

FIRST GUEST:

We thank you, sorceress; you charm our hearts.
Of all the happy pleasures life supplies,
To love alone does music yield in sweetness;
But love itself is melody . . . You see,
Your sullen guest, Don Carlos, too, is moved.

SECOND GUEST:

What sounds! What depth of feeling in the words!
Who wrote them, Laura dear?

LAURA:

Don Juan himself.

DON CARLOS:

What's that? Don Juan!

LAURA:

He wrote them long ago,
My ever-faithful friend, my fickle love.

DON CARLOS:

Your friend's a godless scoundrel and a wretch,
And you're a fool!

LAURA:

Have you gone raving mad?
Take care: though Spanish grandee you may be,
I'll have my servants in to slit your throat.

DON CARLOS:

Then call them now.

FIRST GUEST:

Oh, Laura, stop it, please!
Don Carlos, hold your rage; she doesn't know . . .

LAURA:

Know what? That in a duel, and honorably,
Don Juan his brother killed? He should have slain
Don Carlos here.

DON CARLOS:

I've been a fool to rage.

LAURA:

Aha! Since you yourself admit your guilt,
We'll make our peace.

DON CARLOS:

Forgive me, Laura, please.
The fault was mine. But try to understand:
I cannot hear that name with mute indifference . . .

LAURA:

And yet am I to blame that every moment
I find that very name upon my lips?

GUEST:

Come, Laura, prove your anger quite dispelled.
Another song.

LAURA:

All right, a parting song.
It's late, and you must leave. Now let me see? . . .
I have the song.
(She sings.)

ALL:

Incomparable! What charm!

LAURA:

Now, gentlemen, good night.

ALL:

Good night, dear Laura.

(They leave. Laura detains Don Carlos.)

LAURA:

You madman, you! You'll stay with me tonight.
I've taken quite a fancy to your looks;
The way you ground your teeth when you abused me
Quite called to mind Don Juan.

DON CARLOS:

That lucky man!
You loved him then?

(Laura nods.)

Very much?

LAURA:

Very much.

DON CARLOS:

And love him even now?

LAURA:

This very moment?
Oh no . . . I never love two men at once;
Just now . . . it's you I love.

DON CARLOS:

But tell me, Laura,
How old you are.

LAURA:

I turned eighteen this year.

DON CARLOS:

You're young tonight . . . and young shall you remain
For five or six more years. For six more years
Will men, enamored, crowd the path you walk,
Caress and cherish you, and make you gifts,
Amuse you with their nightly serenades,
And strike each other down in murky alleys
To win your love. But when your time has passed,
When eyes have dimmed and wrinkled lids are dark,
When strands of gray have streaked your lovely hair,
And men have called you old and turned away,
What then will you reply?

LAURA:

Why ask me that?
Why think about such things? What talk is this?
Or do you always have such morbid thoughts?
Come here ... let's step outside. How soft the sky;
How warm and still the evening air ... the night
Of laurel and of lemon smells; the moon ...
All gleaming in the deep and darkling blue ...
The watchman calling out his long *All's well!* ...
While far away—in Paris to the north—
The sky, perhaps, is overcast with clouds,
A cold wind blows, and chilling rain descends;
But what is that to us? O Carlos, come ...
I order you to smile. That's better now!

DON CARLOS:

You charming devil!
(A knock at the door.)

DON JUAN:

Laura, open up!

LAURA:

Whose voice is that? Who's there?

DON JUAN:

Unlock the door ...

LAURA:

It couldn't be! ... O God! ...
(She opens the door. Don Juan enters.)

DON JUAN:

Hello.

LAURA:

Don Juan! ...
(She throws her arms around his neck.)

DON CARLOS:

What's this! Don Juan!

DON JUAN:

My sweet, my lovely girl!
(He kisses her.)
Who's with you there? Who is this man?

DON CARLOS:

It's I,
Don Carlos here.

DON JUAN:

An unexpected meeting!
Come morning, sir, I'm at your service.

DON CARLOS:

No!
This very moment . . . now!

LAURA:

Don Carlos, stop!
You're not upon the street but in my house—
Please leave at once.

DON CARLOS (not listening):

I'm still at your disposal.
I do believe, you have your sword.

DON JUAN:

Well, then,
Impatient friend, lay on!
(They fight.)

LAURA:

O God! Don Juan! . . .
(She throws herself on the bed. Don Carlos falls.)

DON JUAN:

Get up, my dear; it's finished now.

LAURA:

Well, then?
He's dead? How marvelous! And in my room!
And what am I to do, you devil's rake?
And how shall I be rid of him?

DON JUAN:

Perhaps
He's still alive?

LAURA (examining the body):

Oh yes! Just look, you fiend,
You didn't miss . . . you pierced him through the heart.
There's not a drop of blood, nor does he breathe . . .
What now, I say?

DON JUAN:

There's nothing to be done.
He called it on himself.

LAURA:

O God, Don Juan,
You vex me so. These constant escapades,
Whose fault is never yours! . . . But where've you been?
And when did you return?

DON JUAN:

I've just arrived—
And secretly at that; I've not been pardoned.

LAURA:

And right away you thought about your Laura?
How sweet that you remembered. But alas,
I don't believe a word. You happened by
And chanced to see the house.

DON JUAN:

Sweet Laura, no,
Ask Leporello then. I've taken rooms
Outside of town—some wretched inn—and came
Into Madrid for you alone.
(He kisses her.)

LAURA:

My sweet! . . .
Oh, stop . . . before the dead! But what of him?

DON JUAN:

Just let him lie: before the break of day
I'll wrap him in my cloak and cart him off
And drop him at a crossroad.

LAURA:

But take care,
Be sure that no one sees you in the light.
What luck you didn't come a moment sooner!
Your friends were here for supper and, in fact,
Had barely even left when you appeared.
Imagine if you'd come while they were here!

DON JUAN:

But tell me, Laura, had you loved him long?

LAURA:

Loved whom? You must be mad.

DON JUAN:

Oh, come, confess:
How often, since I left, have you been faithless?
How many have you loved?

LAURA:

And you, you rogue?

DON JUAN:

Confess . . . Ah no, we'll tell each other after.

SCENE III

The Commander's statue

DON JUAN:

All augurs well. Since having slain Don Carlos,
I've taken refuge here and have assumed
The guise of simple monk. Each day I see
My charming widow, who begins—I think—
To notice me as well. We still remain
On strictly formal terms, but I intend
To speak with her today. The time has come!
Yet how shall I begin? "I dare intrude" . . . ?
Perhaps "Señora" . . . ? Bah! I'll have no plan,
I'll say whatever comes into my mind.
I'll improvise my tender song of love . . .
She'll be here soon. Without her, to be sure,
The good Commander here seems rather bored.
But what a huge colossus they've erected!
Whereas in life he seemed quite small and frail.
Why, standing tiptoe here, that puny man
Could hardly reach a hand to touch his nose.
That day we met behind the Escuriál,
He fell upon my sword and stood transfixed,
A dragonfly upon a pin—and yet,
The man was proud and brave and had great heart.
But here she comes.

(Dona Anna enters.)

DONA ANNA:

Again he's here . . . Good father,
I fear that I disturb your meditations—
Forgive me, please.

DON JUAN:

Oh no, it's I, Señora,
Should beg forgiveness here of you. Perchance
I hinder you from pouring out your grief.

DONA ANNA:

No, father, all my grief lies deep within;
And here with you, the better may my prayers
To Heaven rise. Indeed, I'd be most grateful
To have you, father, join your voice with mine.

DON JUAN:

To me . . . to me you offer such a boon!
O Dona Anna, I'm unfit for this.
These sinful lips of mine would never dare
To join with yours in holy supplication.
I dare but gaze—with reverence from afar—
When, bowing in a silent show of grief,
You drape with raven locks the pallid stone,
And it appears that I have just beheld
An angel come in secret to this tomb.
And then I find within this troubled heart
No hint of prayer—but only speechless wonder:
How happy he, I think, whose frigid grave
Is warmed by such an angel's airy sighs
And watered by her sweet and loving tears.

DONA ANNA:

How strange I find these words you speak!

DON JUAN:

Señora?

DONA ANNA:

I haven't . . . you forget . . .

DON JUAN:

That I am naught
But simple monk? That my unworthy voice
Ought never to be heard in such a place?

DONA ANNA:
It seemed to me . . . Have I misunderstood?
DON JUAN:
So then you've guessed; you know the truth, I see!
DONA ANNA:
What truth is this?
DON JUAN:
That I am not a monk.
I beg you on my knees for your forgiveness.
DONA ANNA:
O God! Get up, get up . . . Who are you then?
DON JUAN:
A wretch, the victim of my hopeless passion.
DONA ANNA:
My God! To speak such things before this tomb!
Pray leave at once.
DON JUAN:
One minute, Dona Anna,
I beg of you!
DONA ANNA:
But what if someone came! . . .
DON JUAN:
The gates are locked. One minute, please! I beg!
DONA ANNA:
Well, what? What is it that you want?
DON JUAN:
To die.
Oh, let me die this moment at your feet,
And let my wretched dust be buried here;
Oh, not beside these ashes that you love
But somewhere farther off—before the gate,
Inside the very entrance to this place,
That you might there caress my sorry grave
With touch of gentle foot or flowing cloak
When coming here to grace this noble tomb
With lowered head and softly falling tears.
DONA ANNA:
You must be mad.

DON JUAN:

O lady, do you think
Such craving for the end a sign of madness?
If I were truly mad, 'twould be my wish
To stay alive, for then I'd have the hope
Of touching with my tender love your heart;
If I were truly mad, why then I'd come
To stand beneath your balcony at night
And haunt your very sleep with serenades.
No longer would I try to hide or flee,
But rather would I seek to catch your eye.
If I were truly mad, I'd not endure
In silence so much pain . . .

DONA ANNA:

And this is how
You hold your tongue?

DON JUAN:

Mere chance, my lady, chance,
Has made me speak—or else you'd not have known
The secret sorrow deep within my heart.

DONA ANNA:

And have you loved me so for very long?

DON JUAN:

I know not, lady, whether long or not.
I only know that since that time alone
Have I perceived the preciousness of life
Or understood what happiness might mean.

DONA ANNA:

Withdraw, I pray . . . I find you dangerous.

DON JUAN:

How so . . . how so?

DONA ANNA:

I'm frightened by your words.

DON JUAN:

I'll hold my tongue, but do not drive away
A man whose only joy is in your face.
I entertain no hopes or fond illusions,
No claims do I advance but one alone:

That I may see your face if I be doomed
To stay upon this earth.

DONA ANNA:

Withdraw . . . Such words,
Such ravings are unfit for where we are.
Tomorrow you may call. And if you swear
To hold me as before in full respect,
I'll see you then—at evening, after dark.
I have not entertained or seen a soul
Since I've been widowed . . .

DON JUAN:

Angel Dona Anna!
May God console your heart, as you today
Have eased the heart of one who greatly suffers.

DONA ANNA:

Now go, I say.

DON JUAN:

One moment more, I pray.

DONA ANNA:

Then I must leave . . . for as it is my mind
Is now untuned to prayer. Your worldly words
Have quite unnerved my heart. I've grown unused
To hear such talk. Tomorrow, though . . . tomorrow—
I'll see you then.

DON JUAN:

I scarcely dare believe . . .
I hardly dare surrender to my joy . . .
Until tomorrow then! Not here, not here!
And not by stealth!

DONA ANNA:

Tomorrow, yes tomorrow.
And your true name?

DON JUAN:

Diego de Calvado.

DONA ANNA:

Farewell then, Don Diego.
(She leaves.)

DON JUAN:

Leporello!

(Leporello enters.)

LEPORELLO:

Your pleasure, sir?

DON JUAN:

My dearest Leporello!
I'm happy, man! "At evening . . . after dark . . ."
Make ready, Leporello, for tomorrow . . .
I'm happy as a child!

LEPORELLO:

You spoke with her?
And she, perhaps, responded to you kindly?
Or did you, master, give her then your blessing?

DON JUAN:

No, Leporello, no! An assignation,
An assignation, do you hear!

LEPORELLO:

Ye gods!
O widows, are you all the same?

DON JUAN:

I'm happy!
I want to sing, to hug the great wide world!

LEPORELLO:

And what might the Commander have to say?

DON JUAN:

You think, my friend, that he'll be jealous now?
I have my doubt; the man was always sane,
And surely since he died, he must have cooled.

LEPORELLO:

But cast your eye upon his statue there.

DON JUAN:

Why so?

LEPORELLO:

It looks on you, or so it seems,
In anger.

DON JUAN:

Go, good Leporello then,
And say that I invite it to my house,
Or rather Dona Anna's, on the morrow.

LEPORELLO:

Invite the statue! Why?

DON JUAN:

O Leporello,
It's not for conversation, to be sure—
But bid the statue come to Dona Anna's
At evening after dark . . . and there to stand
The watch beside her door.

LEPORELLO:

Be careful, sir,
With whom you jest!

DON JUAN:

Go to!

LEPORELLO:

But sir . . .

DON JUAN:

Go to.

LEPORELLO:

O statue most illustrious and great!
My master here, Don Juan, most humbly begs
That you tomorrow come . . . O Lord, I can't,
I'm true afraid.

DON JUAN:

You cur! You'll pay!

LEPORELLO:

All right.
My master here, Don Juan, has bid you come
Tomorrow after dark . . . to take the watch . . .
Outside your lady's door . . .
(The statue nods assent.)
Ah! Ah!

DON JUAN:

What's there?

LEPORELLO:

O God! I'll die!

DON JUAN:

What's wrong?

LEPORELLO (nodding his head):

The statue! Ah! . . .

DON JUAN:

You bow!

LEPORELLO:

Not I, but it!

DON JUAN:

What nonsense this?

LEPORELLO:

Go look you for yourself.

DON JUAN:

Take care, you knave.

(He turns to the statue.)

Commander, I invite you to your widow's,
Tomorrow after dark . . . where I shall be . . .
To stand the watch. What say you, will you come?

(The statue nods again.)

Almighty God!

LEPORELLO:

I told you so . . .

DON JUAN:

Let's go.

SCENE IV

Dona Anna's room

DON JUAN and DONA ANNA

DONA ANNA:

I welcome you, Don Diego; but I fear
My mournful conversation may well prove
Too trying for a guest: a widowed wife,
I constantly lament my grievous loss . . .
And weep, like April, even as I smile.
But why so mute?

DON JUAN:

I feel a wordless joy
In being here alone with you at last,
My lovely Dona Anna . . . in your house!
And not before that lucky dead man's tomb,
No longer seeing you upon your knees
Before your marble spouse.

DONA ANNA:

Are you, Don Diego,
So jealous . . . that my husband in his grave
Can cause you pain?

DON JUAN:

I cannot have such thoughts.
Your husband was the man you chose.

DONA ANNA:

Oh no,
My mother gave my hand to Don Alvaro,
For we were poor, and Don Alvaro rich.

DON JUAN:

The lucky man! He brought but worthless wealth
To lay before an angel—and for this
He tasted all the joys of paradise!
If I had known you then, with what elation
My rank and all my riches I'd have paid,
Yes, all . . . for just one gracious glance from you.
I would have been your slave and held you sacred;
Your every wish I would have learned to guess,
To grant them ere they came, to make your life
One constant, magic realm of all desires.
But Fate, alas, had something else in store.

DONA ANNA:

Don Diego, say no more: I do but sin
To heed your words. I cannot love again;
A widow must be true beyond the grave.
If only you could know how Don Alvaro
Adored me once! And he himself, I'm sure,
Would never have received a woman's love
Had he been so bereft. He would have kept
His marriage vows for life.

DON JUAN:

O Dona Anna,
Torment my heart no more with recollections
Of him you wed. You've punished me enough,
Although, perhaps, I've earned it well.

DONA ANNA:

How so?
You are not tied, I think, by holy bonds
To someone else—and in your loving thus
You do no wrong to Heaven or to me.

DON JUAN:

To you! O God!

DONA ANNA:

You surely don't feel guilt
On my account? Or tell me why?

DON JUAN:

Of this
I cannot speak.

DONA ANNA:

What is this, Don Diego?
You've done me wrong? How so? I beg you, answer.

DON JUAN:

I will not speak!

DONA ANNA:

Don Diego, this is strange:
I ask . . . demand . . . that you reply.

DON JUAN:

No! Never!

DONA ANNA:

So this is how you serve my every wish?
And what did you just now so boldly claim?
That you'd give all to be my willing slave.
You anger me, Don Diego; now reply:
Of what are you to blame?

DON JUAN:

I dare not speak.
You'll look at me with hatred and revulsion.

DONA ANNA:

No, no. I pardon you before you speak,
But know I must.

DON JUAN:

You should not wish to know
The terrible and fatal thing I've done.

DONA ANNA:

The fatal thing! You torture me, Don Diego;
I have to know . . . What is it you conceal?
And how can you have given me offense?
I knew you not . . . I have no enemies,
Nor none I had. The man who slew my spouse,
But only he.

DON JUAN (to himself):

The denouement approaches!
(To Dona Anna.)
You never knew the hapless wretch Don Juan,
Is that not so?

DONA ANNA:

In all my living days
I never saw him, no.

DON JUAN:

And does your heart
Nurse hatred of the man?

DONA ANNA:

So honor bids.
But you're attempting to evade my question;
Now answer me, Don Diego, if you please . . .
I must insist.

DON JUAN:

And what if you should chance
To meet Don Juan?

DONA ANNA:

Why then I'd thrust a dagger
Inside the villain's heart.

DON JUAN:

O Dona Anna!
Then thrust your dagger here!

DONA ANNA:

Good Lord, Don Diego!

What's this?

DON JUAN:

I'm not Don Diego . . . I'm Don Juan.

DONA ANNA:

O God! It can't be so, I don't believe it.

DON JUAN:

Don Juan am I.

DONA ANNA:

It can't be true.

DON JUAN:

It's true,
I killed your husband—and regret it not;
I feel no true repentance in my soul.

DONA ANNA:

What's this I hear? Oh no! It cannot be.

DON JUAN:

Don Juan am I, and I'm in love with you.

DONA ANNA (fainting):

Where am I! Where? I'm faint . . . I'm faint . . .

DON JUAN:

Good Lord!
What's wrong with her? What is it, Dona Anna?
Wake up, wake up, come, rouse yourself; your Diego,
Your loving slave, is at your feet.

DONA ANNA:

Oh, leave!

(Weakly.)

My greatest foe . . . You took away my life . . .
My very life . . . my life . . .

DON JUAN:

Sweet creature, speak!
And I'll requite you for the blow I struck.
Pronounce my sentence as I kneel before you:
At your command . . . I die; or bid me breathe
For you alone.

DONA ANNA:

So this is then Don Juan . . .

DON JUAN:

No doubt you've often heard the man described
As villain or as fiend. O Doná Anna . . .
Such ill repute may well in part be true:
My weary conscience bears a heavy load
Of evil deeds. For all too many years
I've been the most devoted slave of lust;
But ever since the day I saw your face
I've been reborn, returned once more to life.
In loving you, I've learned to love true goodness,
And now for once I bend my trembling knees
And kneel in awe before almighty virtue.

DONA ANNA:

Ah yes, Don Juan is eloquent, I know;
I've heard of his seductive way with words.
They say that you're a godless and depraved,
Inhuman fiend. How many hapless women
Have you destroyed?

DON JUAN:

But not a one till now
Have I in truth adored.

DONA ANNA:

Should I believe
That now at last Don Juan has come to love
And not to seek another of his victims?

DON JUAN:

Had I intended, lady, to deceive you,
Would I have made confession or revealed
The very name you cannot bear to hear?
What kind of plot or craftiness is this?

DONA ANNA:

Who knows your heart? Why visit me at all?
You might have been detected on the way,
And then you would have met . . . not me but death.

DON JUAN:

I fear not death. For one sweet moment here
I'd give my life without complaint.

DONA ANNA:

But how,

You reckless man, will you escape from here?

DON JUAN (kissing her hand):

So even you can find within your heart
Some pity for Don Juan! O Dona Anna,
Have you no hatred in your angel's soul?

DONA ANNA:

I wish with all my heart that I could hate you!
But I'm afraid . . . that you and I must part.

DON JUAN:

And when shall we two meet again?

DONA ANNA:

Who knows?

One day, perhaps.

DON JUAN:

Tomorrow?

DONA ANNA:

Where?

DON JUAN:

Right here.

DONA ANNA:

Alas, Don Juan, how weak my woman's heart.

DON JUAN:

In pledge of your forgiveness . . . one brief kiss . . .

DONA ANNA:

It's late . . . it's late.

DON JUAN:

One cold, one quiet kiss . . .

DONA ANNA:

As you will have it so . . . one kiss I grant . . .
(A knock at the door.)
What noise was that? . . . Conceal yourself, Don Juan!

DON JUAN:

Farewell . . . until we meet, my tender friend.
(He leaves, then rushes in again.)
Ah no!

DONA ANNA:

What is it? Ah! . . .
(The statue of the Commander enters. Dona Anna faints.)

STATUE:

You summoned me.

DON JUAN:

O God! O Dona Anna!

STATUE:

Let her be.
It's finished. Do you tremble now, Don Juan?

DON JUAN:

Oh no. I called you here . . . and bid you welcome.

STATUE:

Then come . . . your hand.

DON JUAN:

Ah, yes . . . my hand. O God!
How cold and hard his mighty fist of stone!
Away from me . . . Let go . . . Let go my hand . . .
I perish . . . All is done . . . O Dona Anna! . . .
(They sink into the ground.)

A Feast in Time of Plague

Translated by James E. Falen

An excerpt from John Wilson's tragedy, *The City of the Plague.*

A street; a table, laid for a feast

Several men and women celebrants

A YOUNG MAN:

Most honored Chairman! I would speak
Of one whose memory we revere,
A man whose jests and comic tales,
Whose pointed wit and observations,
So caustic with their mocking air,
Enlivened many past occasions
And drove away the gloom with which
Our guest, the Plague, has now infected
So many of our brightest minds.
But two days since we hailed with mirth
Those tales of his, and so tonight,
Amid our feast, let's not forget
Our Jackson now. Here stands his chair,
The empty seat as if awaiting
That merry man—but now he's gone
To lie beneath the chilly earth . . .
Although his vivid voice remains,
Unsilenced yet within the grave.

But we are many still alive
And have tonight no cause to grieve.
So I propose for Jackson's sake
A ringing toast and shouts of cheer,
As if he lived.

MASTER OF REVELS:

He was the first
To leave our band, and so let's drink
A silent toast.

YOUNG MAN:

So be it then.
(All drink in silence.)

MASTER OF REVELS:

Your voice, dear Mary, can evoke
The dark, rich sounds of native song;
So sing us, Mary, something sad,
That we may then more madly still
To mirth return, like one who wakes
From some dark dream to earth again.

MARY (sings):

Long ago our land was blessed:
Peaceful, rich, and gay;
People then on days of rest
Filled the church to pray.
Children's voices full of cheer
Through the schoolyard rang;
In the fields both far and near
Scythe and sickle sang.

Now the church deserted stands;
School is locked and dark.
Overgrown are all our lands;
Empty groves are stark.
Now the village, bare as bone,
Seems an empty shell;
All is still—the graves alone
Thrive and toll the bell.

Endless carts of dead appear;

Now the living cry,
Calling down in mortal fear
Mercy from on high.
Endless corpses all demand
Plots of hallowed ground;
Graves like frightened cattle stand
Crowded close all round.

~

If my youth is doomed to go
Early into night,
Edmund, whom I treasure so,
Edmund, my delight,
Don't approach your Jenny's bier,
Please, I beg, be kind.
Do not kiss these lips once dear;
Follow far behind.

~

Leave the village then, I pray,
Find some place of peace;
Dull your pain and go away,
Bring your soul release.
When the plague has passed, my love,
Pay my dust its due;
Even, Edmund, up above,
Jenny will be true.

MASTER OF REVELS:

We thank you, Mary, pensive lass,
We thank you for your mournful air.
In former days some plague like ours
Attacked your lovely hills and vales,
And woeful moans back then arose
Above your streams and purling brooks,
Which now once more in joy and peace
Meander through your native realm.
And now that dreadful year that took
So many brave and noble souls
Has only left the barest trace
In this your simple, rustic song,
So touching and so sad . . . There's naught

Could move us more at this our feast
Than sounds remembered by the heart.

MARY:
If only I had never learned
To sing such songs so far from home!
My parents loved their Mary's voice,
And even now I seem to hear
Myself in song outside our door.
My voice was sweeter then and sang
In tones more pure and true.

LOUISA:
Such songs
Are out of fashion now. And yet
There still are simple souls who pine
At women's tears . . . and deem them real.
Our Mary thinks a tearful eye
Invincible, but if she thought
Her laughter so, then be assured,
She'd laugh and laugh. But Walsingham
Has praised these shrieking northern belles,
And so she moans. Oh, how I loathe
These Scottish heads of flaxen hair!

MASTER OF REVELS:
Be still. I hear the wagon wheels.
(A cart goes by, laden with corpses and driven by a black man.)

MASTER OF REVELS:
Louisa swoons! To hear her talk,
You'd think her heart was like a man's.
The cruel prove weaker than the soft,
And dread can strike the fiercest soul.
Some water, Mary . . . She'll come round.

MARY:
Come, sister of my shame and woe,
Lean back on me.

LOUISA (regaining consciousness):
I thought I saw
Some dreadful thing—all black . . . white-eyed . . .
That called me to its cart . . . and there
The dead lay deep . . . and babbled words . . .

Some strange and unfamiliar tongue . . .
But tell me, did I only dream?
Or did that cart go by?

YOUNG MAN:

Louisa!
Lift up your heart. Although our street
Is refuge safe enough from death,
A place for feasts, where grief is banned,
That somber cart, as you well know,
Has right to travel where it will,
And let it pass we must. But now,
Good Walsingham, let's cancel strife
And all these women's fainting spells.
Come, sing a rash and lively song,
No tune composed of Scottish grief—
But reckless, bacchanalian song,
One fit for friends and flaming cups!

MASTER OF REVELS:

I know no songs like this. I'll sing
A hymn to plagues. I wrote the thing
Last night when we had quit the feast.
A strange, compulsive need for rhyme,
Quite new to me, then gripped my soul.
My throaty voice well suits the song . . .

VOICES FROM THE CROWD:

A hymn to plagues! Let's hear it then!
A hymn to plagues! Bravo! Well done!

MASTER OF REVELS (sings):

When mighty Winter from the North,
Like warrior chieftain, marches forth
To lead herself her ragged host
Of frosts and snows against the land,
Our glasses ring in hearty toast
And crackling chimneys warm our band.

~

The Plague herself, that fearsome Queen,
Has now arrived upon the scene
To reap corruption's rich reward.
All day and night with dreadful spade

She taps the battened window board.
But where to turn? Where summon aid?

~

As we from prankster Winter hide,
We'll greet the Plague locked up inside.
We'll light the flame and pour the wine,
We'll drown our thoughts and gaily jest,
And as we dance and as we dine,
We'll praise the reign of Empress Pest.

~

There's rapture on the battleground,
And where the black abyss is found,
And on the raging ocean main,
Amid the stormy waves of death,
And in the desert hurricane,
And in the Plague's pernicious breath.

~

For all that threatens to destroy
Conceals a strange and savage joy—
Perhaps for mortal man a glow
That promises eternal life.
And happy he who comes to know
This rapture found in storm and strife.

~

So hail to you, repellent Pest!
You strike no fear within our breast;
We are not crushed by your design.
So fill the foaming glasses high,
We'll sip the rosy maiden wine
And kiss the lips where plague may lie!
(An aged priest appears.)

PRIEST:

This godless feast! You godless men!
With revels and with wanton songs
You mock the dark and gruesome hush
Sent forth by death across the land!
At dreadful funeral rites I pray
Before the pale and weeping crowd,
While your repulsive sinful play

Disturbs the graveyard's silent peace
And shakes the earth where dead men sleep.
Had not old men's and women's prayers
Redeemed our common pit of death,
I might have thought that fiends had come
To torture sinners' godless souls
And drag them, cackling, off to Hell.

SEVERAL VOICES:

He speaks of Hell as one who knows.
Be gone, old man, you've lost your way.

PRIEST:

I charge you by the sacred blood
Of Him who suffered for our sins
To halt this monstrous feast, if still
You hope to meet by Heaven's grace
The souls of those you loved and lost.
Disperse, I say, and get you home!

MASTER OF REVELS:

Our homes are sad—youth treasures mirth.

PRIEST:

Can that be you, good Walsingham?
Who on your knees but three weeks since
Embraced your mother's corpse and sobbed?
Who howled and beat upon her grave?
Or think you that she doesn't weep
Great bitter tears in Heaven now
To see her son at such a feast,
This feast of vice, to hear your voice
In shameless song—all this amid
Our holy prayers and anguished sighs?
Come with me now!

MASTER OF REVELS:

Why come you here
To cause me pain? I cannot leave
To take your path. What holds me here
Is foul despair and memories dread,
Awareness of my lawless ways,
The horror of the deathly hush
That now prevails within my house—

And yes, these fresh and frenzied revels,
The blesséd poison of this cup,
And kisses sweet (forgive me, Lord)
From this depraved but lovely wretch . . .
My mother's shade will call me back
No more . . . Too late . . . I hear your plea
And know you struggle for my soul . . .
Too late . . . Depart, old man, in peace;
But cursed be all who follow thee.

MANY VOICES:
Bravo! Well said! Our worthy chief!
You've heard the sermon. Leave us, priest!

PRIEST:
Mathilda's blesséd spirit calls!

MASTER OF REVELS (rising):
Oh, raise your pale, decrepit hand
And swear to God to leave unspoke
That name entombed forevermore!
Oh, could I from those deathless eyes
Conceal this scene! She thought me once
A proud and pure . . . a noble man,
And in my arms she savored joy . . .
Where am I now? My blesséd light!
I see you . . . but my sinful soul
Can reach you there no more . . .

A WOMAN S VOICE:
He's mad—
He babbles of his buried wife.

PRIEST:
Come with me now . . .

MASTER OF REVELS:
In Heaven's name,
Good father, leave.

PRIEST:
God save your soul.
Farewell, my son.

(He leaves. The feast goes on. The Master of Revels stays, lost in thought.)

Selected Bibliography

Editions and Translations of Alexander Pushkin's Works

Nabokov, Vladimir. *Three Russian Poets: Translations of Pushkin, Lermontov, and Tyutchev.* Norfolk: New Directions, 1944.

Pushkin, Alexander. *Complete Prose Fiction.* Translated by Paul Debreczeny. Stanford, Calif.: Stanford University Press, 1983.

———. *The Complete Works of Alexander Pushkin.* 15 vols. Norfolk: Milner and Company Limited, 1999.

———. *Eugene Onegin.* Translated by Charles Johnston. London: Penguin Books, 1979.

———. *The Letters of Alexander Pushkin.* 3 vols. in 1. Edited and translated by J. Thomas Shaw. Madison: University of Wisconsin Press, 1969.

———. *The Little Tragedies.* Translated by Nancy K. Anderson. New Haven, Conn.: Yale University Press, 2000.

Pushkin, Aleksandr. *Dramaticheskie proizvedeniia.* Edited by Dmitrii P. Iakubovich. Vol. 7 of *Polnoe sobranie sochinenii.* Moscow: Akademiia Nauk SSSR, 1935.

———. *Malen'kie tragedii. Opery russkikh kompozitorov.* St. Petersburg: Kompozitor, 1999.

———. *Polnoe sobranie sochinenii.* 17 vols. Moscow: Akademiia Nauk SSSR, 1937–58.

Other Works Cited

Aikhenval'd, Iurii. *Pushkin.* Moscow: Nauchnoe slovo, 1908.

———. *Pushkin.* Moscow: Izdatel'stvo tovarishchestva "Mir," 1916.

Akhmatova, Anna. "*Kamennyi gost'* Pushkina." In *O Pushkine: Stat'i i zametki.* Edited by Emma G. Gernshtein. Leningrad: Sovetskii pisatel', 1977.

———. "*Kamennyi gost'* Pushkina." In *Pushkin: Issledovaniia i materialy.* Vol. 2. Moscow-Leningrad: Izdatel'stvo Akademii Nauk SSSR, 1958.

———. "*Kamennyi gost'* Pushkina." In *Sochineniia.* Edited by G. P. Struve and B. A. Filipoff. Washington, D.C.: Interlanguage Literary Associates, 1965–83. 2: 257–74.

———. "Pushkin's *Stone Guest.*" In *My Half Century: Selected Prose.* Edited by Ronald Meyer. Translated by Janet Tucker. Ann Arbor: Ardis, 1992. 200–214.

Alekseev, Mikhail P. "A. S. Pushkin." In *Shekspir i russkaia kul'tura.* Edited by M. P. Alekseev. Moscow-Leningrad: Nauka, 1965. 162–200.

———. "Kommentarii k 'Motsartu i Sal'eri.'" In Aleksandr Pushkin, *Dramaticheskie proizvedeniia.* Edited by Dmitrii P. Iakubovich. Vol. 7 of *Polnoe sobranie sochinenii.* Moscow: Akademiia Nauk SSSR, 1935.

———. *Pushkin. Sravnitel'no-istoricheskie issledovaniia.* Leningrad: Nauka, 1984.

Alexandrov, Vladimir E. "Correlations in Pushkin's *Malen'kie tragedii.*" *Canadian Slavonic Papers* 20, no. 2 (June 1978): 176–93.

Allen, Elizabeth Cheresh. *Beyond Realism: Turgenev's Poetics of Secular Salvation.* Stanford, Calif.: Stanford University Press, 1992.

Anderson, Nancy K. "Critical Essays." In Alexander Pushkin, *The Little Tragedies.* Translated by Nancy K. Anderson. New Haven, Conn.: Yale University Press, 2000.

Anikin, Andrei V. "'Vse kupliu'—skazalo zlato." In *Muza i mamona: Sotsial'no-ekonomicheskie motivy u Pushkina.* Moscow: Mysl', 1989. 112–27.

Ardens, Nikolai N. *Dramaturgiia i teatr A. S. Pushkina.* Moscow: Sovetskii pisatel', 1939.

Arinshtein, L. M. "Pushkin i Shenston (k interpretatsii podzagolovka 'Skupogo rytsaria')." *Boldinskiie chteniia* (1980): 87–99.

Bagno, Vsevolod E. "Oppozitsiia 'guliaka prazdnyi' (Avel') i 'ugriumets' (Kain) kak skvoznaia tema tvorchestva Pushkina." In *Rossiia. Zapad. Vostok: Vstrechnye techeniia.* Edited by M. P. Alekseev. St. Petersburg: Nauka, 1996. 224–30.

Bakhtin, Mikhail. *Problems of Dostoevsky's Poetics.* Translated and edited by Caryl Emerson. Minneapolis: University of Minnesota Press, 1984.

Bartenev, Petr. I. *Rasskazy o Pushkine.* Moscow: Izdatel'stvo M. i S. Sabashnikovykh, 1925.

Bayley, John. *Pushkin: A Comparative Commentary.* Cambridge: Cambridge University Press, 1971.

Beliak, Nikolai V., and Mariia N. Virolainen. "'Malen'kie tragedii' kak kul'turnyi epos novoevropeiskoi istorii (Sud'ba lichnosti—sud'ba kul'tury)." In *Pushkin: Issledovaniia i materialy.* Moscow-Leningrad: Izdatel'stvo Akademii Nauk SSSR, 1991. 14: 73–96.

———. "*Motsart i Sal'eri*: Struktura i siuzhet." In *Pushkin: Issledovaniia i materialy.* Moscow-Leningrad: Izdatel'stvo Akademii Nauk SSSR, 1995. 15: 115–19.

Belinskii, Vissarion G. *Polnoe sobranie sochinenii.* Vols. 4, 5. Moscow: Izdatel'stvo Akademii Nauk, 1954.

Bem, A. L. "Boldinskaia osen'." In *O Pushkine: Stat'i.* Uzhgorod: Pismena, 1937. 95–96.

———. "'Skupoi rytsar' v tvorchestve Dostoevskogo (Skhozhdeniia i raskhozhdeniia)." In *U istokov tvorchestva Dostoevskogo.* Vol. 3 of *O Dostoevskom.* Prague: Petropolis, 1936.

Bethea, David M. *Realizing Metaphors: Alexander Pushkin and the Life of the Poet.* Madison: University of Wisconsin Press, 1998.

Bethea, David, and Sergei Davydov. "Pushkin's Saturnine Cupid: The Poetics of Parody in *The Tales of Belkin.*" *PMLA* (January 1981): 8–21.

Blagoi, Dmitrii. "Dostoevskii i Pushkin." In *Dusha v zavetnoi lire: Ocherki zhizni i tvorchestva Pushkina.* Moscow: Sovetskii pisatel', 1977.

———. Excerpt from *Tvorcheskii put' Pushkina (1826–1930).* In *"Motsart i Sal'eri," tragediia A. S. Pushkina. Dvizhenie vo vremeni: Antologiia traktovok i kontseptsii ot Belinskogo do nashikh dnei.* Edited by Valentin S. Nepomniashchii. Pushkin v XX veke series. Moscow: Nasledie, 1997. 3: 337–62.

———. *Masterstvo Pushkina.* Moscow: Sovetskii pisatel', 1955.

———. *Sotsiologiia tvorchestva Pushkina.* 2d ed. Moscow: Mir, 1931.

———. *Tvorcheskii put' Pushkina.* Moscow: Izdatel'stvo Akademii Nauk SSSR, 1950.

———. *Tvorcheskii put' Pushkina.* Moscow: Sovetskii pisatel', 1967.

Bliumenfeld, V. "K problematike 'Motsarta i Sal'eri' Pushkina." Abridged. In *"Motsart i Sal'eri," tragediia A. S. Pushkina. Dvizhenie vo vremeni: Antologiia traktovok i kontseptsii ot Belinskogo do nashikh dnei.* Edited by Valentin S. Nepomniashchii. Pushkin v XX veke series. Moscow: Nasledie, 1997. 3: 272–86.

Bogoslovskii, N. V., ed. *Pushkin o literature.* Moscow: Academia, 1934.

Bondi, Sergei. "Dramaturgiia Pushkina." In *O Pushkine: Stat'i i issledovaniia.* Moscow: Khudozhestvennaia literatura, 1978. 169–241.

Braun, Edward, trans. and ed. *Meyerhold on Theatre.* New York: Hill and Wang, 1969.

Braunbehrens, Volkmar. *Maligned Master: The Real Story of Antonio Salieri.* Translated by Eveline L. Kanes. New York: Fromm International Publishers, 1992.

Brée, Germaine. *Albert Camus.* New York and London: Columbia University Press, 1964.

Brée, Germaine, ed. *Camus: A Collection of Critical Essays.* Englewood Cliffs, N.J.: Prentice-Hall, 1962.

Briggs, A. D. P. Introduction to Alexander Pushkin, *The Complete Works of Alexander Pushkin.* Vol. 6, *Boris Godunov and Other Dramatic Works.* Norfolk: Milner and Company Limited, 1999.

Bronner, Stephen. *Camus: Portrait of a Moralist.* Minneapolis: University of Minnesota Press, 1999.

Brown, William Edward. *A History of Russian Literature of the Romantic Period.* Vol. 3. Ann Arbor: Ardis, 1986.

Brun-Zejmis, Julia. "*Malen'kie tragedii* and *Povesti Belkina*: Western Idolatry and Pushkinian Parodies." *Russian Language Journal* 32, no. 111 (winter 1978): 65–76.

Burrow, John A. *The Ages of Man: A Study in Medieval Writing and Thought.* Oxford: Oxford University Press, 1986.

Butakova, V. "Pushkin i Monten'." *Vremennik pushkinskoi komissii* 3 (1937): 203–14.

Camus, Albert. *The Myth of Sisyphus and Other Essays.* Translated by Justin O'Brien. New York: Vintage Books, 1991.

———. *The Plague.* New York: Alfred A. Knopf, 1948.

Chumakov, Iurii. "Dva fragmenta o siuzhetnoi polifonii *Motsarta i Sal'eri.*" *Boldinskiie chteniia* (1981): 32–43.

———. "Remarka i siuzhet (k istolkovaniiu *Motsarta i Sal'eri*)." *Boldinskiie chteniia* (1979): 48–69.

———. *Stikhotvornaia poetika Pushkina.* St. Petersburg: Gosudarstvennyi Pushkinskii Teatral'nyi Tsentr, 1999.

Clark, David Lee, ed. *Shelley's Prose; or, The Trumpet of a Prophecy.* Albuquerque: University of New Mexico Press, 1966.

Cornwell, Neil, ed. "Aleksandr Pushkin: From Byron to Shakespeare." In *Reference Guide to Russian Literature.* London: Fitzroy Dearborn Publishers, 1998. 18–25.

Cox, Jeffrey. *In the Shadow of Romance: Romantic Tragic Drama in Germany, England, and France.* Athens: Ohio University Press, 1987.

Curtis, Laura A. "Raskolnikov's Sexuality." *Literature and Psychology* 37, nos. 1–2 (1991): 88–106.

Czapska, Maria. *Szkice Mickiewiczowskie.* London: B. Swiderski, 1963.

Dante. *La Divina Commedia.* Edited and annotated by C. H. Grandgent. Revised by Charles S. Singleton. Cambridge, Mass.: Harvard University Press, 1972.

———. *Inferno.* Translated by Allen Mandelbaum. New York: Bantam Books, 1981.

Darkii, Dmitrii. *Malen'kie tragedii Pushkina.* Moscow: Moskovskaia khudozhestvennaia pechatnia, 1915.

Davison, Ray. *Camus: The Challenge of Dostoevsky.* Chicago: Northwestern University Press, 1997.

Davydov, Sergei. "Pushkin's Merry Undertaking and 'The Coffinmaker.'" *Slavic Review* 44, no. 1 (spring 1985): 30–48.

Debreczeny, Paul. *Social Functions of Literature: Alexander Pushkin and Russian Culture.* Stanford, Calif.: Stanford University Press, 1997.

Dolinin, Alexandr. "Zametka k probleme 'Pushkin i Shekspir.' (O podzagolovke 'Skupogo rytsaria')." In *Sbornik statei k 70-letiiu professora Iu. M. Lotmana.* Edited by A. Mal'ts and Iu. Lotman. Tartu: Tartuskii universitet, Kafedra russkoi literatury, 1992. 183–90.

Dolinin, Arkadii S. *Poslednie romany Dostovskogo: Kak sozdavalis' "Podrostok" i "Brat'ia Karamazovy."* Moscow-Leningrad: Sovetskii pisatel', 1963.

Dostoevskii, Fedor M. *Polnoe sobranie sochinenii.* 30 vols. Leningrad: Nauka, 1972–88.

Dostoevsky, F. *The Brothers Karamazov.* New York: Norton, 1976.

Durylin, Sergei. *Pushkin na stsene.* Moscow: Izdatel'stvo Akademii Nauk SSSR, 1951.

Eiges, Iosif. *Muzyka v zhizni i tvorchestve Pushkina.* Moscow: Muzgiz, 1937.

Emerson, Caryl. *Boris Godunov: Transpositions of a Russian Theme.* Bloomington: Indiana University Press, 1986.

Emerson, Ralph Waldo. *Napoleon, or the Man of the World.* Edited by Frank Davidson. Bloomington: Indiana University Press, 1947.

Ermakov, Ivan D. *Etiudy po psikhologii tvorchestva A. S. Pushkina: Opyt organicheskogo ponimaniia "Domika v Kolomne," "Proroka," i "Malen'kikh tragedii."* Moscow-Petrograd: Gosudarstvennoe izdatel'stvo, 1923.

Evdokimova, Svetlana. *Pushkin's Historical Imagination.* New Haven, Conn.: Yale University Press, 1999.

Fedorov, V. "Garmoniia tragedii 'Motsart i Sal'eri' A. S. Pushkina." In *"Motsart i Sal'eri," tragediia A. S. Pushkina. Dvizhenie vo vremeni: Antologiia traktovok i kontseptsii ot Belinskogo do nashikh dnei.* Edited by Valentin S. Nepomniashchii. Pushkin v XX veke series. Moscow: Nasledie, 1997. 3: 597–604.

Feldman, Oleg M. *Sud'ba dramaturgii Pushkina: Boris Godunov, Malen'kie tragedii.* Moscow: Iskusstvo, 1975

Ferguson, Niall. *The House of Rothschild: Money's Prophets, 1798–1848.* New York: Viking, 1998.

Fitch, Brian. *The Narcissistic Text: A Reading of Camus' Fiction.* Toronto: University of Toronto Press, 1982.

Folkenflik, Vivian, ed. and trans. *An Extraordinary Woman: Selected Writings of Germaine de Staël.* New York: Columbia University Press, 1987.

Fomichev, S. A. "Dramaturgiia Pushkina." In *Istoriia russkoi dramaturgii: XVII—pervaia polovina XIX veka.* Leningrad: Nauka, 1982. 261–96.

Fontane, Theodor. *Briefe.* Vol. 3. Edited by K. Schreinert and Ch. Jolles. Berlin: Propylaen Verlag, 1971.

Foucault, Michel. *The Order of Things: An Archeology of the Human Sciences.* New York: Vintage, 1970.

Freud, Sigmund. "Dostoevsky and Parricide." In *Dostoevsky: A Collection of Critical Essays.* Edited by Rene Wellek. Englewood Cliffs, N.J., 1962. 98–111.

Fridman, N. V. *Romantizm v tvorchestve A. S. Pushkina.* Moscow: Prosveshchenie, 1980.

Friedman, Norman. "What Makes a Short Story Short?" *Modern Fiction Studies* 4 (1958): 103–17.

Friedrich, Hugo. *Montaigne.* Translated by Dawn Eng. Berkeley and Los Angeles: University of California Press, 1991.

Fusso, Susanne. "Dostoevsky's Comely Boy: Homoerotic Desire and Aesthetic Strategies in *A Raw Youth.*" *Russian Review* 59 (October 2000): 577–96.

Gal'tseva, Renata A., ed. *Pushkin v russkoi filosofskoi kritike: Konets XIX–pervaia polovina XXvv.* Moscow: "Kniga," 1990.

Garden, Edward, and Nigel Gotteri, eds. *"To My Best Friend": Correspondence between Tchaikovsky and Nadezhda von Meck 1876–1878.* Translated by Galina von Meck. Oxford: Clarendon Press, 1993.

Garkavi, A. M. "*Malen'kie tragedii* Pushkina kak dramaturgicheskii tsikl (kompozitsiia v sviazi s zhanrom i khudozhestvennym metodom)." In *Siuzhet i kompozitsiia literaturnykh i fol'klornykh proizvedenii.* Voronezh: Izdatel'stvo Voronezhskogo universiteta, 1981.

Gasparov, Boris. "Ty sam sebia nedostoin." In *Pushkinskii vremennik.* Leningrad: Nauka, 1977. 115–22.

Gershenzon, Mikhail. *Mudrost' Pushkina.* Moscow: Tovarishchestvo "Knigoizdatel'stvo pisatelei v Moskve," 1919.

Gillespie, David. "New Versions of Old Classics: Recent Cinematic Interpretations of Russian Literature." In *Russia on Reels: The Russian Idea in Post-Soviet Cinema.* Edited by Birgit Beumers. London: I. B. Tauris, 1999. 114–24.

Ginzburg, L. "Pushkin i liricheskii geroi russkogo romantizma." In *Pushkin: Issledovaniia i materially*. Moscow-Leningrad: Izdatel'stvo Akademii Nauk SSSR, 1962. 4: 140–54.

Girard, René. "The Plague in Literature and Myth." In *Theories of Myth: Literary Criticism and Myth*. Edited by R. Segal. New York: Garland, 1966. 155–72.

Glebov, Gl. "Filosofiia prirody v teoreticheskikh vyskazyvaniiakh i tvorcheskoi praktike Pushkina." *Pushkin. Vremennik pushkinskoi komissii* 2 (1936): 185–207.

Golstein, Vladimir. "Pushkin's *Mozart and Salieri* as the Parable of Salvation." *Russian Literature* 29, no. 2 (1991): 155–76.

———. "Sekrety 'Pikovoi damy.'" In *Transactions/Zapiski Russkoi Akademicheskoi gruppy v SShA* 30 (1999–2000): 99–125.

Gomolicki, Leon. *Dziennik pobytu Adama Mickiewicza w Rosji 1824–1829*. Warsaw: Wiedza, 1949.

Gorodetskii, Boris P. *Dramaturgiia Pushkina*. Moscow: Akademiia Nauk, 1953.

Greenberg, Mitchell. *Subjectivity and Subjection in Seventeenth Century Drama and Prose*. Cambridge: Cambridge University Press, 1992.

Greenleaf, Monika. *Pushkin and Romantic Fashion: Fragment, Elegy, Orient, Irony*. Stanford, Calif.: Stanford University Press, 1995.

Gregg, Richard. "The Eudaemonic Theme in Pushkin's 'Little Tragedies.'" In *Alexander Pushkin: A Symposium on the 175th Anniversary of His Birth*. Edited by Andrej Kodjak and Kiril Taranovsky. New York: New York University Press, 1976. 178–95.

Griboedov, Aleksandr S. *Sochineniia*. Moscow: Goslitizdat, 1953.

Gukasova, A. G. Excerpt from *Boldinskii period v tvorchestve A. S. Pushkina*. In *"Motsart i Sal'eri," tragediia A. S. Pushkina. Dvizhenie vo vremeni: Antologiia traktovok i kontseptsii ot Belinskogo do nashikh dnei*. Edited by Valentin S. Nepomniashchii. Pushkin v XX veke series. Moscow: Nasledie, 1997. 3: 287–94.

Gukovskii, Grigorii A. *Pushkin i problemy realisticheskogo stilia*. Moscow: Gosudarstvennoe izdatel'stvo khudozhestvennoi literatury, 1957.

Hodgdon, Barbara. "Replicating Richard: Body Doubles, Body Politics." *Theatre Journal* 50, no. 2 (May 1998): 207–26.

Hodge, Thomas P. *A Double Garland: Poetry and Art-song in Early Nineteenth-Century Russia*. Evanston, Ill.: Northwestern University Press, 2000.

Hoffman, E. T. A. "Don Juan: Eine fabelhafte Begebenheit die sich mit einem reisenden Enthusiasten zugetragen." In *Fantasie- und Nachtstücke*. Sämtliche Werke. Vols. 1–5. Edited by Georg von Maassen and Georg Ellinger, with an afterword by Walter Müller-Seidel. Munich: Winkler-Verlag, 1960–65. 1: 67–78.

Iakubovich, Dmitrii P. "Skupoi rytsar'." In Aleksandr Pushkin, *Dramaticheskie proizvedeniia*. Edited by Dmitrii P. Iakubovich. *Polnoe sobranie sochinenii*. Moscow: Akademiia Nauk SSSR, 1935. 7: 506–22.

Iof'ev, M. I. *Profili iskusstva: Literatura, teatr, zhivopis', estrada, kino*. Moscow: Iskusstvo, 1965.

Isaakian, Georgii. "Russkoe 'Kol'tso.'" *Muzykal'naia Akademiia* 2 (1999): 22–30.

Ishchuk-Fadeeva, N. I. "*Stseny* kak osobyi dramaticheskii zhanr: *Malen'kie tragedii* A. S. Pushkina." In *Pushkin: Problemy poetiki*. Edited by V. Baevskii and Iu. M. Nikishov. Tver': Tverskoi gosudarstvennyi universitet, 1992. 84–97.

Jackson, H. J., ed. *Samuel Taylor Coleridge.* Oxford: Oxford University Press, 1985.

Jackson, Robert Louis. "Miltonic Imagery and Design in Pushkin's *Mozart and Salieri*: The Russian Satan." In *American Contributions to the Seventh International Congress of Slavists.* Edited by Victor Terras. The Hague: Mouton, 1973. 1: 261–69.

———. "Moral-Philosophical Subtext in Pushkin's *Kamennyi gost'*." *Scando-Slavica* 35 (1989): 17–24.

———. "Napoleon in Russian Literature." *Yale French Studies,* no. 26 (1960–61): 106–18.

———. "The Temptation and the Transaction: 'A Gentle Creature.'" In *The Art of Dostoevsky: Deliriums and Nocturnes.* Princeton, N.J.: Princeton University Press, 1981.

Jakobson, Roman. "The Statue in Pushkin's Poetic Mythology." In *Language in Literature.* Cambridge, Mass.: Belknap Press, 1987. 318–68.

Iakovlev, N. "Pir vo vremia chumy." In Aleksandr Pushkin, *Dramaticheskie proizvedeniia.* Edited by Dmitrii P. Iakubovich. *Polnoe sobranie sochinenii.* Moscow: Akademiia Nauk SSSR, 1935. 7: 579-609.

Kahler, Erich, *The Inward Turn of Narrative.* Translated from the German by Richard and Clara Winston. Foreword by Joseph Frank. Princeton, N.J.: Princeton University Press, 1973.

Karpiak, Robert. "Pushkin's *Little Tragedies*: The Controversies in Criticism." *Canadian Slavonic Papers* 22 (1980): 80–91.

Kazakova, L. A. "*Malen'kie tragedii* A. S. Pushkina kak khudozhestvennaia tselostnost'." Aftoreferat kandidatskoi dissertatsii, Novgorodskii gosudarstvennyi universitet, Novgorod, 1999.

Kibal'nik, Sergei. *Khudozhestvennaia filosofiia Pushkina.* St. Petersburg: "Petropolis," 1998.

———. "Tema smerti. Problema religioznosti tvorchestva Pushkina." In *Khudozhestvennaia filosofiia Pushkina.* St. Petersburg: Dm. Bulanin, 1999. 158–83.

Kino: Entsiklopedicheskii slovar'. Moscow: Sovetskaia entsiklopediia, 1986.

Kiui, Ts. A. *Izbrannye stat'i.* Leningrad: GosMuzIzdat, 1952.

———. "Moskovskaia Chastnaia Russkaia Opera. 'Motsart i Sal'eri' A. S. Pushkina i N. A. Rimskogo-Korsakova." *Novosti i birzhevaia gazeta,* 12 March 1899.

———. "Vliianie Pushkina na nashikh kompozitorov i na ikh vokal'nyi stil'." *Novosti i birzhevaia gazeta,* 26 May 1899.

Knapp, Liza. *The Annihilation of Inertia: Dostoevsky and Metaphysics.* Evanston, Ill.: Northwestern University Press, 1996.

Kostalevskaia, Marina. "Aurum Vulgi." *Zapiski Russkoi Akademicheskoi Gruppy v SShA/Transactions of the Association of Russian-American Scholars in the USA* 20 (1988): 91–114.

———. "Duet—diada—duel'." *Moskovskii pushkinist.* Moscow: Nasledie, 1996. 2: 40–56.

———. "Duet—diada—duel' ('Motsart i Sal'eri')." In *"Motsart i Sal'eri," tragediia A. S. Pushkina. Dvizhenie vo vremeni: Antologiia traktovok i kontseptsii ot Belinskogo do nashikh dnei.* Edited by Valentin S. Nepomniashchii. Pushkin v XX veke series. Moscow: Nasledie, 1997. 3: 807–21.

Kotliarevskii, N. "*Kamennyi gost'.*" In *Biblioteka velikikh pisatelei. Pushkin.* Vol. 3. Edited by S. A. Vengerov. St. Petersburg: Izdanie Brokgauz-Efron, 1909.

Kuchera, Henry. "Pushkin and Don Juan." In *For Roman Jakobson: Essays on the Occasion of His Sixtieth Birthday, 11 October 1956.* Compiled by Morris Halle et al. The Hague: Mouton, 1956. 273–84.

Lazaresku, O. G. *Boldinskie dramy A. S. Pushkina: Problemy poetiki zhanra.* Petrozavodsk: N.p., 1997.

Leavy, Barbara Fass. *To Blight with Plague.* New York and London: New York University Press, 1992.

Levin, Iurii D. "Metafora v 'Skupom rytsare.'" *Russkaia rech'* 3 (1969): 17–28.

———. "Pushkin." In *Shekspir i russkaia literatura XIX veka.* Edited by M. P. Alekseev. Leningrad: Nauka, 1988. 32–62.

Levkovich, Ia. L. "Vnov' ia posetil..." In *Stikhotvoreniia Pushkina 1820–1830-kh godov.* Edited by Nikolai V. Izmailov. Leningrad: Nauka, 1974. 306–23.

Lipking, Lawrence. *The Life of the Poet: Beginning and Ending Poetic Careers.* Chicago: University of Chicago Press, 1981.

Literaturnaia gazeta, no. 71. St. Petersburg: Izdatel'stvo Borodina, 1830.

Loewen, Donald. "Disguised as Translation: Religion and Re-creation in Pushkin's 'A Feast in Time of Plague.'" *Slavic and East European Journal* 40 (1996): 45–62.

Lotman, Iurii. M. "Iz razmyshlenii nad tvorcheskoi evoliutsiei Pushkina (1830 goda)." In *Izbrannye stat'i.* Tallin: "Aleksandra," 1992. 2: 463–78.

———. "Opyt rekonstruktsii pushkinskogo siuzheta ob Iisuse." In *Pushkin.* St. Petersburg: "Iskusstvo-SPB," 1995. 281–92.

———. "Pushkin: Etapy tvorchestva." In *V shkole poeticheskogo slova: Pushkin, Lermontov, Gogol.* Moscow: Prosviashchenie, 1988. 6–30.

———. "Tipologicheskaia kharakteristika realizma pozdnego Pushkina." In *V shkole poeticheskogo slova: Pushkin, Lermontov, Gogol.* Moscow: Prosviashchenie, 1988. 124–58.

Maimin, Evgenii A. "Filosofskaia poeziia Pushkina i liubomudrov (k razlichiiu khudozhestvennykh metodov)." In *Pushkin: Issledovaniia i materially.* Moscow-Leningrad: Izdatel'stvo Akademii Nauk SSSR, 1969. 6: 112–14.

———. "Polifonicheskii roman Dostoevskogo i pushkinskaia traditsiia." In *Kul'turnoe nasledie drevnei Rusi: Istoki, stanovlenie, traditsii.* Edited by V. G. Bazanov. Moscow: Nauka, 1976. 312–14.

Makogonenko, Georgii P. *Tvorchestvo Pushkina v 1830 gody (1830–1833).* Leningrad: Khudozhestvennaia literatura, 1974.

Maloff, Nicholas. "Pushkin's Dramas in Russian Music." Ph.D. dissertation, University of Pittsburgh, 1976.

Mandelbaum, Allen, and Anthony Oldcorn, eds. *Lectura Dantis: Inferno.* Berkeley and Los Angeles: University of California Press, 1998.

Mandelshtam, Nadezhda. *Mozart and Salieri.* Translated by Robert A. McLean. Ann Arbor: Ardis, 1973.

Manvell, Roger. *Theater and Film: A Comparative Study of the Two Forms of Dramatic Art, and of the Problems of Adaptation of Stage Plays into Film.* Cranbury, N.J.: Associated University Presses, 1979.

May, Charles E. *The New Short Story Theories*. Athens: Ohio University Press, 1994.

Meierkhold, Vsevolod E. *Stat'i, pis'ma, rechi, besedy*. Moscow: Iskusstvo, 1968.

Mickiewicz, Adam. *Dziela*. 16 vols. Warsaw: Czytelnik, 1955.

Minskii, N. "Skupoi rytsar'." In *Biblioteka velikikh pisatelei. Pushkin*. Vol. 3. Edited by S. A. Vengerov. St. Petersburg: Izdanie Brokgauz-Efron, 1909.

Mitina, L. S. "Tragedii Pushkina: Zhanrovyi aspect." Aftoreferat kandidatskoi dissertatsii, Moscow, 1989.

Modzalevskii, B. L. *Biblioteka A. S. Pushkina: Bibliograficheskoe opisanie*. Moscow: Izdatel'stvo "Kniga," 1988.

Molière. *Don Juan, or, The Statue at the Banquet*. Translated by Wallace Fowlie. Great Neck, N.Y.: Barron's Educational Series, 1964.

Montaigne, Michel. *Selected Essays*. Edited by Blanchard Bates. New York: Modern Library, 1949.

Monter, Barbara Heldt. "Love and Death in Pushkin's 'Little Tragedies.'" *Russian Literature Triquarterly*, no. 3 (spring 1972): 206–14.

Moretti, Franco. *The Way of the World: The Bildungsroman in European Culture*. London: Verso, 1987.

Moskvicheva, Galina V. "Osobennosti konflikta v tragedii Pushkina *Motsart i Sal'eri*." *Boldinskie chteniia* (1993): 114–26.

———. "Problema zhanra *Malen'kikh tragedii* A. S. Pushkina." *Boldinskiie chteniia* (1991): 47–61.

———. "Tragicheskaia kolliziia v *Kammenom goste* A. S. Pushkina." *Boldinskie chteniia* (1994): 36–48.

Moskvitianin 9 (1841).

Murat, Ines. *Napoleon and the American Dream*. Baton Rouge: Louisiana State University Press, 1981.

Murianov, Mikhail F. "U istokov pushkinskoi filosofii vremeni." In *Iz simvolov i allegorii Pushkina*. Moscow: Nasledie, 1996. 155–200.

"Muzykal'nye zametki." *St. Peterburgskie vedomosti*, 28 March 1868.

Nabokov, Vladimir. *Three Russian Poets: Translations of Pushkin, Lermontov, and Tyutchev*. Norfolk: New Directions, 1944.

Neff, Lyle. "César Cui's Opera *Feast in Time of Plague/Pir vo vremia chumy*." Prefatory note to a new English singing version of the text in *Pushkin Review/Pushkinskii vestnik* 1 (1998): 121–48.

Nepomniashchii, Valentin S. Excerpts from "Simfoniia zhizni (o tetralogii Pushkina)" and "O malen'kikh tragediiakh." In *"Motsart i Sal'eri," tragediia A. S. Pushkina. Dvizhenie vo vremeni: Antologiia traktovok i kontseptsii ot Belinskogo do nashikh dnei*. Edited by Valentin S. Nepomniashchii. Pushkin v XX veke series. Moscow: Nasledie, 1997. 3: 331–36.

———. "Iz zametok sostavitelia pri podgotovke etoi knigi." In *"Motsart i Sal'eri," tragediia A. S. Pushkina. Dvizhenie vo vremeni: Antologiia traktovok i kontseptsii ot Belinskogo do nashikh dnei*. Edited by Valentin S. Nepomniashchii. Pushkin v XX veke series. Moscow: Nasledie, 1997. 3: 843–915.

———. "Simfoniia zhizni (o tetralogii Pushkina)." *Voprosy literatury* 2 (1962): 128–29.

Nepomniashchii, Valentin S., ed. *"Motsart i Sal'eri," tragediia A. S. Pushkina.*

Dvizhenie vo vremeni: Antologiia traktovok i kontseptsii ot Belinskogo do nashikh dnei. Vol. 3, Pushkin v XX veke series. Moscow: Nasledie, 1997.

Novikova, Marina. *Pushkinskii kosmos: Iazycheskaia i khristianskaia traditsii v tvorchestve Pushkina.* Moscow: Nasledie, 1995.

Nusinov, Isaak M. *Istoriia literaturnogo geroiia.* Moscow: Khudozhestvennaia literatura, 1958.

———. "Tragediia skuposti." In *Istoriia literaturnogo geroiia.* Edited by Isaak M. Nusinov. Moscow: Khudozhestvennaia literatura, 1958.

O'Bell, Leslie. *Pushkin's "Egyptian Nights": The Biography of a Work.* Ann Arbor: Ardis, 1984.

Odinokov, Viktor G. *Khudozhestvenno-istoricheskii opyt v poetike russkikh pisatelei.* Novosibirsk: Novosibirskii gosudarstvennyi universitet, 1990.

Odoevskii, Vladimir F. *Muzykal'no-literaturnoe nasledie.* Moscow: Gosudarstvennoe muzykal'noe izdatel'stvo, 1956.

Ospovat, L. S. "'Kamennyi gost' kak opyt dialogizatsii tvorcheskogo soznaniia." In *Pushkin: Issledovaniia i materially.* Moscow-Leningrad: Izdatel'stvo Akademii Nauk SSSR, 1995. 15: 25–59.

Ossovskii, Aleksandr. "S. V. Rakhmaninov." In *Vospominaniia o Rakhmaninove.* Edited by Z. A. Apetian. 3d ed. Moscow: Muzyka, 1967. 1: 388–89.

Oxenhandler, Neal. *Looking for Heroes in Postwar France: Albert Camus, Max Jacob, Simone Weil.* Hanover, N.H.: Dartmouth College, University Press of New England, 1996.

Panofsky, Erwin. "Father Time." In *Studies in Iconology: Humanistic Themes in the Art of Renaissance.* New York: Icon Editions, Harper and Row, 1972. 69–93.

———. "Titian's *Allegory of Prudence*: A Postscript." In *Meaning in the Visual Arts.* Chicago: University of Chicago Press, 1985. 146–68.

Proffer, Carl R. "Pushkin and Parricide: The Miserly Knight." *American Imago* 25, no. 4 (winter 1968): 347–53.

Proskurin, Oleg. "Chem pakhnut chervontsy? Ob odnom temnom meste v 'Skupom rytsare.'" In *Poeziia Pushkina, ili podvizhnyi palimpsest.* Moscow: Novoe literaturnoe obozrenie, 1999. 348–76.

Pushkinskii kinoslovar'. Moscow: Sovremennye tetradi, 1999.

Quinones, Ricardo J. *The Changes of Cain: Violence and the Lost Brother in Cain and Abel Literature.* Princeton, N.J.: Princeton University Press, 1991.

———. "Montaigne." In *The Renaissance Discovery of Time.* Cambridge, Mass.: Harvard University Press, 1972. 204–43.

Rabinow, Paul, ed. *The Foucault Reader.* New York: Pantheon Books, 1984.

Rabinowitz, Peter. "Rimskii and Salieri." In *O Rus! Studia litteraria slavica in honorem Hugh McLean.* Edited by Simon Karlinsky, James L. Rice, and Barry P. Scherr. Oakland, Calif.: Berkeley Slavic Specialties, 1995. 67–68.

Raskol'nikov, Feliks. "'Pir vo vremia chumy' v svete problemy demonizma u Pushkina." *Pushkin Review/Pushkinskii vestnik* 3 (2000): 1–11.

Rassadin, Stanislav B. *Dramaturg Pushkin: Poetika, idei, evoliutsiia.* Moscow: Iskusstvo, 1977.

Reid, Robert. *Pushkin's Mozart and Salieri: Themes, Character, Sociology.* Amsterdam: Rodopi, 1995.

Retsepter. V. "Ia shel k tebe..." In *"Motsart i Sal'eri," tragediia A. S. Pushkina. Dvizhenie vo vremeni: Antologiia traktovok i kontseptsii ot Belinskogo do nashikh dnei.* Edited by Valentin S. Nepomniashchii. Pushkin v XX veke series. Moscow: Nasledie, 1997. 3: 363–73.

Rhein, Phillip. *Albert Camus.* Boston: Twayne Publishers, 1989.

Richardson, Alan. *A Mental Theater: Poetic Drama and Consciousness in the Romantic Age.* University Park: Pennsylvania State University Press, 1988.

Rimsky-Korsakov, Nikolay A. *My Musical Life.* Translated by Judah A. Joffe. New York: Vienna House/Knopf, 1972.

Rizzuto, Anthony. *Camus: Love and Sexuality.* Gainesville: University Press of Florida, 1998.

Rocks, James. "Camus Reads Defoe: *A Journal of the Plague Year* as a Source of *The Plague.*" *Tulane Studies in English* 15 (1967): 81–87.

Rosen, Nathan. "Breaking out of the Underground: The 'Failure' of 'A Raw Youth.'" *Modern Fiction Studies* 4, no. 3 (fall 1958): 225–39.

Rozanov, M. N. "Puskin i Dante." In *Puskin i ego sovremenniki* 37. Leningrad, 1928. 11–41.

———. "Zametka o 'Skupom rytsare' Pushkina." In *Sbornik statei v chest' professora Sobolevskogo.* Edited by V. N. Perets. Leningrad: Akademiia Nauk SSSR, 1927. 253–56.

Ruskin, John. *Unto This Last: Four Essays on the First Principles of Political Economy.* Vol. 12, *Works.* New York: John Wiley and Sons, 1885.

Rybak, L. *Kak rozhdalis' fil'my Mikhaila Shveitsera.* Moscow: Soiuz kinematografistov SSSR, 1984.

Savage, D. S. "The Idea of *The Gambler.*" In *Dostoevsky: New Perspectives.* Edited by Robert Louis Jackson. Englewood Cliffs, N.J.: Prentice-Hall, 1984. 111–25.

Schlegel, August Wilhelm. "From Lectures on Dramatic Art and Literature." In *German Romantic Criticism.* Edited by A. Leslie Wilson. New York: Continuum, 1982. 175–218.

Schlegel, Friedrich. "Athenäum Fragments #116, 139, 238." In *The Romantic Manifesto: An Anthology.* Edited by Larry H. Peer. New York: Peter Lang, 1988. 11–13.

Schmid, Wolf. *Puskins Prosa in poetischer Lektüre: Die erzählungen Belkins.* Munich: Wilhelm Fink Verlag, 1991.

Schoenbaum, Samuel. *William Shakespeare: A Compact Documentary Life.* Rev. ed. New York: Oxford University Press, 1987.

Seeley, Frank F. "The Problem of *Kamennyi Gost'.*" *Slavonic and East European Review* 41, no. 97 (June 1963): 362–67.

Semerchuk, Vladimir. "Mezhdu poetikoi i ideologiei. Pushkin v igrovom kino: Dve strategii ekranizatsii." In *Pushkinskii kinoslovar'.* Moscow: Sovremennye tetradi, 1999. 246–53.

Shakespeare, William. *Richard III.* New Penguin Shakespeare. Edited by E. A. J. Honigmann. London: Penguin, 1968.

Shakh-Azizova, T. K. "Pushkin kak teatral'naia problema." In *Pushkin i sovremennaia kul'tura.* Edited by E. P. Chelyshev. Moscow: Nauka, 1996. 226–32.

Shapiro, Michael. "Journey to the Metonymic Pole: The Structure of Pushkin's 'Little Tragedies.'" In *From Los Angeles to Kiev: Papers on the Occasion of the*

Ninth International Congress of Slavists. UCLA Slavic Studies 7. Edited by Vladimir Markov and Dean S. Worth. Columbus, Ohio: Slavica, 1983. 169–206.

Shapiro, Michael, and Marianne Shapiro. *Figuration in Verbal Art.* Princeton, N.J.: Princeton University Press, 1988.

Shatzmiller, Joseph. *Shylock Reconsidered: Jews, Moneylending, and Medieval Society.* Berkeley and Los Angeles: University of California Press, 1990.

Shaw, Thomas. "Dramas: Malen'kie Tragedii." In *Pushkin's Poetics of the Unexpected.* Columbus, Ohio: Slavica, 1993. 239–66.

Shelley, Percy Bysshe. *"A Defence of Poetry" and "A Letter to Lord Ellenborough."* London: Porcupine Press, 1973.

Shervinskii, Sergei V. *Ritm i smysl: k izucheniiu poetiki Pushkina.* Moscow: Izdatel'stvo Akademii Nauk SSSR, 1961.

Shik, Aleksandr. *Odesskii Pushkin.* Paris: Dom knigi, 1938.

Simmel, Georg. *The Philosophy of Money.* Edited by David Frisby. Translated by Tom Bottomore, David Frisby, and Kaethe Mengelberg. 2d enlarged ed. London: Routledge and Kegan Paul, 1990.

Siniavskii, Andrei D. *Progulki s Pushkinym.* London: OPI, 1975.

Smirnov, I. P. *Psikhodiakhronologika: Psikhoistoriia russkoi literatury ot romantizma do nashikh dnei.* Series editor, I. D. Prokhorova. Moscow: NLO, 1994.

Solov'ev, V. "Opyt dramaticheskikh izuchenii (k istorii literaturnoi evoliutsii Pushkina)." *Voprosy literatury* 5 (1974): 143–57.

Sonnet, Esther. "From *Emma* to *Clueless*: Taste, Pleasure, and the Scene of History." In *Adaptations: From Text to Screen, Screen to Text.* Edited by Deborah Cartmell and Imelda Whelehan. London: Routledge, 1999. 51–62.

Stafford, William. *The Mozart Myths: A Critical Reassessment.* Stanford, Calif.: Stanford University Press, 1991.

Stanislavskii, Konstantin. *Sobranie sochinenii v 8 tomakh.* Moscow: Iskusstvo, 1954–56.

Stendhal. *The Lives of Haydn, Mozart, and Metastasio.* Translated by Richard N. Coe. London: Calder and Boyars, 1972.

Stepanov, L. A. "*Skupoi rytsar'* A. S. Pushkina: Transformatsiia traditsii v tvorcheskom protsesse." *Filologiia-philologica* 3 (1993): 32–34.

Stephanson, Raymond. "The Plague Narratives of Defoe and Camus: Illness as Metaphor." *Modern Language Quarterly* 48, no. 3 (1987): 224–41.

Taborisskaia, E. M. "*Malen'kie tragedii* Pushkina kak tsikl (nekotorye aspekty poetiki)." In *Pushkinskii sbornik.* Edited by E. A. Maimin. Leningrad: LGPI im. A. I. Gertsena, 1977.

Taruskin, Richard. *Defining Russia Musically.* Princeton, N.J.: Princeton University Press, 1997.

———. *Opera and Drama in Russia as Preached and Practiced in the 1860s.* Ann Arbor: UMI Research Press, 1981.

Taylor, Charles. *Sources of the Self: The Making of the Modern Identity.* Cambridge, Mass.: Harvard University Press, 1989.

Terras, Victor. "Introduction." In A. S. Pushkin, *The Little Tragedies.* Letchworth: Bradda Books, 1966.

———. "Pushkin's 'Feast during the Plague' and Its Original: A Structural

Confrontation." In *Alexander Pushkin: Symposium on the 175th Anniversary of His Birth.* Edited by Andrej Kodjak and Kiril Taranovsky. New York: New York University Press, 1976. 206–20.

Thody, Philip. *Albert Camus.* New York: St. Martin's Press, 1989.

Thorslev, Peter. *The Byronic Hero: Types and Prototypes.* Minneapolis: University of Minnesota Press, 1962.

Tiupa, Valerii I. "Novatorstvo avtorskogo soznaniia v tsikle 'Malen'kikh tragedii.'" *Boldinskie chteniia* (1987): 127–35.

Tocqueville, Alexis de. *Democracy in America.* Vol. 2. New York: Vintage Books, 1945.

Tolstoi, Lev. *Polnoe sobranie sochinenii.* 90 vols. Moscow: Gosudarstvennoe izdatel'stvo khudozhestvennoi literatury, 1935–64.

Tomashevskii, Boris. "*Kamennyi gost'.*" In Aleksandr Pushkin, *Dramaticheskie proizvedeniia.* Edited by Dmitrii P. Iakubovich. *Polnoe sobranie sochinenii.* Moscow: Akademiia Nauk SSSR, 1935. 7: 547–48.

———. "'Malen'kie tragedii' Pushkina i Mol'er." In *Pushkin i Frantsiia.* Leningrad: Sovetskii pisatel', 1960. 262–314.

———. "Pushkin." In A. S. Pushkin, *Stikhotvoreniia v trekh tomakh.* Bol'shaia seriia Biblioteki poeta. 2d ed., vol. 1. Leningrad: Sovetskii pisatel', 1955.

Tsvetaeva, Marina. "Art in the Light of Conscience." In *English Essays on Poetry by Marina Tsvetaeva.* Translated by Angela Livingstone. Cambridge, Mass.: Harvard University Press, 1992. 149–83.

———. "Iskusstvo pri svete sovesti" (1933). In Marina Tsvetaeva, *Sobranie sochinenii.* 7 vols. Moscow: Ellis-Lak, 1994.

Tsuker, A. "K kontseptsii 'Skupogo rytsaria.'" *Sovetskaia muzyka* 7 (1985): 92–97.

Tynianov, Iurii. *Pushkin i sovremenniki.* Moscow: Nauka, 1968.

Ustiuzhanin, Dmitrii L. *Malen'kie tragedii A. S. Pushkina.* Moscow: Khudozhestvennaia literatura, 1974.

Varshavskii, Iakov. "Est' upoenie v boiu..." *Teatr* 12 (1980): 55–60.

Vatsuro, Vadim E. "Introduction." In A. S. Pushkin, *Povesti Belkina.* Moscow: "Kniga," 1981.

———. "Pushkin i Dante." In *Pushkinskaia pora.* St. Petersburg: Akademicheskii proekt, 2000. 235–53.

———. "'Skazka o zolotom petushke' (Opyt analiza siuzhetnoi semantiki)." In *Pushkin: Issledovaniia i materially.* Moscow-Leningrad: Izdatel'stvo Akademii Nauk SSSR, 1995. 15: 122–34.

Vil'k, Evgenii A. "Malen'kie tragedii—odna bol'shaia tragediia?" In *Materialy Chetvertoi mezhdunarodnoi Pushkinskoi konferentsii.* St. Petersburg: N.p., 1997.

Vol'f, Abram. *Khronika Peterburgskikh teatrov s kontsa 1826 do nachala 1855 goda.* Vols. 1–2. St. Petersburg: R. Golike, 1877.

Voltaire. *Candide, ou l'optimisme.* In *Roman et contes.* Bibliothèque de la pléiade. Edited by Frédérik Deloffre and Jacques van den Heuvel. Dijon: Editions Gallimard, 1979. 145–233.

Watt, Ian P. *Myths of Modern Individualism: Faust, Don Quixote, Don Juan, Robinson Crusoe.* Cambridge: Cambridge University Press, 1996.

Wilson, John. *Oxford Prize Poems: The City of the Plague.* New York and London: Garland, 1979.

Woll, Josephine. "'Mozart and Salieri' and the Concept of Tragedy." *Canadian American Slavic Studies* 10, no. 2 (summer 1976): 250–63.

Worthen, William B. "Drama, Performativity, Performance." *PMLA* 113, no. 5 (October 1998): 1093–1107.

Zhukovskii, Vasilii. *Polnoe sobranie sochinenii v 3 tomakh.* Petrograd: Literaturno-izdatel'skii otdel Komissariata narodnago prosvieshcheniia, 1918.

Contributors Biographies

DAVID M. BETHEA is the Vilas Research Professor of Slavic Languages and Literature at the University of Wisconsin–Madison. He is the author of *Khodasevich: His Life and Art*, *The Shape of Apocalypse in Modern Russian Fiction*, *Joseph Brodsky and the Creation of Exile*, and *Realizing Metaphors: Alexander Pushkin and the Life of the Poet* and the editor of *Pushkin Today* and *The Pushkin Handbook* (coedited with Alexander Dolinin and Alexander Ospovat). His interests include classical and modern Russian poetry, and at present he is working on a creative biography of Pushkin.

SERGEI DAVYDOV teaches Russian literature at Middlebury College, Vermont. He holds a Ph.D. from Yale and is the author of numerous studies on Pushkin, Dostoevsky, Nabokov, and literary theory. He has written a book, *Teksty-Matreshki Vladimira Nabokova*, and is working on another about Pushkin.

CARYL EMERSON is A. Watson Armour III University Professor of Slavic Languages and Literatures at Princeton University, with a coappointment in comparative literature. She is a translator and critic of the Russian literary critic and philosopher Mikhail Bakhtin and has published widely on nineteenth-century Russian literature (Pushkin, Dostoevsky, Tolstoy, Chekhov), on the history of literary criticism, and on Russian opera and vocal music. Most recently, she is the author of

The First Hundred Years of Mikhail Bakhtin (1997) and a brief biography of Modest Musorgsky (1999).

SVETLANA EVDOKIMOVA is associate professor of Slavic languages and comparative literature at Brown University. She is the author of *Alexander Pushkin's Historical Imagination* (1999) and of a wide range of articles on nineteenth-century Russian literature (Pushkin, Gogol, Tolstoy, Chekhov). Most recently, she authored an article on the problem of infantilism in *The Cherry Orchard* and an essay on Tolstoy's sense of an ending for *Approaches to Teaching Tolstoy's Anna Karenina*, edited by Liza Knapp and Amy Mandelker. At present, she is working on a monograph about Chekhov and the Russian intelligentsia, tentatively entitled "The Creation of Anton Chekhov."

JAMES E. FALEN received his doctorate in Russian at the University of Pennsylvania in Philadelphia. He spent thirty years on the faculty at the University of Tennessee in Knoxville and is now an emeritus professor. His main publications include *Isaak Babel: Russian Master of the Short Story*, a translation of Pushkin's novel in verse, *Eugene Onegin* (in *The Complete Pushkin*), and translations of a number of lyrics as well as *The Little Tragedies* and other works that also appear in *The Complete Pushkin.*

SUSANNE FUSSO is professor of Russian language and literature at Wesleyan University. She is the author of *Designing Dead Souls: An Anatomy of Disorder in Gogol.* She is now working on a book about sexuality in Dostoevsky's art and thought.

VLADIMIR GOLSTEIN is visiting associate professor of Russian language and literature at Brown University. He is the author of *Lermontov's Narratives of Heroism* and of numerous articles on nineteenth- and twentieth-century Russian authors, including Pushkin, Lermontov, Gogol, Dostoevsky, Tolstoy, and Tsvetaeva. His interests include modern Russian poetry and Russian culture. He is currently completing a monograph on the generation conflicts in Russian literature and culture.

MONIKA GREENLEAF is chairman of the Slavic Department and also associate professor of comparative literature at Stanford University. She is the author of *Pushkin and Romantic Fashion: Fragment, Elegy,*

Orient, Irony and coeditor, together with Stephen Moeller-Sally, of *Russian Subjects: Empire, Nation, and the Culture of the Golden Age.* She has written on Catherine the Great's multiple memoirs and the theory and practice of eighteenth-century autobiography, the poetics of empire and subjectivity in Batiushkov's lyrical poetry, Pushkin's Byronic apprenticeship, cultural differentials in Mickiewicz's comic epic *Pan Tadeusz* and Pushkin's novel in verse *Eugene Onegin*, the burial of Pushkin in Gogol's Pl'iushkin, Tynianov, montage, and the theory of the fragment, fathers and imposters in Nabokov's *Gift*, and Tsvetaeva's comic prose. She is soon to complete a book, *Art of the Debut*, on the Pushkin function in the comic works of Gogol, Tsvetaeva, and Nabokov. She is working on a book-length study of Catherine the Great as author and her inscription of Russia into the genres of the eighteenth-century public sphere.

ROBERT LOUIS JACKSON is B. E. Bensinger Professor Emeritus of Slavic Languages and Literatures at Yale University. Author of several books on Dostoevsky, he has written articles on Pushkin, Gogol, Turgenev, Tolstoy, Chekhov, Solzhenitsyn, and other Russian writers of the nineteenth and twentieth centuries. He is preparing a book on Chekhov's short stories. Jackson was a founder and president of the International Dostoevsky Society.

SOFYA KHAGI holds a master's degree in comparative literature from Dartmouth College and is a doctoral candidate in Slavic languages and literatures at Brown University. She is working on her dissertation on linguistic skepticism in nineteenth- and twentieth-century Russian poetry. She has authored an article, "Art as Aping: The Uses of Dialogism in Timur Kibirov," which appeared in the *Russian Review* (2002).

VLADIMIR MARKOVICH is professor of Russian literature at the Saint-Petersburg State University, St. Petersburg, Russia. He has published widely on nineteenth-century Russian literature and on the history of literary criticism. He is the author of several monographs, including *Man in the Novels of Turgenev, Turgenev and the Russian Realist Novel of the Nineteenth Century, St. Petersburg Tales of Nikolai Gogol*, and *Pushkin and Lermontov in the History of Russian Literature,* and of more than one hundred articles on modern Russian literature from romanticism to Gertsen and Goncharov to Chekhov.

His interests include the history of literary criticism, narratology, and hermeneutics.

STEPHANIE SANDLER has written on Pushkin, on gender issues in Russian literature, and on contemporary Russian poetry and culture. Recent publications include two edited volumes, *Rereading Russian Poetry* and *Self and Story in Russian History*, the latter coedited with Laura Engelstein. Her study of myths of Pushkin in Russian culture is forthcoming from Stanford University Press. She is professor of Slavic languages and literatures at Harvard University.

Index

PUBLICATIONS OF THE WISCONSIN CENTER FOR PUSHKIN STUDIES

David Bethea, Alexander Dolinin, Thomas Shaw
Series Editors

Realizing Metaphors: Alexander Pushkin and the Life of the Poet
David M. Bethea

Alexander Pushkin's Little Tragedies: *The Poetics of Brevity*
edited by Svetlana Evdokimova

Pushkin's Tatiana
Olga Hasty

The Imperial Sublime: A Russian Poetics of Empire
Harsha Ram

Pushkin and the Genres of Madness: The Masterpieces of 1833
Gary Rosenshield